RURAL PROTEST ON PRINCE EDWARD ISLAND: FROM BRITISH COLONIZATION TO THE ESCHEAT MOVEMENT

Who has the more legitimate claim to land, settlers who occupy and improve it with their labour, or landlords who claim ownership on the basis of imperial grants? This question of property rights, and their construction, was at the heart of rural protest on Prince Edward Island for a century. Tenants resisted landlord claims by squatting and refusing to pay rent. They fought for their vision of a just rural order through petitions, meetings, rallies, electoral campaigns, and direct action. Landlords responded with their own collective action to protect their interests. In *Rural Protest on Prince Edward Island* Rusty Bittermann examines this conflict and the dynamic of rural protest on the Island from its establishment as a British colony in the 1760s to the early 1840s.

The focus of Bittermann's study is the remarkable mass movement known as the Escheat movement, which emerged in the 1830s in the context of growing popular challenges elsewhere in the Atlantic World. The Escheat movement aimed at resolving the land question in favour of tenants by having the state revoke (escheat) the large grants of land that created landlordism on the Island. Although it ultimately gained control of the assembly in the late 1830s, the Escheat movement did not produce the land policies that tenants and their allies advocated. The movement did, however, synthesize years of rural protest and produce a persistent legacy of language and ideas concerning land, justice, and the rights of small producers that helped make landlordism on the Island unsustainable in the long term. *Rural Protest on Prince Edward Island* is a comprehensive and fascinating examination of an important, but often overlooked, period in the history of Canada's smallest province.

RUSTY BITTERMANN is an associate professor in the Department of History at St. Thomas University.

RUSTY BITTERMANN

Rural Protest on Prince Edward Island

From British Colonization to the Escheat Movement

UNIVERSITY OF TORONTO PRESS
Toronto Buffalo London

ISBN 978-0-8020-0439-0 (cloth)
ISBN 978-0-8020-7229-0 (paper)

Publication cataloguing information is available from Library and Archives Canada.

Cover image: map drawn by Samuel Holland, reproduced in smaller scale from James Munro, ed., *Acts of the Privy Council of England, Colonial Series, Vol. V, A.D. 1768–1783* (London, 1912)

We wish to acknowledge the land on which the University of Toronto Press operates. This land is the traditional territory of the Wendat, the Anishnaabeg, the Haudenosaunee, the Métis, and the Mississaugas of the Credit First Nation.

This book has been published with the help of a grant from the Federation for the Humanities and Social Sciences, through the Awards to Scholarly Publications Program, using funds provided by the Social Sciences and Humanities Research Council of Canada.

University of Toronto Press acknowledges the financial support of the Government of Canada, the Canada Council for the Arts, and the Ontario Arts Council, an agency of the Government of Ontario, for its publishing activities.

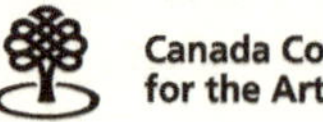

Conseil des Arts
du Canada

Funded by the Government of Canada | Financé par le gouvernement du Canada | Canada

to Kim and Karen,

who fought the good fight and died too young,

and

to our parents, Ann and Norm, who taught us what matters

Contents

Maps and Tables

Maps

Tables

Acknowledgments

This study has been long in the making. I have been assisted by the efforts of many kind people. My apologies in advance to those who deserve to be acknowledged and who are not. The failure lies with my memory and not with a lack of gratitude.

Donnie MacGillivray first drew my attention to rural protest on Prince Edward Island. I am grateful to him for that (I think) and to the many historians whose work on Island and regional history provided a foundation for this study. I also benefited enormously from the support of the intellectual communities associated with the Atlantic Canada Workshop and the Atlantic Canada Studies Conference. They epitomize the best in academic engagement and they helped to keep me going. I and others owe a huge debt to the scholars whose contributions to the *Dictionary of Canadian Biography* have transformed the writing of history in Canada. Thank you.

I have been assisted along the way by helpful (and patient) people at many libraries and archives, indeed too many to name. A few, however, deserve special note. The wonderful staff at the Public Archives of Prince Edward Island were (and are) extraordinary. Spending time in their company was almost enough to make winter travel to Charlottetown in the years before the bridge a matter of pleasant anticipation. It is a wonder more people do not do Island history simply to have the benefit of their support and company. The staff at the Public Archives of Nova Scotia and the Scottish Record Office were invariably friendly and supportive as well, far beyond the call of duty. At the University of New Brunswick's Harriet Irving Library, Katherine Hilder provided essential assistance with the complexities of the Loyalist Collection.

Many people have read all or parts of this study along the way and offered words of advice and encouragement. I am particularly indebted to Harry Baglole, Phil Buckner, Ernie Forbes, David Frank, Allan Greer, Gerry Hallowell, Craig Heron, Matthew Hatvany, Margaret McCallum, Del Muise, Rosemary Ommer, Jim Richardson, Ian Ross Robertson, Danny Samson, Peter Thomas, Don Wright, and Graeme Wynn in this regard. David Frank guided my work on the core of this study when it was a doctoral thesis, and I am grateful to him for his enthusiastic support and for his wise guidance on the crafts of research and writing. I am grateful too for the insightful advice of the anonymous reviewers who read this manuscript for the University of Toronto Press and the Social Science Federation. Margaret McCallum holds the record for reading more drafts of this study than anyone else. And she survived the experience. As well, she offered invaluable advice every time. Len Husband and the good people at the University of Toronto Press have my thanks for their many efforts to make this a better manuscript.

RURAL PROTEST ON PRINCE EDWARD ISLAND

Introduction

On the morning of 8 November 1837, rural Islanders began to assemble opposite George Sentiner's tavern on the outskirts of Georgetown in eastern Prince Edward Island. They were coming to show their dissatisfaction with government policies that gave landlords control of most of the colony's resources and that relegated two-thirds of the population to the status of tenants or squatters. Those travelling from distant parts of the colony arrived in long processions with flags and pipers; the assembled crowd greeted them with great shouts of welcome and celebratory musket fire. By noon more than two thousand had gathered for the largest mass demonstration to that date in Island history. As the open-air public meeting got underway, agrarian leaders gave rousing speeches emphasizing the injustice of the status quo and questioning the legitimacy of landlords' titles to large Island estates. Some also articulated the threat implicit in the firearms and the numbers assembled. The final resolution of the day phrased it bluntly: upholding 'a system of injustice will bring the government into contempt, and the people to disturbance.'[1] Those gathered at Sentiner's to support the most formidable popular protest against landlordism in the history of the colony were raising fundamental questions about the relationship between state authority and property rights in land. This study examines the history of this challenge, which has come to be known as the Escheat movement, and its antecedents.

The land question that was the focus of popular dissatisfaction on Prince Edward Island in the 1830s had been a matter of contention for more than half a century. It had its roots in the British imperial decision, following conquest of the island from the French in the Seven Years' War, to expel most of its small population and to use large land grants of the island's 1.4 million acres as a means to develop the expanding imperial frontier.[2] A British survey team divided the island into townships of roughly twenty thousand acres each, and in 1767 these were allocated to worthy Britons on the condition that they establish settlers on their holdings and pay an annual rent to the Crown, a quit rent. As was the case in other North American colonies where this strategy of frontier development was adopted, the system proved unstable and was unpopular with settlers, as proprietors failed to fulfil the terms of their grants – thus placing their titles in doubt – and rural residents came to resist the burden of landlords. Rural protest on Prince Edward Island in the late eighteenth and nineteenth centuries is thus part of the broader story of settler resistance to large proprietorial grants and landlordism in colonial and post-colonial North America.[3]

Settler opposition to landlordism on Prince Edward Island assumed different forms at different times in the eighteenth and nineteenth centuries. Farm-level resistance, such as squatting, rent refusals, and the use of landlord assets without permission or payment, provided a persistent backdrop for more organized challenges that waxed and waned across more than a century of landlordism. With the establishment of Prince Edward Island as a separate British colony in 1769 and the creation of a House of Assembly in 1773, resistance to landlordism became part of formal politics on the Island. The first significant organized challenge took shape in the 1790s in the wake of the American Revolution and the movement of Loyalist refugees to maritime British North America. The specific goal of the protests of the 1790s was to induce the Crown to escheat – revoke – proprietorial grants and redistribute lands to settlers in fee simple grants. An underlying assumption of the protest movement was that the state had a responsibility to bring property relations on the Island in line with settlers' perceptions of a just social and economic order. An escheat would provide a means to this end.

The rural protest movement that developed on Prince Edward Island in the 1830s had its roots in settler resistance to landlordism in the eighteenth century and in the first decades of the nineteenth century. It owes its name – the Escheat movement – to contemporary usage. Because the leaders of the movement advocated state resumption of proprietorial grants, as had agrarian leaders in earlier periods, and because they advanced this cause on the hustings and in the Island legislature, those associated with it came to be known as the 'Escheat Party' or 'Escheators.' The movement's opponents, who helped establish the labels, shortened these to the 'cheat party' and 'cheator' when they sought to characterize its advocates as unprincipled people seeking to deprive landlords of their lawful property. The label is problematic, both because it has the potential to conflate different moments of rural protest on the Island and because it misrepresents the factions and positions of 1830s and 1840s – a matter not unrelated to the political origins of the labels. There were people who advocated escheat proceedings yet were not advocates of sweeping land reform. At the same time, proponents of a radical change in the structure of land ownership did not think exclusively in terms of an escheat strategy. What united those gathered at Sentiner's was not so much their belief in the efficacy of an escheat as their insistence on the injustice of the status quo and the need for a fundamental overhaul of the colony's land system. In this study I use 'Escheat,' spelled with an upper case 'E,' to refer to the movement that took shape in the early 1830s and that advanced this position. When spelled with a lower case 'e,' 'escheat' simply refers to the process whereby title to land reverts to the Crown.

Besides drawing from a history of rural protest on the Island, the Escheat movement of the 1830s unfolded within a broader set of popular challenges to the status quo arising in British North America, the British Empire, and the Atlantic world. At the time of the mass meeting at Sentiner's, countrypeople in homespun were holding similar meetings to express concern with the distribution of land and power in Lower Canada, five hundred miles to the west of Prince Edward Island. Two weeks before the demonstration at Sentiner's, Dr Cyrille Coté and other Patriote leaders spoke to four thousand people at a six-county rally in St-Charles, east of Montreal. Casting his eyes over the multitude that had gathered there with banners, flags, and firearms, Coté spoke of the imminence of a day when they would be free from the oppression they suffered and from the burden of rents and tithes. He spoke too of the parallel struggle that was occurring on Prince Edward Island, suggesting that a rebellion was well under way there and that Patriotes needed to emulate the militancy that was rising elsewhere.[4] He also spoke of developments in Upper Canada, where tensions were mounting as colonists, determined to alter the structures under which they lived, were forming political unions, drilling, and assembling in mass rallies such as the one at Sentiner's.[5] A week after Escheat's great protest meeting, William Lyon Mackenzie, leader of the radical reformers in Upper Canada, published a draft of a new constitution for that colony, one that embodied sweeping changes in the distribution of political power and of land ownership.[6] Far to the east of Prince Edward Island, in the imperial centre, other challenges to the status quo were under way. The first edition of the Chartist newspaper the *Northern Star* appeared on British streets in November 1837, heralding the popular challenge that Dorothy Thompson has characterized as coming 'nearer to being a mass rebellion than any other movement' in modern British history.[7]

Had those challenging the status quo elsewhere in British North America and in the Imperial centre in these years achieved greater success, the Islanders gathered at Sentiner's, and at the other meetings organized by Escheators, might have realized a future closer to their dreams. In the event, their unborn children would reach adulthood before Island residents realized the immediate goal of a comprehensive change in property relations. The change, though it came slowly, owed much to the struggles and achievements of the men and women who participated in the rural protest movement that emerged on the Island in the 1830s, as well as to those who challenged existing concentrations of landed wealth and power elsewhere in the British Empire. Although the Escheat movement failed to eliminate landlordism in the second quarter of the nineteenth century, it left a lasting legacy of language and ideas concerning a just social order that would, in time, help bring landlordism to a close.

The history of the Escheat movement is, in part, the history of a series of remarkable popular achievements. Despite many obstacles, including poor roads, dispersed settlement, a population divided by religion, ethnicity, and language, and the concerted opposition of landlords, land agents, and leading members of the Island's business and professional community, the Escheat movement managed to draw settlers from all parts of the colony into a coherent movement of protest that combined the efforts of squatters, tenants, and freeholders. This study looks at the means whereby thousands of Islanders, from a variety of ethnic backgrounds, some speaking French, others Irish Gaelic, others Scots Gaelic, and yet others English, forged the strongest challenge to the status quo that the colony had ever seen. It explores their construction of an alternative vision of how the colony might develop, and their vision of a more democratic society in which the state would maintain legitimacy by acting on behalf of the interests of small producers. It details how petitions, meetings, rallies, electoral campaigns, and direct action were all used to force a reorientation in Island politics and to make rural concerns about land distribution the central public issue of the 1830s and of subsequent decades. As well, it examines how Escheators succeeded in achieving power in the only state institution directly open to popular control, even though property qualifications for assembly membership, a restricted franchise, and undemocratic districting impeded their efforts. These were no small feats.

It is also a study of failure and its causes. Despite remarkable organizational achievements, the creation of a flexible, multifaceted strategy for change, and victories in the political arena, the Escheat movement was unable to achieve its immediate goals. Some of the reasons for this lie with the growth of opposition to the movement on the Island and in the Imperial centre, as well as with unfavourable changes in the broader context that had once fostered the Escheat challenge. Other causes of failure lie with the limitations of the movement's tactics, given how power was allocated within existing state structures.

Chapters 1 to 3 of this study explore the history of the land question on the Island in the years prior to the emergence of the Escheat movement. Chapters 4 and 5 focus on the emergence of the Escheat challenge in the political arena and in the countryside in the first half of the 1830s. Chapter 6 examines the collective action of landlords and their allies as they sought to defend their interests in these years. Chapters 7 to 9 track the continuing growth of organized rural protest, culminating in Escheat's successful bid to win control of the Island House of Assembly in 1838, despite concerted efforts to suppress the movement. Chapter 10 examines the four years that Escheators held power in the House of Assembly, the obstacles they encountered in trying to use this position to usher in land reform, and their loss of control of the assembly in 1842.

1 The Eighteenth-Century Roots of Rural Protest

The grievances that led thousands of colonists to participate in the Escheat movement were rooted in land policies established by the British in the 1760s. The manner in which colonists chose to express their dissatisfaction was shaped by a long history of settler resistance. It drew from a repertoire of protest that began to emerge on the Island in the early decades of its history as a British colony and from beliefs concerning settler rights that had developed over many years.

Prince Edward Island, called Île St-Jean, and then Saint John's Island, before being given its current name in 1799, first came under British rule following the collapse of French rule in North America during the Seven Years' War.[1] It was then a small part of a new British North American frontier stretching from the Floridas along the lands to the west of the Appalachians to the Great Lakes and around to the Gulf of St Lawrence. British policies concerning the Island's development reflected the challenges confronting Imperial planners as they sought to manage this vast territory and to incorporate it within Imperial structures. Needing to organize and secure new lands at minimal cost, and if possible by means that would avoid the social and political problems that were developing in some of the older British North American colonies, the men of the Board of Trade looked favourably on schemes that used private capital to provide for government and develop the frontier. As well, they sought arrangements that would encourage the development of landed aristocracies. British plans for Prince Edward Island addressed both of these goals. In addition, they provided a means to distribute the spoils of war in ways that would strengthen government support, using land as patronage.[2]

With the end of the Seven Years' War, there was a rush to exploit the new territory that had become available for settlement on the margins of Britain's North American empire. Opportunities created on the frontier by peace and the restructuring of political boundaries attracted land companies, merchants, government officials, military officers, and other prominent individuals interested in frontier speculations, as well as people of more humble station interested in farm making. These were years during which speculators engrossed more than a million and a half acres of the Floridas, lobbied unsuccessfully for the grant of tens of millions of acres west of the Appalachians, and acquired hundreds of thousands of acres of what is now Vermont.[3] The land history of Prince Edward Island belongs to these developments. British officers serving in the St Lawrence theatre during the conflict spread word of the region's resources and helped generate a speculative surge at the end of the war. Postwar policies for the development of the Island reflected these pressures.

Under the direction of Samuel Holland, surveyor general of Quebec and the northern district of North America, a survey was begun in 1765. The survey assessed the improvements brought about by French occupation and use of the colony, which were layered upon First Nations' use of the island. Prince Edward Island was divided into three counties, with land set aside in each for royalties that would contain the county seat (see map 1.1) The remainder of the lands in each county were subdivided into townships of roughly twenty thousand acres and distributed in 1767 to military men and other land seekers. Except for one lot that was reserved for the Crown and two that were granted to merchants with existing Island investments, a lottery determined which township went to which recipient.[4] The grants themselves were issued in Nova Scotia and later on Prince Edward Island, upon request. Some grants were issued in Nova Scotia and reissued on Prince Edward Island, some appear never to have been issued, and others were not issued until as late as 1795.[5] Recipients of these grants were expected to bear the cost of settling the Island and providing for government; the reward of frontier land was coupled with an obligation to help carry the burden of empire. Because the Imperial government was concerned with the 'intention and ability' of potential proprietors to 'make settlement' on their Island lands, the Board of Trade required those seeking to become Island proprietors, or their agents, to appear personally before the Board of Trade in June 1767 to indicate 'what they had to

Map 1.1. Samuel Holland's plan

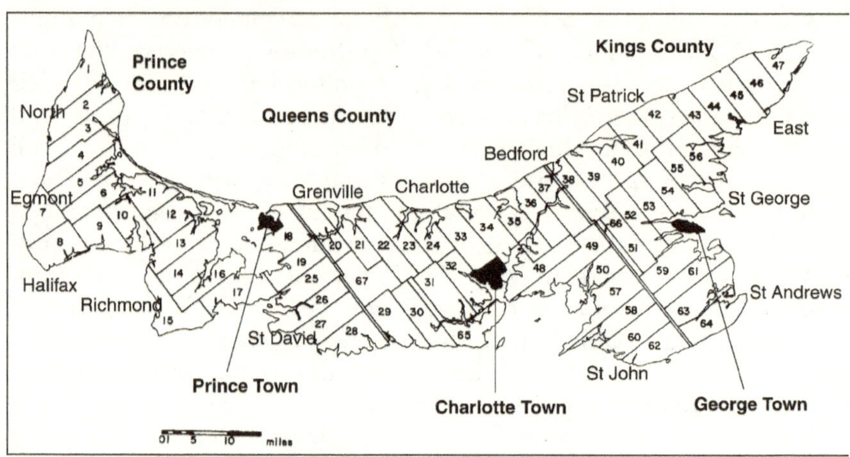

Source: Drawn from map by Samuel Holland and reproduced in James Munro, ed., *Acts of the Privy Council of England, Colonial Series*, Vol. 5

offer in support of their petitions' for colonial land.[6] Grantees were required to settle their lots with foreign Protestants – these people to be drawn from Europe or other parts of North America – at the rate of one hundred settlers per township, and to pay annual quit rents of between two and six shillings per hundred acres to the Crown. One-third of their holdings were to be settled in the proper proportions within four years and all within ten. In most of the grants, the Crown reserved a five-hundred-foot-wide belt of land above the high-water mark to be used to support a fishery.

The Imperial government's policies for land distribution in Prince Edward Island during the postwar speculative boom were neither unique nor anachronistic. Royal quit rents, such as those established on the Island, had been a part of financing in British colonies since 1625, and they remained an aspect of land policy in the non-rebelling colonies well into the nineteenth century.[7] The distribution of large tracts of frontier land to speculators in advance of significant settlement was a common practice in British North America, just as it was in the North American colonies of other European powers, and it would continue on the continent for years to come, persisting in government dealings with land companies and in the financing of railways.[8] Nor was the coupling of land ownership with obligations to develop it an unusual idea or one whose time had passed. Large tracts of land were similarly distributed in other colonies; comparable policies governed the distribution of Crown land to homesteaders into the twentieth century. Those receiving Crown grants of small tracts of land in British North America in the late eighteenth and early nineteenth centuries were required both to pay quit rents and to settle and improve their land.[9] The Dominion Lands Act of 1872, which established the terms whereby thousands of men gained access to lands on the western prairies, made the granting of land provisional on occupancy and cultivation of the soil.[10]

Nor is it useful to conceptualize the land tenure system that the British established on Prince Edward Island as 'neo-feudal.' Certainly, all the European-derived systems of land tenure in North America contain feudal elements. But this characterization, which has roots in the history of resistance to landlordism on Prince Edward Island, suggests more, particularly when coupled with a historiography that has exaggerated the significance of anachronistic thinking in Imperial planning for the Island.[11] How best to define 'feudal' has been a matter of much controversy, but whether we take feudalism to be a system combining 'the right to revenues from the land with the right to exercise authority' or as a mode of production in which rents were extracted by 'non-economic forms of compulsion,' or focus on the personal bonds of mutual obligation that sustained it, there was little that was 'feudal' about the system of land tenure that was established on Prince Edward Island.[12] While royal quit rents did assert the 'feudal position of the Crown,' the development of quit rent systems in the British colonies of North America, with the rents paid either to a proprietor or to the Crown, was part of the spread of modern, post-feudal forms of land tenure to the New World.[13] Historically the emergence of quit rents in the British countryside was an indication of the decline of feudal relations, in that they represented the replacement of tenure by personal service with tenure by the payment of cash.[14] And while there were aspects of a feudal revival in the powers of governance that were granted in proprietary colonies such as Pennsylvania, Maryland, and the Carolinas, no such powers were granted to the proprietors who received grants on Prince Edward Island.[15] Initially the Island came under the jurisdiction of the Crown colony of Nova Scotia. When, as of 1769, proprietorial petitioning led to its establishment as a separate colony, Prince Edward Island became a Crown colony in its own right.

Proprietors had no legislative or judicial powers; these lay with the Crown. While many of the proprietors who concerned themselves with organizing settlement chose to rent rather than sell their lands, the establishment of the mode of tenure within townships was a matter of proprietorial choice; it was not stipulated in the terms of the township grants. A few proprietors attempted to cast themselves as feudal lords, but their ability to do so depended upon the willingness of tenants to assume leases that committed them – for example – to grind all their grain at the landlord's mill and provide labour for his estate; it rested on contracts that tenants could refuse.[16] Proprietors who chose to do so could and did sell land to settlers. In any case, neither the lease nor the sale of land for money provides evidence of feudal practice. The law that governed landlord/tenant relations on the Island was, except when modified by colonial statutes, the same body of law that as of 1773 governed the relations between British farmers and their landlords. The circumstances that offended settlers on Prince Edward Island, and that inspired many to contest the status quo, related to the concentration of economic resources in the hands of a few as private property as well as to the maintenance of this enormous power by the force of law. The system that had been established was fully in keeping with the ways of a capitalist order.

British land policy on Prince Edward Island in the years after the Seven Years' War was, thus, consistent with general patterns of land tenure in North America. The most anomalous practices on the British North American frontier in this period were not those affecting Prince Edward Island, but those governing land tenure in Newfoundland and Quebec. In Newfoundland, Imperial authorities impeded the establishment of private property rights in land; in Quebec, they chose to maintain the seigneurial system the French had established.[17] Imperial policy on Prince Edward Island was similar to that governing land distribution in Nova Scotia, to which it was annexed at the end of the Seven Years' War, when land policy was formulated for the Island. Both Nova Scotia and Prince Edward Island experienced a great land boom after the Seven Years' War as speculators sought to benefit from the opportunities offered by a reorganized empire and to make profits from the improvements left by the expulsion of most of the region's thirteen thousand Acadians.[18] And in both there was a flurry of land-granting activity. Less than two years before the imperial government decided to allocate 1.4 million acres on Prince Edward Island in a single day, Nova Scotian's government had distributed 3 million acres in large grants over the course of seventeen days.[19] These grants, like those later issued for land on Prince Edward Island, required proprietors to pay quit rents and to settle their lands. Joshua Mauger's grant for 100,000 acres along the Saint John River in what is now New Brunswick, for instance, required him to pay quit rents of one shilling for each fifty acres, beginning ten years after the date of the grant, and to establish Protestants who would 'plant, cultivate, improve or inclose' one-third of the grant within ten years. Two-thirds was to be settled and improved within twenty years and all within thirty.[20]

During these years, however, Nova Scotia and Prince Edward Island differed in subtle but important ways in their land policies; these differences contributed to the emergence of contrasting patterns of development by the end of the eighteenth century. The distribution of land in Nova Scotia, while occurring within a policy framework established by Imperial authorities, was a local initiative: the government in Halifax determined the detailed terms of the grants and who would receive them. In the case of Prince Edward Island these decisions were made by the Imperial government. Also, Nova Scotia had a longer history of British rule and colonial land policy, which meant that legislation regulating the recovery of Crown grants was in place prior to the great distribution of grants in the 1760s – in other words, prior to the first deadlines for meeting settlement conditions. Indeed, there was a history of escheat actions. This was not the case on Prince Edward Island after it ceased to be part of Nova Scotia. As well, the massive distribution of Nova Scotian lands in the third quarter of the nineteenth century, large as it was, did not encompass all the province's resources. Undistributed Crown lands remained, and earlier grants had placed other properties in private hands. When Prince Edward Island was established as a separate colony, the Island differed from Nova Scotia in being a jurisdiction without private lands pre-dating the 1767 grants and without a significant quantity of Crown land. With the exception of land set aside for three county seats, a landlocked six-thousand-acre lot that had been reserved for the Crown, and land retained for fishery reserves, churches, glebes, schools, wharves, fortifications, naval yards, and roads, the proprietorial allocations of 1767 were the basis of all title on Prince Edward Island subsequent to the property rights of Mi'kmaq and Acadians, which the British ignored.[21]

As in other regions of North America where large tracts of land were granted with settlement and quit rent conditions, the history of these grants in Nova Scotia and Prince Edward Island was one of proprietorial failure. Few grantees undertook to meet their obligations. Although quit rents trickled in from some proprietors, most did not pay.[22] Around half a dozen of the hundred or so proprietors who received Island lands undertook developmental schemes in the years between the lottery of 1767 and the beginning of the American Revolution.[23] Captain Robert Stewart, the son of a Church of Scotland minister, brought perhaps eighty Scots to his family's portion of Lot 18 on Malpeque Bay, in part by promising free land there for those who would pay their own passage.[24] James Montgomery, lord advocate of Scotland and recipient of one lot in the original lottery, purchased yet more townships and recruited fifty indentured servants in Scotland to work on a commercial flax operation he sought to develop on Lot 34 in north-central Queens County. He also attracted a few dozen tenants to settle near a commercial timber operation he established at Three Rivers in Kings County.[25] Captain John Macdonald of Glenaladale, chief of a cadet branch of Clan Ranald, and his brother Donald, purchased Lot 36 from Montgomery and, with the aid of the Scottish Catholic Church, organized the movement of roughly two hundred Catholics from the Highlands to Prince Edward Island.[26] Robert Clark and Robert Campbell, Londoners with mercantile connections, worked together to develop an English settlement on Lot 21 in northwestern Queens County, combining commercial goals with a desire to provide a refuge for English Quakers.[27] And Irish-born Thomas Desbrisay, the colony's lieutenant-governor from 1769 to 1784 and an active speculator and promoter, attracted perhaps two hundred settlers to property he held on Lots 31 and 33 in Queens County – though most did not stay in these townships – by placing advertisements in northern Irish newspapers.[28] These ventures, coupled with less organized movements of people into and about the region, increased the Island's population from roughly five hundred at the time of Holland's survey to between thirteen and fifteen hundred at the outbreak of the American Revolution.[29]

Although proprietors like Montgomery, Clark, and the Macdonalds could argue that they and/or their backers had spent thousands of pounds and thus helped advance the settlement of the colony, neither these few active proprietors nor the scores of inactive ones could claim that they had adhered to the terms of their grants. Proprietors were allowed four years to settle one-third of their lands with the appropriate number of foreign Protestants and ten years to settle the whole of their grants at the ratio stipulated by the original terms. None ever did. Nor could any honestly claim to have attempted to meet these terms.

The proprietorial activity that did occur was shaped by commercial and religious considerations rather than by a concern to meet the conditions of these grants. And the considerable costs that some incurred in advancing their projects were due to the expense of these particular endeavours, and were not – as proprietors would later contend – an indication of the unreasonable burdens placed on them by the terms of the Crown grants. Had proprietors been seriously concerned about meeting their settlement requirements, they would have recruited Protestant immigrants from Europe or other American colonies. And had they wanted to establish a sufficient number of settlers on their properties at the least personal expense, more would have followed Captain Stewart's lead – that is, they would have offered free land to entice settlers to pay their own costs of immigration and settlement. Given the different course that proprietors followed, however, as of 1772, Island grants allocated by lottery in 1767 and granted the following year had, by their terms, 'become forfeited to His Majesty His Heirs & Successors, and ... [were] void and of none Effect.'[30] In short, most of the grants were subject to escheat prior to the American Revolution, and the argument for mitigating circumstances and good intent, even in the cases of active proprietors, was thin.

The concentration of land ownership on the Island would no doubt have become a matter of settler complaint under any circumstances. That the landlords' economic power was based on conditional grants that had become void shortly after they were issued compounded the reasons for grievance. So too did the emergence of a different pattern of land history in Nova Scotia. There, and in the new colony of New Brunswick – which was carved out of Nova Scotia in 1784 – when proprietors failed to fulfil the conditions of their grants, their lands were escheated. The Nova Scotia government began resuming the grants of the 1760s on the eve of the American Revolution. Local officials interested in land speculation and accustomed to local procedures for escheating and regranting land initiated the process. With the movement of thousands of refugees northward following the defeat of British forces in the American Revolution, the resumption of the grants of the 1760s accelerated. One and a half million acres were escheated in greater Nova Scotia between 1783 and 1788; this enabled the government to provide incoming Loyalists with tracts of Crown land. As well, land on Cape Breton Island, which had previously been off limits to settlement, was made available to the new immigrants by Crown grant.[31]

Thus, land tenure in adjacent regions of British North America shifted significantly in the 1770s and 1780s, as large grants were resumed by the Crown and regranted in smaller lots, and as new areas opened for agricultural settlement. Meanwhile, circumstances on Prince Edward Island remained relatively static. Land speculators within government circles stripped some proprietors of their holdings by prosecuting them for quit rent arrears and then purchasing their townships at distraint auctions of dubious legality, but this simply changed the composition of proprietorial ranks and further muddied the question of title.[32] The American Revolution brought no big shifts in land policy. Neither Guy Carleton, who as British commander-and-chief at New York oversaw arrangements for the evacuation of Loyalists from the rebelling colonies, nor the various Loyalist agents who visited the Maritimes to make local arrangements, nor the authorities in the Imperial centre who responded to the postwar crisis, paid much attention to the possibility of accommodating significant numbers of Loyalists on Prince Edward Island. The small scale of the colony and the absence of extensive Crown lands no doubt had something to do with this. What initiatives did occur in response to the Loyalist influx were private initiatives tailored to meet private needs. In 1783, Prince Edward Island's governor, Walter Patterson, and a number of his associates – who, like him, had acquired distrained lands recently auctioned for quit rent arrears – along with several other proprietors, offered collectively to provide 100,000 acres of free land for the benefit of Loyalist settlers.[33] On Prince Edward Island, American refugees were to be provided with land by private charity rather than government grant – although the Island government was left with the task of arranging the transfer of these lands. In the process, old and new proprietors alike hoped to strengthen their tenuous claims to Island lands and to shore up their title to the conditional grants of the 1760s.

The events of the American Revolution and of the Imperial restructuring that followed, that saw Prince Edward Island diverge from the broader regional pattern of Crown resumption of the large grants of the 1760s, provided the backdrop for the first coherent challenge to the Island's land tenure system. Some of the five hundred or so Loyalists who moved to the colony in the years after the war assumed a significant role in this protest as many of them soon became entangled in the problems and complications of the land system on the Island. But the discontent that they came to feel, and that they helped articulate, predated their arrival and the organized protests of the 1790s. Behind the development of a political challenge to the proprietorial system at the end of the eighteenth century lay years of inchoate resistance to the Imperial plan for the Island.

British policy, expressed in the Cartesian order of Samuel Holland's survey, indicated one way of conceptualizing the Island's land and of organizing life upon it. It was a way fully in keeping with the confident rationalism of Imperial elites. Straight lines were drawn across the irregular arrangements of hill and marsh and across the meanderings of river and stream. And a social plan of comparable lineaments was sketched out whereby a stable hierarchical society would take shape on the Imperial frontier, with settlers answering to proprietors and proprietors to the Crown. Life as it was lived on the Island at the time of Holland's survey and in the years thereafter represented another way of relating to the land. And it carried with it a challenge to Imperial plans and to those who sought to benefit from their implementation. In theory, every parcel of land was part of a numbered lot whose owner held the appropriate title documents, and anyone who wanted to make use of that parcel might do so only with the owner's permission and under their conditions. In fact, these spatial and social projections remained, for the most part, simply that during the first decades of British rule: projections. The Island's Mi'kmaq residents, who had been left out of British planning for the colony, continued to gain their livelihood by seasonal movements that linked the varied resources of river, coastal, and inland sites, both on and off the Island; they paid little heed to the new British claims of property ownership.[34] The Acadians, who persisted despite the deportations, tended to follow similar strategies.[35] There were, of course, a few nodes of proprietorial enterprise, places where aspects of the structures envisaged by Imperial planners were being articulated, but for decades after the lottery of 1767, most Island land lay outside of active proprietorial control. And many of those who had begun Island living as part of these enterprises soon moved elsewhere. Most of the eighty or so Scots whom Captain Robert Stewart brought to his lands on Lot 18 left to take up abandoned Acadian lands on the other side of Malpeque Bay.[36] The same held with immigrants attracted to other proprietorial operations.

Settlers tended to move on as they gained a local understanding of Island circumstances and of the situation in adjacent colonies.[37] The land that Island residents knew was one where geography and the labour of earlier inhabitants had produced scattered opportunities – old Acadian clearings stretching back from coast and river, pockets of marsh that would yield a regular supply of hay, and sheltered coves and bays with mussels and oysters and possibilities for pursuing the fishery. It was a land of curves and irregularities, where livelihoods were gained by exploiting differences in the local environment. As well, it was a land lacking in formal control. Across much of the Island during the early years of British rule, occupation and use had a greater local significance than did title. Alexander MacLean's description of how he came to hold the land that he farmed on Lot 55 in Kings County reflected a common experience: he 'saw the place vacant and liked it, and so took it.' He did not trouble with the details of titular owners and 'got no leave' from any landlord.[38] His was a common story in the eighteenth and early nineteenth centuries.[39]

The possibilities for obtaining unmediated access to resources, and the traditions associated with doing so, persisted well into the nineteenth century. As early as the late eighteenth century, though, these opportunities were becoming constricted as settlement increased and the structures of Imperial and proprietorial control became better established. With the development of a colonial capital in Charlottetown and the establishment of a council and a Supreme Court in 1770 and a House of Assembly in 1773, government became more tangible, and those possessing grants increasingly had means whereby they might uphold their property claims.[40] As well, the expansion of settlement increased the competition for resources among Island residents. Securing legal claim to the land they used, or sought to use, began to matter more to settlers as the colony's population grew. Doing so, though, was problematic. In some cases the owners of township grants took no interest in their property, and those who settled on these people's lots, while free from the burden of rents, lacked the means for securing their position. And especially in the more valuable townships, where proprietors interested in actively managing their lands were assuming control, Islanders had to conform to these men's demands. Settlers seeking to benefit from the soil and locale of the lots along the Hillsborough River northeast of Charlottetown, for instance, had to enter into agreements with landlords such as James Montgomery, John Macdonald, or Thomas Desbrisay, or their agents. And many found the cost of access, whether by purchase or lease, to be beyond their means. As John Macdonald noted, his fellow proprietors tended to 'expect too high rents.'[41] For a variety of reasons, the settler world of use, need, and local circumstance was not easily reconciled with the Imperial and proprietorial world of numbered lots, large-scale holdings, and the prerogatives of landed wealth.

Organized opposition to the land system, when it emerged in the late eighteenth century, and as it persisted into the following century, reflected a popular desire to bring the structures supported by the state in line with local needs and ways, rather than vice versa. It was in this sense part of a common frontier experience of resistance to metropolitan organization and domination.[42] Although the property claims of those holding township grants posed an obstacle to achieving these ends, the unfulfilled conditions of these grants and the patterns of Crown resumption in adjacent colonies suggested ways around this problem. If big proprietorial grants could be reclaimed in Nova Scotia and New Brunswick and the land within them distributed in small parcels to new settlers and their existing occupants, why not on Prince Edward Island as well?

The possibility of escheat proceedings was first raised as a political issue on Prince Edward Island in 1790, during the election of a new House of Assembly. It emerged at that time on the heels of massive escheats in Nova Scotia and New Brunswick. As well, it emerged in the context of significant changes in Island politics occasioned by postwar immigration, the arrival of a new chief executive, Lieutenant-Governor[43] Edmund Fanning, and a shift in power among contending clusters of the Island's elite. The election, held at a time when the Island probably had fewer than four thousand inhabitants, pitted a party formed around the Island's first governor, Walter Patterson, against another formed around the families of Chief Justice Peter Stewart (the younger brother of Captain Robert Stewart) and Thomas Desbrisay. Land policy became an issue during the election when some members of the latter party sought votes by promising to arrange for the establishment of a court of escheat on the Island and the redistribution of proprietorial land in small tracts to settlers.[44] Several years later, Joseph Robinson, who had been speaker of the House of Assembly after the election, and subsequently was appointed to council by Fanning, launched a campaign to achieve these ends.

Much of what we know about the thinking informing this early escheat movement comes from a manifesto that Robinson wrote and that was widely circulated around the countryside in draft form.[45] Robinson was a Loyalist from South Carolina who had served with distinction there as an officer during the early years of armed conflict and had become a lieutenant-colonel in the South Carolina Royalists. At the invitation of Lieutenant-Governor Fanning, a fellow Loyalist with first-hand knowledge of life in the Carolinas, Robinson moved from

New Brunswick to Prince Edward Island in 1789. His relationship to Fanning and to the prominent families associated with the lieutenant-governor is not clear. In terms of education, background, and leadership skills, Robinson had reason to believe himself equal to any on the Island. His actual circumstances, though, left much to be desired. While others held comfortable salaried positions, his work as a member of council and as an assistant Supreme Court judge was unpaid. And while some of those associated with the Stewart/Desbrisay party – Fanning in time included – were landlords, Robinson, who had once owned a back-country plantation, was struggling with the difficulties of being James Montgomery's tenant. This may help explain why he came to associate himself with the cause of those settlers who were dissatisfied with the status quo, and why he articulated their grievances as well as his own.[46]

Robinson's manifesto described the tension between the settlers' world and the proprietorial order and called for an end to landlordism on the Island.[47] Robinson challenged the fairness and justice of the proprietors' demands, and the Imperial land policies that supported those demands, by speaking to the realities of daily life in rural communities. It was not possible, he argued, for tenants to meet the rents that landlords were demanding in a place where farming was only possible for five months of the year and in a wilderness environment where farm making required generations of unrelenting work. Because rents were too heavy a burden under these circumstances, tenants inevitably fell into arrears and were vulnerable to being evicted and thus to losing all their improvements – their cleared fields, fences, houses, and barns. The settlers' world could not, he argued, be reconciled with the plans and projections of the Imperial government and the proprietors, people who in general had no direct experience of the colony. Furthermore, he noted, there was no longer a legal basis for this project, as the proprietors of township grants had not fulfilled the conditions of their grants. The legitimate claims of ownership, he contended, lay with those who were investing their labour in the land and not with those who clung to township grants that were now void. He placed the history of land tenure on the Island in the context of British policy elsewhere in North America, noting that a similar proprietorial system in the Carolinas had been swept away with the introduction of new Imperial policies in the early eighteenth century and that comparable things had happened as a result of major escheats in Nova Scotia.[48] In his discussions of the land question, Robinson also noted the simplicity of the escheat process in

New Brunswick and described how escheats were effected there through existing Chancery Court procedures.[49]

Robinson's manifesto, which was distributed about the Island by his son-in-law Robert Hodgson, who had also been elected to the assembly in 1790, called on Islanders to petition the house for a court of escheat. Other assemblymen and local magistrates convened meetings around the Island where the manifesto was discussed and petitions constructed.[50] In the wake of these rural meetings and the ensuing petitions to the house, the assembly prepared a report on the Island's land situation and sent it, along with a petition for the establishment of a Court of Escheat, to the Imperial government.[51] Settlers made plans, which never came to fruition, to send Robinson to Britain to make the case for a general escheat.[52] Public discussion of the land question and the organization of political initiatives fostered other modes of protest as well. Widespread rent resistance emerged in tandem with the petition campaign, and so too did resistance to militia service.[53] In the late summer of 1797, a year after Robinson's manifesto had given rise to public meetings in the countryside, members of the Prince County militia used the occasion of a muster to link military affairs with the land question.[54] While obeying orders to assemble in a Princetown field, they refused to fall into ranks or to follow their officer's commands. Instead, the rank and file held a meeting a few hundred yards from their officers and then sent three 'commissioners or delegates' to relay their sentiments. The government, the militiamen insisted, needed to grant them titles to their lands equivalent to those available to settlers in Nova Scotia. Under such circumstances 'they would obey the militia laws, but not otherwise.' Similar resistance occurred among the Acadians at Grand Rustico and in communities elsewhere on the Island.[55]

These challenges, not surprisingly, generated alarm in some circles. John Hill, at times a resident landlord and a key player in the Island's mercantile development, was deeply disturbed by the course of events in the colony and appalled that government officers were 'conniving at the peasantry being invited to discuss so delicate a subject' as property rights and 'a division of lands.' The Island's rural residents, he claimed, were developing 'wild ideas about natural rights.' Escheat, he noted in a letter to the Colonial Office, had become 'the general subject of conversation among the lowest classes and even labourers have asserted that no man ought to be a tenant on the Island.'[56] John Macdonald, who was wrestling for power with his own difficult tenantry, suggested that principles were being disseminated on the Island 'which may vie with the like which have laid France to ruins.'[57] Even Lieutenant-Governor Fanning, who had reason to downplay the tensions on the Island, and whom some were blaming for allowing Robinson to challenge landlordism in the colony, acknowledged to his superiors in London that Island affairs had some similarities with unsettling events occurring elsewhere in the final decades of the eighteenth century. In the fall of 1797 he wrote that the colony was being shaken by the actions of 'restless individuals' who, like those 'in many other parts of the World,' were being drawn to 'a profligate spirit of falsehood and calumny evidently leveled at exciting a contempt of constituted authorities and bearing a threatening aspect against the peace of society.'[58]

Recent accounts of this period of Island history have tended to downplay evidence of popular radicalism and have instead emphasized the extent to which the discussion of land policy was a matter of political manoeuvring among the upper classes. In the first half-century of the Island's existence as a British colony, the land question was, Jack Bumsted has argued, 'not really a popular issue at all, but one created by contending factions of elites (chiefly officials and would-be officials) for their own political, economic, and social advantage.'[59] The research sustaining this position provides a useful corrective to earlier accounts, which cast various members of the Island's establishment – men who were often proprietors themselves – as defenders of the interests of Islanders who worked the soil and as proponents of a new system of land tenure. And it tellingly challenges the thinking of those who have conceptualized Island land politics as a seamless popular struggle to throw off the yoke of landlordism. Nonetheless, focusing too narrowly on elites obscures matters of importance other than political leadership. Elites did not 'create' the land question. Rather, at various times and for a variety of reasons, some chose to address rural problems and to articulate popular perceptions. Their political choices were the product of broader forces.[60] Nor did elites always have it within their power to keep popular agitation within channels of their choosing.[61] In the case of the militia revolts of 1797, the commanding officer of the Prince County units was none other than Joseph Robinson. While he certainly agreed with the call for land grants equivalent to those being issued in Nova Scotia, and was an advocate of rent resistance, it seems unlikely – particularly given his bitter experience of civil war in the Carolinas – that he would have approved of this method of agitating the issue.

Those among the Island's upper classes who spoke of democratic stirrings on the Island and growing popular unrest were not simply paranoid. The land agitation of the 1790s did have a popular dimension, and as these people were well aware, various members of the elite were fuelling it and legitimating popular perceptions concerning property rights and justice. John Macdonald, who like Robinson was an exceptionally well-educated and astute observer, spoke to the broader significance of the events of the 1790s. He believed firmly that the land agitation was being manipulated by cronies of Fanning to serve their own short-term, selfish interests; at the same time, though, he suggested that it would yet have long-term consequences: 'It may be reasonably supposed that the embers of so general a combustion, though smothered for a time, may revive hereafter.'[62] The key word in his fire metaphor is 'general.' Seeing the extent of the escheat agitation – of which Macdonald had grassroots knowledge – he correctly sensed its significance to popular thinking and to the formation of enduring traditions.

In the short term, the challenges of the 1790s were checked and ultimately petered out. Fanning dealt with the militia revolts by confronting the mutinous rural units with an armed force composed of his key government officers, the sheriff, other civil and peace officers, the 'principal gentlemen in and about Charlottetown,' and a detachment of light horse mustered from among Charlottetown's militia.[63] By such means, and by compromises whereby none of the resisters were prosecuted, the militia units were persuaded to call a halt to overt acts of rebellion. Landlords dampened rent resistance by initiating legal proceedings.

Although the rural mobilization of the 1790s called for an escheat of proprietorial lands, and although the House of Assembly's subsequent appeal to the imperial government highlighted the benefits that escheats had produced in Nova Scotia and New Brunswick, when the Imperial government addressed Island grievances in the early nineteenth century, quit rent collection was its primary concern. That the imperial response was so long in coming had much to do with the difficulties of transportation in the late eighteenth century, Prince Edward Island's limited profile in imperial affairs, and the disruptions of war. That popular demands for land reform came to be translated into imperial policies designed to foster quit rent collection had much to do with the exertions of the Speaker of the House of Assembly, John Stewart, son of Chief Justice Peter Stewart, and his allies. Although Robinson's escheat manifesto had focused on the burdens that the

Imperial land system imposed on farm-making tenants and had advocated sweeping the proprietorial structure away in its entirety, the evidence the assembly submitted to the secretary of state opened up other possibilities. This evidence included a complex categorization of Island lots on the basis of their existing populations and the settlement initiatives some proprietors had undertaken. Although irrelevant if there was to be a general escheat, the breakdown could provide the basis for a partial escheat of the most sparsely populated lots. Whether such an escheat would be of much benefit to settlers on other lots was unclear. The House of Assembly evidence also provided data for producing a graduated taxation scale to deal with mounting quit rent arrears.

Stewart subsequently shaped the Imperial response to the assembly's initiatives by travelling to London in 1800 and appealing to the Colonial Office.[64] What Stewart sought was imperial backing for quit rent collection. In his account of land issues in *An Account of Prince Edward Island,* which he published in 1806, he framed his objections to a general escheat in terms of its potential to cause injury to proprietors who had invested in the Island; also, he objected to a limited escheat and the regranting of land in small tracts as this would undermine the ability of landlords to sell and lease land elsewhere on the Island.[65] The efforts of Stewart and the Island's colonial agents in London, William Knox and his son Thomas,[66] lay behind the Imperial government's new land policies for the Island, which were sent to Fanning in August 1802. The dispatch focused primarily on quit rent collection and on the enforcement of a graduated scale for the collection of arrears, this scale to extend from four to fifteen years, depending on the extent to which proprietors had settled their holdings. All proprietors would get a remission of arrears of more than fifteen years. The terms of the graduated scale tended to blur the distinction between settlement requirements, which were enforceable by escheat, and quit rent requirements, which were enforceable by distraint and the sale of sufficient property to pay the outstanding quit rent debt.[67] Lord Hobart provided draft legislation to support quit rent collection, and instructed Fanning to seek advice from Nova Scotia on escheat procedures and to move without delay.[68]

Hobart's dispatch failed to generate escheat proceedings, and in time a popular tradition emerged that blamed Fanning – who had become a landlord over the course of his administration – for the defeat of the escheat initiatives.[69] Certainly Fanning helped inflate some of the settlement statistics sent to the Colonial Office, but he did recommend that the legislature pass an escheat bill, as Hobart instructed, and he submitted the act to London in the spring of 1803, along with quit rent recovery legislation.[70] Indeed, as Bumsted's research has revealed, Fanning appears to have assented to the escheat act before submitting it to the Colonial Office.[71] Two years after passage of the act, however, the House of Assembly was still making inquiries as to whether the bill had received Imperial approval.[72] It had not, nor would it ever. Without positive Imperial support for initiating escheat proceedings, neither Fanning nor his successor, Lieutenant-Governor DesBarres, who assumed office in 1804, would proceed to recover forfeited grants. The drift away from the popular demand for an escheat of forfeited grants, though, had begun long before as the assembly framed its initial appeal to the Colonial Office.

The real beneficiaries of the escheat agitation of the 1790s proved to be government officers – primarily members of the Stewart/Desbrisay clique – who channelled popular pressure for an escheat into the new, albeit brief, Imperial resolve to enforce quit rent collection. This ultimately helped generate a significant flow of quit rents, which permitted a number of key Island figures, some of whom were owed back salaries payable from quit rent returns, to realize handsome sums. The official accounts of John Stewart, who occupied the lucrative post of collector of quit rents, and whose books were widely thought to have underrepresented his personal returns, indicate that in excess of £2,000 had moved into Stewart and Desbrisay hands by the first years of the nineteenth century.[73] As well, the threat of escheat, combined with demands for quit rent arrears, prompted many proprietors to sell their Island properties. Roughly one-third of the Island's lands changed hands in the aftermath of the events of the turn of the century.[74]

One of the legacies of the events of the 1790s was greater concentration of landholdings as a handful of individuals began to acquire vast grants at discount prices. As well, a more active proprietorial community emerged, as some of those speculating in Island lands began to pay a good deal of attention to their new acquisitions. John Hill, who had become a proprietor in the late 1770s, enlarged his holdings and his mercantile activities in western Prince County, ultimately creating an estate of nearly 100,000 acres. John Cambridge, who had been involved in various London-based mercantile schemes for the Island's development since the 1780s and who had served as Robert Clark's land agent, acquired the holdings of a number of proprietors and deepened his involvement in the economy of eastern Kings County. In time his estate, too, would grow to 100,000 acres. And Jonathan Worrell, a Barbadian planter who had retired to England, began assembling an estate for two of his sons, Charles and Edward, around St Peters in northern Kings County. It, too, would in time encompass roughly 100,000 acres. Most significantly, Thomas Douglas, the 5th Earl of Selkirk, began acquiring more than 150,000 acres and organized the movement of eight hundred Highlanders to land he held around Orwell Bay in southeastern Queens County.[75]

At a popular level, the challenges of the 1790s ended in disappointment. Certainly there were achievements, as well as a lasting legacy in terms of ideas and tactics. Robinson's pamphlet and the public discussions it generated helped validate the settlers' world that had emerged despite the Imperial plan, and served to clarify settler claims that use-based property rights had a greater legitimacy than those derived from the deeds issued following the allocations of 1767. As well, a broad repertoire of collective actions had been developed for advancing public calls for land reform. All of this would prove of lasting importance to ongoing rural attempts to alter land structures on the Island. The hopes and struggles of the 1790s, however, had led to little of immediate consequence for farm-making settlers. Life on the land in the early nineteenth century continued, in most cases, to revolve around reconciling the challenges of carving out a frontier living with the demands of those who claimed the land on the basis of titles derived from the Imperial allocations of 1767.

2 Land Issues in a Changing Context, 1800–1824

The Escheat movement of the 1830s drew not just from the protest traditions of the years after the American Revolution, but from the experiences of settlers and political leaders in the intervening years as well. The early years of the nineteenth century brought increased immigration to Prince Edward Island and with it yet more tensions arising from conflicting visions of an appropriate rural order. Shifts in estate ownership, coupled with economic growth, helped generate greater interest among proprietors in actively managing the Island's lands. In this, however, landlords continued to encounter difficulties and resistance. As the early nineteenth century unfolded, it became increasingly clear that the land question that had begun to take shape in the eighteenth century had an enduring quality and that it would persist despite the changes fostered by economic growth and by the arrival of waves of new settlers and despite significant shifts in Island politics.

Rent rolls provide insight into the texture of life in the countryside in the early nineteenth century. Those from Township 24, which stretches back from the shores of Rustico Bay in north-central Queens County, reveal how tenants went about making a living and meeting rent demands and how this changed in tandem with economic changes on the Island. In the summer of 1805 the agent made a survey of those occupying farms on the estate. Most of the settlers he visited had resided in the township for many years without paying any rent – a common practice in the early years of the Island's history as a British colony. Some were Acadians with a long history of Island residence. Others were recent immigrants from the British Isles. At farmstead after farmstead the agent took account of the years of residency and calculated the rents owing. Fermain Martin's case was not unusual. As of October 1805, according to the land agent's books, the Martin household owed £35 sterling in arrears for fourteen years of rent at £2/10 per 100 acres – half the rental rate demanded on a number of other Island estates at this time. The agent appears to have offered a 50 per cent abatement to all who agreed to pay their arrears, so this debt in fact worked out to be £17/10.[1]

The rent rolls for Lot 24 show that by October 1808 the Martins' debts had been compounded by the addition of another £7/10 in annual rents. To meet these demands, the Martins sold the land agent two heifers and an ox. These fetched roughly £10 – a good price, reflecting the buoyant economy of those years. As well, various members of the household sold their labour to pay the rent. Joseph Martin, a married son, hired out with his horses in the spring (probably for ploughing), mowed hay in the summer, and worked at sail making and boat building at other times of the year. His daughters and son dug potatoes and reaped grain. As well, he and his widowed mother set handwork against their rental debts, Joseph selling a dozen handspikes and his mother hose and mitts. These activities, which involved more than forty days of labour, earned the household another £10 that could be put against their arrears, leaving them £5 in debt as of the fall of 1808.[2]

The rent books for Lot 24 show similar patterns elsewhere. Tenants paid their rents by selling livestock, produce, handicrafts, and labour. The land agent purchased labour on a contract basis as well as on a daily basis. Peter Martin earned £9 by squaring more than twenty-four tons of pine in the winter of 1809. Francis Blanchard earned £1 by transporting goods in his boat to New London fifteen miles to the west, and John Peters earned five shillings by driving a flock of sheep to Charlottetown in the winter of 1810.[3] Tenants paid rents as well by selling fish and timber. While most households listed on the rent rolls for Lot 24 for the first decade of the nineteenth century managed, like the Martins, to meet a good part of the rents they owed by a combination of activities, they were not uniformly successful, nor did all tenants persuade the land agent of their good intentions. In some cases tenants had to give up parts of their farms to reduce their arrears; in others they were ejected entirely.[4] The rent books for Lot 24 highlight the substantial burden that rents placed on rural households and the significant risks stemming from arrears. The ongoing resistance to landlordism on the Island was grounded in these farm-level realities, played out in the various townships of the colony.

Besides providing a window on tenant life on one of the Island's many estates, the rent books for Lot 24 record a momentous change in the social and economic history of Prince Edward Island: the growth of the timber trade in the early nineteenth century. During the Napoleonic Wars, Britain lost its traditional source of timber when, following France's defeat of Prussia in 1806, Napoleon closed the Baltic ports to English shipping. Timber prices soared, and this, coupled with tariffs that favoured imports from British North America, gave rise to a booming timber trade on Prince Edward Island and elsewhere in British North America.[5] In 1805 and 1806 the land agent for Lot 24 collected less than £2 of rent in wood products. In 1807 more than £27 of rents were paid in timber, and yet more was earned in loading the vessels that came to pick up the loads. Over the following years, credits for deliveries of wood, for squaring (and resquaring) pine and hardwood, for sawing boards, and for rafting and loading timber became central to settlers' strategies for paying rents on the estate.

The expansion of the timber industry brought big changes to Prince Edward Island. In 1810, John Macdonald wrote to Lord Selkirk that the 'Island is in thrice a better state all over, than it was when your Lordship left it' in 1804. By 1809, Islanders were expecting two hundred vessels to call for cargoes of wood during the season.[6] The demand for timber drew entrepreneurs, capital, and, ultimately, waves of new settlers to the colony; at the same time, the increased traffic in vessels moving wood to British ports facilitated a reverse movement of immigrants. In the 1790s roughly four thousand people inhabited the colony; by 1814 the population had more than doubled. The colony's new lieutenant-governor, J.F.W. DesBarres, who replaced Edmund Fanning in 1805, reported that wage rates on the Island also doubled between 1805 and 1810. Besides helping established settlers pay their rents, these developments attracted many of modest means to the Island to begin the costly task of farm making.[7] They soon found themselves challenged to meet the demands of their landlords, who did not wait until the land was cleared and productive before demanding rent. The growth associated with the timber trade drew other types of immigrants as well. New merchants and professionals came, too, and many initially found themselves on the outside of established networks of power and patronage.

These years of growth and change provided the context for a new challenge to the status quo and for the continuing politicization of land grievances. The challenge began, innocuously enough, in 1806, with the formation of an association for promoting improvement on the Island.

The key player in the birth of this organization was J.B. Palmer, a Dublin attorney who had lived and worked in London before accepting a position as a land agent and immigrating to the Island in 1802.[8] Initially called the Farming Society, this group soon came to be called the Society of Loyal Electors.[9] Palmer, who was full of grand plans for developing the Island's resources (and advancing his own precarious fortunes), failed to gain a platform for the cause of improvement when he lost an election to the House of Assembly the year he arrived.[10] The campaign should have taught him the importance of the land question to Island politics. The election, which was called a few months after the arrival of the dispatch from Lord Hobart requesting passage of escheat legislation, allowed candidates associated with agitating the land issue to claim that they had orchestrated a land settlement of great value and to reap the rewards of the public's perception of their policies.[11] One of the successful candidates in Prince County, where Palmer ran, entered the assembly with written instructions to press for a general escheat and not settle for anything less. Candidates such as J.B. Palmer, who were not identified with the escheat cause or who did not promise to promote it, appear to have fared less well.[12]

It was on the eve of the next general election, in 1806, that Palmer helped organize the Society of Loyal Electors. He contended that the model for the association was the Dublin Society, which since its founding in 1731 had inspired the formation of many comparable improvement-oriented associations elsewhere in the British Isles and in Europe.[13] Palmer's claim is consistent with what we know of his thinking and of the Society of Loyal Electors during its early years. Like the Dublin Society, the Loyal Electors appear to have gathered together a 'public spirited middle class' dissatisfied with the status quo and interested in new intellectual developments and in promoting economic growth and change.[14] The Society of Loyal Electors was not a strong presence during the election of 1806, and its members did not emerge as a significant force in the new House of Assembly. Palmer ran for one of the Charlottetown seats on an improvement-oriented platform and again lost.[15] The society survived the election, however. Initially, it had between thirty and forty members. Although one of its opponents described it as lacking any 'person of rank or respectability' and consisting 'chiefly ... of Mechanics,' it found support among merchants and professionals living in and around Charlottetown, as well as artisans.[16] It came to include other lawyers, such as William Roubel; merchants such as Samuel Nelson and Elisha LePage; Highlanders from the tacksmen class such as C.D. Rankin and Angus Macaulay, who had recruited men for the military and for immigrant schemes; and, fortunately for the society, James Bagnall, editor of the *Weekly Recorder*, who gave the society sympathetic coverage in his paper when it began publication in 1810.[17] As originally organized, the society met monthly at Bagnall's Tavern in Charlottetown. In keeping with its urban character, the president of the Loyal Electors was called the 'Lord Mayor.' Other members were 'aldermen,' and yet others were known by similar titles associated with city government.[18] The 'Lord Mayor,' reported Captain John Macdonald of Glenaladale disparagingly, presided with a 'parcel of sticks formed in the shape of a mace before him.'[19]

Although the organization began as an urban group concerned with the cause of 'improvement,' by the early 1810s it had broadened its appeal and begun establishing branches in rural communities and providing French and Gaelic translations of its members' writings.[20] It was aided in its rural organizing by the movement of Loyalists and country magistrates into its ranks.[21] As it broadened its base, it increasingly came to be associated with settlers' demands for escheat and for fundamental land reform, although this was never its only concern. Whatever the original intentions of the men who founded the Society of Loyal Electors, they had learned that in order to gain a following they would have to adapt their program to prevailing rural sentiments. This brought about changes in the character of the society and led it, ultimately, to serve as a vehicle for the hopes generated by the escheat movement of the 1790s.[22]

Despite their attempts at rural organization and their appeal to escheat sentiments, the Loyal Electors again failed to get a majority in the assembly elections of 1812. Even so, they doubled their representation in a bitterly contested election that saw some of their opponents driven from the hustings by angry mobs, both in Charlottetown and on Lord Selkirk's property in Queens County.[23] The society won majorities in Prince and Queens counties, where the escheat movement of the 1790s appears to have been strongest; however, it failed to gain any seats in Kings County.[24]

Over time, then, the Society of Loyal Electors assumed a character quite different from that of the Dublin Society, which Palmer claimed was its model. This claim, made at a moment when the group was under severe attack for being a subversive body, may have been true of the original organization, but was belied by the shape the organization took in its later years. Roubel, a British attorney who had started out on the Island as a land agent and become a leading light of the society after joining it in 1809, contended that the appropriate parallel was the Essex political club that had supported the election of John Archer Houblon to the British House of Commons in 1810.[25] Roubel's claim was in keeping with the political direction the Loyal Electors followed; but it was also part of a defence of the society against charges of being unconstitutional, and it must be considered in this light. The society's opponents among the governing elite contended that the more appropriate parallel was the United Irish, the Jacobin organizations, or the British corresponding clubs.[26] Regarding the latter, they were particularly struck by the similarity between the British corresponding club model and the way the Loyal Electors were guiding the establishment of affiliated societies in the countryside.[27] There is, of course, no single answer concerning the relevant model. What becomes clear from the contemporary discussions of the Society of Loyal Electors is that educated Islanders were familiar with the wide variety of societies and clubs that had arisen in Britain, Europe, and America to further the claims and interests of various groups and that they – supporters and opponents alike – were capable of seeing how aspects of these developments might be adapted to Island circumstances.[28]

As a result of the political challenge organized by the Loyal Electors, new members of the merchant and professional community, new government officers, and new settlers alike were integrated into ongoing patterns of conflict. Much of what emerged reflected and reinforced the issues that had arisen in the 1790s. Of particular importance, new members of the leading ranks of the society took up the claim that proprietorial titles were unsound. Such messages were, no doubt, constantly being conveyed to new tenants by older settlers. Lord Selkirk reported in 1803 that the process had begun even before the three boatloads of immigrants he had brought from the Highlands had disembarked. Almost immediately on their arrival, he noted in his diary, 'country people had been on board circulating disadvantageous stories' concerning the land situation and escheat.[29] Countrypeople, John Macdonald reported in 1810, 'teach and bias all new comers' concerning the land question.[30] Such stories prompted some land agents to take out advertisements denying claims concerning the absence of valid proprietorial titles.[31] Popular views on the weakness of landlord titles gained additional credence when that weakness was proclaimed in public by leading members of Island society. Equally as important, prominent figures among the Loyal Electors reiterated the message that the state could and should align land policy with settlers' aspirations and that effective representation in the House of Assembly would ensure that this happened. As with the escheat agitation of the mid-1790s, some settlers made an abortive attempt to raise a fund to send a spokesperson to England to present land grievances to Imperial officials. J.B. Palmer was to be the delegate, and it appears that he was to focus particularly on the grievances of Loyalists.[32]

While the Loyal Electors built on existing traditions, they also broke new ground with their organizational methods. In part these were a product of the economic changes that were transforming the colony. The use the society made of Bagnall's newspaper to disseminate its views was a reflection not just of creative organizing but of the increasing maturity of the Island's press. The society also used celebratory dinners as a means to attract public attention and to herald victories over opponents – a tactic that probably reflected, among other things, changes in the size and sophistication of Charlottetown.[33] More importantly, the Loyal Electors were the first political society with elected officers and regular monthly meetings. This mode of organization provided a considerable degree of coherence to the society's political challenge. Indeed, some Islanders, foreseeing imminent conflict with the United States, wondered whether the society was becoming an alternative government capable of assuming power should Imperial authorities lose control of the colony.[34] As well, the society developed the idea of extending itself by having the Charlottetown group function as a corresponding society associated with rural branches. By such means, a coordinated Island-wide movement could be maintained. In a move of questionable legality, society members also considered establishing a committee – some saw it as a secret body – that would operate on its own during the intervals between monthly meetings.[35]

By the second decade of the nineteenth century, developments in the colony had contributed to the establishment of an Island version of the broader repertoire and pattern of popular politics that was emerging around the North Atlantic.[36] In terms of organizing strategies, we see the importance of petitions, manifestos, public meetings, celebratory dinners, newspaper reports, election campaigns, and political societies for focusing concern and for drawing together associations of people with shared grievances. In addition, the state was coming to be seen as a focus of protest and as the potential source of ameliorative change.[37] There are also parallels between the Island experience and what was occurring elsewhere around the Atlantic with regard to the aspirations that were being articulated. Although descriptions were heavily laden with proscriptions in the writings of those who spoke of the 'levelling' and 'democratic' tendencies at work in the colony, there is no doubt that egalitarian dreams were gaining currency and power. The popular call for a general escheat was in fact a call for a great levelling that would eliminate landlords altogether. The fact that 'the lowest classes' were discussing property rights and participating in political campaigns for change was, as John Hill noted at the time, fraught with significance.

Island settlers were asking for nothing more radical than what had already been established in Nova Scotia and New Brunswick by governmental directives; even so, their protests had a radical edge. The goal of land reformers was parity with land policies in adjacent colonies, and they repeatedly emphasized this aspect of their agitation as it presented their protest in a favourable light; but the process they followed for achieving this end, as the movement's critics noted, challenged central aspects of the established order by raising fundamental questions about the relationship between citizens and the state and the role of the state in the distribution of property. It was one thing, as in the case of Nova Scotia and New Brunswick, for government officers to decide it was appropriate, or necessary, for the state to reclaim grants that it had made and to then regrant them. It was quite another to redistribute land because of rural pressure to do so and to permit the state to act as an instrument for the realization of popular conceptions of a just apportionment of property.

Island observers among the elite noted worrisome international parallels. The situation in the spring of 1812, Abbé LeSeuer contended, increasingly reminded him of 'the state of France in the years 1789 and 1790.' LeSeuer had fled the French Revolution and so had a first-hand familiarity with popular protest. In Prince Edward Island as in France, he contended, the populace was being inflamed by rhetoric concerning the rights of the poor. He feared that if the organizations that were fanning the flames were not soon suppressed, things would 'soon turn out here as they did in my unfortunate country.'[38] The Chief Justice at this time, Caesar Colclough, worried about the similarities between developments on the Island in the early nineteenth century and the prelude to the United Irish rising, which he had helped suppress in his native country. Reports that the Society of Loyal Electors was 'attempting to gain over the soldiery' stationed on the Island were fitted into his memories of insurrection at home. Local Jacobins, he suggested, were acting as 'I know was done in Ireland in 1798.'[39] Others drew parallels with revolutionary challenges elsewhere. No doubt the rhetoric was in part aimed at justifying the suppression of the Loyal Electors, but there was a genuine fear among some of the elite that the established order was breaking down on the Island and that the colony was on the verge of a civil conflict that might endanger their property and their lives.[40] From their perspective, Island developments were kin to other unsettling events.[41] As Chief Justice Robert Thorpe phrased it in the early nineteenth century, the 'levelling Republican Spirit' on the Island was part of a broader force that was 'spreading misery over half the world.'[42]

The bitterly contested election of 1812 proved to be a turning point in the Island's political history. It marked the beginning of the end of a particularly creative period during which important linkages were established between formal politics and rural grievances. The rise of the Society of Loyal Electors, tainted as it was by association with democratic and levelling forces, set off alarms both on the Island and in Britain – alarms that eventually led to the curtain being brought down on these developments. Faced with urgent appeals from prominent Islanders, complaints from the colony's non-resident landlords, and the outbreak of war with the United States, which heightened concerns about maintaining authority within the colony, the Colonial Office recalled Lieutenant-Governor DesBarres, who had allowed the society to become a force on the Island. His replacement, Charles Douglass Smith, worked to dampen political debate and to quash democratic stirrings.

When Smith arrived on the Island in the summer of 1813, he believed that a firm hand would be necessary to deal with the existing state of affairs.[43] When he convened the assembly for the first time in November 1813, he saw threats everywhere and believed he could discern the Society of Loyal Electors' influence in the assembly. Claiming that the interest shown by the members in his handling of the colony's accounts was a reflection of the society's sway over the assembly, he abruptly prorogued it and set about devising ways to govern without popular input for as long as possible. The Society of Loyal Electors was, he informed Secretary of State Lord Bathurst, a 'club' of 'very dangerous principles.' The group was formed 'upon the plan and *principles* of the United Irish and connected I am strongly persuaded with the Irish in the United States of America.' Although no longer operating openly, they were 'as active as they dare to be' and remained a potent force.[44] Believing that democratic and levelling forces were at work in the colony, Smith sought to close the forums that sustained them and to reinforce the structures of hierarchy. He defended an earlier decision of the mayor of Charlottetown, J.F. Holland, to have the Supreme Court open with an elaborate procession through town, led by law officers bearing tin replicas of halberds and battleaxes and followed by the court officers in their robes, as a necessary step towards restoring a proper sense of deference in Island society. Commonfolk, 'the vulgar,' needed to be 'forcibly reminded almost daily of the proper respect due to ranks and offices,' and most particularly so 'on this side of the Atlantic.'[45] More importantly, Smith argued the following year, if the proper ordering of society was to be sustained, 'landed proprietors should be countenanced and supported in every possible degree by government against the attempts of democratic levellers' who kept 'stirring up sedition' by agitating the 'question of an Agrarian Law.'[46]

Whatever his original intentions, Smith's policies would in time drive the landlords and land agents he sought to make the mainstay of his government into the ranks of the opposition. Unable or unwilling to work with the assembly that was elected in 1812, or with subsequent assemblies elected in 1818 and 1820, he had to look beyond the legislature for sources of revenue. Permanent revenue acts had been passed in 1785 and 1795 to tax imports of wine, spirits, and beer, but the limited funds these provided were to be used exclusively for internal improvements.[47] Had Smith been able to work with the men who dominated the lower house, he might have obtained more revenues from trade. Because he could not, he was almost inevitably drawn towards policies that would provide resources for the government by, in some fashion, turning Island lands into a state resource.

Smith explored three initiatives in this regard. The first was to enforce the regular collection of quit rents. He described this as an 'absolute necessity,' given the how difficult it was to acquire revenues from the House of Assembly. He also considered levying taxes by working with a grand jury and justices of the peace – men whose appointments lay with the lieutenant-governor in council and the Chief Justice – to establish county rates. By this means, he thought he could quickly raise monies and demonstrate to the house that it was dispensable.[48] As well, he explored the possibility of reclaiming proprietorial grants. Indeed, by June 1815 he had become an advocate of the idea of a court of escheat. A risk with this policy was that it would undermine landlords' property claims and fan tenant unrest; however, Smith assured the Colonial Office that rural expectations of free grants were a thing of the past and that there were no grounds for believing that a court of escheat would pose a general threat to property. Smith suggested selling escheated lands to immigrants, thus providing the government with revenues outside the control of the House of Assembly. As well – as became clear with later dispatches – Smith planned to distribute newly acquired Crown lands among his allies. Escheated properties would provide the lieutenant-governor with badly needed patronage.[49]

Smith's plans for raising monies without working with the House of Assembly set him on a collision course with the Island's proprietors and their agents, the men he saw as his natural allies. In the spring of 1816 he began preparing for escheat proceedings.[50] It has been suggested that Smith's initiatives gained him a popular following.[51] Certainly this was not his intention. His acts were rooted in his continuing interest in enhancing the governor's powers by broadening the revenues and patronage at his disposal. They were also stimulated by directives emanating from the Colonial Office. Behind the latter, which concerned Lot 55 – a township that appeared to be without a proprietorial claimant – lay the lobbying efforts of one of the Island's most prominent families, the Stewarts, who hoped to obtain it.[52] Smith also took steps in the fall of 1816 to establish more active quit rent collection. In both cases he was concerned that the proceedings be conducted in ways that preserved the executive's power and did not concede rights to the legislature.[53]

Implementation of Smith's escheat and quit rent policies began in 1818.[54] He ordered inquests in February and then again in May, leading to the escheats of Lots 55 and 15. As Nova Scotia's solicitor general had noted when he advised Island authorities on how to conduct escheat proceedings, proving non-fulfilment of the terms of the grants was easy: it simply required summoning witnesses who would testify to the non-cultivated state of the township in question.[55] That done, the land was revested in the Crown. While it might be desirable to have local legislation for the regulation of escheat proceedings, it was possible – as Smith demonstrated – for the executive to initiate proceedings without it. His actions lent credibility to the arguments Joseph Robinson had made in the 1790s, when he advocated escheat proceedings and noted the ease with which they were conducted in New Brunswick. Progress was rapid with quit rent collection as well. Legal proceedings enforcing demands for rents and arrears quickly generated a significant flow of revenues from the Island's smallholders, who, some argued, were quite willing to pay their due provided that proprietors did as well.[56] The Crown, Smith reportedly jubilantly in February 1818, 'will soon have reliable revenue to direct as it sees fit.' By March he was claiming to have collected in one month one-fifth of the sum of quit rents that had been collected in the previous twenty-six years. As he noted in his February dispatch, landlords and their agents were far less forthcoming with their quit rents than were smallholders. Although proprietors and their representatives were collecting land rents from the Island's tenantry, the receivers of these revenues were not in turn fulfilling their obligations to the government.[57]

Although Smith's intentions were to strengthen the power of the Crown and to sustain a hierarchical order, his actions had different results. Not surprisingly, his proceedings generated a great stir throughout the Island. Smallholders scrambled to find the cash to pay their quit rents, as failure to pay on time could result in additional legal costs. Agents and resident proprietors looked for the larger sums to cover the rents due on thousands of acres and gathered for meetings and dinner parties to consider how they would respond to the demands.[58] As quit rent collection proceeded, rumours spread that Smith intended to sell lands for quit rent arrears and escheat yet more lots.[59] Even before he actually held escheat inquests, proprietors reported that news of his plans had affected 'the public mind' and 'totally prevented the selling or letting of land.'[60] Subsequent steps to protect the land claims of squatters who resided on escheated lots must have caused many to hope for more government action.[61] Perhaps Smith saw the proceedings as a means to regain the initiative in the conduct of the Island's administration; others saw them as evidence that the old dream of an escheat could become a reality.

Still others saw Smith's actions as proof of the need to check his power. Evidence of the effectiveness of their counter-exertions began to emerge in the summer of 1818: a dispatch from Lord Bathurst brought an end to Smith's quit rent collections and to his plans to escheat yet more townships. Ongoing lobbying by proprietors for changes in Imperial land policy had led to promises of alterations in the spring of 1816.[62] Urgent appeals from those feeling the sting of Smith's initiatives induced Lord Bathurst to publicize the Colonial Office's new policy concerning Island lands. Effective as of 1816, quit rents that, since Holland's original survey, had been graduated on the basis of land quality, were now all to be at the same rate – two shillings per hundred acres, the rate that used to apply only to the poorest lands. Those who had paid at a higher rate were to receive refunds, and proprietors owing more than £20 were to have the option of paying in Britain. As well, Bathurst announced a fundamental change in the settlement terms of the original grants. Landlords had long lobbied for new deeds in which the settlement requirements of 1767 would be dropped altogether, thus eliminating the threat of escheat. While not going this far, Bathurst's new policy relieved proprietors of the obligation to settle their lands with foreign Protestants – settlers of any sort would do – and gave them until 1826 to meet the hundred-settlers-per-township requirement that was supposed to have been met ten years after the grants were issued. The changes, posted on the last day of July 1818 and printed in Island papers a week later, represented a major victory for proprietors and a serious blow to Smith's credibility in the colony.[63] But they also reaffirmed fundamental features of the Island's original grants: quit rents and settlement requirements still mattered.

A significant realignment of forces had begun to emerge as Smith moved to implement his land policies, and it picked up momentum in the years following Lord Bathurst's 1818 dispatch. When he first arrived on the Island, Smith had found support among the Stewart and Desbrisay families and had aided them in their struggles against the Loyal Electors. As he laid plans for an escheat and the enforcement of quit rents, it was clear that a chasm was growing between the lieutenant-governor and his earliest allies. In a dispatch concerning the distribution of escheated lands, Smith noted that there were two or three families on the Island 'very much connected that grasp at everything,' including the opportunity to gain Crown land. In 1819 he made the same point concerning the distribution of offices: 'The families of Desbrisay and Stewart in this Island have grasped at, and for a long continuance of years have held at different times almost every office under the Crown in this colony, either by themselves or their immediate connections, and it is absolutely necessary to put an end to this system.' Had the Colonial Office provided him with the patronage necessary to gain new allies among prominent Islanders, and had he had the good sense to spread what little he had beyond the confines of his own family, perhaps Smith would have been able to withstand the enmity that was developing among his old allies. As it was, the ranks of his enemies swelled more rapidly than those of his friends, and a rapprochement was developing among the various anti-Smith forces. Men who had been important members of the Loyal Electors were beginning to work hand and glove with their old enemies and with landed interests.

Leading figures in the Island's merchant and professional community in the summer of 1818 joined forces with a broad spectrum of the residents of the Island's three royalties and with landlords to complain about quit rent policy. The petition forwarded to Smith bore the names of a number of former members of the Society of Loyal Electors.[64] To a considerable extent the emerging alliance was held together by shared anti-Smith sentiments and by the short-term interests of the parties involved. Lord Selkirk's agent reported in the summer of 1819 that faction was disappearing and being replaced by 'one feeling': 'unmixed detestation of Lieutenant-Governor Smith' and of his oppressive administration.[65] The possibility of a more lasting coalition, though, was taking shape as well. A meeting held in the late fall of 1817 suggested the grounds on which a more permanent working alliance might be built. Held ostensibly to bring together all those interested in promoting the fisheries, settlement, and public credit, the message of the meeting was that economic development on the Island had been retarded due to a lack of cooperation between proprietors and local capitalists and that by working together through the House of Assembly they could stimulate growth. The committee struck to promote these ends included representatives from the mercantile and professional community as well as the landed community. Some among the participants had once been members of the Society of Loyal Electors.[66]

Not all of the central figures associated with the Loyal Electors joined in this new alliance. Indeed, some spoke out against it. Angus Macaulay, who had become Speaker of the House after the 1818 election and who was a leader of the Highland community established on Lord Selkirk's estate, though he publicly opposed Smith over his treatment of the assembly, was nevertheless vehement in his denunciation of the new alliance between government officers and members of the landed and commercial communities. It was, he claimed, acting to thwart the interests of countrypeople.[67] Privately he suggested to Smith that the lieutentant-governor's noisy opponents did not have solid support in the countryside.[68] Yet another of the Loyal Electors from the tacksmen class, Coun Douly Rankin, also arrayed himself against the new coalition that was taking shape. Rankin came to serve as deputy receiver of quit rents under Smith and was active in upholding the governor's quit rent policies.[69] Their voices joined with those which claimed that Smith's land policies were in fact good for the general populace and that collection of quit rents would most hurt the land speculators. While all Island landowners would have to bear some of the burden of the tax, this was, Smith's supporters argued, a small price to pay for increased revenues for local improvements.[70]

The new political alignments taking shape on the Island at this time would prove to be enduring insofar as they pitted an alliance interested in state-fostered economic growth against those who maintained that the need for fundamental land reform was the central issue on the Island. The main political project in the short term, though, proved to be a campaign to have Smith removed from office. In the spring of 1819, leading men from the ranks of the Island's landlords, merchants, professionals, and government officers formulated plans for holding meetings in all three counties to prepare petitions calling for the governor's recall and to draw up affidavits to substantiate their complaints.[71] Smith's handling of land issues provided the primary focus for those rallying opposition, but other issues were important as well, including Smith's disdain for the House of Assembly.

Smith's decision to again attempt to enforce quit rent collection in the winter of 1822–3 drew the wrath of landlords, merchants, artisans, and other residents of the towns and royalties holding town lots, as well as smallholders in the countryside, as crudely organized collection procedures led to judgments against thousands of acres of land. In accordance with plans that members of the Island's elite had first formulated in 1819, mass meetings were held in all three counties in the spring of 1823. The names on the requisition to the sheriff calling for the protest meetings read like a who's who of proprietors, merchants, and professionals. Backing the call were landlords such as Donald Macdonald and Edward Worrell, agents such as John and Charles Stewart, Thomas Owen, and William Cooper, and merchants and shipbuilders such as Angus and Hugh Macdonald, Benjamin Webster, William Pope, Samuel Nelson, and George Dalrymple.[72] Despite the efforts of some rural leaders, such as Angus Macaulay, to dissuade people from joining the campaign, the meetings were well attended and gave credence to the claim that Smith had lost the confidence of the Island's population.[73] Documents produced at these meetings were published in the *Prince Edward Island Register* that fall, and a subscription was begun to raise £500 so that John Stewart might carry Island grievances to Britain and present them there in person.[74] Smith responded to the publicity by bringing charges against the editor and others associated with the challenge. He was, however, unable to follow through on the guilty verdicts pronounced in the Court of Chancery, where Smith himself had acted as the presiding judge. Fearing that he lacked the military strength necessary to sustain his judgments in the face of widespread opposition, Smith released the men without delivering a sentence.[75]

The evidence Stewart took to Britain in the fall of 1823 persuaded James Stephen, the Colonial Office's legal advisor, that a number of the charges of misconduct could not be effectively rebutted. Smith, in consequence, was dismissed the following year, and Colonel John Ready appointed as his replacement.[76] While it may be true, as Phil Buckner has argued, that Bathurst's decision to dismiss Smith hinged entirely on James Stephen's consideration of the legal case against him, and was unrelated to proprietors' pressure and the popular clamour raised against Smith, this was not how matters were viewed in the colony.[77] From an Island perspective, the change of governors and policies appeared to be the result of a mass campaign, backed by newspaper coverage, petitions, the complaints of the House of Assembly, affidavits substantiating specific incidents of grievance, and the dispatch of an informed delegate to the Colonial Office.

The first quarter of the nineteenth century enlarged the repertoire of popular protest on the Island and provided evidence, whether correctly read or not, that well-orchestrated mass protests could gain the attention of authorities in London and effect changes. Events in these years also demonstrated that the terms of the Island's eighteenth-century land grants were still relevant – indeed, that the grants could be revested in the Crown through escheats. Furthermore, Lord Bathurst's dispatch of 1818 set the clock ticking on the land issue yet again, in that it gave landlords a new ultimatum concerning the settlement conditions in their grants.

3 The Limitations of Developmental Politics, 1824–1831

The change of administration in 1824 brought with it a substantial change in the political climate on the Island, as Smith's autocracy gave way to participatory politics and the House of Assembly assumed a greater profile in Island affairs. The dominant political agenda that emerged in the late 1820s concerned how the state might foster economic growth in the colony. This project had drawn the interest of a broad array of the Island's elite in the previous decade and had the potential to generate wide support. The challenges of funding state-led growth, however, proved divisive; among other things, landed and mercantile interests tended to have different views concerning how best to raise state revenues. As well, the development project failed to directly address the concerns of a significant portion of the Island's growing population – specifically, their concerns about land tenure. Thus, over time, calls for escheat and land reform grew stronger and more persistent, while the political alliance supporting development policies began to fragment. In the process, the outlines of a three-way political dynamic began to emerge: landlords and their allies, leading members the Island's growing mercantile community, and representatives of tenants and small freeholders all vied with one another for control of state policy.[1]

Prior to his appointment as lieutenant-governor of Prince Edward Island, John Ready had served as an official in Lower Canada's government during the Richmond and Dalhousie administrations and had been on friendly terms with reformers there such as John Neilson and Louis-Joseph Papineau.[2] He would prove a friend to those interested in political reform on the Island as well. Ready regularly convened the Island's House of Assembly and sought to work through it rather than without it. He lent his support to initiatives he thought constructive and capable of sustaining a consensus in the colony and gaining support at home; and as best he could, he dampened initiatives he thought divisive. The new assembly's interest in investigating the wrongs of Smith's regime and in settling scores with Smith's supporters fell in the latter category. So, too, did policies designed to assert the assembly's powers vis-à-vis the appointed Legislative Council, although Ready was sympathetic to a series of initiatives taken by the assembly in an attempt to uphold its right to control appropriations. By contrast, measures tailored to foster the colony's economic development had the potential to gain broad support both in the colony and at home. The election rhetoric in the fall of 1824 had been full of calls for the state to take a hand in agriculture, the fishery, roads, schools, and currency reform.[3] Ready worked diligently to nurture these initiatives when they emerged in the 12th Assembly.[4]

The newly elected 12th General Assembly, which gathered in 1825, reflected the social and economic changes on the Island since the end of the Napoleonic Wars. By the mid-1820s the colony's population had grown to roughly twenty thousand as hundreds of new immigrants, most of them from the British Isles, added their numbers to the natural growth of the resident population. And while agriculture was a mainstay of the domestic economies of most households, timber and an emergent shipbuilding industry had become central to many of them as well. In 1824 an Island newspaper estimated that perhaps one thousand Islanders – approximately one-twentieth of the total population and perhaps one-fifth of the adult male population – were working in the shipyards.[5] Yet more earned wages cutting and hauling wood for shipbuilding and the timber trade. Over the course of the nineteenth century, the men who controlled these industries assumed an ever larger profile in Island society and in the lower house. Those elected to the assembly included a sprinkling of land agents and a pair each of doctors and lawyers.[6] The majority of assemblymen made an income through mercantile activities; most were players in the timber trade and the burgeoning shipbuilding industry. Indeed, more than one-third of the eighteen members of the house were involved in vessel construction.[7]

The dividing lines between those playing a leading role in the growing mercantile and industrial economies and those who held positions of prominence in Island society by other means were far from crisp. Some landlords took a prominent part in developing the Island's commercial and industrial potential. Lemuel Cambridge's family, for instance, held roughly 100,000 acres of land, while also investing in the shipbuilding and sawmilling industries and constructing a brewery.[8] Thomas Owen, who was closely associated with the Cambridge family, supported himself as a land agent, merchant, and shipbuilder – a not uncommon mixture of occupations.[9] And it is worth noting that the assembly elected John Stewart, a central figure in the old politics of the colony and a master at getting ahead through non-commercial means, as Speaker of the House. Nonetheless, it was clear that the assembly was dominated by men associated with the growing mercantile economy.

Over the second half of the 1820s these men – like many of their counterparts elsewhere in British North America – promoted policies that would assign the state a more active role in fostering economic growth.[10] In establishing a politics of development, they strengthened their own positions within state structures. Enhancing and controlling government revenues was of central importance to their plans, though the extensive legislation of the 12th General Assembly highlighted other concerns as well, including the regulation of labour, the protection of shipping, the standardization of weights and measures relative to export economies, and legal reforms.[11]

Government monies were derived from three main sources: an annual grant from Westminster, which paid the salaries of the major office holders in the colony; permanent duties on imported wine, spirits, and beer, supplemented by small sums derived from various sorts of government licences and fees; and duties and taxes imposed for a limited term by the assembly.[12] The Imperial government determined how the parliamentary grant would be used; monies raised through licences and the permanent revenue acts were, within the limits imposed by statute, allocated at the discretion of the lieutenant-governor and the appointed Executive Council, which advised him. Only insofar as the assembly raised monies through additional annual revenue acts did it constitutionally have control over any government expenditures. However, enlarging the assembly's economic power by imposing additional tariffs or taxes required the approval of the Legislative Council, the governor and, ultimately, the Imperial government. It also required potential sources of revenue.

In keeping with the pattern emerging elsewhere in British North America, the Island's assembly sought and was granted a greater role in government affairs. The Imperial government's representative was willing not simply to permit political debate in the house but to augment the assembly's power and influence in Island society by placing some of the permanent revenue at its disposal and by backing its plans for raising additional revenues.[13] With the support of Lieutenant-Governor Ready, the 12th General Assembly moved to stimulate the settlement and development of the colony through extensive government expenditures on infrastructure. During the latter years of Lieutenant-Governor Smith's regime, surpluses had accumulated in the treasury, and Lieutenant-Governor Ready made some of these available to the assembly for road improvement projects during the first years of his administration.[14] Island observers talked of a revolution in transportation in the second half of the decade.[15]

Those promoting these initiatives saw many benefits stemming from government investments in infrastructure. With road construction there were of course the direct advantages of improved lines of transportation, but beyond this, highways would also open up the largely unpopulated interior of the colony. During the first quarter of the nineteenth century, agricultural settlement had been restricted primarily to the coastline and to the lands bordering the Hillsborough and other major rivers. Road construction provided a way to expand the region supporting agrarian activities and promised an improved agricultural economy as the better lands of the interior were brought into production.[16] Also, and importantly for Island entrepreneurs, roads opened up new sources of supply for the timber, lumber, and shipbuilding industries.[17] Furthermore, as assemblymen noted, government investments of any sort did much to stimulate the economy. Prince Edward Island, unlike Nova Scotia, did not receive the economic benefits of British military expenditures. Local leaders suggested that the Island government could help fill this vacuum through wise expenditures of state funds. Road construction and investments in wharves and government buildings would put money into circulation and provide work opportunities for new and old settlers alike. Advocates also claimed that these expenditures would improve the Island's image and make it more attractive both to immigrants and to investment capital.[18]

The developmental plans of the leading politicians of the 12th Assembly probably would have required new sources of revenue under ordinary circumstances. Cyclical trends in the Atlantic economy, though, made this particularly urgent, as external market conditions beyond the control of local entrepreneurs were bringing about the collapse of the most important sectors of Prince Edward Island's export economy. The timber trade and the trade in Island-built ships, which together accounted for 92 per cent of the enumerated exports in 1825 and 85 per cent in 1826, declined precipitously in the latter years of the decade.[19]

Timber exports in 1828 were roughly one-third of what they had been in 1823. Even more importantly, ship construction, which had accounted for 78 per cent of the enumerated value of Island exports in 1826, plummeted from a peak of more than 9,200 tons that year to roughly 2,400 in 1830.[20] Exacerbating the fall in exports was a substantial decline in the profits being made per vessel and per ton of timber. In 1824, for instance, exports of pine timber were valued at £1 per ton; the following year they were valued at 15 shillings per ton. Over the same period, the estimated value of hardwood timber fell from 17/6 per ton to 15 shillings per ton.[21] Island-built shipping that was being valued at £10 per ton at the end of 1825 was being figured at £8 per ton the following year.[22] Thus the striking gross declines in exports do not capture the full impact of these declines on the colony's economic life.

Growth and improvement in the agricultural sector during Ready's regime – a development that has often been linked with Ready's personal interest in agricultural improvement – was in part a response to the near collapse of the timber and shipbuilding industries.[23] Some agricultural improvers suggested that the decline of the timber-based industries might in fact be a blessing and that the colony's economy was finally shifting to a more secure footing, with the growth in agricultural exports and increase in the percentage of improved land per farm. But even if this were so, the immediate repercussions were grim.[24]

Increasing the funds available to the state was a key problem for Island development prior to the depression of the late 1820s, and many of the ideas the 12th Assembly explored had been considered before. Except for the two lots that Lieutenant-Governor Smith had escheated, there was little Crown land on Prince Edward Island and thus little timber revenue and limited potential for acquiring money through land sales. Apart from the parliamentary grant, revenues were almost entirely derived from import tariffs, and these sums of course depended on the volume of trade. As export returns fell off, so too did imports and consequently government revenues, even as the assembly imposed additional tariffs.[25] A £4,000 surplus in funds that had accumulated during the final years of the Smith regime went quickly.[26]

To deal with the dilemma of increasing expectations for government expenditures at a time of declining revenues, the assembly would have to either increase the percentage and breadth of the tax on imports or find other sources of government funds. It adopted both strategies, enlarging the cut taken by duties even while pursuing alternatives. Not all of the assembly's revenue initiatives met with Imperial approval.

New duties on wine, liquor, tobacco, and tea were confirmed, but the Imperial government blocked a duty on all imports as well as an attempt to levy duties on molasses and sugar.[27] The assembly also initiated legislation permitting the issue of £8,000 of treasury notes.[28] As well, it explored the possibility of a land tax. Soon after taking office, the 12th Assembly petitioned Ready for an end to quit rent claims and for his assistance in persuading the Colonial Office to permit the replacement of this burden with a land tax of a comparable scale that could be used to sustain internal improvements.[29] Ultimately, the legislature passed a statute imposing a tax of two shillings per hundred acres on township lands and a tax on lots within the three royalties as well. Under the terms of the act, which would be in force for five years, these measures would only come into effect if the imperial government suspended the collection of quit rents during the period of the act. The monies raised by the act were to be used in the construction of public buildings.[30] The 12th Assembly also developed legislation that had the potential to fund highway construction by passing much of the cost of building new roads onto those landowners who would benefit from the construction. The same act provided compensation for those suffering damages from highway construction and provided a framework for the government to use the clauses in the original grants that reserved land for highways. Its most important clauses permitted Island juries to assess the extent to which land had increased in value because of highway construction and to force proprietors to contribute to the cost of road construction on the basis of this assessment.[31]

The assembly's development legislation promised to increase the resources available for investment in colonial infrastructure, to draw new monies into the Island economy, and to deal at least temporarily with the nagging issue of quit rents. Moreover, these initiatives would help sustain a political coalition drawn together by the possibilities of state-induced economic growth. For all these reasons, Ready supported the legislature's economic initiatives and recommended them to his superiors in the Colonial Office.[32]

There were, though, divisive aspects of these initiatives. While there was a relatively broad consensus, both on the Island and in Britain, on the central importance of fostering economic growth in the colony, divisions emerged over how the costs of development were to be allocated and who was to control that development.[33] For the Imperial authorities, the land tax proposal, contingent as it was on an abatement in the collection of quit rents, entailed a loss of revenue and a further devolution of power to a colonial assembly. As well, it had to be considered in light of the relationship between quit rents and the cost of carrying the civil list and contextualized in terms of outstanding quit rent issues in other British North American colonies. For large landowners, policies such as the highways and land tax bills entailed out-of-pocket costs for programs over which they could exercise little control. Had there been a broad and equitable distribution of land ownership on Prince Edward Island, state policies that imposed a developmental burden on landowners and that gave discretionary control over these resources to local juries, the colonial legislature, and colonial officials would not in all likelihood have occasioned significant controversy. Perhaps they would not have had as much appeal in the colony either.[34] The structure of land ownership on the Island, though, ensured that these policies would generate resistance even among those with an interest in their purported ends, for in essence the development program advanced by the majority of the House of Assembly entailed passing much of the cost of infrastructure expansion onto landlords, many of whom were not resident on the Island. The issue of infrastructure costs would prove to be a wedge issue, one soon to divide many of the Island's landlords – speculators, simple rentiers, and those involved in the commercial development of their estates alike – from those who were not landlords. As a result, the politics of development that took shape on the Island in the late 1820s would generate opposition not only from tenants, who felt that their needs were being ignored, but also from landed interests, who objected to carrying the burden of increased state expenditures.

By the late 1820s, land ownership on the Island was highly concentrated. Because few of the original sixty-seven townships remained unbroken through subdivision among heirs or the sale of small freeholds, it is difficult to specify precisely the distribution of land ownership, but a general picture can be sketched. At the top of the landholding hierarchy were eighteen or so great proprietors, those holding their land in lot-size (twenty-thousand-acre) portions or more. The six largest of these holdings – those assembled or held by the Earl of Selkirk, John Cambridge, John Hill, James Montgomery, Laurence Sulivan (a London resident who was an important figure in the War Office), and Edward and Charles Worrell – each contained the better part of four or more townships and collectively accounted for somewhere between one-third and one-half of the Island's land.[35] The rest of the largest proprietors held one or two townships each. There was also a more numerous class of lesser landlords. The distinction between resident proprietors and non-resident ones was blurred by the movement of these people to and from the Island and by family-based economic strategies that spanned the Atlantic. If we define the entire proprietorial class as those possessing five hundred acres or more of Island land – the definition Escheators ultimately proposed – slightly more than half the eighty or so people with such holdings in the 1830s were Island residents.[36] Below them was a reasonably numerous class of small freeholders – roughly one-third of the rural population – who collectively owned around 19 per cent of Island lands.[37]

These were the people who would feel the impact of the development costs that the assembly was seeking to place on the Island landowners. Clearly though, the extent of the burden varied markedly among this group. The land tax of two shillings per hundred acres proposed by the assembly would cost the average freeholder precisely that – two shillings per year – the value of half a bushel of wheat or half a yard of homespun.[38] For a great proprietor such as Lord Selkirk, though, two shillings on every hundred acres represented an annual levy of well over £100. In theory, the land tax was in lieu of quit rents that would otherwise have been due, and thus were not an extra burden; but in practice, land taxes were sure to be collected whereas quit rents often were not. Added to this, if the assembly's legislation were sustained, would be the costs assessed by local juries against landowners for the construction of new roads. It was likely that the initiatives proposed by the 12th Assembly would substantially increase the overheads of the great proprietors. So the landlords and their agents attempted to halt these measures, both on the Island and later in the Privy Council when they were submitted for Imperial approval.[39]

Plans for growth may have absorbed the mercantile community and Lieutenant-Governor Ready, but distribution – specifically, the distribution of land – was the central concern in the countryside, where people continued to hope that the state would act to redress the land question. Lieutenant-Governor Smith had escheated two townships in 1818, and this no doubt helped keep the possibility of more escheats alive; proprietors had been unable to overturn these, and there were other lots whose circumstances seemed comparable to those of townships 15 and 55.[40] Significant as well was the deadline that Lord Bathurst imposed in 1818, which gave proprietors until December 1826 to fulfil their settlement requirements. Although landlords do not appear to have taken this new policy seriously, rural expectations of change in the structure of land ownership increased as this deadline approached.[41]

Appeals for an escheat of proprietorial lands and for the formation of a party that would work through the legislature to achieve this goal emerged during the 1824 election. An advertisement in the *Prince Edward Island Register* called on voters to ask candidates whether they supported an escheat and to vote only for those who would commit themselves to such a program and work to make forfeited proprietorial lands available to Island farmers in small grants.[42] Those attempting to make escheat an election issue appear to have met with little success; the big winners of the election were those who had been prominent in ousting Smith. If escheat advocates had any voice at all in the assembly, it was that of Angus Macaulay, who had been one of the leading figures in the Society of Loyal Electors. The twelve-to-four vote that defeated Macaulay's bid to again become Speaker of the House was revealing – the position was given instead to John Stewart, who had led the campaign against Smith.[43] Macaulay would be politically isolated in the 12th Assembly, often voting alone or with one or two other members against the majority. After the assembly convened in 1825, Macaulay placed a petition before the house from eight hundred Island inhabitants asking that no new settlement indulgences be granted to Island proprietors and requesting a general escheat of proprietorial holdings and the regranting of these lands in small tracts to those who worked them.[44] Although he lacked the support necessary to advance the escheat issue in the house, the petition demonstrated that escheat continued to have advocates in the countryside of Kings and Queens counties.[45] Had Macaulay lived to see the 1830 election, perhaps he would have assumed a larger role in building a party around the escheat issue.

It is not difficult to appreciate the appeal that escheat had among the rural population of Prince Edward Island. About one-third of these people held their lands as freeholders; the remainder were tenants or squatters. For the majority who were not freeholders, escheat offered the possibility of gaining ownership of their lands at little or no cost. For freeholders who were purchasing their lands from proprietors by instalment and finding it difficult to make payments, an escheat offered an end to these burdens. As well, for freeholders and the tenant and squatter population alike, escheat might provide cheap fee simple access to new lands, either for themselves or for their offspring or other relatives. The underlying assumption, which stretched back to the escheat agitation of the eighteenth century, was that once lands were revested in the Crown, the government would make them available to the present occupants – or to newcomers in the case of unsettled lands – on terms that were much better than those currently being offered through lease or sale by the Island's proprietors. Although small freeholders had reason to embrace the idea of an escheat, they also had grounds for concern about escheat actions that touched on the townships in which they held land, as such proceedings might, depending on the practices governing them, undermine their own titles. For this reason, measures to protect the land claims of smallholders came to be part of the platform of those advocating a general escheat.

For squatters and leaseholders, escheat held out the possibility not only of providing something they did not possess – the chance to gain freehold title to their land – but also an assurance of retaining something they currently held that they might otherwise lose – occupancy of their farms. Squatters and leaseholders without written contracts – perhaps one-third of tenants – were chronically vulnerable to eviction from their lands by proprietors. At least in theory, tenants with written leases were safe from arbitrary ejectment provided they could stay abreast of the rent payments required by their contracts. Accumulating arrears, though, seem to have always been a fact of life for most of the Island's tenantry. In large part this was because of the enormous labour and costs involved in clearing lands and establishing new farms in the colony. Settlers, as Joseph Robinson had noted in the 1790s, typically found that farm making strained their resources to the limit and that they lacked the additional resources necessary to meet annual rents. Those with short leases would lose their improvements if their landlord did not renew their leases, regardless of whether they had been regular in their rent payments.

The difficulty of making rent payments, which in the second quarter of the nineteenth century typically amounted to £5 per hundred acres, was not always immediately evident to new tenants. Leases for wilderness lots usually had graduated rents whereby tenants paid little or no rent for the first few years of farm making and came to pay full rents only in the fifth or sixth year of the lease. The terms, of course, varied from proprietor to proprietor. For the capital-poor immigrants who had begun to arrive on the Island in increasing numbers after the Napoleonic Wars, these terms looked attractive. A rent of one shilling per acre would have appeared a bargain relative to land rents in the British Isles, and buying freehold land on Prince Edward Island entailed an outlay of from half a pound to one pound per acre – a cost beyond the reach of most. Leasing, unlike squatting, seemed to offer respectability and security of tenure, and for those with little capital, there were few options in any case. To move to a colony where lands might be obtained directly from the Crown required yet new expenditures of money, and as settlement expanded in the region during the early nineteenth century, the Crown lands that were available in nearby colonies were increasingly of marginal agricultural value.[46]

At some point, though, tenants who had entered into wilderness lands on easy terms had to face the problem of meeting full rents. And settlers entering into leases in the second and third decades of the nineteenth century, unlike those in earlier years, typically did not have the advantage of the use of Acadian improvements, or easy access to salt marsh hay, or an abundant open landscape where their cattle might find rich pasture. Over time, as the best land was taken, farm making became in many ways more difficult. A rent of one shilling per acre on a hundred-acre holding was no small sum. Such a land rent amounted to fifty times the burden imposed by quit rents. Measured by the value of agricultural production in the 1820s, this represented an annual claim on the value of one hundred bushels of oats or ten sheep. Measured in wage labour, it represented forty days of work at 2/6 per day or thirty-three at 3 shillings per day.[47] Even with graduated leases, full rents had to be paid on wilderness farms long before much of their acreage could be brought into production. Assuming that a tenant family managed to clear and improve land at a rate of two acres per year and that the lease called for full rents at the end of five years, the real cost for the ten acres of land that could produce a return at this point in farm making would be ten shillings per acre.

Periods of economic depression, such as that of the late 1820s, made paying rents yet more of a burden. So long as there was demand for Island timber and the Island's shipyards were busy, wages might be gained in the woods and along the shore to help cover household expenses and meet rental payments. The collapse of these economies in the second half of the 1820s, though, placed great pressure on rural households as the sources of off-farm wages necessary for sustenance and rent payments dried up.

By the 1830s many tenants were facing substantial arrears. Evidence from the rent rolls for Montgomery's Lots 12, 30, 34, 51, and 59 show arrears amounting to roughly £3,400 in 1832–3, or a debt of approximately £15 per tenant.[48] The figures include people who had just become tenants and who had yet to pay full rents. As well, they include people who occupied lands on the Montgomery estate without having taken a lease, but who were nonetheless listed as being in arrears since the date of their occupancy. More revealing is a subset of data concerning those among Montgomery's tenantry who were long-term leaseholders. The mean value of arrears on the forty-seven holdings on Montgomery's estate where written leases had been executed in 1822 or earlier was roughly six years' rent or, given an average annual rental of £5, roughly £30. That would be the equivalent of roughly sixty sheep or six hundred bushels of oats – a substantial debt for a farm family.[49]

Tenants in arrears were vulnerable to the seizure of their livestock and goods for payment of back rents. Landlords or their agents might, when they chose, proceed by means of distress to recover rents owing. Rent books from Lot 24 show the day-to-day workings of the system. As of the mid-1820s, Charles Blackier owed, according to his landlord's books, more than £60 in back rents and accumulated interest. In November 1828 his landlord recovered nearly £15 of this debt by having law officers seize and auction off the movable possessions on Blackier's farm. The cost of these distress proceedings, £1/3/6, was added to the debit column of Blackier's rental account. Similar proceedings were instituted against Joseph LeClear, who owed £6/10 in arrears, and Altanas Ducett, who owed £11/2.[50]

Arrears could cost tenants their farms too, as proprietors and their agents might proceed by eviction, a possibility that became increasingly attractive to landlords once immigration increased after the Napoleonic Wars. In Blackier's case, distress proceedings led to the recovery of only a fraction of the arrears his landlord claimed. In 1835, Blackier was forced to give up half his farm in return for a £17/5 credit against his debts.[51] Had he not been behind in his rents, Blackier might have – had he chosen, and had his landlord not created obstacles – sold his leasehold interest on his own terms and in accordance with his own timetable; but he was denied this means to recoup the value of his improvements. His neighbour, Lorain Ducette, was served with a notice of eviction, avoidable only if he could raise the £43 in back rent his landlord claimed.[52] By such means, landlords could profit from the value of the improvements that tenants were making to the land, including the fields, fences, houses, and outbuildings they had constructed for themselves. Indeed, it was the value of the improvements made by tenants that kept many landlords from worrying unduly about mounting arrears. Tenants might minimize their movable assets, or manage in some fashion to hide them when distress proceedings were rumoured, but they could not effectively guard the value of their farm improvements. The Island's tenantry 'may be poor,' noted the absentee landlord

Robert Stewart, drawing on insights his brother had gained from a visit to the colony, but 'almost all are solvent ... for the lands cleared by them are of more value than any claims the landlord can have against them.'[53] As with farm households elsewhere in northeastern North America in this era, much of the return accruing to the labour of Prince Edward Island's tenants accumulated not in cash or movable assets but in the increasing value of the farm property itself.[54]

With care, a clever landlord moving against tenants with large arrears might capture both the value of a tenant's movable assets and the value the tenants had added to their lands. Writing to George Young in 1838, Lemuel Cambridge – son of the great proprietor John Cambridge and an agent for others – noted a singular failure in his timing with tenants on Lots 3, 4, and 5 a few years earlier. Had he acted at the correct moment, he lamented, he might have distrained on them and

> collected a large portion of the arrears as most had tolerable good stock of cattle but the almost entire failure of the crops the following years rendered the people to such a state of want that they were obligated to dispose of most all they had to secure sustenance ... It was my contention to have removed most of the tenants from their present farms and disposed of their improvements to a better class of farmers by which means I would have realised the greater part of the back rent with a prospect of being paid in the future.[55]

Not all landlords and agents thought as Lemuel Cambridge did, but his observation underlines the threat that faced tenants with substantial arrears.

Support for the politics of escheat, which was again growing in the countryside, and for the politics of development were not necessarily mutually exclusive. They did, however, offer hope or threats to different clienteles, and separately they held the potential for different alignments in Island politics. The development initiatives proposed by the assembly offered something to the colony's tenantry and small freeholders in the way of improved roads and employment opportunities. They did not, however, directly address fundamental problems of rural life – specifically, those related to land access and the power of the proprietors. Certainly a buoyant economy would benefit tenants who were struggling to meet current rents and arrears. An escheat, though, would eliminate the problem altogether. So long as proprietors remained in control of the lands that most Islanders relied on for their living, tenants would remain vulnerable to losing their holdings at some point in the future when the chronically unstable regional economy – which relied on external markets for Island exports – left them short of the monies necessary for rent. As well, growth and prosperity would not solve the problems that small freeholders, tenants, and squatters alike confronted when they considered the futures of their sons and daughters. If proprietors continued to monopolize Island lands, they would be free to set new and more costly terms of access and to reap the advantages of prosperity at the expense of yet another generation of Island farmers. For those seeking to make a living from the land, the problem was that proprietors possessed the power – regardless of the economic context – to appropriate much of the value created by their tenants' labour. Without a redistribution of resources, economic growth would not resolve this inequity; indeed, insofar as it would increase competition for land, it might exacerbate it. As well, as some prescient observers seem to have realized, the greater developmental burden the assembly sought to pass on to proprietors through taxes and road assessments would ultimately be borne by the Island's tenantry, since landlords could, and would, pass on their costs.[56]

Surely, as well, the talk of economic development and 'improvement' must have had a disturbing resonance among a rural population composed in large part of families and their descendants who had been driven to emigrate by rent hikes, clearances, and other changes that 'improvement' brought to the countryside of the British Isles.[57] Some of this discomfort would have been visceral, but in addition, there were rational grounds for worrying about what the commercial development of the Island might bring if it occurred in a context in which landlordism prevailed. Many rural Islanders must have pondered whether once more they might be laying the foundations for a commercial agriculture in which they would be marginalized. Lemuel Cambridge's plan amounted to a clearance of impecunious tenants, to be replaced with 'a better class of farmers. Such plans threatened a large portion of the rural Islanders who were vulnerable to eviction either because they held no leases, or because their leases would soon expire, or because they were in arrears.

An escheat of proprietorial grants held out exceedingly attractive possibilities for most of the rural population; but for many reasons, such policies were potentially damaging to the interests of many of those who supported the cause of development. Some among that causes's supporters were small-scale landlords; others were agents who faced immediate direct losses should landlordism be abolished. Others benefited from the proprietorial regime more indirectly, deriving income from Island estates by providing services as lawyers, surveyors, and brokers for the produce submitted to pay rents. For those entertaining dreams of government office, association with escheat policies could draw the wrath of prominent British proprietors who had influence in government circles. So could advocacy of land taxes, but being associated with those challenging the legitimacy of proprietorial titles was riskier. Men such as the Earl of Selkirk, Viscount Melville, and the Earl of Westmorland could be useful allies or, alternatively, damaging detractors. The same may have been true in the case of employment with British commercial houses doing business on the Island. Certainly as well, escheat was distasteful to some because they adhered to the ideals of landed society.[58] Indeed, as Island history repeatedly demonstrated, more than a few upwardly mobile residents of the colony aspired to landlord status themselves and purchased estates when they could. For some, though, there were potential compensations: escheat proceedings might stimulate the rural economy and provide new opportunities for small-scale land speculation. As well, the paperwork involved in a major transfer of land would enhance the fees of office for the government officials handling these matters and provide business for lawyers and surveyors.

By 1830, political developments that had been coalescing in the period since Ready came to office were coming to a head. Bills relating to crucial aspects of the assembly's development policy were being considered in London, or they were on their way, and the leading proprietors were moving – albeit slowly – to protect themselves from the potential challenges that some of these initiatives posed to their concerns. In the countryside of Prince Edward Island, the idea of land reform through an escheat of proprietorial holdings was again gaining currency. Challenges to the policies proposed by the men of the 12th assembly were gathering at both ends of the social spectrum.

Coupled with these local developments were the ripple effects of changes occurring elsewhere. As the editor of the *Royal Gazette* (which was both a commercial paper and the record of official news) noted in October 1830, Islanders were living in 'the era of great events.'[59] The immediate cause for this pronouncement was the news that the July Revolution in France had triggered a similar uprising in Spain – a report that proved to be premature. Even so, the observation was a fair reflection of the broader transitions occurring in the Atlantic world as aristocratic rule crumbled and new contenders for power entered the political arena.[60] Momentous shifts were under way, and their reverberations were heard and felt on colonial Prince Edward Island. One of these, the successful struggle for Catholic emancipation in Britain, directly induced a greater democratization of colonial politics. In the second half of the 1820s the Island assembly had rejected local appeals to enfranchise Catholics, who were roughly one-third of the population, but after British law was changed under pressure from the mass movement organized by Daniel O'Connell, discriminatory electoral laws were abolished on Prince Edward Island as well.[61] As a consequence, many of the Island's adult Catholic males were able to vote and hold elected office for the first time in the elections in September and October 1830, occasioned by the death of George IV.

The fall election provided yet more evidence of the new political alignments that were taking shape on the Island. At polling time the land tax act and highways compensation act still awaited Imperial approval. They reflected the orientation of the policies adopted by the 12th Assembly, as did the extra import duties it had imposed and its expenditures for infrastructure development, and some of those supporting the assembly's development initiatives thought it useful to advertise this on the hustings in 1830.[62] Others, though, challenged the choices the assembly had made. In Kings County, William Cooper supported the government's new infrastructure investments but argued that they needed to be supported by taxes on land rather than on commerce, as the costs appropriately belonged to 'those who receive the greatest share of the benefit.' More importantly, he challenged the developmental focus of the assembly's legislation, arguing that it did not speak to the primary concerns of the rural population: 'I have always heard that those great proprietary Grants were the *only* grievances in the country, and though a great deal has been said, there is nothing done in it yet.' Laws were needed, Cooper argued, 'to protect the poor but industrious settlers from the exactions of the great landed proprietors.' People 'cannot exist without land. Land is essential to their very existence; yet in this country a few individuals are allowed to monopolize nearly the whole of it. If ever laws were wanted for the protection of the people, surely justice calls for them here.'[63]

It seems that there were attempts to focus politics on the escheat issue in Queens County, too, just as in 1824. An advertisement in the *Royal Gazette* notifying Queens County voters that there was to be a meeting at John Crisp's house in Rustico to nominate candidates for the assembly was, in all likelihood, a call to advance the cause of land reform.[64] A year and a half later, as the Escheat movement began to assume a more prominent profile in Island affairs, Crisp drew up the first escheat manifesto to be issued from Queens County.[65] The land issue probably played a significant role in making the Queens County election particularly acrimonious. Four seats were at stake, and the winner of the last position was a Catholic resident landlord, Donald Macdonald, son of Captain John Macdonald, who squeezed out a Protestant newcomer, John Willock, by a narrow margin.[66] Willock challenged the election results and, following success in a new election, became a proponent of escheat in the House of Assembly.[67] George Dalrymple, who was a victor in this second election as well, and who been endorsed by electoral meetings at Crisp's house and in Belfast, became an ardent advocate of a limited escheat.[68]

William Cooper, though, failed in his electoral bid in Kings County, coming in fifth in the race for four Kings County seats. Like many of the others who ran for a seat that year, Cooper was a newcomer to electoral politics, and his decision to run was taken at the last minute. Since his arrival on the Island in 1818 he had come to reside at Bay Fortune in northeastern Kings County, where, among other things, he served as Lord James Townshend's land agent for the lot, taking a small part in the agitation that unseated Lieutenant-Governor Smith in the mid-1820s.[69] He does not at this point seem to have had a substantial profile beyond his local community. This would change, however, as events proved the truth of his contention that the politics of development were failing to address the central grievance of rural voters. As the stirrings in Queens and Kings counties suggested, demands for land reform would not easily be brushed aside.

4 Escheat Enters the Political Arena, 1831–1833

Economic growth and development were central issues in the proceedings of the 12th General Assembly in the second half of the 1820s and the first session of the 13th in 1831. This began to change in subsequent sessions as the house took up the land question. Land reform, and the possibility of escheat actions to achieve it, became a central issue in the assembly after William Cooper joined the house when it met in January 1832 and forcefully articulated the issue. Cooper's advocacy of land reform then and in later years would have been of little consequence, though, had discussion of land reform in the assembly not set in motion important changes in rural perceptions. Consideration of the land question in the legislature, amplified by newspaper coverage, gave rise to great hopes that solutions to the fundamental problems confronting the rural majority would emerge out of the political process in the very near future. Debates in the assembly, as well as at public meetings called to respond to the escheat discussions in the house, heightened awareness of shared experiences among the subordinate rural population and helped build Island-wide alliances that spanned identities rooted in local, ethnic, religious, and personal loyalties. State structures were the focus of agrarian plans for bringing about change; these structures also did much to facilitate the construction of a rural social movement with the breadth necessary to challenge the status quo.[1]

The intrusion of the land question into the deliberations of the assembly beginning in the winter session of 1832 would have enormous consequences for Island politics. In part this was because that question would persist as a central feature of Island political debate; absent a comprehensive solution to landlord/tenant tensions, it simply would not go away. As well, the discussion of the land question that began in the early 1830s profoundly shaped how people thought about, and described, the issue for decades thereafter.

A Kings County by-election, held in July of 1831, gave Cooper a seat in the assembly for the first time and provides a useful view of rural politics in the early years of the Escheat movement.[2] Much emerged in the course of the campaign that was of general significance concerning the challenges faced by those who wanted to reorient Island politics and sought to sustain the call for land reform in the political arena.

Even in an era in which elections typically were rough and boisterous male events, the by-election of July 1831 was notable for its violence.[3] One witness before a committee of the House of Assembly struck to investigate the proceedings testified: 'I never saw such an Election as that, and hope never will again.'[4] Voting was a public event, with those claiming to hold a forty-shilling freehold or leasehold mounting the hustings – a raised platform bearing the various electoral officers – and declaring their vote in the presence of all assembled.[5] Voting was restricted to heads of households who met the property requirements; the crowds present during polling contained a broader cross-section of the population, who by their cheers, jeers, and physical actions could influence the election. At the Kings County by-election, members of the crowd that had assembled to witness the voting tore down the hustings during the final day of voting. After polling was resumed again in an adjacent barn, they resorted to violence to force a premature final closing of the polls. Cooper, who was winning by a substantial margin at the time the polls were closed, was, according to some who witnessed the day's events, fortunate to escape the turmoil with his life.

The election was occasioned by the death of the incumbent, John Macdonald, and although contested by four candidates it was fundamentally a race between two: Angus Macdonald of Black Bush (Lot 44) and William Cooper of Bay Fortune.[6] Campaigning under the electoral banner 'Our country's freedom and farmers' rights,' Cooper reiterated the call for land reform he had sounded in the 1830 election.[7] To a certain extent the contest, like many others of the day, broke along regional lines. Polling was conducted for two days at Georgetown on the southeast coast of Kings County on 13 and 14 July and continued for two days at St Peters on the north coast one week later. Cooper drew the support of the southeastern portions of the county and, consequently, carried the voting conducted in Georgetown. By the end of the polling there he had 199 votes and Macdonald only 19.[8] It was reported that a vessel loaded with neighbours and supporters from Bay Fortune had sailed down the coast and played a prominent role in sustaining Cooper's cause on the southern hustings.[9] Macdonald, 'a stranger at Georgetown,' required the assistance of a local man to identify the people of the area and determine whose voting rights to challenge.[10] Squatters and other household heads who did not have a forty-shilling holding, mature sons who had access to land only through their fathers, and people who had not resided in the county for six months were all ineligible to vote but could be pointed out only by someone with good local knowledge. When Macdonald's actions, or those of his few supporters, drew the crowd's displeasure, it was Cooper who possessed the personal authority to maintain order. The situation was reversed in St Peters the following week. There it was Cooper who required the assistance of a local scrutineer, and there the crowds were intensely hostile to his cause. The 'mob' surrounding the hustings, estimated at around 150 people, intimidated and assaulted Cooper's supporters. At St Peters, however, no local authority acted effectively to contain the violence. Cooper gained an additional 118 votes while Macdonald collected nearly double that.[11] Macdonald's votes were insufficient to overcome Cooper's lead, and mounting evidence that Cooper would prevail appears to have triggered a crescendo of violence that forced the premature closure of the polls, opening up the possibility of a new election.

The particular bitterness of the affray at St Peters may reflect, in part, the role that ethnic and religious divisions played in the contest. Cooper, a Scottish Protestant with an English wife, had complained after the 1830 election that religion had been used against him during that campaign – a tactic that seems to have bedevilled John Willock's candidacy the previous year as well – and that at the last minute he had lost the votes of Catholics who otherwise would have supported him.[12] His complaint echoed concerns expressed by some Islanders prior to the 1830 election that religious cleavages might come to dominate the colony's politics in the post-emancipation era.[13] Others had immediately replied that Cooper's contentions were an insult to the Irish and Scottish Catholics of the county.[14] During the polling at Georgetown in the 1831 by-election the issue emerged again as a rumour spread that Cooper's supporters had insulted Daniel Brenan, a recently elected Irish Catholic assemblyman from Kings County. Brenan, a Charlottetown merchant, was a prominent member of the Island's Irish community.[15] Many in the crowd at St Peters were also Irish Catholics, and Dr Conroy, a recent immigrant from Ireland, reported that they sought to avenge the affront supposedly given to Brenan, their compatriot.[16] In the violence that followed, Irishmen such as Thomas Hogan, Richard Cullen, and Michael Scully played a central role. Indeed, Hogan appears to have acted as crowd captain. Others named as playing a significant part in the rioting at St Peters were Highlanders lending their support to Angus Macdonald's candidacy.[17]

Localism and ethnic and religious loyalties were mutually reinforcing. While Scots predominated in the county as a whole, there was a significant Irish population in and around St Peters; indeed, it seems they were numerically predominant in the near townships.[18] Settlers of English extraction – an even smaller minority in the county as a whole – were only lightly sprinkled among the Scots and Irish in the north of the county but had a significant profile in a number of the townships in the south.[19] The religious composition of the population varied as well between those settlements along the northern tier of the county and those to the south. Catholics were three-quarters of the population of the northern townships but a minority in the rest of the county.[20] The patterns of settlement in Kings County reflected broader Island realities in that similar ethnic and religious clusterings were to be found elsewhere across the colony.

There was most definitely another force at play in this election. Charles Worrell, whose estate covered tens of thousands of acres around St Peters Bay, clearly played a critical off-stage role in the events. In elections earlier in the century when Worrell himself sought office, land agents had assembled tenants and led them to the polls to support his cause, with banners flying and bagpipes skirling.[21] In July 1831, with Angus Macdonald's election at stake and Worrell now a member of the council, changing times and new circumstances called for more subtle measures. When the polling moved to St Peters, Worrell sent men as far as East Point, thirty miles away, to gather voters for Macdonald's cause; he also personally visited others of his own tenantry asking whether they had voted and demanding arrears from some who had not supported Macdonald.[22] By the end of the first day of voting at St Peters, the results suggested that Cooper would prevail. Did Worrell then help plan a riot for the following day with the intention of stopping the polling, perhaps even destroying the poll books, and ensuring a new election? And did he engage Scully, who was his servant, and Hogan, who had once served as his miller, to disrupt the election? Clearly, some of those participating in the hearings later conducted by the assembly's

Committee of Privileges and Elections thought the answer was yes. A polling clerk testified under oath that Dr Conroy had informed him that the riot had been planned the night before it took place. Conroy, though, denied this charge and also denied that Worrell had been involved in supplying rum to the crowd.[23]

Worrell, who had been present during the polling and had on occasion exercised his personal power to quiet things down, appears to have been absent in the last hours of the final day's voting, when the hustings were torn down and the civil authorities required assistance. Deputy Sheriff John Sims, who was serving as the returning officer, swore in special constables to keep the peace. Yet power at St Peters did not rest with those carrying the authority of the law, but rather – insofar as there were figures capable of quelling the unrest – with local figures wielding personal authority. In the heat of the final riot, which brought the voting to an end, Sims relied on a prominent resident proprietor, Donald Macdonald of Glenaladale (Captain John's son), to assist him in subduing the violence. Sims refused to leave the barn where the final voting had taken place, and where he and the other officials had sought shelter from a hail of sticks and stones, unless Macdonald accompanied him and spoke to the rioters. Certainly Macdonald possessed a fluency in Gaelic that Sims perhaps did not have, but Sims also needed Macdonald for the personal authority he carried.[24]

Although most of the colony's elite resided in Charlottetown, the countryside was dotted with men like Worrell and Macdonald and others of lesser stature who carried weight because of the resources they controlled and the personal power relationships they had established with area residents. Many of those in and about St Peters knew Charles Worrell not just as a landlord but as the owner of a store, mills, and shipyards and as a justice of the peace. He was landlord, merchant, employer, and a representative of Charlottetown's law and administration all in one and therefore a force to be reckoned with in northern Kings County.[25] When the polling came to St Peters it was being conducted on Worrell turf, and he had made it abundantly clear that he did not want Cooper to be returned. Whether or not Worrell directly conspired in the violence that closed the polls, and whether or not the events at St Peters amounted to rioting by permission, the central reality was that men like Worrell had a good deal of power over local affairs and that they exercised it.[26] When they stood against the call for land reform, as Worrell did, they presented a formidable obstacle to those who were seeking to organize politics around the issue.

Local, paternal, ethnic, and religious loyalties had the potential to impede the development of issue-focused, class-based politics everywhere in the colony. The rural protest movement that emerged in the 1830s succeeded in developing an Island-wide profile despite this, and it did so not so much by displacing localism as by building on aspects of it.

Cooper's ability to function as a guiding force in agrarian politics was grounded in the solid support he drew from his own community in and about Bay Fortune. His success in advocating land reform owed much to the political activism and militancy of his neighbours there and to the close relationships he maintained within his local constituency. After narrowly losing the 1830 election, he won all the subsequent elections he contested in the 1830s and 1840s, and he maintained his popularity at the polls long after the Escheat movement had ceased to be a dominant force in Island politics. Cooper had the backing of important families in the district – including the Dingwells, Douglases, Aitkens, Morrows, and Coffins – but clearly he was also able to establish a lasting rapport with a broader rural constituency. The beginnings of this relationship appear to date back to the 1820s, when he served as Lord Townshend's land agent for Lot 56 – a seemingly inauspicious start for a man who would gain fame as an advocate of the tenantry. The previous agent, Edward Abell, had been murdered in 1819 by a tenant enraged by Abell's seizure of his horse for back rents.[27] The tenant, Patrick Pearce, escaped from the Island. That Cooper was able to assume Abell's job yet gain the respect and support of the tenantry suggests that he was a man with remarkable personal skills. His background with the merchant marine and the navy probably was an asset in a community that had its face to the sea and many of whose residents were Highlanders imbued with military traditions. When Cooper settled on the Island a few years after the end of the Napoleonic Wars, he was in his early thirties and recently married. Behind him lay twenty years of life at sea, including ten as a captain in the merchant marine plying the trade routes of the Baltic, the North Atlantic, and the Mediterranean and Black Seas. He was a literate and well-travelled man who knew something about the command of men, so it is perhaps not surprising that he would assume a significant profile in his community.[28]

The evidence suggests that Cooper's perception of his role as agent and his understanding of the appropriate relationship between landlord and tenant may have had something too to do with the support he was able to gain from the rural people of Bay Fortune. It is not clear how

Townshend came to choose Cooper as his agent. There may have been a maritime connection, as they were roughly the same age and had both been sea captains, or they may have made contact in London, where Cooper's wife originally lived.[29] Nor is it clear what Townshend expected from Cooper following the murder of Edward Abell. After meeting Townshend in London at the assumption of his agency, Cooper came away believing that Townshend's primary concern was that his estate – which was but sparsely populated – be settled and that the agent ensure the 'kind treatment of his tenantry.'[30] Cooper's assertion in this regard was penned nearly twenty years after the meeting, but it is very much in keeping with the portrait of the young Captain Townshend provided by the British naval officer and novelist Captain Marryat, who described him as a benign master concerned with the peopling of his lands.[31]

These were the principles that Cooper seems to have acted upon. Over the years of his employment he greatly increased the numbers on Lord Townshend's rent rolls even while acting to ensure the provision of a variety of services for the tenantry. Living on the estate, Cooper assumed a paternalistic role among those resident on Lot 56. He arranged for the construction of a grist mill, worked hard to find markets for local goods, and saw to it that rents could be paid in labour, timber, or agricultural goods. This flexibility was important to tenants in the cash-poor Island economy. In 1825 Cooper organized the building of a brigantine, the *Hackmatack*, for sale abroad, as a way, he claimed, 'to make a remittance' to Lord Townshend in Britain. These efforts, combined with the role he assumed as a local peacemaker, doctor, and sustainer of those in need, made him an important and, it would appear, popular person in and around Bay Fortune. They also brought him into conflict with Lord Townshend and those who advised him, as some of Cooper's initiatives became costly speculations in the troubled second half of the 1820s. Ultimately Cooper was dismissed from his post with Lord Townshend and replaced by an agent residing in Charlottetown, who, Townshend thought, would more effectively ensure the flow of rent monies homewards.[32]

Cooper's advocacy of land reform might usefully be seen as an extension of the role he had assumed in his community as a resident land agent. By the 1830s, though, he was no longer trying to achieve his ends within proprietorial structures; he had begun to perceive these structures themselves as the central problem.[33] Given his own experiences and background, it is not surprising that some of Cooper's early speeches in favour of escheat were framed in terms of a paternal order that had failed. What was wrong on Prince Edward Island, he suggested during his first term in the house, was that proprietors had forgotten their social obligations. The Island's landlords, he argued, had turned their backs on the 'people they ought to support and cherish.' They were refusing to use their possessions to provide 'employment and bread to the industrious.' Instead they were acting to 'strip those who they do employ of the greater part of their earnings.'[34] Cooper's understanding of landlord/tenant relations and of his role within this structure had been rooted in notions of reciprocity. Landlords were supposed to look after the needs of their tenantry and to provide the basic services and resources necessary for tenants to sustain themselves and meet their obligations; tenants, in turn, paid their rents. As an agent, Cooper appears to have tried to be an intermediary in this sort of relationship, lobbying for and organizing estate improvements that would aid those resident on Lot 56, while informing his employer of the difficulties the tenantry were experiencing in raising the monies necessary to pay their rents. As his own relationship with Lord Townshend and his advisors deteriorated, and as he found himself being held personally responsible for the debts incurred in ventures related to the estate, his perspective began to shift from that of an intermediary to one closer to that of the tenantry.

Many of the approaches to problems that Cooper took as a land agent re-emerged in his activities as an Escheat advocate. It is probably significant for later developments at Bay Fortune that he communicated collectively with Lot 56's tenantry on important matters concerning his agency. For instance, after he returned from sailing the *Hackmatack* to Britain for sale, he convened a public meeting in order to pass on the news that Lord Townshend had refused to assume the costs of a grist mill that Cooper had constructed on the lot and that all future rents would have to be received in cash or treasury bills.[35] In the 1830s, public meetings in Bay Fortune would do much to guide and maintain the momentum of Escheat agitation. As an agent Cooper took part in the Island-wide meetings of 1823 – meetings that, in the absence of a regularly functioning assembly, served to articulate public grievances and to generate pressure for the removal of Lieutenant-Governor Smith.[36] In the following decade he would play a central role in establishing similar, but more democratically organized, meetings to advance the Escheat cause, working outside the officially sanctioned governmental structures when they proved unresponsive to Escheat demands. As an agent he attempted to arrange a hearing for tenant grievances by organizing local meetings to draw up petitions to send to Lord Townshend.[37] After he was dismissed as a land agent, he continued to organize these sorts of activities in his community, but in his new circumstances the possibilities for petition and political action were much broader.

Failed paternalism, exploitation, and the pressing needs of the Island's tenantry were not, however, the themes that dominated the proceedings of the 13th General Assembly before Cooper joined the house. Instead the house concerned itself with economic progress, defence of its prerogatives, legal reforms, urban improvements, and the development of a more secure niche for itself. While there were many new faces in the 13th Assembly, the objectives the house pursued during its first year of proceedings tended to be a continuation of those adopted by its predecessor. Catholic emancipation did not occasion a sudden shift in political policy. When the assembly members convened for their first session in 1831, the highway compensation act and land tax act, passed in 1829 and 1830, still awaited Imperial approval. As had the previous assembly, the 13th pressed Lieutenant-Governor Ready and the Imperial government for speedy royal assent for this important legislation.[38]

Beyond this, the assembly sought to solidify and extend its de facto power over appropriations by eliminating the permanent impost bills the assembly had passed in 1785 and 1795. To this end, the house, following in the footsteps of the previous assembly, petitioned the king for permission to revoke these eighteenth-century bills.[39] The only mention of escheat during the first session of the new assembly came when John Willock joined with two resident landlords, Thomas Compton and Hugh Macdonald, to vote against a petition to the lieutenant-governor asking for speedy approval of the land tax bill passed by the 12th Assembly. Compton and Macdonald opposed the land tax as an attack on property. Willock joined them in opposition because, he argued, legislation of this sort might give current proprietors a greater claim to their lands and impede subsequent actions of escheat.[40]

By the time the house reconvened in early January 1832, a new lieutenant-governor, Aretas Young, had replaced Colonel Ready. He informed the legislature that news still had not been received concerning the fate of the bills passed in 1829 and 1830 and sent for royal assent. In mid-January he informed the assembly that the highways bill had received royal assent; the first assessments of costs under the new highways bill began in the second quarter of 1832.[41] Confirmation of the land tax bill was not received until the house met again the following January.[42] Well before it received confirmation of the first land tax initiative – a product of the deliberations of the late 1820s – the 13th Assembly passed a second supplementary land tax bill, which – much to the members' consternation – was tabled for a year by the Legislative Council.[43] The assembly protested this by petitioning the king; however, its opportunities to respond effectively to the council's parry were limited by its inability to block supply. In general, the development program crafted by the 12th Assembly and pursued by the 13th in its early sessions was proceeding at a crawl and remained vulnerable to opposition from the Legislative Council, the lieutenant-governor, and/or those who might challenge legislation when it reached the Colonial Office.

Of greater moment in the proceedings of the assembly was the beginning of a discussion in the house regarding the possibilities of an escheat. On 19 January 1832 the Committee of Privileges and Elections narrowly declared Cooper the victor in the Kings County by-election. The following day he took his seat in the house. Ten days later, George Dalrymple introduced a motion, which gained the support of the majority, calling for the establishment of a committee to inquire into 'whether any and what lots or townships of land on this Island are liable to escheat.'[44] Cooper and Dalrymple became members of this committee, along with three others. Dalrymple was an improvement-minded entrepreneur who owned grain and carding mills and who ran a Charlottetown pharmacy. Charles Binns was a Charlottetown lawyer and businessman. Thomas Owen was a land agent and merchant involved in the shipbuilding industry and closely associated with the Cambridges. John Brecken was the scion of a wealthy Loyalist merchant family; he acted as a private banker for many in the colony before the Bank of British North America established itself on the Island.[45] After hearing testimony – including discussion of the escheat proceedings of 1818 – and inquiring into the history of the land question in the colony, the committee recommended that the house send a petition to the lieutenant-governor calling for the establishment of a court of escheat and that it frame a bill to facilitate its creation. All but two members of the house supported this motion, as well as a subsequent motion on the committee's report calling for the establishment of a court of escheat.[46]

The timing of this initiative and the speeches some members made concerning it strongly suggest that many of those who supported escheat at this time were motivated principally by the desire to pre-empt

Cooper by initiating a moderate proposal for land reform.[47] Dalrymple, who had been a member of the previous assembly, raised the escheat question in the house only after Cooper assumed a seat. In making his motion, Dalrymple pointedly differentiated himself from radical positions that seemed to be gaining ground in the countryside by assuring the house that he maintained a 'sacred regard' for the rights of private property and that he strongly opposed 'any visionary scheme being carried into execution.'[48] Certainly this was also the message in the remarks Daniel Brenan made in explaining his support for the formation of a committee to investigate escheat. It was necessary, he argued, to 'quiet the minds of the public, and to prevent them being made subservient to the wishes of the designing.'[49] His comments were aimed at Cooper and others, whom he maintained were, for 'vile political purpose,' fanning 'generally prevalent' rural sentiments which held that tenants had as much right to the land as their landlords. Cooper would respond directly to Brenan's attack in his first major escheat speech two months later. It is possible that some, such as John Willock and perhaps Dalrymple as well, had promised their rural constituents during the campaigning for the 1830 election that they would support escheat policies.[50] Willock, who had opposed the land taxes in the first session of the 13th Assembly because they might strengthen landlords' titles, spoke strongly in favour of an escheat in the second, arguing that many of the proprietors were 'no better than blood suckers.'[51] It is also possible that others publicly supported escheat, out of fear that they would lose electoral support if it became an issue in the house and if they did not do so. Some appear to have taken such a stand while working in other forums to defeat the measure.[52]

The repercussions of these developments are clearer than the specific motives, mixed or otherwise, that led the majority of the assembly to initiate escheat legislation in 1832. Discussion of escheat in the house heightened awareness of rural grievances throughout the colony and generated great hopes that substantial land reform was possible and might even be imminent. Consideration of the escheat issue in the house in the winter and early spring of 1832 gave enormous impetus to aspirations that had been simmering in the countryside for years and set the stage for a reorientation of Island politics around the land question. Public discussion forced assemblymen to take a position on the matter and permitted rural constituents to judge where their legislators stood on policy that was potentially very important to them. During the initial discussions of escheat, three positions emerged.

A minority were willing to publicly declare their opposition to the establishment of a court of escheat. Two resident landlords, Hugh Macdonald and Thomas Compton, articulated this position. Thomas Compton had assumed ownership of part of Lot 17 from his father, Colonel Harry Compton, a veteran of the suppression of the Irish Rebellion of 1798 who had lost two brothers in the conflict. Thomas Compton was born in England, came to the colony with his father at the turn of the century, and took over the estate when his father retired to France in the 1820s. Compton had initially supported the establishment of a committee to inquire into the escheat issue, stating that he would be glad to see the escheat of lands where the proprietors had not lived up to the conditions of their grants. However, he ultimately changed his stand and voted against the escheat initiatives that emerged from the committee's proceedings. Hugh Macdonald was the son of Andrew Macdonald, a prosperous merchant from Arisaig, Scotland, who had purchased 10,000 acres of land around Three Rivers in Kings County and established a mercantile operation there in the early nineteenth century after hearing favourable reports of the colony from his relative, Captain John Macdonald of Glenaladale. The family subsequently obtained yet more land elsewhere on the Island. Hugh Macdonald followed in his father's footsteps as a landlord and as a merchant in the timber and shipbuilding industries. Compton and Macdonald's position would in time receive the firm backing of the absentee landlord community. Given the extent of dissatisfaction on the Island concerning the prevailing land system, it is not surprising that few assemblymen were willing to go on record as being opposed to any escheat proceedings whatsoever.[53]

A majority, led in part by Dalrymple, coalesced around an appeal for a partial escheat that would see the confiscation of some of the least settled Island lots. Integrating their position with the politics of development that had emerged in the proceedings of the 12th Assembly, they argued that it was necessary for the government to escheat undeveloped townships so that the economic progress of the colony would not be retarded. Landlords who had let their lands lie idle, they contended, were obstructing the potential flow of new immigrants and in so doing impeding the ability of the colonial government to raise the revenues necessary to sustain the growth of the Island's infrastructure. Titling their legislation 'A Bill to Encourage the Settlement and Improvement of Lands in this Island and to Regulate the Proceedings of a Court of Escheats Therein,' they spoke in terms of the imperatives of growth and improvement. A selective escheat of the least settled lots, they contended, would induce new investments, 'improve trade,' and 'encourage the introduction of emigrants and thereby the cultivation of the soil.'[54] Because the legislation did not seek to overthrow the prevailing structure of land tenure on the Island, prominent members of the 13th Assembly such as Charles Binns, Thomas Owen, and Daniel Brenan could, without any inconsistency, follow Dalrymple in advocating escheat proceedings while at the same time calling for the extension of the activities of the New Brunswick Land Company to Prince Edward Island, with its plans for corporate landlordism.[55]

In social terms, a partial escheat program stood a chance of gaining the middle ground in Island politics. It would, obviously, draw the opposition of some of those associated with proprietorial interests, but it would not necessarily alienate all of them. Townships with significant numbers of settlers would not be affected by an escheat, and thus many landlords and most land agents would be spared the impact of confiscation – agencies were, by and large, rooted in the management of townships that had substantial numbers of tenants. Indeed, depending on how it was arranged, a partial escheat might afford new investment opportunities for proprietors or would-be proprietors, as well as new employment opportunities for agents. Insofar as it would act as a spur to new settlement and investment and help broaden the tax base, a partial escheat obviously would appeal to the merchant and professional community. Thus it was a policy that many of those in the assembly who had a foot in both rentier and commercial activities could support. Moreover, such a policy offered something to the Island's relatively numerous small freeholders, in that it might make new freehold lands available to them and to their sons and daughters without in any way threatening their own titles. Opposition would of course emerge from landlords threatened by confiscation and, at the other end of the social spectrum, from tenants, squatters, and freeholders, who sought more wide-ranging land reforms.

A third position also emerged from the debate on the issue in the house. It amounted to a call – this one sustained at this time by Cooper alone – for the broadest possible escheat, to extinguish proprietorial tenure throughout the colony and place Island lands in the hands of those who worked them. While he supported the legislation to establish a court of escheat drawn up by Dalrymple, Binns, Owen, Brenan, and Joseph Pope, Cooper made it clear in his first major speech to the house that his objectives differed from those of his fellow assemblymen. After careful consideration he had concluded that 'nothing less than a general Escheat will do justice to, or satisfy, the inhabitants of this Island.'[56] Cooper's position addressed the needs of a rural population that was labouring to clear land, improve their farms, and make ends meet under the burden of rents that at best were an additional hardship and at worst, if arrears became too great, a threat to their claim to their hard-earned improvements. As well, Cooper articulated the rural belief that Brenan had deprecated: that tenants had as strong a claim to the land as their landlords. Brenan had warned the house about those who were 'wafted on Eagle's Wings' by the visionary notion of expropriating the proprietors.[57] To this, Cooper replied: 'I have heard a prattle about soaring on eagle's wings; if it means a person that sympathises with the wrongs and distress of the poor tenantry, I am the man!'[58]

Although Cooper, like the partial escheators, indulged in complex legal and historical arguments to support his case for expropriation on the basis of non-fulfilment of the original grants, he offered a markedly different and broader rationale for the initiatives he was proposing. Dalrymple and his allies framed their position in terms of obstacles to economic growth, and advocated a partial escheat as a corrective for stagnation; Cooper spoke of the need to secure basic justice for the tenantry. Where Dalrymple and his allies emphasized economic development, Cooper stressed distribution. None of the catchwords and objectives of the majority of the assembly – progress, improvement, economic growth, greater immigration, commercial prosperity – figured in his speech. These were not the issues that preoccupied him, nor by extension the constituency he sought to represent. A general escheat was necessary, he contended, to secure 'the people's rights' to the product of their labour and most fundamentally to provide 'justice.' He employed the latter word ten times in his short, two-thousand-word speech.[59]

Moving beyond legalistic discussion of the terms of the eighteenth-century grants to a more general discussion of justice and property rights, Cooper drew from a number of sources to construct an argument for state intervention in the distribution of land. Citing classical precedents, he defended the thinking of those who had constructed the Roman agrarian laws establishing a low ceiling on the amount of land that any individual might hold.[60] Similar measures, he contended, were necessary on Prince Edward Island, because without such restrictions 'the liberties of the people' were in jeopardy; 'there cannot be a greater power given to one man over another than the right of a landlord over poor tenants.' His contention that the concentration of landownership led to oppression and tyranny and posed a threat to liberty paralleled the arguments agrarian leaders would make in Lower Canada and New York later in the 1830s and in the 1840s.[61] While all accumulation was potentially threatening, none was more so than the accumulation of land. Those who engrossed the soil were uniquely placed to capture the labour of others. 'There cannot,' he argued, 'be a greater monopoly of the labour of man, than by holding the possession of large tracts of land.' With such power, proprietors could appropriate the wealth the settler population was creating. Like those speaking on behalf of subordinate rural populations elsewhere in North America in the late eighteenth and early nineteenth centuries, Cooper drew from a labour theory of value to argue that rural people had legitimate property claims that their representatives needed to defend. And it was, he maintained, the job of the state to do so. Arguing against liberals in the assembly who might adhere to the notion that 'all restriction was against the principles of justice,' he contended that restriction was necessary to secure justice for ordinary people.[62]

Cooper's proposal spoke directly to the attitudes and needs of the majority of Islanders – the tenants and squatters. A partial escheat would do little or nothing for them, for by definition the lots targeted for confiscation under that plan were to be those lacking settlers. A partial escheat did not offer relief from the burden of rents on the lots that already had substantial settlement, and it did not promise relief to those whose farms were in jeopardy because they were unable to pay arrears. At best, a partial escheat might offer the existing tenantry the chance to give up their past improvements and begin the land-clearing process all over again as freeholders. Cooper's call for a general escheat, by contrast, offered tenants and squatters the hope of realizing clear ownership of the lands they had improved and were currently working, and it offered all tenants relief from the burdens and threats posed by rents. As well, it offered relief to freeholders who were still making land payments to proprietors and – because it would open up access to land everywhere – opportunities for all to settle their sons and daughters on nearby holdings. What it gained in its appeal to the interests of subordinate countrypeople, though, it lost elsewhere as it challenged the interests of those who benefited from landlordism. In addition, a general escheat, unless it was defined clearly in a way that secured freeholders' interests, could easily be construed by the Island's small freeholders as a threat to the security of their own titles.

Although their objectives, rhetoric, and rationales differed, Cooper and the members of the 13th Assembly advocating a partial escheat agreed on some matters. The calls for a partial escheat and a general escheat were rooted in similar claims concerning the failure of proprietors to fulfil the terms of their original land grants, and both entailed the establishment of a court of escheat to adjudicate this matter. Initially, too, except for the voices of two resident proprietors, there appeared to be a consensus in the House of Assembly concerning the history of the land question. There seemed to be broad agreement in the 13th Assembly that the terms of the eighteenth-century grants had been at best but incompletely fulfilled by the Island's original landlords and that in general they had chosen to dispose of their lands to speculators for 'trifling consideration' rather than live up to the stipulations in their deeds. The new class of landlords that had emerged, the majority argued, had no just claims on the Crown – they were profit seekers, not worthy patriots who had sustained the British cause in the Seven Years' War and who had been rewarded with lands for their troubles. The strategy of these landlords, they contended, had been to turn essentially worthless grants, for which they had paid little, into valuable claims by deceiving the Crown about the real situation prevailing on Prince Edward Island. Over the years, landlords had been involved in misrepresentation and deception regarding the state of settlement on the Island and also regarding their efforts to abide by the terms of their grants; thus they had defeated attempts by the colonial assembly to escheat unsettled lands early in the nineteenth century by giving 'false statements' to the Colonial Office. Had it not been for their perfidious interference in the administration of Island affairs, the majority argued, the structure of land ownership in the colony would have been more equitably arranged years earlier.[63]

The assembly was dominated by moderates, who were concerned about maintaining much of the status quo as they advanced the pace of economic development in the colony; yet the rhetoric they employed inadvertently supported a more radical position in the countryside. The contentions aired in the house reinforced popular ideas about the wrongdoings of proprietors and the weaknesses of proprietorial claims to title. Island residents were able to follow the first stirrings of the escheat issue in the house through the *Royal Gazette*, which reprinted the proceedings of the assembly, including evidence bearing on the terms of the original grants and concerning the assembly's attempts to initiate an escheat in the late eighteenth and early nineteenth centuries. In the countryside the investigations were followed closely. Newspapers, noted W.H. Williams of Bay Fortune, were 'almost worn out with the handing from one to another.'[64] Vere Beck, a resident of Cape Bear who had immigrated from southeast England in 1813, reported that transportation problems and the scarcity of cash made it difficult in normal times for those in his district to regularly see the paper, but that when escheat was raised in the house those going to town made it a point to return with multiple copies of the latest issue. When a neighbour was expected back from Charlottetown, Beck observed, 'he is hardly allowed to refresh himself before his house is crowded.'[65] Beck personally made it a point to obtain a copy of every paper containing the proceedings of the assembly that year; he regretted only that the debates were not more fully reported. Illiteracy, the presence of many non-English speakers, and a level of poverty that put newspaper subscriptions out of reach of most rural Islanders ensured that in much of the countryside, following the printed news was a collective task; papers were passed about, read aloud, and translated for the benefit of those who did not speak English.[66] Because the assembly's proceedings were published in the newspaper, the audience for the debates in the house was potentially colony-wide. As Beck and others noted, discussion of the escheat question drew the rapt attention of people in distant parts of the Island.

As the escheat drama unfolded in the assembly, one of the things rural residents sought to discern was the true character of the actors who represented them in Charlottetown. Fuller reporting of the debates, Beck noted, would permit people to form a better opinion concerning 'who are really and truly its [Escheat's] steady and determined advocates and worthy of our future confidence.'[67] Audience response to events in the assembly might then be better expressed in subsequent elections. Cooper, who read his major speeches in the house from a written text, provided James Haszard, the editor of the *Royal Gazette*, with a copy of his stirring call for a general escheat; this was reprinted on page one of the final issue of the *Royal Gazette* dealing with the proceedings of the second session of the 13th Assembly.[68]

Rural communities showed their support for the house's land initiatives by drawing up petitions in favour of an escheat and in support of their elected representatives. The residents of Bay Fortune, Cooper's district, provided a model for how people might respond to the issues being aired in the assembly. Shortly after the house finished its proceedings on the escheat issue, a committee of Bay Fortune residents called a local public meeting to consider the land question. It passed resolutions providing strong support for a general escheat and resolved that a petition be drawn up asking the lieutenant-governor to establish a court of escheat *and* to protect the tenantry from proprietorial demands pending official expropriation. It was, they contended, 'as clear as the sun at noon, that the Grantees, and their Assigns, by evil counsels and combinations against our Rights and Privileges have circumvented and intercepted His Majesty's most gracious and beneficent intentions towards his most faithful and loyal people.'[69] Royal paternalism had been thwarted by a landlord conspiracy. Bay Fortune residents submitted a report of the meeting and a list of the resolutions passed to the *Royal Gazette*, and once again, the paper played a role in broadening the audience for the escheat cause.

Publication of the proceedings of the Bay Fortune meeting helped generate similar public meetings elsewhere on the Island in the spring and summer of 1832 (see map 4.1). Gatherings at Bear River and St Peters affirmed their support of the Bay Fortune resolutions.[70] A fourth Kings County escheat meeting was held at Cape Bear.[71] The residents of New London passed similar resolutions of their own and drew up an escheat petition bearing 470 signatures. The New London escheat committee's correspondent to the *Royal Gazette* enlarged on the Bay Fortune committee's interpretation of current events by noting that Prince Edward Island, too, was beginning to participate in the reforms that were altering the shape of society in other parts of the world. Besides arguing that the proprietors had not fulfilled the terms of their grants and thus had no legal claim to their lands, the New London correspondent contended that rents were an unmanageable burden that had to be discarded. The difficulties of making a farm in the wilderness had been compounded by the collapse of the shipbuilding and timber industries, which 'were done, never again to revive'; and the rural majority, which was deep in arrears, was only going to fall deeper into debt as opportunities for wage work continued to decline. To save themselves from 'bondage and poverty,' rural Islanders needed to 'meet and consult each others views' and 'pursue an orderly and steady course, in their endeavours to free themselves, their country, and their offspring.'[72] An escheat meeting at Rustico Ferry drew two hundred residents from the communities of Rustico, Cavendish, and New Glasgow. John Crisp, the man who had hosted meetings to nominate representatives for Queens County in the 1830 elections, acted as secre-

Map 4.1. Escheat meetings, 1832

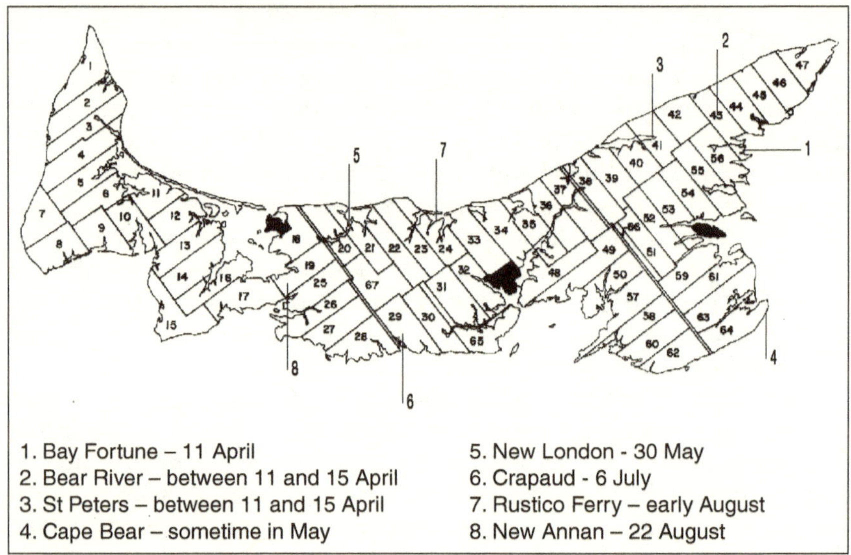

Source: *Royal Gazette*, 1832

tary for the gathering.[73] More moderate lists of resolutions supporting escheat were passed at this meeting and at others held at Crapaud and New Annan.[74]

Within months of the assembly's consideration of the land question, then, escheat had become a matter of public debate and there was an Island-wide campaign to petition and agitate for a court of escheat. Cooper's supporters in Bay Fortune, having been the first to hold a public meeting and publish a set of resolutions, helped set the tone of the escheat organizations that emerged elsewhere both by their example and through correspondence with agrarian activists in other townships.[75] The Bay Fortune group played an especially prominent role in combating written opposition as it emerged in the columns of the *Royal Gazette* and in other publications.[76] It also took an active hand in circulating copies of statements on the escheat issue written by Cooper, Beck, and the Dingwells of Bay Fortune, and explored the possibility of bringing these out in pamphlet form with a printing of five hundred copies.[77] It is not clear whether this particular pamphlet was printed; however, such publications were assembled and circulated by escheat organizations later in the 1830s.[78]

Most of the escheat meetings held in 1832 advocated a general escheat, and even the more moderate lists of resolutions passed assumed that the establishment of a court of escheat would sweep away the vast majority of proprietorial holdings and place their inhabitants in freehold possession of the lands. The key issue dividing proponents of escheat in the countryside was not so much the extent of landlord holdings that needed to be reclaimed, but the appropriate means of achieving their goal. With the escheat debate being conducted at the community level, the positions adopted varied from locale to locale. Extant records of escheat meetings suggest that in general, Kings County escheat activists adopted a more militant stance than their counterparts elsewhere. The resolutions of the original Bay Fortune meeting of April 1832 called not just for political initiatives but for a form of direct action – rent resistance. One of the resolutions asserted that tenants could no longer 'acknowledge' the proprietors as landlords, for their claims were rooted in 'deceit and falsehood' and consequently void. The Island's landlords had never fulfilled the conditions of their original grants and therefore lacked legal title to the lands they let. Resistance to rent payment was of course not new, and had been a facet of the escheat agitation of the 1790s, but developments in the political arena now gave it a new aura of legitimacy and helped transform individual reluctance to regularly pay rents into a broader phenomenon with an articulated moral and political justification. Tenants in eastern Kings County moved from passing resolutions calling for rent resistance to establishing collective 'bonds' or 'agreements' to effect this, and there were reports of such agreements elsewhere as well.[79] The resolutions made at public meetings in yet other locales, though, explicitly limited support to constitutional tactics.

The association of the political challenge with direct action, and the involvement of people like Cooper in the organization of rent resistance, drew attacks not just from the political right and the centre, but from the left as well. Jotham Blanchard, editor of Pictou's *Colonial Patriot* and a supporter of Papineau and MacKenzie's struggles in Upper and Lower Canada, lent his pen to the support of the assembly's call for a court of escheat, but at the same time condemned tenant unions. While asserting that 'Agitation' was 'the only mode of obtaining rights from any Government,' Blanchard – whose political position in Nova Scotia had been in keeping with that of British radicals in the Imperial centre – argued that it would be 'equally just for the landlords, if they were strong enough, to combine and drive the tenants from their cultivated leaseholds as for the tenants to combine to withhold rents from the landlords.' Cooper, and those who followed him in arguing for the rights of rural producers to defend the value they were creating with their labour, saw justice and collective action differently.[80]

The growing militancy in the countryside, although stimulated by events in the political arena, found little outlet there in the aftermath of passage of the escheat act in 1832. In September 1832, Islanders were informed that the Colonial Office would not support the assembly's escheat bill and were able to read for themselves the secretary of state's reasons for opposing a court of escheat. While Lord Goderich acknowledged that proof of non-settlement might be sufficient to 'justify a forfeiture under the letter of the Grants,' he argued that such a process would be unfair, for he was informed that some proprietors had sent out more than their necessary share of settlers only to have these people leave their properties and go elsewhere. Discerning whom these proprietors might be and exempting them from confiscation would, Goderich argued, take too long and lead to uncertain results. Beyond this, he admonished tenants to forget any hope they might entertain that an escheat of the township they resided in would result in their gaining access to the lands they occupied for little or nothing. Free grants of Crown lands were a thing of the past, Goderich declared, and should there be an escheat those occupying lands which reverted to the Crown ought to expect to continue in the payment of their present rents.[81]

Publication of Lord Goderich's dispatch fanned rather than allayed the growing agitation. The argument that a court of escheat would damage proprietors who had invested capital to establish settlers on their lots only to have them move elsewhere confirmed the belief widely held among tenants that a proprietorial conspiracy was feeding fabrications to the king's ministers. On one hand, the dispatch was disheartening, for it suggested that governmental intervention to settle the land question in the interests of the tenantry was not imminent. On the other hand, the arguments of the dispatch reinforced the rural version of Island history which saw colonial injustice as the product of conspiratorial intervention in the accurate flow of information between subject and monarch. Goderich's articulation of a version of Island history that saw proprietors as energetic promoters of the welfare of the colony, who required protection from injustices, did not ring true with Island settlers. Rather, it confirmed their belief that once again Imperial policy makers were being 'informed' by a distorted version of history; this left intact the hope that an escheat could ultimately be gained once the

Colonial Office understood Island realities. Indeed, Escheat proponents were buoyed by the fact that Goderich had not denied the possibility of a court of escheat. He had, instead, made a case for it to be equitable and to operate speedily with predictable results. More importantly, though, because the dispatch was framed in terms of a version of Island history that was fully congruent with their version of how unjust policies had been perpetrated in the past, it kept alive the hope – as old as peasants, kings and rural injustices – that things could be set right if accurate information concerning Island circumstances were conveyed directly to those in power in the home government.[82]

The escheat excitement that had grown in the early spring of 1832 with the assembly's discussion of the issue had, as the editor of the *Royal Gazette* noted that fall, 'suffered no abatement' during the summer, and it continued to dominate public discussion in the months after the publication of Goderich's dispatch.[83] Tenants' perceptions that they were victims of a conspiracy to deny them justice were maintained over the course of the fall by the publication of yet more documents bearing on the history of the land question in the early nineteenth century. In the *Royal Gazette* of 16 October 1832, James Haszard published a copy of the dispatch the Colonial Secretary, Lord Hobart, had sent to Lieutenant-Governor Fanning thirty years earlier asking him to arrange for passage of escheat legislation in the colony similar to that prevailing in Nova Scotia. As well, Haszard published other documents submitted to him by 'Fiat Justitia' purporting to show how Fanning, a land agent and proprietor himself, had evaded carrying out these instructions.[84] Fiat Justitia contended that at the turn of the century a cabal, which included proprietors and government officials, had operated to deny an escheat and thereby thwart the king's justice and that, as Goderich's dispatch demonstrated, a cabal was continuing to do so. Haszard, who was of Rhode Island Loyalist stock and who had returned to the United States for a number of years towards the end of the first quarter of the nineteenth century, was sympathetic to the cause of reform in the 1820s and early 1830s. He reviewed the evidence and remarked at length on the 'glaring tissue of misrepresentation and falsehood' that had been 'pawned upon His Majesty's government.' He suggested that his anonymous contributor was closing in on the truth of Island history and the means by which proprietary interests, at the turn of the century, had maintained their control of the colony's lands. Investigation was 'exposing the secret influences which have hitherto operated so banefully on the fortunes of this country.'[85]

Haszard later modified his position concerning the meaning of this evidence and published a letter from Maria Fanning, a resident proprietor, defending her father's conduct, but it is doubtful whether his change of heart and the lengthy arguments that accompanied it were persuasive in the countryside.[86] His own initial comments reveal much about the climate of opinion on the Island at this time – a climate reinforced by the rhetoric emerging from the assembly when it convened again early in 1833. To protest the response it had received from the Colonial Office concerning the escheat legislation of 1832, the assembly framed a petition to the king complaining that Lord Goderich's dispatch was yet another example of the effect that proprietorial misrepresentation was having on colonial policy. The proprietors, it contended, had 'contrived by means of false statements' concocted for 'the most sordid motive' to defeat the continued efforts of the colony's assembly to obtain a just settlement of the land issue.[87]

While the rhetoric was strident, and in keeping with the sentiments expected by a rural audience, the actions of the majority of the house reflected the less enthusiastic position that most in fact supported. Indeed, the minimal nature of the escheat bill itself suggests that the legislature did not expect success.[88] Having initiated legislation aimed at appeasing rural demands for an escheat, and having been blocked by outside forces, they were free, after protesting loudly in the following session of the house, to return to other matters while awaiting a response from the complaint to the Imperial government. Some, no doubt, were relieved that they could shift the blame for the inaction onto the Colonial Office.[89] The gap between the intentions of the majority of the assembly and the aspirations of general escheators in the countryside remained as a latent division. At this point, general escheators and partial escheators alike seemed stymied by the same external obstacles, and the house seemed to be doing all it could to establish a court of escheat and advance rural interests.

The following year, the 1833 session of the assembly turned its attention to yet another land tax scheme, one that one of its key promoters, Joseph Pope, argued would 'answer the end of an escheat.'[90] Pope, who would play a central role in opposing the Escheat movement, was part of a large, Plymouth-based mercantile family that had become involved in Prince Edward Island's timber trade in the years after the Napoleonic Wars. By the early 1830s he was in sole control of the family's extensive operations in and around Bedeque in Prince County; he was also the most prominent merchant west of Charlottetown and a land agent for

Horatio Mann, an absentee American proprietor.[91] When Pope assumed a seat in the assembly in 1830 he was taking up where his father-in-law, Alexander Campbell, had left off, and his positions in the house were very much in keeping with those of the majority of the previous assembly.[92] Pope's initiative was related to a response from the Imperial government to the assembly's requests for revocation of the permanent revenue acts of 1785 and 1795. Like similar requests from the other British North American colonies, it received conditional approval.[93] In a dispatch that was written in November of the previous year and that was laid before the house as it convened early in 1833, Lord Goderich replied that the Imperial government would be willing to revoke the acts whenever the colony decided to assume the financial cost of the civil list.[94] Lord Goderich's original dispatch responding to the escheat bill had suggested that while the Imperial government opposed the escheat legislation, it would look more favourably on a land tax, including one that taxed settled and unsettled lands at an equal rate and thereby acted as an incentive to promote the development of lands being held for speculative purposes. In a major legislative initiative the assembly pursued a union of these two Colonial Office suggestions by drafting and passing a civil list bill that would see the colony assume the cost of the civil establishment through a land tax of 4/6 per hundred acres of township land and additional sums on lots of land in the Island's royalties.[95] If the act passed the upper house and received royal assent, it was to go into effect in the fall of 1837, as the current land tax, which was funding the construction of government buildings, expired. Like the earlier tax, it was contingent on a cessation in quit rents. It was not clear how this bill would intersect with new quit rent policies Lord Goderich had laid out in a more recent dispatch. This communication, which was placed before the house during the 1833 session, indicated how quit rents were to be collected when they resumed in 1838; it also stipulated terms by which landowners could permanently redeem these claims and acquire new grants.[96]

Cooper complained that the assembly had contested Goderich's escheat refusal with an 'apathy' suggesting that the protests had been 'dragged through our teeth against our inclination,' but the issue appeared to have run its course in the house.[97] A motion by Cooper to send a delegate to Britain to press the issue with the home government found no support in the assembly in 1833.[98] Nonetheless, a fundamental shift in Island politics had begun in the spring and summer of 1832 as debate over the land question drew Island politics towards pressing rural issues and as people in the countryside came to believe that their problems and aspirations could be addressed through appropriate political action. With this movement, the political initiative began to shift from the Island's business community, and others who shared their objectives, towards tenants, squatters, and small freeholders and towards a leadership willing to articulate their interests.[99] As the discussion and debate of land issues moved from the House of Assembly into the countryside, a growing sense of colony-wide discontent among tenants and other rural residents began to emerge and with it a determination – as one of the Bay Fortune committee members put it – 'to do something for ourselves.'[100] What the appropriate actions should be at this point was a matter for local experiment. Although the Escheat movement was to a large extent launched from the House of Assembly, it would be kept alive by developments in the countryside.

5 Resistance in the Countryside, 1832–1834

'Reform appears to be the order of the day in almost all parts of the civilized world,' noted the secretary of an Escheat meeting at Rustico Ferry in northern Queens County.[1] He went on to describe the grievances besetting the rural underclasses of the Island and to record a series of resolutions concerned with redressing them. Discussion of the escheat issue in the assembly in the early months of 1832 generated enormous enthusiasm in the countryside. There was a sense that Prince Edward Island was participating in the great changes occurring elsewhere in the Atlantic world. Judging by the petitions and letters that emerged from the countryside in 1832, the fine gradations of support for escheat in the assembly were lost on much of the rural audience. What mattered most was that rural demands were on the agenda and that escheat legislation had passed with a large majority. A growing euphoria followed these developments.[2] On Prince Edward Island in 1832, The Great Hope – rather than *La Grande Peur*, as in the case of revolutionary France – was sweeping through the countryside.[3] Observers spoke of a growing 'excitement' in rural regions during and after the sitting of the assembly.

Sensing that important shifts were underway and that major changes were possible, indeed imminent, tenants increasingly challenged the status quo. In the countryside, the 1832 session of the assembly was followed by widespread rent resistance, diminishing deference to those associated with landlordism, heightened awareness of class oppression, and increasing political activity. This in turn led to open resistance to private and civil authority. Disappointment and disillusionment soon followed, as landlordism proved resilient and the hope of a rapid and revolutionary change in land tenure turned out to be ill founded. Success, if it was to be gained, would require moving beyond enthusiasm and mass resistance towards the construction of more substantial and sustainable means for challenging the status quo.

The Island's new lieutenant-governor, Aretas Young, who had previously held the post of protector of the slaves in Demerara, had been in Prince Edward Island for less than a year when he found himself dealing with growing rural unrest.[4] Several months after the assembly debated and passed escheat legislation, he noted that 'a good deal of excitement' prevailed 'amongst certain classes' in the countryside, who believed that the dream they 'cherished of obtaining their land without any restriction' was about to become a reality, a hope 'kept alive by several addresses to me urging its immediate adoption.'[5] His publication of Lord Goderich's negative response to the assembly's escheat initiative, in September 1832, was an attempt to dampen this hope. What Young did not indicate clearly to his superiors was that the 'excitement' in the countryside went beyond petitions and support for political redress of rural grievances and included rent resistance. In June, two months after the assembly was prorogued for the year, tenants of the resident proprietor Donald Macdonald were refusing to pay him rents and had 'set him at defiance' – a development that, according to landlord sources, resulted from the influence of 'Cooper's principles' on 'the minds of the lower classes.'[6] The absentee proprietor Robert Stewart must have received similar news from the Island at the same time, for in July he wrote to Goderich complaining that since the passage of the escheat act, his tenants had been refusing to pay rent. He claimed as well that rent resistance had become general in the colony as tenants 'anticipated what will be the effect' of the legislation.[7] One of his agents, William Forgan, writing in June, predicted that the excitement in the countryside produced by activities in the assembly would induce 'open resistance' to the 'enforcement of the payment of rents' if escheat hopes were not quickly squelched by prompt action at the Colonial Office.[8] By autumn, Laurence Sulivan's agent, too, was facing tenants who refused to pay rent.[9]

All of these observers noted that rent resistance was intimately connected with events in the political arena. In part, the resistance was anticipatory: the tenants believed that an escheat was inevitable and were acting according to their expectations. Similar anticipatory responses had occurred in the wake of Governor Smith's 1818 escheats. As the residents of the Bay Fortune district somewhat ruefully noted in 1838, they had withheld their rents in the aftermath of the passage of the escheat legislation of 1832 'under the impression that they were to be relieved by the appointment of such a Court.'[10] Moreover, and importantly, developments in the assembly offered moral grounds for a refusal to pay rents. The demand for the establishment of a court of escheat was rooted in various contentions concerning the improper behaviour of Island landlords, ranging from their failure to fulfil the terms of their grants to fraud and deceit. Such assertions were rooted in long-standing rural perceptions; now as they re-emerged from the proceedings of the assembly, those perceptions carried new weight. In part this reflected the power of the printed word in a semi-literate rural society. The documents derived from the activities of the assembly carried authority. As well, the debates in the assembly, their coverage in the papers, and the discussions of them in the rural meetings that followed provided new immigrants with an education in Island traditions concerning the land question and helped bring about a sharing and blending of perceptions emerging from different localities. In these ways the proceedings of the assembly augmented the construction of a common narrative concerning landlord perfidy and in so doing strengthened the foundations for a common response of resistance. Beyond this, rural meetings convened to discuss the activities of the assembly and to formulate political responses provided an organizational basis for considering and launching other initiatives.

Events on a local level in Bay Fortune provide an example of how the initiatives in the assembly intersected with local collective decisions to engage in rent resistance. After the passage of escheat legislation, the residents of Cooper's district held a meeting during which they passed resolutions supporting the actions of the assembly and castigating landlords for their immoral, grasping behaviour. Landlords, they maintained, had forfeited their claim to the land years earlier but had managed to maintain their position by deceiving both the Crown and the Island's rural population. With 'ready made titles, and Lawyers at their side,' they were acting 'to compel the simple but industrious people to acknowledge one Landlord after another, and be torn to pieces with as little mercy as sheep would experience from hungry dogs.' On the basis of all this, they went on to call for rent resistance. Tenants could not 'conscientiously, or with justice to ourselves, acknowledge as landlords those men who by deceit and falsehood' had undermined the king's justice.[11] To pay rent to such people would be to 'become panderers to their guilt.'[12] A collective decision to refuse to pay rents emerged from hope of an imminent escheat and a narrative that provided moral grounds to resist the terms of the leases. A public meeting called to respond to developments in the assembly served as well to ventilate land grievances and coordinate rural responses.

There were reports of similar collective decisions elsewhere. Not surprisingly, evidence concerning these proceedings is thin.[13] Meetings to discuss rent resistance were of uncertain legality, and few gatherings dared to publicize their discussions of these matters as did the residents of Bay Fortune.[14] There are indications, however, that by the spring of 1833, resistance to the payment of rents was widespread. In early March, H.D. Morpeth informed his employers, David and Robert Stewart, that he had visited all their tenants on Lot 47 in Kings County and had written and/or visited all those on Lot 27 in Prince County and that from all of them he still had not received sufficient sums to permit payment even of the annual land taxes the Stewarts now owed. He reported as well that rents were not being paid on the estates of Worrell, Macdonald of Tracadie, the Cambridges, or William Townshend, and he contended that the refusal to pay rents originated with the escheat proceedings of the assembly and the council. Their treatment of the land question, he argued, had encouraged the belief that an escheat would occur, despite Young's publication of Lord Goderich's dispatch. Even in the absence of any significant new developments in the assembly (which had resumed in January 1833), Island tenants clung to this expectation 'with the greatest pertinacity.'[15] Later complaints from Charles Worrell would support Morpeth's contentions with regard to rent resistance on the huge Worrell estate. By the fall of the year John Hill also was complaining that rent resistance on his estate was widespread and that his agent could not raise sufficient monies to permit payments of the first and second instalments of the annual land taxes that were due.[16] While the most militant public statements in favour of rent resistance came from Kings County and the more conservative public statements in favour of responding to the issue solely within constitutional bounds came from parts of Queens and Prince counties, the evidence of land agents attempting to collect rents suggest that significant numbers of tenants across the Island were adhering to a no-rent position after the passage of the escheat act.[17]

Besides refusing to make rent payments, some also were beginning to demonstrate a willingness to use force if need be to protect their farms and their possessions from legal proceedings initiated by landlords (see map 5.1). In the fall of 1832 an Island paper reported that a sheriff's officer attempting to execute processes for rent on Lot 1 in the

Map 5.1. Direct action, 1832 to 1835 (partial list)

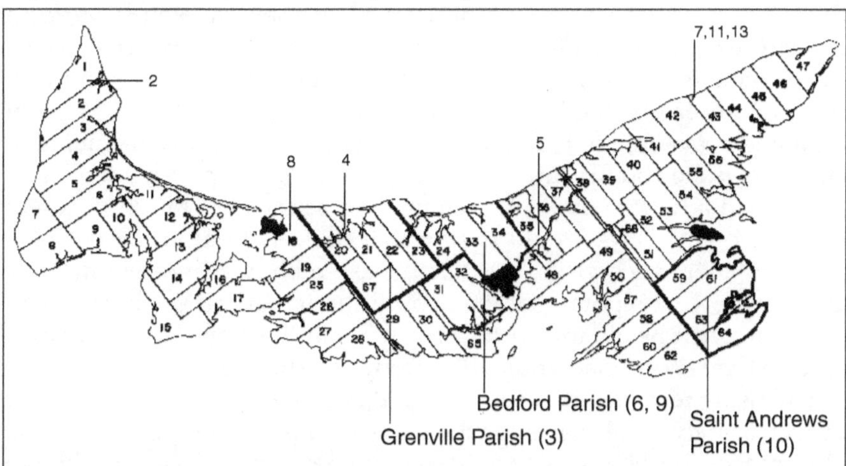

1. Early summer 1832 – Allan and Michael MacDonald assault constable and rescue farming implements (location unknown)
2. Fall 1832 – crowd turns back sheriff's officer, Tignish Bridge
3. 26 February 1833 – William MacKay assaults at bailiff, Grenville Parish
4. 15 June 1833 – Crowd resists officer serving writs, New London
5. 29 June 1833 – Arsonists burn millhouse and premises of resident landlord, Donald Macdonald, Lot 35
6. 25 July 1833 – Malcolm Steel's armed resistance to bailiff acting for Donald Macdonald, Bedford Parish
7. September 1833 – Allan Macdonald and four others assault bailiff, Naufrage
8. 12 December 1833 – Mathew Connick and four others assault constables, Lot 18
9. 15 December 1833 – Alexander MacInnis and Angus MacPhee assault landlord, Donald Macdonald, Bedford Parish
10. 2 April 1834 – John and Catherine Renahau assault constable, Saint Andrews Parish
11. 8 June 1834 – Large crowd turns back posse, Naufrage
12. Fall 1834 – Mary and Margaret Campbell assault constable, Kings County
13. Early January 1835 – Large crowd turns back posse, Naufrage

Source: *Royal Gazette*; *Prince Edward Island Times*; Supreme Court Records, RG 6, PARO

northwestern tip of the Island was met by 'a large armed body' of local residents at the Tignish Bridge and obliged to turn back.[18] Elsewhere rural residents assaulted bailiffs and constables who were distraining for rents and regained the goods and implements the law officers were attempting to carry away.[19] According to a local paper, a boatman sought to intimidate a sheriff's officer and assistant sent to serve writs at Bay Fortune by attempting to capsize them in deep water during a river crossing when he learned of their mission.[20] Morpeth reported early in March 1833 that when he threatened one of the Stewarts' Lot 47 tenants with a visit from the sheriff, the man had told him to tell the law officer that 'he had better bring his coffin with him.'[21] A bit of bluff and bravado, no doubt, but talk of assassination was beginning to circulate in the countryside. According to one Island paper, a tenant on Lot 56 had advised others that killing 'two or three' of the sheriffs sent to enforce land laws would ensure that 'they would not be troubled with any more such visits.'[22] While the assembly was meeting in April 1833, there were reports that the deputy sheriff had been rebuffed with violence when he attempted to serve writs in the New London district and that the sheriff had applied for troops to enforce the law.[23]

The rising tensions in the countryside in 1833 occurred in the context of increasingly bleak news for the escheat cause in the political arena. The publication of Goderich's dispatch in September 1832 had thrown cold water on the escheat initiative, and a more recent communication placed before the house in late January 1833 was even more discouraging.[24] In this latest dispatch, Goderich revealed the Imperial government's new quit rent policy, to take effect after collection was resumed on the Island in 1838, following the five-year suspension that had been decreed with the introduction of a land tax to support the construction of government buildings. When collection began again, proprietors would be permitted to buy the quit rents out for a sum equivalent to fifteen times the annual quit rent rate during the first two years of their resumption. Landlords who chose to exercise this option would be excused from any previous arrears that might have accumulated against their grants and would also be provided with 'a formal release' from all previous settlement provisions. Speaking to the arguments in favour of an escheat that had been advanced by those sustaining the politics of development, Goderich contended that this new arrangement was an appropriate response to the 'common complaint' of Islanders – that land was being left unimproved by speculating landlords and that as a consequence the colony's economic performance was being retarded. The strict enforcement of quit rents that would occur under the new arrangements would, he assured them, make speculating in wilderness lands unprofitable and would ensure that landlords either developed their properties or sold them to others who would. He promised as well that the monies raised by quit rents would be applied solely to the colony's purposes.

In an important speech delivered on 6 April, William Cooper responded bitterly to Goderich's dispatches and to the news that proprietors were to be provided a means to escape all the conditional aspects of their grants.[25] The policy Goderich was enunciating might, as the secretary of state argued, meet the objectives of business people concerned with the Island's economic development, but it threatened to kill any chance the majority of those living in the countryside had of achieving their goals. The agrarian dream underlying demands for an escheat rested on the hope that the existing rights the state maintained over Island grants would be exercised for the benefit of those who actually worked the soil. Because the state retained legal claims to all Island lands, it was possible to conceptualize and formulate an expropriation policy that was in keeping with existing laws and that need not be interpreted as an outright attack on private property. Island lands were, Escheators contended, still the king's property. While the effect of a general escheat as envisioned by the subordinate rural population of the colony would be a redistribution from the rich to the poor and from the parasitic to the industrious, the policy itself could be sustained as a defence of the property rights held by the Crown, provided the state did not relinquish its residual rights to the land by formally releasing proprietors from the obligations contained in the terms of the original grants.

The 'rights and liberties of His Majesty's subjects' on the Island were, Cooper asserted, being imperilled by the 'dangerous design of a party' who, because of the nature of the Island's land system, had been able to 'combine against the labouring class, to deprive them of their labor.' If the state did not intervene, landlords would soon have 'the whole labor of the industrious class of the colonists.' Goderich's policy, Cooper argued, would close the door on any hope the tenantry might entertain of gaining the advantages accruing from their improvement of the land, and this was wrong, as one of the duties of the state was 'to secure the benefits of their own labor to the industrious.' Unless they achieved an escheat – something that Cooper was beginning to see as a right that could not in justice be denied the tenantry – they would in the long term lose their possessions and their farms to the proprietors. In effect, Goderich's policy was offering to sell the tenantry 'as vassals with all their labour' to 'the land jobbers' at a rate of less than five pence per acre, in that proprietors with forfeited titles could, upon payment, receive good deeds to lands the Island's tenantry had spent their lives improving. Drawing a parallel between the rural disturbances occurring synchronically in Ireland and on the Island, Cooper argued that the 'complaints of the people of Ireland and this Island are of the same nature.' Those who worked the soil in both places were victims of insidious land monopolies, and while 'bullets and bayonets' might momentarily silence these protests, state repression was not a realistic long-term policy. The real 'aggressors' in each case, he claimed, were not the rural poor fighting for a livelihood, but the landed classes who were denying them access to a living. Lasting stability could only be gained if land was redistributed so that the majority of the inhabitants had a claim to the soil – a hope that in the case of Prince Edward Island was being dashed by Goderich's actions. What Prince Edward Island needed to do at this moment of crisis, Cooper proposed, was frame a new address to the king that conveyed the true state of affairs in the colony more strongly than the escheat request the house had agreed to the previous week. Cooper also proposed that it be delivered directly to London by a delegate who could ensure that the message was heard.[26]

More conservative assemblymen were aware of the impression that had been made in the countryside by the escheat speeches of Cooper and others in the previous session of the house, and condemned Cooper for the tone of his address. Joseph Pope maintained that such speeches had induced the present unrest among the rural population and recommended that Cooper's latest statement never be published as it might 'produce an open rebellion.'[27] He suggested that it was of no great importance that Goderich was eliminating the possibility of an escheat, and he argued that a land tax, such as the one proposed to sustain assumption of the civil list, could bring about similar results. Thomas Compton and Samuel Green – an English-born merchant, shipbuilder, and commercial farmer who had established his operations on the Island by purchasing land from Thomas Compton's father – continued to condemn Cooper's 'inflammatory' speech; Green argued that should blood be spilled in the unrest that was brewing in the countryside, he hoped that 'those who had been the means of misleading the people would be made to bear their full share of the responsibility.'[28] In the event, James Haszard decided not to publish Cooper's speech in the *Royal Gazette*, and the assembly, unwilling to entertain Cooper's suggestions, sustained instead a motion by Pope regarding the civil list.[29]

Yet, rural resistance to the enforcement of landlords' claims continued to grow after the house adjourned in the spring of 1833. In May the solicitor general, John Lawson, one of David and Robert Stewart's representatives on the Island, informed his employers that it was becoming impossible for law officers to 'serve process' in the countryside, as the Stewarts' tenants and those of others were 'in a complete state of revolt' and were using 'force to prevent the Sheriff or Bailiff from coming among them.'[30] The following month an angry crowd confronted land agent William Mumford when he attempted to serve writs against a dozen or so tenants of the resident landlord, William Cundall. News that Cundall's agent had obtained writs that were to be served in the New London region induced a crowd to gather outside Mumford's house. At least one carried a gun. They demanded that the agent either show the title under which Cundall was asserting his claims or not serve the writs.[31]

By the time the Trinity Term of the Supreme Court began a few weeks after the New London incident, reports of tenant resistance to the payment of rents and to the legal process for collecting arrears were coming in from all three counties. Chief Justice Edward Jarvis took the occasion to address the grand jury on the subject of tenant unrest. Jarvis was the son of Munson Jarvis, a prominent Connecticut Loyalist who had settled in Saint John, New Brunswick, and become a leading merchant and a member of the 'patrician elite' there.[32] After legal training in London, Edward Jarvis held appointments in New Brunswick and Malta before being given the job of Chief Justice of Prince Edward Island in 1828 with a comfortable salary of £700 per year.[33] Jarvis issued a warning to all those who were party to rent resistance: 'Dangerous and illegal combinations,' he informed them, 'existed among certain of the tenantry in this Island to resist the payment of their rents.' Some had 'opposed by force the officers of justice who came to levy by warrant of distress.' Behind these actions, he suggested, was the hand of 'designing and evil disposed persons' who were misleading the tenantry.[34] Rural Islanders should know that 'all combinations to obstruct or defeat the course of public justice were highly illegal, and would, upon indictment and conviction, be punished with great severity.' He warned those involved in physical resistance that should a law officer be killed in the course of one of these confrontations, all would be 'guilty of the high crime of murder' and 'without doubt, suffer the extreme penalty of the law.' If, on the other hand, law officers 'should unfortunately cause the death of any individual, it would be in a measure justifiable homicide, and the officers would be free from punishment.' Jarvis pointed out that if tenants had a legitimate grievance concerning the demand for rents, the appropriate course was to bring it before the courts so that justice might be rendered.[35]

Jarvis's suggestion concerning an appropriate course of action for the Island's tenants was unrealistic for most of them. While there were specific individual problems of title informing landlord/tenant disputes in various regions of the Island, the primary legal challenge raised by the rural Escheat agitation concerned the validity of the titles by which proprietors were claiming rents. Although landlords' titles appeared to support legal claim to rents from the occupants of the soil, close investigation would, many felt, reveal that their titles were void due to non-fulfilment of the conditions laid out in the grants. These beliefs were in keeping with the rhetoric that had emerged in the proceedings of the assembly and, of course, lay behind the agitation for a court of escheat. In this regard, then, the problem with Jarvis's suggestion was that the Colonial Office, for the moment at least, had denied the colony a forum where these claims could be adjudicated.

At best, all that could be done in the Island's Supreme Court was wrangle over details which, in general, were irrelevant to the basic grievances tenants were seeking to correct. At common law, tenants could not contest the titles of their landlords. Proof that a tenant had acknowledged a landlord was sufficient to establish proprietorial claims against a tenant, and proprietorial actions to collect rents could not be challenged by disputing the title sustaining the claim.[36] In Prince Edward Island as in New York State – where tenants were contesting a similar legacy of colonialism – this feature of the common law limited the usefulness of the courts as a forum for considering tenant grievances and helped to divert agitation into other channels.[37] Island tenants, even if they had the time, skills, and resources to investigate the titles of landlords *before* they paid rents and/or acquired leases, were faced with a costly search of public registries in Nova Scotia and Prince Edward Island, as well as private collections of title deeds in Britain and elsewhere, since landlords did not have to register their titles on the Island. Indeed, it would appear that for some lots, landlords never arranged to have the original grants issued.[38] Thus there was no practical way to separate claimants with an unbroken chain of title leading back to the original grants from others with technically flawed claims; and even this, of course, would not have addressed the issue of the validity of the original conditional grants. Because of the confusion over property rights on the Island and over who was legally empowered to act on behalf of various landlords, it was not unheard of for tenants to be approached by multiple claimants to their rents.[39] Island practices that permitted those claiming to be landlords to distrain on rural people without having registered title on the Island, and without the latter ever having entered into a lease, made the legal system, as Joseph Howe noted at a later date, an 'engine of terror.'[40] Faced with such a claim, those working the land could initiate an action of replevin – a legal counter-challenge – and attempt to recover the goods seized, or they could submit. Responding to rental demands in court, though, could involve the tenant in crippling costs.

These problems generated an attempt in 1832 to alter the laws governing title registration on the Island. Tenants petitioned the assembly concerning the problem of multiple land claimants and inadequate mechanisms for tenants to assess landlords' title early in 1832. The 13th General Assembly responded to this by passing a land registry act that made it illegal for proprietors to initiate legal process to collect rent without first having fully recorded their deeds in the Island's registry books and that limited the collection of arrears to six years.[41] Proprietors challenged this legislation when it was submitted to Imperial authorities for review, arguing that it would undermine the property rights of landlords. While acknowledging that there were lapses in the chain of some titles, they complained that the legislation might permit tenants to defeat landlords' claims upon 'some technical defect of title.' In addition, proprietors were worried that public disclosure of the small sums paid for many of the Island's estates might adversely affect the credibility of landlords' claims. Rural residents had long argued that speculators had acquired title to much of the land on the Island for trifling sums because seller and buyer alike were aware that the titles had lost their value due to failure to fulfil settlement terms or pay the quit rents stipulated in the grants. Proprietors were concerned that much evidence appearing to substantiate this argument would have to be recorded on the Island if the bill became law. Beyond this, they argued that the assembly's act violated British law concerning landlord/tenant relations in that it required the landlord to prove his title before he could collect rent. In the event, their arguments carried the day, and the Privy Council refused royal assent to the bill.[42]

Besides the existing law, tenants faced other barriers to the use of the courts as a means for obtaining redress for perceived injustices. It was widely believed that it was impossible for the tenantry to obtain honest legal counsel in the colony, as all Island lawyers were thought to be in some way associated with the proprietors' interests.[43] Court proceedings, then, drew tenants into legal labyrinths with guides whom many tenants believed to be untrustworthy. Moreover, for many of the Acadian,

Highland, and Irish tenants the language of the courts and of the law books was a foreign tongue – a complaint shared by some of the English-speaking tenantry. In addition, there was a perception that Chief Justice Jarvis had little sympathy with the tenant cause. These sentiments, though probably rooted mainly in his public statements and legal judgments, would not have been undermined by advertisements indicating that he was Island agent for the British American Land Company.[44] Legal proceedings also entailed costs and delays that for many were unsustainable. For instance, key court challenges launched in 1829 by relatively prosperous residents of Bay Fortune to determine whether tenants could be made to pay rents on land located beyond their survey lines dragged on through the 1830s and ultimately involved ruinous costs that forced the litigants to abandon their farms.[45]

These problems and perceptions gave rise to agrarian demands for fundamental changes in the Island's legal system – demands that would persist across the years of the Escheat movement. Rural leaders argued that the courts as constituted in the early 1830s served the interests of the wealthy and that what could be sustained as 'law' and what was 'common justice, which a child might understand,' were two different things.[46] Law and justice, one of the Bay Fortune escheat committee wrote in the fall of 1832, 'like other sciences, are so much refined now-a-days, that they are above the comprehension of common mortals, and like specimens of the fine arts, it is only the rich can purchase them.'[47] The grievances of rural Islanders concerning the judicial system paralleled the dissatisfactions voiced by rural producers elsewhere in British North America and in the United States in this era and so, too, did some of the suggested remedies.[48] In January 1833, Cooper proposed legislation that would address some of these problems by creating a system of local 'arbitration courts' that would take over some of the Supreme Court's caseload, particularly in matters concerning debts.[49] The existing court system with all its 'costly appendages and technical terms, which few knew the meaning of and fewer still the use of,' did not provide justice for rural people. Justice, 'the stability and security of all governments,' needed to be made 'cheap and easy of access.'[50] A start in this direction could be made, he argued, by having the government appoint local 'arbitrators,' who would hold office only for a limited time and only if they had renewable certificates of approval signed by a sufficient number of their neighbours. In essence, centralized governmental control over judicial appointments would be a formality; arbitrators would be informally selected by their communities and able to remain in office only so long as they retained local support. Lawyers would have no place in these courts. Different arbitrators would act on behalf of plaintiff and defendant. Cooper's suggestions for legal reform, coming at a time when the assembly was considering expanding the Supreme Court establishment and assuming the cost of yet another judge, represented a call for a more democratic and a less costly way of organizing the judicial system on the Island. In the event, he was unable to find support for his initiative in the 13th Assembly.

Despite the many good reasons rural residents had for eschewing the courts, however, some had no choice. Three days after Jarvis's address to the grand jury, indictments were returned against five individuals accused of fomenting the disturbance in New London. Archibald Campbell, John Burke, Andrew MacPherson, George Stewart, and Thomas Lanigan were charged, 'together with divers other evil disposed persons ... as yet unknown,' with assaulting an officer in the process of serving writs and with causing a riot that blocked the king's highway and lasted half an hour.[51] In their defence, the defendants would claim that they had congregated at the house of William Cundall's land agent simply to demand proof of title.[52] One happened to have a firearm in his possession during this gathering, they argued, because he was a blacksmith and it had been entrusted to him for repair. Certainly there were aspects of the case that reflected specific New London circumstances. The man who appears to have organized the gathering, Archibald Campbell, claimed that he doubted Cundall's title because he believed himself to be the legal heir to the township. Others beyond the community questioned the legitimacy of Cundall's claims.[53] Nonetheless, the confrontation expressed general concerns as well. Residents of the New London district, like those in many other parts of the Island, had organized an escheat meeting in the summer of 1832 and had endorsed the call for a general escheat, arguing that all the lands in the colony in fact had been forfeited to the Crown.[54] Not surprisingly, at least one of the defendants had spoken to Cundall's land agent in terms of the general agitation that was occurring, threateningly mentioning the possibility of a broader rebellion on the Island.[55]

There were ample grounds for the elite to be growing anxious over developments in the countryside. Rent resistance was being organized collectively, and so was some of the resistance to law officers. The tenants who had turned the constables back at the Tignish Bridge had not simply waited for the law to descend upon them; instead, they had repulsed the sheriff at a strategic point on the highway. Similarly, the tenants who accosted Cundall's land agent had left their farms and gone as a group to his house to confront him; they had not waited for him to deliver the writs, one by one, to their dwellings. Those accused of the New London riot, once they had been summoned before the Supreme Court, tried to put the best face on their actions by emphasizing their willingness to submit to valid land claims, but even their own statements strongly suggest that their intentions had been to intimidate the agent, both with their presence and with reminders of the broader movement underway, and to prevent him from serving any writs. Also worth noting is that those who had acted together to confront Cundall's agent were an ethnically diverse group.[56] The bonds and divisions that informed the contentious gathering outside New London were those of class.

After a jury found the New London defendants guilty of riot and assault and resistance to the execution of legal process, the chief justice faced a difficult decision. Jarvis advocated severe punishment as a means to halt the resistance to the law that was growing rapidly in the countryside, and he had already publicly delivered his views concerning the existence of a rural conspiracy. With some of those responsible for tenant resistance in New London under lock and key in the Charlottetown jail, substantial sentences seemed in order. At the same time, though, Jarvis was probably aware of the doubts some members of the Island upper classes had concerning the validity of the Cundall title. In addition, the jury had recommended that the accused be given 'favourable consideration,' and the evidence had not suggested egregious wrongs in the defendants' behaviour.[57] On close examination, the Island-wide conspiracy that was supposedly agitating the countryside seemed in this instance to be driven by relatively innocuous individuals understandably frustrated by local grievances. Before sentencing one of the defendants to four months in jail and the rest to three – terms he considered moderate – Jarvis explained the context in which he viewed their crimes and the reasons for his decisions. A 'determined spirit of opposition to the law, in resisting all proceedings for the recovery of rent by the landlords' was, he declared, afoot on the Island. It was being orchestrated by 'designing persons' who were leading 'their less intelligent and more artless countrymen' into illegal activities. Those being sentenced, falling into the latter category, might be considered for leniency, but should their leaders be brought before the bench they risked receiving the severest penalties under British law: 'General combinations to resist the law, might, under some circumstances, amount to a levying of war against the King, a species of high treason, the most atrocious of all crimes, and punishment for which is death in its most horrible shape.'[58]

Even as the court was sitting, the countryside continued to heat up. On the night of 29 June 1833, fire destroyed the mill house and premises of the Island's high sheriff, Donald Macdonald of Glenaladale. Evidence indicated that the fire had been deliberately set, and Lieutenant-Governor Young offered a reward of £200 for information leading to the conviction of the arsonists and £100 and a 'free pardon' to anyone who was party to it and who would reveal those behind the arson.[59] The structure of this reward suggests that Young, too, believed there was a conspiracy afoot. Besides being sheriff and one of the candidates in the bitterly disputed Queens County election of 1830, Macdonald was an abrasive and heavy-handed landlord engaged in extensive disputes with his tenants. Like other landlords and agents, he was using the legal system to counter rent resistance on his estate and had successfully initiated cases against a number of his tenants during the Trinity Term.

Gains achieved relatively easily in court, though, were challenged and disputed in the countryside in 1833 and 1834. A few weeks after the close of the Supreme Court, Malcolm Steel, one of Donald Macdonald's tenants who had just lost a court battle with his landlord over arrears, confronted John Collings, a law officer distraining for Macdonald. Losing his legal battle had added £19 in court costs to the £27 in arrears Macdonald claimed from his tenant. When Collings arrived to seize livestock to meet the costs of the judgment, Steel was not thinking in terms of a further legal suit. Perhaps he had yet another of the Trinity Term cases in mind. Alexander Smith, another of Macdonald's tenants, had contested the legality of a seizure of his livestock for back rents and for his troubles had been levied an additional £27 in costs.[60] Collings later testified that Steel levelled a gun at him and swore he would shoot him if he did not return the mare and cow he was leading from the farm back to the barn and leave immediately thereafter.[61] Steel's actions, for which he received a month in prison,[62] reflected the growing sense of frustration, and desperation, among much of the tenantry in 1833 and 1834.

Legislative measures initiated by the assembly and supported by escheat meetings and petitions from across the colony had apparently led nowhere. Goderich's dispatch had thrown cold water on the idea of establishing a court of escheat, and a subsequent petition of the assembly rebutting his contentions drew no direct response from the Colonial

Office either in 1833 or in the following year. The 4th session of the 13th Assembly, which began in February 1834, was simply informed that the escheat bill and the petition were under review.[63] Land registry legislation also awaited the decision of the Privy Council. Worse yet was the news that the Colonial Office would permit proprietors to purchase new titles by buying out their quit rents. Rural attitudes had shifted substantially over the months of the escheat debate, and strong expectations of change had been generated by developments both in the assembly and in the countryside. Yet, all the structures that supported landlordism remained in place, and nothing that was taking place in the assembly or in the courts suggested that things were about to improve. Tenants were still legally bound to pay rents to those who demanded them, and landlords were still able to respond to those who resisted by sending law officers out to seize their livestock and goods or by turning them out of their farms. When faced with a landlord (or multiple landlords) with dubious claims, tenants still lacked workable procedures for testing those claims.

Many of those who had resisted the payment of rents following the escheat proceedings of 1832 now faced the additional burden of legal fees, as the costs of law process and distress warrants were being added to the arrears. Some landlords appear to have acted intentionally to ensure that rent resisters faced punitive costs. Lord Townshend's tenants, for instance, were persuaded to come to terms with their landlord in part by a visit from George Dalrymple, who took on the role of intermediary between land agent and tenantry and promised the latter they would have time to get their harvest in before having to pay their arrears. Yet they found themselves saddled with an additional £40 to £50 in legal costs after Townshend's agent, the colonial treasurer T.H. Haviland, sent law officers into the community during the harvest.[64] The Stewarts, too, were instructing their agents to take punitive action against those tenants who had been prominent in rent resistance.[65]

Events in the political arena and in the courts suggested that tenant euphoria had been premature and that rent resistance could prove costly; meanwhile, economic developments were making it difficult for many to readjust. Crop failures and uncooperative weather at harvest time sharply reduced the returns to farmers in 1832 and 1833.[66] Agricultural exports for these years were on average less than two-thirds the value of those of 1831, and the resulting drop in income – and thus the purchasing power that sustained imports – was sharp enough to induce an unexpected deficit in the government accounts for 1833.[67] The returns to agriculture in 1834 were little better. The shipbuilding industry, a key source of wages for the tenantry, had rebounded somewhat from its slump, but production volumes in 1832–4 were still roughly half those of 1826.[68]

The result was ongoing tension and conflict in the countryside, with frustrated and often economically straitened rural dwellers responding defensively to landlord initiatives. Reports from many parts of the Island revealed sporadic resistance to law officers as they served writs or attempted to seize goods or prisoners.[69] What is striking about the pattern revealed in map 5.1 is the geographical breadth of the disturbances. Confrontations were occurring in all three counties; if the reports are a fair reflection of the broader set of conflicts, Kings and Queens counties shared the lead in incidents of physical rent resistance. The number of Supreme Court cases arising from these confrontations does not appear to have been great, but as landlords and agents reasserted their authority to enforce rents, there were sufficient incidents and reports to instil a climate of fear both in the countryside and among those acting on behalf of landlords. Many tenants saw themselves as victims of a conspiracy among proprietors to deny them justice, and many on the other side of the dispute believed that a tenant conspiracy was underway in the countryside. The stage was thus set for violence.

In January 1834 the *Royal Gazette* reported an indictment for what had become a commonplace event. Two men and two women were charged with a rescue and assault in the case of a bailiff distraining for rents on Flora Townshend's estate.[70] The case is of interest for what it reveals about circumstances in the countryside during this period and because it was to become a cause célèbre. In September 1833, Donald McVarish proceeded to Townshend's estate in northern Kings County to serve warrants of distress on some of the residents there.[71] Among those on his list was the household of Isabella and Allan Macdonald, tenants who had been paying rents since 1819 but had stopped paying them during the escheat agitation.[72] McVarish's actions that day as he himself described them speak to the fears held by law officers enforcing landlords' claims in the countryside at this time. As he approached the Macdonald farm he encountered Allan, axe in hand, working on his fences. Instead of acknowledging the purpose of his visit, McVarish wished Allan good morning and proceeded to distrain upon his neighbour. McVarish then made his way back to the Macdonald barn by crossing a fence and working his way through a field of standing grain. He was, he acknowledged later, moving 'pretty fast' at this point.

Having successfully distrained on a stack of their hay – which probably entailed posting a notice defining it as Flora Townshend's property – he attempted to make good his escape. Unfortunately for McVarish, he again encountered Allan, now accompanied by his wife Isabella (who was obviously pregnant), his brother Ronald (who occupied a nearby house), his sister Nancy, and yet another farmer, Archibald McCormick. They demanded to know what he was doing, and when McVarish acknowledged his mission they showered him with abuse. In fear, he pulled a loaded pistol out from his pocket and aimed it at Isabella, who appears to have been the most threatening of those confronting McVarish.[73] At this point some of the men managed to seize McVarish and disarm him. Grasping him by the collar, they led him to the main road and released him after they extracted a promise that he would never return. Except that he was knocked to the ground while being disarmed, the only actual violence to McVarish came at the end of the confrontation, when Isabella, who had accompanied the procession to the road, struck the constable with a board after he was released.

This incident, like many others at the time, was a defensive response to a legal process that tenants thought unjust. Flora Townshend, widow of the resident proprietor and colonial official William Townshend, had initiated the action that sent McVarish on his journey. The two Macdonald households and a neighbour had acted in an ad hoc fashion when he arrived. In his testimony concerning the incident, McVarish did not suggest that they had been prepared and waiting for his visit or that they had in any way attempted to summon others. They had simply responded angrily to his mission, telling him that they 'would not pay a farthing of rent 'till they got a better title' and that under the circumstances they 'would lose their lives rather than their property.'[74]

Things were somewhat different, though, when law officers attempted to serve warrants on those accused of assaulting McVarish. It is not clear what happened when the warrants were first issued out of the Hilary Term of the Supreme Court in January 1834.[75] Come June, the Macdonalds and McCormick were still at large, and the deputy sheriff, John Cambridge Sims, and six armed law officers set out from Charlottetown to northern Kings County to capture them. Leaving on Sunday evening, 8 June, they travelled the St Peters Road by night, picking up two more men along the way. They arrived at the defendants' community, Naufrage, at four the following morning. There, the *Royal Gazette* later reported, they found not a sleeping community, but

> a large body of people, consisting of upwards of a hundred men and boys, and a large number of women. Several of them had muskets, and others were provided with iron pikes, attached to the end of poles, and the remainder were armed with pitchforks, altogether presenting a very formidable array. The Deputy Sheriff desiring his party to halt, went forward and addressed this armed mob, stating to them the object of his mission, and the danger they would incur by offering resistance. Whereupon he was told at once to be off; that it was in vain for him to attempt to execute the warrant, for they were determined to die to a man, before they would allow one of the parties named in it to be apprehended. Mr. Sims, finding all expostulation in vain, and their numbers were rapidly increasing, deemed it prudent to return, without attempting to use force, which there can be little doubt, from the hostile attitude of his opponents, would have been attended with fatal consequences to himself and his party.[76]

This was not the spur-of-the-moment action of a few neighbours, but the organized resistance of a community informed by accurate intelligence concerning the movement of law officers. Like the earlier confrontation with McVarish, it was strictly defensive. The residents of Naufrage had gathered in large numbers, men and women alike, to prevent the law from being applied in their community. Judging from petitions later submitted by the residents of Naufrage, this assembly – like the contentious gathering in New London – was composed of people of differing ethnic backgrounds.[77]

The scale of resistance to legal process in this case inspired considerable alarm among the Island's elite and ultimately among the absentee proprietors in Britain as they learned about it from the *Royal Gazette* and from their agents. Lieutenant-Governor Young was in England to receive a knighthood at the time of the Naufrage confrontation, but was notified of the incident. Chief Justice Jarvis wrote informing him of the particulars, arguing that it proved that a 'spirit of resistance' remained prevalent among the tenantry. The 'instigators of these deluded people,' he confided to the lieutenant-governor, 'assure them that they will not be suffered to remain unmolested until they have killed some sheriff's officers.' Unless the organizers of resistance, who were as yet 'too wary to be detected,' were apprehended and subjected to 'severe and exemplary punishment,' tenant unrest would, he thought, become bloody.[78] Young received notice of the confrontation as well from the absentee proprietor Robert Stewart, who lived in London and who contacted the lieutenant-governor during his stay in England to draw his attention to the Naufrage affair, passing on a copy of the June *Royal Gazette*, which described it.[79] Stewart had been following the growth of rent resistance on the Island with increasing concern, and encouraging the Colonial Office to insist on a firmer policy for its suppression. News of the Naufrage incident now caused him to advise more decisive action.[80] In a series of letters to the Colonial Office, supported by evidence drawn from correspondence with his Island agents, Stewart accused the Island government of 'apathy, not to call it by a harsher name,' when it came to enforcing 'the authority of the law,' and demanded that Island authorities be instructed to act to ensure the immediate suppression of resistance to land law.[81] As matters stood, he complained, it was impossible to enforce the legal proceedings necessary to collect rent.[82]

Tenant resistance to the landlords' use of the law had been able to develop as it had at Naufrage, and elsewhere, in large part because the government lacked suitable means for efficiently dealing with problems of this nature. While some of the dilatoriness in suppressing rent resistance may have reflected the sympathy that Lieutenant-Governor Young – and perhaps others in positions of power – felt for the tenantry, there were practical limits to the state's power. Enforcement of the law was entrusted to a small number of annually appointed non-professionals. They in turn could deputize others of the citizenry to assist them if the need arose, but in the case of widespread civil disobedience, such as that manifested at Naufrage, the weakness of this means of response quickly became apparent. In normal times the personal authority of the individuals who filled law enforcement offices and of others who might be deputized, combined with the power of the legal establishment itself, was sufficient to enforce the law. But the 1830s were not normal times when it came to laws concerning land and rents. When authority and deference broke down, as they did at Naufrage, what mattered was the skill, strength, and motivation of the physical force the state could muster.[83] Even though the sheriff's party at Naufrage was on horseback and better armed than the tenantry they were confronting, they enjoyed no clear superiority in physical force. They were working at a considerable distance from Charlottetown, and in a region where most residents were hostile to their purpose, so they had good reason to simply go through the motions of attempting to enforce the law without hazarding a physical confrontation.

Because enforcement of the law depended on non-professionals and on the participation and consent of common citizens, law officers often found it difficult to prevail over protests that were rooted in a popular cause.[84] It seems that as rent resistance grew in the 1830s, some of those called on to enforce landlords' claims became increasingly reluctant to do so. Two constables had refused to assist the deputy sheriff in the clash at Naufrage.[85] Whether they had been motivated by fear, or sympathy, or something else, law officers were being fined for failing to serve legal documents on recalcitrant tenants. Lieutenant-Governor Young made a point of travelling around the Island and reviewing the militia units of the various districts in the summer and fall of 1833, but there were serious doubts about the reliability of this force should civil unrest deepen.[86] Most militiamen were tenants, and the rank and file of militia units had refused to obey orders at various times in the past. Few of the militia officers had assumed or would assume a significant profile in the Escheat movement, but there were significant exceptions, the most notable of whom was William Cooper.[87] There was talk of raising a cavalry force that could act as an aid to the civil power, but again, there were concerns about how to ensure that the members of such a force would be 'faithful' participants.[88] In cases of popular resistance to the law, the obvious fallback was to use troops to back the civil power. It was felt – not without reason – that a well-armed, disciplined soldiery could overawe rural resistance such as that at Naufrage. One of the problems facing colonial authorities was that even if they chose to exercise this option, there were very few soldiers available on the Island in the early 1830s. In those years the Island was garrisoned by a rifle brigade of forty men, who were rotated annually and drawn from units at Halifax. Because desertions were chronic, even these small numbers were not always available for service. In the summer of 1834, as the Naufrage case flared up, Island papers reported that five men – 12 per cent of a new garrison that had just arrived on the Island – had already deserted.[89]

Faced with continuing unrest in the countryside in the summer of 1834, Lieutenant-Governor Young decided to augment the military option and requested that additional soldiers be sent to the Island. Even before he learned of the Naufrage incident, Young, while he was home on leave, had discussed the need for more troops with officials at the Colonial Office. When he received news of the incident from Jarvis in July, he passed the chief justice's report on to the Colonial Office to reinforce his request that yet another company be temporarily stationed on the Island. Young appears to have believed that their presence in Charlottetown alone might serve to restore the appropriate balance of power in the countryside. Once the rural Islanders knew that significant numbers of soldiers could easily be sent into their districts, he reasoned, they would be less open in their resistance to legal process.[90]

Young himself had travelled extensively about the Island on his arrival and had spoken with those petitioning for land reform. He recognized that things were becoming increasingly tense in the countryside. He did not, however, accept the alarmist positions adopted by some of the Island elite and by many of the absentee landlords, who viewed the state of affairs in the months and years after the escheat bill as a rural rebellion. The governor's differences were no doubt rooted in both needs and perceptions. Understandably, Young wanted to appear as an administrator who was presiding over a properly functioning colony. Landlords and agents, on the other hand, given the prevailing circumstances, had much to gain if soldiers could be drawn into the countryside to intimidate the tenantry and facilitate the resumption of rental payments. Reports of a tenant revolt might help bring this about. Certainly, local law enforcement officers would benefit from having troops available to support them, but Young resisted having the military readily available for such purposes. In the summer of 1833, when the high sheriff, the resident landlord Donald Macdonald, applied to the commanding officer of the garrison for a soldier to flog a prisoner, Young made a point of reminding this prominent Islander of the appropriate chain of command and the distinction between his job and that of the military. In a tart note, Young informed Macdonald that he was never to apply to 'the Military to aid the Civil Power in the execution of any duty without having my express sanction for so doing.'[91] Later, when there was yet more resistance at Naufrage and the civil power was rebuffed once again, Young was equally firm in asserting his authority over the use of troops and in insisting that civil authorities could not draw on the military except in the most dire circumstances. The persistent question was always this: How much resistance to the enforcement of landlords' claims would justify the use of troops? Or, to cast it differently, how much cost and risk was the state willing to incur to uphold property laws that lacked legitimacy in the countryside?

The growing possibility that greater force would be used by the Island authorities to ensure law enforcement in land disputes troubled the Island's tenantry, particularly those of northern Kings County, who continued to harbour the individuals who had been indicted in January. Shortly after returning to the colony in late September 1834, Young received petitions from the rural residents in and around Naufrage. At a number of public meetings they had hammered out a collective statement of their problems and principles. They had also directed petitions to the president of the council, George Wright, before Young's return and to the lieutenant-governor after, requesting executive intervention to deal with what they saw as an unjust and intolerable situation. At a meeting held at the head of St Peters Bay during Young's absence, they gathered to determine the 'best measures for the proceedings of those stiled [*sic*] Rioters of Naufrage.'[92] Those people who had been branded with this epithet, they stated, had merely been seeking 'common justice' and had been forced into the appearance of insurrection for lack of any legal means of securing their rights. Multiple claimants were demanding rents in the district, and the petitioners asked that all legal proceedings be halted until a court was established in which the justice of these land claims could be tested.

A second document produced by the inhabitants of northern Kings County complained of the oppression arising from multiple claimants for rents and the absence of any adequate means for tenants to determine which proprietor, if any, had a valid title.[93] Were they to pay two rival claimants, they contended, 'a third and a fourth will be encouraged to make a claim.' And if they paid neither, 'both are at liberty to distrain under pretence of seeking their own.' They moved beyond the specifics of multiple claimants, though, to assert – in a statement very close to the ideas Cooper had been advancing – that perhaps none of these would-be landlords had 'so just a claim as the man who has spent his skill, strength and years on the cultivation of the soil.' Faced with what they construed to be unjust and impossible demands, they asked that the executive intervene to stop law proceedings relating to land and to order an investigation of proprietors' titles, for as it was they had to either submit to demands that violated 'common justice' or assume the posture of rebels and risk the attack of 'a militia force and the loss of our lives and that of our wives and children.' They described themselves as loyal subjects who wanted to fulfil their responsibilities, but added that the workings of the legal system were forcing them to resist the state insofar as the laws regarding land were concerned. A third petition, this one from the inhabitants of Lot 47, complained of the problems induced by multiple claimants and of the costs the township's residents were having to bear because of the legal actions initiated by David Stewart.[94]

The petitions were, of course, framed to put the actions of the tenants in northern Kings County in the best possible light. They spoke to the matters the petitioners thought would get a sympathetic hearing and glossed over other issues. Certainly, some of the tensions in the district, such as those around New London earlier, related to the problem of multiple claimants and details concerning the validity of specific deeds, but these were endemic problems and their existence does not fully explain why landlord/tenant relations had become so strained at this particular moment. David Stewart's tenants had attorned to him – acknowledged him as their landlord – when he visited the Island in 1831; two years later they were, to Stewart's amazement, denying his claim to the land, refusing rents, and threatening those who came to collect them.[95] Duncan Stewart was one of those who had been a target of the legal actions the tenants of Lot 47 complained about, and had signed the petition to the lieutenant-governor requesting that Young put a stop to any further legal proceedings. This was the man who had told David Stewart's land agent that if he was going to send in the sheriff he should instruct him to bring his coffin with him. David Stewart had encountered no such bravado when he visited the Island a few years earlier. At that time he claimed that one of his tenants on Lot 27 had thrown his hat in the air in jubilation on hearing that his landlord had arrived.[96] Flora Townshend's tenants, Isabella and Allan Macdonald, whose particular case of rent resistance was at the core of the Naufrage conflict, had paid their rent regularly between 1819 and 1831 before they, and their neighbours, stopped paying rents. Like tenants elsewhere, those of the Naufrage district had joined in the anti-proprietorial excitement and enthusiasm of 1832. A couple of years later, with a landlord counter-attack in full motion and effective land legislation still a dream, they found themselves stranded and vulnerable.

Having come to believe that landlords' demands were invalid and that proprietorial use of the court system was unjust, tenants were not willing to readily yield. On the other hand, even when they succeeded in physically rebuffing attempts to arrest residents, distrain on property, or eject the occupants of farms, they were uneasy with actions that lay outside legally prescribed behaviour and with appearing to oppose the state. As well, continuing rumours that authorities in Charlottetown were going to send a military force into northern Kings County were troubling and demoralizing. The correspondence of land agents and landlords – much of which ultimately rang alarm bells in the Colonial Office – continued to speak in late 1834 in terms of a rebellious tenantry that was dominating the countryside and defying the forces of law. The reality was that the spontaneous wave of tenant resistance to the proprietorial system that had swelled in 1832 had lost much of its force. Developments in the political arena no longer suggested that an escheat was imminent, and in the absence of a well-developed strategy for achieving land reform through prolonged struggle, proprietors' initiatives and successes in the legal and legislative spheres had, by the latter part of 1834, seriously diminished the initial momentum the Escheat movement had achieved.[97]

6 Organizing Proprietors, 1831–1834

Writing to a business acquaintance in May 1833, David Stewart shared his relief that the threat of escheat on Prince Edward Island had substantially diminished over the last few months. Much hard work had gone into turning aside the threat confronting his family's investments in the colony, and he wrote with a consciousness of the peril they had narrowly avoided: 'It is extremely doubtful whether the Escheat Act passed by the Legislature of the Colony would not have received Royal Allowance, had it not been for the exertions of my brother, Mr. Bainbridge, the colonial agent, Mr. MacGregor, and our other friends.'[1] Vigilance nonetheless had to be maintained to ensure that the state continued to sustain their interests. Within the month his brother, Robert, began coordinating resistance to the civil establishment act, which Joseph Pope and others had just carried through the more recent sitting of the Island legislature and which was expected to be submitted to the Colonial Office shortly.[2] As the Stewarts knew, dangerous challenges to proprietorial interests could come from pressures originating with tenants and small freeholders or from the colony's mercantile community. The escheat act had been carried through the legislature with the support of both, albeit with different intentions concerning the breadth of its application and with different degrees of enthusiasm. The imperial government's response to these initiatives would depend on how successfully contending interests brought pressure to bear on those who determined policy. Landlords, the Island's business community, and the subordinate rural population, held competing visions of the future but shared a common focus on the state as a central agent for realizing their plans; this meant that the struggle to define the role of the state and to control state policy was vitally important to the interests of each.

Much of the historiography bearing on early-nineteenth-century Prince Edward Island assumes that Imperial policy was almost always formulated in the interests of the colony's landlords. Given the prominence in British society of some of those who owned Island estates and the importance of the landed elite in British politics, the argument goes, the colony's proprietors had little to fear from policy makers at the highest echelons of Imperial planning and could by and large rest confident that state policies would meet their needs. Initiatives launched in the Island legislature, therefore, were necessarily doomed to failure if they violated the landlords' interests and sensibilities. As the Stewart letter suggests, such conclusions underestimate the efforts that were necessary to achieve these results. Landlord power in the Colonial Office and Privy Council in the 1830s seems in retrospect to have been unassailable in part because of the very effective organizational work that the landlords put into maintaining their influence. Proprietors' interests required active protection in the 1830s, even in London. The early checks that the Escheat movement received from the Colonial Office with Goderich's responses to the escheat act and to new policies on quit rents, and the Privy Council's refusal to give royal assent to the land title bill, were the product of determined countervailing collective action by a handful of landlords.

The coalition of proprietors, government officers, and members of the merchant community that had contributed to the overthrow of Lieutenant-Governor Smith in the early 1820s drifted apart once Smith was removed from office in 1824. With the escheat agitation of the 1830s, landlords and land agents again took steps to revitalize their own community and to defend their own interests. This renewed activity by proprietors was initially triggered not by calls for land reform emanating from the countryside, but by the legislative initiatives of increasingly assertive leaders of the Island's mercantile community. There had been a certain tranquility in land politics in the early years of the Ready regime, but this surface calm had masked growing tensions. With the decline of autocracy on the Island and the reopening of the political process after 1824, members of the colonial business community began to realize that they would benefit from gaining partial control of the local state. With the support of Lieutenant-Governor Ready and the compliance, by and large, of the Legislative Council, the assembly initiated legislation such as the highway compensation act and the land tax bill, which passed the cost of infrastructure development in the colony on to those with landed wealth. Most members of the assembly at this time were from the ranks of the mercantile and professional community, so that body closely reflected their concerns.

The proprietors' reactions to these developments were initially somewhat ineffectual, in part because of the decline of some of those who had in the past been most active. John Hill and John Cambridge, whose involvement in proprietorial politics stretched back to the eigtheenth century, were in their seventies and eighties, and the estates of each were in serious financial straits.[3] John Stewart, who had artfully played multiple roles in proprietorial and anti-proprietorial politics in the past, and who had assumed a leadership position in the movement to remove Lieutenant-Governor Smith, had turned seventy in 1828 and was slipping toward madness and death by the beginning of the new decade.[4] The colony's growing mercantile community was generating dynamic young leaders such as George Dalrymple, Joseph Pope, and Daniel Brenan; by contrast, proprietorial interests seemed moribund. Charles Worrell, a lawyer by training, did what he could to generate opposition to the assembly's anti-proprietorial legislation, but as a bachelor living on his estate rather than in Charlottetown, and without established interfamilial ties with other prominent Islanders, he did so with limited effectiveness.[5] In Britain his brother Edward, as well as a few of the proprietary agents resident in London, moved to activate the landlords' defences. But these early responses by landlords to the potentially damaging initiatives of the 12th Assembly were decidedly lacklustre.[6]

The possibilities for landlord collective action received an important boost in the early 1830s when David and Robert Stewart joined the ranks of the great proprietors. The Stewarts were the offspring of a prosperous farm household in Perthshire, Scotland, and had made their way in the world by acquiring training in law and science, moving into the professional ranks as surveyors and estate managers.[7] Although their business entailed work in Ireland, Scotland, and England, they resided in the Bloomsbury district of London and conducted their business from there.[8] Their neighbours around Russell Street, a few blocks from the British Museum, included members of the professional elite – engineers, surveyors, surgeons, architects, attorneys, scientists, and builders – that was assuming an ever greater profile in Great Britain as the nation entered the industrial age.[9] In 1820 the Stewarts purchased fourteen thousand acres of Lot 47 in eastern Kings County.[10] The low per acre cost of questionable township titles permitted them to assume the role of great landlords on Prince Edward Island and to deal with some of Britain's landed elite in that capacity. In the early 1830s they expanded their interests enormously by purchasing a number of townships that had previously been part of the Selkirk and Montgomery estates. Convinced by the events of their times that North America was 'arising' while Britain was becoming 'a sinking country,' the Stewarts had determined to transfer their assets to the other side of the Atlantic.[11] After extensive travels in eastern North America in 1831, David Stewart returned to Britain believing Prince Edward Island to be 'ideal for establishing a respectable family estate.'[12] While on the Island he arranged for the purchase of fifty thousand acres of land. This was supplemented by the acquisition of yet another twenty thousand acres immediately after his return, as the Stewarts moved to fulfil a plan for assembling an estate of a hundred thousand acres.[13]

The Stewarts knew they had become great proprietors in a time of crisis and they acted energetically to shore up the position of the Island's landlords. At the time they made their purchases they were already aware of the problems the developmental bills crafted by the 12th Assembly posed, and they understood that Montgomery's agent had agreed to sell at bargain prices in the belief that these lots might soon be lost through an escheat.[14] While on the Island arranging to enlarge their estate, David informed himself more fully of political developments there. He met with resident proprietors such as Charles Worrell, Donald Macdonald, and Hugh Macdonald, as well as several land agents and government officers such as T.H. Haviland, the colonial treasurer, member of the council, and agent for George Seymour and Lord Townshend; Fade Goff, coroner and Crown clerk, soon to be a member of the council, and agent for George Birnie; Thomas Owen, shipbuilder, merchant, member of the assembly, and agent for the Cambridges; William Forgan, agent for the Earl of Selkirk; and John Lewellin, former member of the assembly and agent for the Cambridges and Laurence Sulivan. On the basis of these meetings he developed a fuller understanding of the significance of events on the Island for proprietary interests; he promised interested Island parties that he would call a meeting of the absentee proprietors in London when he returned there.[15] As well, he worked with a number of Islanders to prepare a memorial against the highway compensation act, which would bill proprietors for some of the costs of new road construction.[16] The political positions each of these people attempted to assume in their discussions with David Stewart are unclear, but, as he astutely noted in a letter to the Earl of Selkirk shortly after his return, Charles Worrell was the only office holder on the Island who could be fully trusted in the cause of the 'extensive landed proprietors.'[17]

As the Stewarts rapidly came to realize, landed interests on the Island were as much threatened by the 'apathy of the principal proprietors' resident in Britain as by external threats.[18] Many of the absentees, they discovered, did not 'consider [Island] property to be worth much.'[19] This stemmed from a long history of challenges to landlord interests in the colony, and from the difficulties many had experienced trying to manage their estates profitably from afar. Also, some landlords were aware how weak the deeds were that sustained their property claims. For others their Island properties were of little importance. For instance, the township or two of colonial land that Lord Melville and Lord Westmorland had acquired by marriage to the elder and younger Saunders sisters respectively (the heirs of Admiral Saunders) were relatively insignificant assets in the Saunders's inheritance. Indeed, Prince Edward Island lands seem to have been forgotten altogether in the sisters' marriage settlements, though they came to be of more interest to the sisters and their families later on.[20] Nor did the Island properties owned by Sir Thomas Sorell loom large in his busy life as a diplomat.[21] Smaller proprietors such as the Langtons of Lincolnshire, on the other hand, often lacked the resources necessary to maintain effective control of their property.[22]

The Stewarts took a different approach to the management of their estate. Having acquired holdings that placed them among the largest of the great proprietors, they took a keen interest in Island affairs. They had purchased their extensive holdings for relatively little, paying roughly £1,000 per twenty thousand acre township at a time when a good freehold farm of two hundred acres in the adjoining colonies might fetch £200 or £300 and when tenants were paying annual rents at a rate equal to or greater than the one shilling per acre that the Stewarts had paid for their acquisitions.[23] Their expenditures nonetheless were a substantial investment for them and represented the core of the family's plans for the future. On the basis of his visit to the Island, David Stewart decided that one requirement for success was to assume residency in the colony, and it was his intention to move there with his family in the early 1830s.[24] Success also required good relations with those in government to ensure that the state would act to maintain the interests of the great proprietors. As the Stewarts knew when they made their purchases, landlords' titles were cheap in the second quarter of the nineteenth century because they were vulnerable to challenges on a number of fronts.[25] To turn their deeds into solid assets, the family would have to place a member on the Island to ensure an annual flow of income from rents and from selling stumpage to timber operators. More importantly, they would have to make a concerted political effort to translate provisional deeds of questionable worth into unchallengeable claims to private property, while ensuring that the costs of holding vast tracts of land did not become too burdensome. The Stewarts, more than most proprietors, were willing to devote considerable effort – and money if necessary – to ensure that their newly acquired deeds were strengthened over time.

Discerning vulnerability and weakness in proprietors' attitudes and behaviour, the Stewarts and a small cluster of people associated with them moved with great energy to shore up the landlords' position in the early 1830s. Landlords living in Britain had banded together in the past. Indeed, collective action by landlords predated the allocation of land in 1767; requests for Island land had been organized before that year by groups of potential proprietors.[26] The separation of Prince Edward Island from Nova Scotia had also been the result of proprietorial collective action.[27] And in the years that followed, proprietors had gathered, and consulted with one another, to formulate common policies concerning their estates, particularly when their interests were threatened. As a London lawyer associated with Prince Edward Island's landed interests phrased it in 1814 to George Seymour after he assumed ownership of his family's property on the Island, 'the proprietors resident in this country occasionally meet to confer on the promotion of their interests.'[28] Such certainly was the case at times of crisis during the Smith regime.[29] The challenges of the late 1820s, though, seemed to be passing by without such meetings and without adequate collective responses. Charles and Edward Worrell, working from Prince Edward Island and Britain respectively, did what they could to protect their interests, but the landlords' ranks were in disarray and lacked in effective leadership.

Over the scattered protests of proprietors on and off the Island, the highway compensation act received royal assent late in 1830, before the Stewarts assumed a substantial interest in Island affairs. Its passage, the Stewarts argued after David returned from the Island in 1831, carried a lesson for proprietors: if they did not become more vigilant, they stood to lose their stake in the colony as the political initiatives of others undercut the value of their deeds. Shortly after returning to Britain in the fall of 1831, David Stewart wrote to the Earl of Selkirk to underscore the need to check each bill passed by the Island assembly with the utmost care before it received royal assent.[30] Effective resistance to challenges to landed interests required good intelligence. A few days after writing to Selkirk, David wrote to Charles Worrell asking that he keep him abreast of developments and that he forward him a copy of the assembly's highway compensation act and 'other objectionable acts or bills' as soon as possible, for 'it is indispensably necessary that I should have all possible knowledge.'[31] The following day he wrote as well to John Stewart and John Lawson, who was the Stewarts' attorney and the colony's solicitor general, requesting that they too keep him well informed concerning Island developments, and reiterating the promise he had made to his allies on the Island that he would hold a meeting with the other proprietors resident in the London area.[32]

Good intelligence concerning Island developments was useful, though, only if it was followed by effective responses. Although David Stewart had to delay convening his meeting of London-based proprietors (the Reform Bill was dominating public affairs to the exclusion of all other issues), the Stewarts acted on an individual basis to inform other proprietors, such as Thomas Sorell and the Earl of Selkirk, of the perils of the assembly's bills. They passed on the information they were receiving from their own sources and from the Worrells, and they spoke of the need for more effective action by proprietors.[33] News of the land registry and escheat bills arrived just as the Reform Bill was entering the last leg of its long journey to royal assent. On receiving a copy of the *Royal Gazette* containing reports of the assembly's final proceedings, along with a copy of Cooper's escheat speech, the Stewarts quickly contacted others. Sending a copy of pertinent newspaper articles on to Andrew Colvile, the 5th Earl of Selkirk's brother-in-law and manager of the Selkirk estate, the Stewarts observed that landed property would be of 'little or no value' on the Island if they did not move immediately to counteract the assembly's proceedings.[34] Writing of his concerns that same day to Edward Worrell, Robert Stewart mentioned the necessity of getting together to formulate a response.[35]

These initiatives may well have triggered the letter that Colvile penned to the Colonial Secretary, Lord Goderich, a few days later, in which he complained of the unfairness of the assembly's escheat measures.[36] The Earl of Selkirk's family was aware of the threats to their property on the

Island and had the profile and skills necessary to make their concerns known at the Colonial Office. Colvile was an able administrator and businessman. As a key player in the negotiations that led to the merger of the Hudson's Bay Company and the North West Company and as chairman of the West India Committee, he was a familiar figure at the Colonial Office.[37] As well, and at least as importantly, the Earl of Selkirk's family possessed considerable wealth, prestige, and power, even if their North American ventures had generated enormous debts.[38] Colvile's letter to the Colonial Office in May was sitting on Lieutenant-Governor Young's desk in Charlottetown in July with a query concerning the validity of its content and the extent of the estate in question.[39] The speed of this initiative reflected both Colvile's ability to highlight an issue and the Colonial Office's lack of information concerning events on Prince Edward Island. It is interesting that Colvile's letter had spoken to the specifics of Lord Selkirk's case and not to the general orientation of the legislation or to the damage it would cause all landlords. Indeed, it asked only that the Selkirk estate be exempted from escheat proceedings and allowed until 1835 to meet the settlement requirements of the original grants.[40] Colvile had argued that Selkirk's Lot 10 did not have a sufficiently large population because it lacked adequate roads and, more generally, because others had lured Selkirk's settlers away from the estate. Lieutenant-Governor Young lacked the knowledge to respond to the second argument, but his reply to the Colonial Office rebutted the first quite effectively.[41]

Colvile and the Earl of Selkirk may have expected – perhaps too sanguinely – that their individualistic approach would succeed, but acting alone promised to be less useful to landlords possessed of lesser stature and weaker claims. For the Stewarts, the Worrells, and various other figures, effective responses would require joint action. As a group they stood a better chance of achieving their ends, especially if they could incorporate the most prominent absentee proprietors. Participation in such a group would bring more prominent proprietors who did not have the time or the incentive to invest great attention in their Island lands the advantage of the energy that others, such as the Stewarts, were giving to their properties. And landowners of the Stewarts' class could increase the likelihood of an attentive reception at the Colonial Office by linking their cause to that of better-connected proprietors. With the Reform Bill finally headed towards resolution and news of escheat agitation generating yet more cause for concern, the Stewarts and a handful of others organized a meeting in London of those who had a stake in landlordism on Prince Edward Island. In late May, Edward Worrell, the Stewarts, and William Waller, a lawyer resident in London who had once been the colony's attorney general and who acted as agent for a number of prominent landlords, arranged a meeting to discuss the escheat challenge and to formulate a common response.[42]

By July a collective memorial opposing the escheat bill and the land registry bill was in Lord Goderich's hands. This massive document delineated the Island's history from the landlords' perspective; it also laid out their arguments against the most recent acts of the assembly by offering excerpts from Edward Worrell's and David and Robert Stewart's correspondence. By this time the proprietors had retained legal counsel to assess the land registry bill, and with the memorial they enclosed their solicitor's negative judgment concerning its legality.[43] Just as collective action on the Island was supported by the construction of a common narrative, so too was that of the proprietors. The memorial told the story of proprietors saddled with grants requiring impossible obligations, inept and perfidious colonial administrators, and grasping tenants and smallholders seeking to strip them of their assets. The costs of arranging for the movement of settlers from Protestant Europe or from other colonies in North America to the Island had been 'found to exceed' the value of the lands that might thereby be secured; furthermore, the quit rent obligations of the grants had proven to be 'a grievous burthen' to settlers. Misrule by the colony's local government, most recently during Smith's regime, had 'prevented the settlement and prosperity of the Island.' Escheat proceedings instituted during Smith's administration had victimized proprietors, some of whom 'were minor female orphans,' and had caused many settlers to leave. Despite these obstacles, landlords had done their best, incurring 'great expense in making improvements and settling emigrants on their lands,' and in doing so had brought the population of the Island as a whole beyond that which would have resulted from minimal adherence to the settlement terms of their original grants. The memorial admitted that there were some townships that lacked the requisite number of settlers, but it also contended that it 'would have been considered highly grievous to new settlers not to have allowed them a choice of location.' Proof of the importance of proprietors' efforts to develop the colony could be found in the fact that the escheated townships were now the least settled and improved in the colony. Proprietors, the memorial concluded, needed to be protected from the designs of a grasping assembly, which was composed of tenants and small freeholders. Given another five years, proprietors would ensure the settlement of their townships in accordance with the numbers stipulated in the original grants.[44]

The main contours of this narrative would be referred to constantly during the coming events, even though the particular account it gave was poorly constructed, suggesting both haste and a lack of adequate knowledge. The memorial was submitted to the Colonial Office by John MacGregor, a proprietor and agent who had once been a prominent member of Island society and who was the author of the highly acclaimed *Historical and descriptive sketches of the Maritime colonies of British North America*; however, it was probably a Stewart production. It was weakened by a number of easily refuted factual errors, such as the claim that the two escheated townships were the least developed on the Island. Far more accurate, but less useful as a promotional narrative, was the brief history of the land question that had been written for the proprietors' legal counsel and that was included with his legal opinion. The history appended to the legal judgment acknowledged that the significant sums some proprietors had expended had in large part been directed towards establishing mercantile operations and that 'not one township in the Island complied with the conditions of the original grants either to the letter or even in ... spirit, so that the whole of the Island may be said to have long since been forfeited.'[45] There was no suggestion that the proprietors had ever seriously attempted to fulfil the requirements of their grants; there was only the claim – which was true enough – that some had spent, and lost, substantial sums in a variety of attempts to make something of their holdings and that in the process these landlords had advanced the settlement of the Island.

The memorial of 1832 was the product of proprietors' collective efforts; furthermore, it rested on arguments that only worked in collective terms. When he wrote individually to the Colonial Office, Andrew Colvile could argue that 5th Earl of Selkirk had in fact arranged for the movement of significant numbers of settlers to the colony but that some of them had been lured away from his holdings. Even ignoring the fact that the Earl of Selkirk had been able to acquire these lands cheaply because the deeds had long since become of dubious value owing to non-fulfilment of their original terms, these sorts of arguments were not ones that all proprietors could make to defend themselves from threat of escheat proceedings. There were many proprietors whose lots had never received a hint of the attention that the Earl of Selkirk devoted to his. The memorial sidestepped this by dealing with landlord efforts in general and with the problems proprietors as a class had faced, and then arguing that all should be protected from the imminent threat of escheat proceedings.

The meeting held in May 1832 and the memorial presented in July represented significant first steps towards establishing effective proprietorial activism. Within days of the signing of Goderich's dispatch of 1 August instructing Lieutenant-Governor Young not to establish a court of escheat, proprietors were aware of their success, and in time they could take satisfaction in watching some of their arguments re-emerge in the text of the colonial secretary's communication.[46] Proprietorial collective action had shown great promise, yet it remained tentative and vulnerable, and major challenges still required resolution. Although Goderich's dispatch momentarily checked the hopes for an escheat, neither proprietors nor escheat advocates believed it had entirely closed the door on the possibility. Nor was there any reason to believe that the assembly was not drafting new legislation that would be damaging to proprietors' interests. The Stewarts' Bloomsbury residence was by now evolving into a clearing house for landlords and agents interested in intelligence concerning Island developments, but coordination among proprietors was still informal and sporadic; the possibility of a return to the haphazard, disparate responses that had prevailed in the late 1820s was very real. Moreover, most proprietors – including some of the potentially most useful figures – remained outside the organization the Stewarts and their associates were attempting to establish. None of the signatures affixed to the memorial of 1832 would have carried much weight at the Colonial Office. The Stewarts, the Worrells, and John Hill had signed as great proprietors. Three lesser proprietors also signed: John MacGregor, the aging John Stewart (who was in town), and George Birnie, John Stewart's son-in-law.[47] Birnie was a one-time Island resident who had acted as an Island agent for his family's London-based mercantile business earlier in the century. His holdings on the Island were modest, and by the 1830s his debts in the colony rivalled his assets.[48] James Montgomery's name appeared on the document because John Stewart signed as his agent, besides signing on behalf of his family members, Captain Peter Stewart and Mrs Mary Stewart. Thomas Sorell's agent was induced to sign on his behalf as well. John MacGregor assured Lord Goderich that but for the rush of time, Andrew Colvile would have signed as trustee of the Selkirk estate and Henry Winchester would have signed on his own behalf.[49] This was no doubt true, but the fact remained that their signatures were not there, nor were those of other prominent individuals such as Lord Westmorland, Lord Melville, Lord Townshend, or Laurence Sulivan, who might have lent more weight to the cause.

In the months and years after the summer of 1832, proprietorial activism became broader and better organized, in part in response to a growing interest in immigration and development schemes for colonial lands. Emigration, and the possibility of vast state expenditures to subsidize the movement of people to the colonies, was an urgent topic for parliamentary debate and committee hearings, and in financial circles the investment opportunities such movements of labour might afford drew renewed interest in the colonial land market.[50] The Stewarts' recent heavy investments in Prince Edward Island land and their close attention to political and economic events in the colony were closely linked with this broader trend. Although they sometimes talked about developing a comfortable family estate for themselves, they were deeply involved in more impersonal corporate approaches to the economic and social organization of the New World countryside. As professional estate managers associated with the rationalization of agriculture and land use in Britain in the years after the close of the Napoleonic Wars, the Stewarts were thoroughly aware of the transformations occurring in the countryside of the British Isles and of the 'redundant population' that was swelling in the rural districts. Like many of their contemporaries, they thought they saw the possibility both for solutions to the human misery they were witnessing (and abetting) and for the creation of profitable enterprises that would unite the surplus population of the Old World with the underused resources of the New. What was needed to resolve the crisis that had arrived in the wake of 'improvements' in the British countryside was for large-scale capital, and capitalist organization, to transform the project of emigration and settlement into an efficient and integrated business venture. Entrepreneurs had developed the Canada Company and the British American Land Company to exploit these possibilities in the interior of British North America.[51] Similar schemes now emerged for the development of the Maritime colonies.[52]

Those associated with Prince Edward Island's proprietorial circles also took an interest in these ideas, and the Stewarts were, not surprisingly, at the forefront of these developments. Even before David ventured westward in 1831, the Stewarts had been in touch with capitalists involved in developmental schemes along the Atlantic rim of British North America, and after his return they became yet more involved with British joint-stock company projects to develop eastern British

North America.[53] David was a shareholder in the General Mining Association (GMA), a London-based firm capitalized at £400,000 and possessing exclusive rights to Nova Scotia's minerals, and he had a significant profile in corporate affairs. Stewart spent time with Richard Smith, manager of the company's Nova Scotian operations, while he was in the colonies, touring GMA facilities in Nova Scotia and Cape Breton and considering plans to expand the coal trade.[54] During his stay in Pictou he arranged for the purchase of more than one thousand acres of additional land for the association there.[55] As well, he considered with his experienced eye the best route for a canal connecting Cape Breton's Bras d'Or Lake with the Atlantic at St Peter's – a matter of some import to the GMA, which hoped to integrate its mainland and Cape Breton operations.[56] It seems that some of his travels in the United States and elsewhere in British North America were conducted to explore the broader context for the GMA's prospects. On his return, David took an active – albeit apparently unsuccessful – part in advising the company on organizational changes and on opportunities for expansion.[57] Besides having an interest in the GMA, the Stewarts played a significant role – along with the Cunards, whom they knew through the GMA and who were one of the most important merchant families in the Maritimes – in the organization of what would become known as the New Brunswick and Nova Scotia Land Company. They invested £500 in shares in this company early in 1832 and obtained one of its nine directorships, in the hope that the scheme would come to embrace immigration and settlement in all three Maritime provinces.[58] These corporate developments caused some proprietors who had lost interest in their Island properties to reconsider their positions. The Montgomerys, for example, had supposedly been eager to sell off their Island estate to avoid paying quit rents and land taxes, and had feared they might lose some of their holdings to escheat proceedings; now, in the early 1830s, having heard about the formation of a land company in the region, they began to value their estate in the colony more highly.[59]

Powerful challenges, though, had to be overcome if these grand schemes were to be realized. The Stewarts and those associated with them were dreaming of vast projects for the capitalist development of Prince Edward Island and adjacent areas of British North America; others in the colony itself had different dreams. Although the proprietors had succeed in halting the escheat initiative at the highest echelons of government, rural dwellers continued to hope for farms free from the burden of landlords. Reports of rent resistance continued to trickle in after Goderich's first dispatch was published and became a deluge after his second was published early in 1833. Threatening as well, from a landlord's perspective, were the ongoing machinations of members of the Island's mercantile community, who had dreams of locally controlled economic development, funded in large part by taxes on landed wealth. As well, in Britain the Imperial government's quit rent policy remained a worry for landlords. Quit rents had been suspended for the five years during which land taxes were being levied to subsidize the construction of public buildings on the Island, but they were due to be reinstituted in 1838. The proprietors' memorial of 1832 had described quit rents as a burden to settlers in the colony, but the truth was that they fell most heavily on big landed interests. The rate of quit rents was roughly one-fiftieth the rate of land rents, and while they were a nuisance for smallholders and tenants, they were a serious burden only for those with vast tracts of land. In particular, they were a burden to proprietors with sparsely settled lots, as leases often assigned the payment of quit rents on settled lands to the resident tenantry.

Given that state policies would in large part determine the viability of their dreams, the most active proprietors moved with determination to take the initiative on colonial matters of importance to them. Lord Goderich's anti-escheat dispatch was still working its way westward when some of the Island's landlords approached him again in a successful attempt to more decisively resolve the problems with their deeds and to prepare the ground for the large-scale development schemes that were under way. Linking the quit rent issue with the challenges they were facing over their titles, they inquired concerning the terms under which they might commute their quit rents and in the process convert their conditional grants into fresh fee simple grants. By striking a deal, the proprietors could rid themselves, in one fell swoop, of a number of nagging problems: quit rents, unfulfilled settlement terms, fishery reserves that gave the Crown claims to the first five hundred feet landward of the high water mark on most grants, and, perhaps, weak linkages in their claims of title. John MacGregor and Robert Stewart pressed the initiative on behalf of an unspecified group of other landlords, ultimately gaining from Lord Goderich a statement of conditions for such a deal.[60] His dispatch of 27 January 1833 setting out the terms under which proprietors could redeem their quit rents and obtain new grants was the outcome of vigorous lobbying and negotiating on behalf of proprietors, spearheaded by MacGregor and Stewart. This dispatch is what inspired William Cooper's fiery speech to the assembly in April demanding that the house act strongly and quickly to check what he perceived as a conspiracy at the highest levels of government to deny justice to the rural population of the colony.

The Stewarts' involvement in the planning and investments for a massive capitalist immigration scheme permitted them to argue persuasively for favourable policy changes concerning Island lands on the basis that the public interest would be served through the resulting movement of people to the colony and through the economic development that would result. Robert's argument made to Lord Goderich about escheat and quit rents and the need to clear up the ambiguities over title on Prince Edward Island emphasized that this groundwork was necessary to their plans for promoting rapid growth on Prince Edward Island and elsewhere in the Maritimes. Besides being true – the land company directors were reputedly thinking in terms of moving between ten and thirty thousand immigrants per year[61] – this argument was well tailored to find a receptive audience. At a time when the British government was exploring state subsidies to broaden emigration, schemes such as the Stewarts' had potential appeal to those whose concern for fiscal restraint made them view emigration as a matter for private capital. Moreover, the settlement and economic development of Prince Edward Island was, Lord Goderich indicated to Lieutenant-Governor Young, the Colonial Office's primary concern for the colony at this time.[62]

The proprietors' initiatives of 1832 were fairly successful in the short term. The Colonial Office instructed Lieutenant-Governor Young not to act on the escheat bill, and although the fate of the land registry act remained unresolved, the bill had not been confirmed. Indeed, after getting yet another legal judgment on the matter early in 1833, the Colonial Office would recommend that royal assent be denied.[63] As well, Lord Goderich had responded favourably to attempts to establish workable terms under which proprietors might translate conditional grants into fee simple holdings. John Hill still entertained the hope of getting all that he wanted by way of title without sacrificing any money for quit rents; others, though, recognized a good offer when they saw one.[64] Writing on his own behalf and on that of those associated with him, Robert Stewart informed the under-secretary of state, Lord Howick, in March 1833 that they intended to 'accede' to the conditions for redeeming their quit rents and acquiring new grants that had been laid out by Lord Goderich.[65] The terms of agreement, while favourable, had not given all that the Stewarts and some of the others sought: they had failed to reach agreement for fee simple rights over the lands that had initially been set aside in their grants for fishery reserves, only for control of these lands by means of short-term Crown leases. Lieutenant-Governor Young had scuttled this part of the plan by noting that the terms of the original grants specifically reserved the shoreline for the King's 'subjects' and that the rights to these lands were public and could not simply be transferred to the proprietors by royal prerogative.[66] His observation was later reinforced by a concurring opinion from the Colonial Office's legal expert, James Stephen.[67] This was a small but significant detail in the broader struggle concerning property rights and the use of state power.

Events in 1833 pointed to the need for ongoing proprietorial activism. The reports of rent resistance and physical resistance to land agents and law officers in the countryside suggested that much remained to be done to re-establish proprietorial hegemony in rural Prince Edward Island. Some landlords believed that in order to maintain the ability to enforce the collection of rents from their estates, they would have to compel the colonial government to uphold landlords' claims with greater resolution and force. Those like the Stewarts who were involved in massive corporate schemes for the colony's development worried at least as much about the bad publicity arising from escheat agitation as they did about the direct effects of rent resistance (that is, on cash flow). The success of their projects depended on investors' confidence in the stability of local social and political structures. Whether the New Brunswick and Nova Scotia Land Company would invest its capital on Prince Edward Island depended in part on perceptions of the colony's social and political situation. News of the agitation in rural Prince Edward Island threatened to scare capital away and to reduce the speculative value of their assets. In addition, the Island's assembly was continuing to take worrisome measures. The session of the assembly that sat between January and April 1833 produced an address to the king rebutting the arguments underpinning Lord Goderich's position on escheat and demanding, once again, that a court of escheat be established on the Island.[68] The same session produced another piece of legislation that proprietors considered dangerous to their interests: the civil establishment act, which, besides levying yet another land tax, threatened to undercut the quit rent deal that had just been arranged with Lord Goderich.[69]

In May 1833, a year after the meeting that had given rise to the memorial of 1832, a second proprietorial gathering was held at the

Stewart residence. Its main purpose was to plan a collective response to the civil establishment act, which had just been passed. In attendance were the key players in the production of the 1832 memorial – the Stewarts, Edward Worrell, John MacGregor, and William Waller. Two useful additions, Henry Winchester and George Seymour, joined the group this time.[70] Winchester, who owned Lot 54, was a nephew of the great proprietor John Cambridge.[71] He had been a London alderman since 1826 and for a brief time in the early 1830s had been the MP for Maidstone in Kent.[72] A Tory who had made himself exceedingly unpopular among reformers during his term as Lord Mayor of the City of London in the mid-1830s,[73] Winchester was an active force in city and national politics and apparently had useful contacts in conservative circles.[74] George Seymour was the owner of Lot 13, which had been purchased by his grandfather, the Marquess of Hertford. Seymour inherited it from his father, Vice-Admiral Hugh Seymour-Conley. After a distinguished naval career during the Napoleonic Wars, Seymour became sergeant-at-arms to the House of Lords. With the ascension of William IV, he assumed the position of master of the robes as well.[75] His family, naval, and political connections made him a valuable addition to the group.

The approach taken by the Bloomsbury group of proprietors the previous year provided a model for dealing with the 1833 legislative challenges. With the escheat act and land registry act, the proprietors had used the printed versions of the bills that were published in the Charlottetown *Royal Gazette* at the close of the legislature's sitting to quickly prepare a case against them while the governor's copies of the acts were still on their way to the Colonial Office. Indeed, in 1832 this approach had succeeded so well that the anti-escheat dispatch was on its way back to Lieutenant-Governor Young before the official copy of the bill reached Britain.[76] The proprietors intended to follow the same procedure with the Civil Establishment Act.[77] Working from the version of the act published in Island newspapers, the Bloomsbury group drew up a memorial opposing the legislation. With this in hand, they awaited word that the Prince Edward Island packet had arrived so that they might submit their brief at an opportune moment after the Colonial Office had received the act and respond immediately to any new developments that had taken place.[78] Andrew Colvile did not attend the proprietors' meeting, though Robert Stewart had attempted to attract him with the news that George Seymour would be there.[79] Colvile, however, stayed in close touch with the Stewarts and insisted on revising passages in the memorial.[80] Seymour made inquiries for the group directly with the new colonial secretary, Lord Stanley, and gained assurances that the civil establishment act would not receive royal assent without the proprietors having a chance to present their case.[81]

Although the proprietors' group enjoyed early successes at the Colonial Office, disturbing news came to light in the summer of 1833, at a time when action over the civil establishment act was pending. First, for those associated with the New Brunswick and Nova Scotia Land Company project, there was the discovery that the new colonial secretary would not accept certain aspects of a deal the company had hammered out with Lord Goderich for New Brunswick lands.[82] Bad news in itself for those involved in this scheme, the refusal suggested that Lord Stanley might act unfavourably in other matters bearing specifically on Prince Edward Island. That same month the Stewarts learned that the version of Goderich's anti-escheat dispatch published in the Charlottetown *Royal Gazette* had not been an exact copy of the communication sent to the Island. Left out had been an important section indicating that the Colonial Office would entertain a land tax that fell equally on wilderness and cultivated lands as an alternative to an escheat. The Stewarts suspected that this had been done intentionally in order to prevent the proprietors from finding out which policies were under consideration and fighting them.[83] These developments highlighted the need to broaden the proprietors' group so that it might bring greater pressure to bear on the policy makers at the Colonial Office. The Stewarts instructed Waller to make sure that Winchester and Seymour were informed of the full content of the Goderich communication and that Lord Townshend and the Earl of Westmorland were sent full copies of the objectionable dispatch in question.[84]

The memorial against the civil establishment act that the Bloomsbury group submitted to the Colonial Office in early September indicated that their ranks had grown.[85] Besides those who had signed the 1832 memorial, the signatories of 1833 included Winchester; Sir George Seymour; the 10th Earl of Westmorland, former Lord-Lieutenant of Ireland and Lord Privy Seal until the fall of the Liverpool administration;[86] Laurence Sulivan, deputy secretary of war, brother-in-law of Viscount Palmerston, and owner of four townships;[87] and Samuel Smith Hill, John Hill's son and a newly appointed member of the Island council. In addition, land agents and lawyers signed on behalf of Lord Townshend, the Cambridges, and Thomas Sorell. Robert Stewart signed for Andrew Colvile. The memorialists contended that the act was designed to defeat the agreement on quit rents that had been worked out with Goderich and, as well, that it was 'an unprovoked and violent attack upon the sacred rights of property.' They claimed that the legislation would force proprietors to sell their lands at ruinous prices in order to meet the rate of taxation – roughly £45 per twenty thousand acre township per year. Alleging an anti-proprietor 'combination' among legislators and the tenantry, they demanded that the Imperial government stop this act and put an end to attacks on their property. John Hill's relationship with the emergent group was uneasy, in part because he, unlike the others, still believed it possible to avoid the costs of quit rents altogether. Differing with the Stewarts and others over the wording of the memorial, he refused to sign it, even though his son had, and instead sent a production of his own.[88]

Proprietors also pressured officials at the Colonial Office through numerous interviews and private letters.[89] Seymour enjoyed easy access to the Colonial Secretary, and the Stewarts appear to have developed a working relationship with Thomas F. Elliot, who had recently been appointed a senior clerk in the Colonial Office and who had worked briefly with the emigration committee established by Goderich in 1831.[90] It seems that Elliot advised the Stewarts on how to better substantiate some of the appeals they were making to the Colonial Office. Meanwhile the Stewarts worked through Elliot to deal with the quit rent issue and to provide the Colonial Office with up-to-date information on tenant unrest on the Island, lending him the latest issues of the *Royal Gazette* when they contained pertinent news.[91] Perhaps it was the Stewarts' command of Island intelligence that prompted the Colonial Office to request that Lieutenant-Governor Young ensure that Downing Street was regularly supplied with copies of the Island paper so that it at least would know as much as the Stewarts from this source.[92] Besides writing many letters themselves and discussing Island issues with the lower echelons of Colonial Office officials, the Stewarts did their best to encourage others to write individually.[93]

Two years after the first proprietors' meeting of 1832, the modes of proprietorial collective action were becoming routinized. In the spring of 1834 yet another landlord meeting was called to prepare yet another memorial.[94] This one requested that the Colonial Office rescind the highway compensation act.[95] Once more, the Stewarts played a central role in airing the issue, coordinating the meeting, drawing up the petition, and circulating the memorial for signatures; they paid particular attention to ensure that important figures such as the Earl of Westmorland, Laurence Sulivan, and Henry Winchester were included in the group.[96] This particular initiative met with some resistance from Seymour, who, though he met at Bloomsbury with Colvile, Worrell, Waller, and the Stewarts, chose not to sign the memorial. Apparently he did not feel that he was well enough informed concerning the issue and was unwilling to simply trust others' judgment on the matter.[97]

Continuing discussions of the civil establishment act with officials in the Colonial Office in the winter of 1833–4 brought rejection of the act in late May, but this did not lay to rest the issue of colonial land taxes that would fall equally on developed and wilderness lands.[98] Colvile, Seymour, and the Earl of Westmorland all met with Lord Stanley on the matter; they came away disturbed.[99] The problem, as Seymour summarized it, was that Stanley was too concerned with his 'double duty'; though he acknowledged that it was his job to protect the property of 'fellow subjects' – men like Seymour, Colvile, and the Earl of Westmorland – he was at least as concerned, if not more so, to fulfil his broader public duty.[100] The public issue he raised with the proprietors who spoke with him was that of Imperial revenues and the need for steps to reduce the burden of parliamentary grants for colonial government. Reading between the lines, the proprietors concluded that if their investment concerns clashed with broader governmental objectives, they could not be guaranteed a sympathetic hearing from Lord Stanley, despite their shared class interests in protecting landed property. It had been, as Seymour noted in a letter to Waller, an 'unsatisfactory conversation.'[101]

Spring and summer brought other disturbing developments as Great Britain received news of continuing rent resistance in the colony. The Stewarts found it difficult to reconcile continuing reports of tenant resistance with the apparent lack of action on the part of colonial authorities to maintain law and order. The Island's tenantry attributed the dissonance between their notions of British justice and what they saw happening about them on the Island to a lack of knowledge of colonial affairs in Britain; similarly, the Stewarts and other landlords had persuaded themselves that the Imperial authorities would act differently if only the real situation on the Island were not being hidden from the Colonial Office. And, again like the tenantry, they believed that if accurate information concerning Island affairs could be placed before the appropriate ministers, the Imperial government would intervene to end the abuses of justice suffered by the proprietors. Working with

Colvile and Seymour, Robert Stewart supplied extracts from letters he had received from them concerning rent resistance on the Island to use in enlightening the men at the Colonial Office and effecting a change in how landlords' rights in the colony were enforced.[102] When in July Lieutenant-Governor Young arrived in Britain to be knighted, proprietors used the occasion to lobby him for more effective action on behalf of their interests.[103] July also brought news of the serious confrontation at Naufrage.

In August 1834 some of the men who had been meeting at the Stewarts' residence decided to institutionalize the Bloomsbury group and establish a formal association to protect proprietors' interests on Prince Edward Island.[104] The purpose of the group was to promote landlord interests by aiding immigration and maintaining a favourable image of the colony in the British Isles, and as well to afford proprietors the means to 'unite to resist the wanton attacks constantly and systematically made upon their property.'[105] It had both development and defensive objectives. The first official meeting of the Prince Edward Island Association was held on 1 September 1834.[106] Though 'not very numerously' peopled, it was, as Robert Stewart later reported, 'respectably attended.'[107] Thomas Sorell, Edward Worrell, George Birnie, Mr Gray, William Waller, Mr Todd,[108] and the Stewarts attended. Henry Winchester stopped in the following day. John Bainbridge regretted that as the paid agent of the Island's assembly he could not, at least for the moment, attend official meetings.[109]

With a core group established, the Stewarts hoped that the membership could be expanded to include the most prominent Island proprietors. Their concern was not so much to recruit those who owned extensive properties or who had in the past shown significant interest in Island affairs, but rather to attract those whose names would draw attention in official circles. Writing to Waller, the new association's secretary, Robert Stewart indicated the need to enlist Colvile, Seymour, Sulivan, the Earl of Westmorland, and Viscount Melville, for with such luminaries 'we must carry some weight at the Colonial Office.'[110] John Hill, he felt, should if possible be kept out of the group, as he represented more of a public relations liability than an asset.[111] What, in his opinion, was important at this point in the affairs of Island proprietors was to keep pressure on the Colonial Office to ensure that state policy reflected the interests of the colony's landlords. As Robert Stewart noted in a letter to Waller after the association was founded, 'they [the

Colonial Office] shall not be allowed to rest in quiet, the ball is now started and it must be kept moving.'[112]

The Prince Edward Island Association (PEIA) was to be the instrument for maintaining and strengthening the momentum of the proprietorial activism that had emerged in recent years. It provided an organizational core for ongoing collective action by proprietors as needs arose, and the Stewarts and others hoped that it would soon include the names of prominent British citizens. Behind the appearances, though, was a very modest reality. The PEIA was to meet at the end of every month, but the meeting scheduled for 29 October had to be an unofficial one, for lack of the five members necessary to form a quorum. At the November meeting, those in attendance decided that henceforth the presence of three rather than five members would be sufficient for an official meeting.[113] Despite the small numbers, though, the association allowed the Stewarts and a few others closely associated with them to appear to be acting on behalf of the wishes of a broader proprietary group. Besides involving itself in lobbying efforts, in the early months of its existence the association sought to establish a repository for pertinent documents and newspapers from the colony.[114] It also worked to ensure broad publicity for a book that Sulivan's agent, John Lewellin, had published on the potential of the Island for British immigrants.[115] As well, it explored the possibility of new initiatives to promote the economic development of the Island, including the establishment of a London-based joint stock bank on the Island and a grain trade between the colony and Great Britain, this to be organized by the proprietors.[116]

The Stewarts had much at stake in protecting and advancing proprietors' interests on Prince Edward Island, and they took a central role in organizing landlord activities in the 1830s and promoting their vision of the colony's future. They were consummate orchestrators. Besides repeatedly writing and petitioning the Colonial Office themselves, and establishing the PEIA, they spent much time attempting to coordinate the activities of others and coaching them in the relevant issues. They supplied documents and briefing papers to those preparing to lobby Colonial Office officials. They wrote artful letters under pseudonyms for submission to English and Irish papers, extolling the virtues of immigration to Prince Edward Island and rebutting negative reports. They employed contacts they knew from their estate work to recruit immigrants for the colony.[117]

The Stewarts also sought to coordinate political affairs on the Island itself. While the highway compensation act remained a concern, they wrote to one of their agents on the Island, William Forgan, instructing him to draw up a memorial against the act and to circulate it among the colony's proprietors and land agents. Then he was to submit it to Lieutenant-Governor Young, whence it would make its way back to the Colonial Secretary as an apparently independent supplement to the memorial he would be receiving from British proprietors and agents.[118] As Robert Stewart explained to the Haligonian George R. Young – an important new friend who was to become a close business associate – arranging for petitions to be sent from a variety of quarters spurred government action. Even should a petition originate from 'a place with only half a dozen huts on the coast ... no one here will know but there may be a thousand people.'[119] The Stewarts also worked with sympathizers on the Island assembly to orchestrate the passage of more favourable legislation. One such initiative appears to have been an 1834 amendment to the highway compensation act. By the terms of the new bill, proprietors would be permitted to pay their costs of new road construction with the labour of their tenants rather than by remitting cash to the Island treasury. The Stewarts were delighted with this development and thanked their attorney, John Lawson, the solicitor general and a member of the assembly, for this coup.[120]

The Stewarts' overtures to Island politicians were a reminder that there were areas for convergence between the interests of proprietors and those of the colony's commercial leaders. The Stewarts worked assiduously to emphasize these zones. Insofar as the legislation that had emerged in the late 1820s and early 1830s had been tailored to promote enhanced levels of economic growth, landlords like the Stewarts and those associated with them could argue persuasively that the program they were developing would bring the Island's mercantile and professional communities much of what they wanted. Indeed, the joint stock company schemes they were involved with, their plans for moving tens of thousands of immigrants to the Maritimes, and their interest in establishing banks and an organized grain trade promised injections of capital and rates of growth far greater than what might be realized through local investments and taxation schemes. Aggressive proprietorial capitalism of this sort also offered a way for prominent Islanders who had one foot in a growing commercial economy and another in rentier activities to reconcile their positions. Many government officers and key members of the mercantile and professional communities – men such as Thomas Owen, Samuel Nelson, Ewen Cameron, Joseph

Pope, George Dalrymple, T.H. Haviland, and John Lawson – were also land agents. Although they stood to gain from an expansion of the commercial economy and would have preferred that the public monies necessary to ensure its growth be drawn from landed wealth, they stood to lose an important source of income if the proprietorial system was eliminated altogether. Landlordism rooted in simple rent extraction or passive land speculation posed a dilemma for commercial men, who derived income from the proprietorial system; a merger of landlordism with capitalist development, of the sort the Stewarts and others were advocating in the early 1830s, offered these people a more consistent position.

The attractiveness of such overtures depended both on the ability of these dynamic landlords to deliver the transformations they promised and on the motives behind the politics of development that had emerged in the Island's assembly in the second half of the 1820s. Some critics charged that the purpose of the development legislation was to transfer landownership from the great proprietors to prominent Islanders with an interest in land speculation by forcing landlords holding large estates to sell off their holdings bit by bit in order to meet the costs of new taxes and the assessed amounts due on road construction – or scare them into selling out altogether. If so, the plans of those associated with the PEIA would not meet these objectives.[121] And likewise, if the legislative efforts of those who dominated the 13th assembly were rooted in a desire to achieve not just growth but control and direction over development in the colony, the capitalist projects emerging from the proprietorial group might not effectively satisfy their aspirations. Modification of the legislation aimed at placing portions of the colony's landed wealth in government hands through taxation or expropriation might, as the Stewarts argued, permit proprietors to use their landed wealth as collateral to draw more capital to the colony. It would do so, though, in a way that left effective control of much of the capitalist development on the Island in private hands other than those of the men who dominated the assembly. On the other hand, using the colonial government as the agent for capitalist expansion offered a broad section of the Island's commercial community a way to gain greater control over the pace and direction of development. As far as road construction was concerned, for instance, the PEIA advocated structures that would permit landlords or land companies to determine the timing and nature of transportation improvements. By contrast, the developmental bills that the colonial legislature had passed in the late 1820s permitted the assembly, in conjunction with the lieutenant-governor, to control new road construction. Beyond these issues, the leaders of the colonial mercantile community had to consider their political position on the Island at a time when pressures from popular forces were growing. While a convergence of interests between landlords and leading members of the Island's commercial community might be fruitful in economic terms, the appearance of collusion could be costly in political terms. Maintaining their own development program, on the other hand, would permit the members of the assembly to claim independence from the proprietors' control and afford better opportunities for withstanding the pressures that were developing among subordinate classes in the countryside.

Achieving effective control over the state was central to the aspirations of proprietors, leaders of the Island's commercial and professional community, and the subordinate rural population alike. In the second quarter of the nineteenth century, the efforts of some of the Island's leading commercial and professional men to use their influence within the colonial state to achieve shared goals stimulated collective responses from these other contenders for power. Those who articulated agrarian dreams increasingly challenged the politics of development. Discussion of escheat in the assembly in 1832 revealed the enormous power that the politics of land reform might have in the countryside. The stirrings that followed were in large part spontaneous and inchoate, but the sorts of organization and coordination that would permit these rural rumblings to gain force were evident. As well, people in the countryside were increasingly persuaded that formal politics held the hope for ameliorative changes in the material conditions of rural life.

The development of proprietorial collective action in this same period, though drawing on a much smaller constituency, proved much more effective in contesting the colonial commercial and professional community's use of the state. At the end of the 1820s, landlord interests had been in disarray; when proprietors' voices were heard concerning ongoing policy decisions, they were the voices of individuals responding to the initiatives of others. By mid-decade, though, the situation had changed with the formation of a dynamic proprietorial association. While focused primarily on decision making in the Colonial Office and Privy Council, where their resources could be used most effectively, proprietors' activism included as well exertions to influence the executive, council, and assembly on the Island and to maintain allies within the commercial and professional communities. Central to this was the development of a robust new landlordism that would embrace vast developmental projects and promise the injection of great sums of capital into the economy of Prince Edward Island and the adjacent colonies. While agrarian enthusiasm and the hope of an easy political salvation surged and then ebbed in the countryside, others were hammering together structures for creating a different sort of order.

7 Organizing Escheat, 1834–1836

In the aftermath of the assembly proceedings of 1832, the Escheat movement had appeared stronger than it was. Conversely, the subsequent decline of agrarian advocacy in the assembly and the collapse of organized rent resistance suggested a moribundity that was not the case. Certainly, the hope of a quick and easy victory was gone, but the movement was not dead. In the second half of the 1830s, Escheat advocates retraced many of the steps that agrarian activists had taken earlier in the decade. They did so, though, with less optimism for immediate success and with more attention to establishing a solid foundation for advancing rural concerns.

The increasing strength of the movement developed along two interrelated lines. First, Escheat gained greater organizational coherence and independence. In the first half of the decade, Escheat agitation had been closely linked to events in the assembly; in the second half, Escheators began to develop their own formal structures for debating land issues and coordinating collective action. These permitted a greater freedom in determining the shape and pace of the agrarian challenge and reduced Escheat's dependence on circumstances in the formal political arena. Relatedly, as the movement developed organizational structures its advocates developed greater self-confidence and a more coherent set of ideas concerning how the countryside should be organized. To borrow the conceptualization of Lawrence Goodwyn, Escheat began to develop a 'movement culture' of considerable force.[1]

The revival of Escheat politics in the mid-1830s was tightly linked to electoral reforms instituted by the 13th General Assembly. The most important of these was legislation shortening the assembly's term from seven to four years. Had it not been for this change, voters hoping for greater attention to land reform would not have been able to express this concern at the polls in 1834. The assembly considered other electoral reforms as well, relating to districting, voting procedures, and the breadth of the franchise. In part, members were responding to broader forces reshaping politics in Britain and elsewhere in the Atlantic world at this time; the assembly included advocates of universal manhood suffrage, voting by ballot, annual parliaments, and proportional representation who wished to institute these reforms on the Island. But electoral reform was an issue for the assembly as well because rapid population growth on Prince Edward Island after the Napoleonic Wars was exposing problems with earlier electoral structures.

Legislation from the 1780s gave each of the Island's three royalties two seats in the house. By the early 1830s the distribution of population growth was making this increasingly inappropriate. Princetown and Georgetown, which had a combined population of roughly seven hundred, had four seats in the house, while the three counties, which had populations of roughly 10,000 each, had the same – four members per county.[2] Disproportional representation coupled with restrictive (albeit low) property qualifications in the royalty elections (and laws that allowed people with holdings in multiple ridings to cast multiple votes) gave those with property in these royalties, and an interest in swaying the votes of others, an easy way to make their influence felt in the composition of the assembly. For instance, the winning candidate in the Georgetown election of 1830 was the resident proprietor and shipbuilder Hugh Macdonald; he won his seat with a total of twenty votes. The other Georgetown seat was gained with fifteen.[3] Yet George Dalrymple and John Willock, who topped the polls for Queens County, gained their seats with more than nine hundred votes each.[4]

Although there were calls for significant electoral changes in the early 1830s, the reforms passed by the 13th Assembly were relatively modest. Cooper introduced a petition from Kings County calling for the elimination of the Island's rotten boroughs and for a broadening of the franchise.[5] While accepting the right of Charlottetown, with a population of 2,500, to elect two members to the assembly, the petition contested the justice of permitting Princetown and Georgetown to retain their two seats each. Cooper's suggestion was not popular with the members from the royalties and failed to attract a majority. After wide-ranging debate, the most significant new development was legislation introduced by George Dalrymple reducing the term of the assembly to four years; this is how 1834 came to be an election year. It was, Dalrymple contended, a measure fully in line with the political philosophy espoused by the 'friends and supporters of freedom in Great Britain' who had constructed the first reform administration.[6] Revealing the extent to which he viewed his political advocacy in international terms, he noted that it was also in keeping with the aspirations of liberals shedding blood for political freedom in Italy, Poland and Russia.[7]

The election of 1834 made it clear that there were growing doubts about the politics of development pursued by the 13th Assembly. Some critics argued that the government was becoming both too active and too costly; others, that it had not done enough to address the basic needs of most Islanders. These were not necessarily conflicting perspectives. It could be argued, as William Cooper did, that the government had fallen far short of the expectations raised by its rhetoric and by the broader context of reform, even though in some spheres it had engineered a costly growth of the state's profile. Cooper charged that over the course of the term of the 13th Assembly, Prince Edward Island had gained, 'five sub-collectors of customs, two or three additional road commissioners, twelve commissioners of impost,' and numerous other patronage positions: 'These are the glorious reforms progressing in our Island.'[8] Judging from the attacks of others and the many defensive statements of members of the 13th Assembly, Cooper's contention that the colony was experiencing reform politics as a costly expansion of government offices and patronage reflected rural sentiments.[9] Bigger and more expensive government – even if it was in large part to be paid for by taxes on proprietors – ran against the inclinations of many rural Islanders, especially when they considered that many of the expenditures had been for urban buildings, urban wharves, and offices that were distributed in large part among the prominent of Charlottetown and the other nodes of commerce. At the time of the 1834 election, in part because of failures in the agricultural economy, increased government expenditures had outstripped revenues and left the treasury with unexpected deficits. These were matters of concern to proprietors and to their allies as well.

On at least some of the hustings, the other significant issue was escheat – the unfulfilled dream that many considered the main point of reform politics on the Island. The enormous enthusiasm and hope generated by the escheat legislation of 1832 had diminished owing to the machinations of proprietors working through the Colonial Office and the lethargic treatment the issue had received in the house in 1833 and 1834, but the issue had not gone away. Cooper and others in Kings

County still believed it to be a viable policy that required vigorous agitation, and they were joined in this by others elsewhere. In Kings County, Escheat supporters, recognizing the potentially fragmenting effects of regional loyalties, coordinated forces to ensure that the politics of land reform would prevail over localism. Escheat advocates held nomination meetings across the county, and those attending these meetings agreed informally to cast one of their four votes for their own regional candidate and to reserve their remaining three for those chosen as appropriate agrarian leaders by other districts.[10] The strategy resulted in the election of four members who supported escheat initiatives in the 14th Assembly. Peter McCallum of St Peters Bay and Daniel Brenan were relatively moderate by Kings County standards, while John Le Lacheur of Murray Harbour and William Cooper took more radical agrarian positions. Le Lacheur, who was born on Guernsey in 1793 and who immigrated to Prince Edward Island in the first years of the nineteenth century, was, like most leaders in the Escheat movement, a labouring tenant farmer.[11] A cooper by trade, he brought a keen intelligence and a facility with language to the Escheat cause. Le Lacheur's love of language was apparent in his speeches. Although most Escheat leaders were condemned as illiterates by the Island elite, Lieutenant-Governor Henry Vere Huntley later singled out Le Lacheur as an exception, as one of the few 'who can spell correctly.'[12] Articulating notions of class that were to emerge more starkly in the politics of ensuing years, Le Lacheur gave a rousing speech on the hustings concerning the relations between 'working bees' and 'drones.' For too long, he declared, 'the former had all the work, while the drones ate up the substance.' It was time, he contended, that 'something were done for the interests of the poor,' and he believed that political action was an appropriate tool for accomplishing these ends.[13]

Escheat advocates were not as successful in other counties. Abercrombie Willock, who promoted himself as someone who had brought rural grievances to the attention of Ireland's Daniel O'Connell, seems to have been the only candidate in Queens County who openly based his campaign on an Escheat platform, and he lost.[14] Except for George Dalrymple, a relatively conservative group of candidates were returned from Queens, including Lord Selkirk's land agent, William Douse. Willock, believing that an overt anti-escheat statement would doom Douse's candidacy, attempted to get one by asking Douse directly whether he would support an escheat in the 14th Assembly. Douse, realizing the peril, adroitly talked around the issue, ultimately declaring with Delphic clarity that he would support 'every measure of public utility.'[15] There are no reports concerning which issues were discussed on the hustings in Prince County, but the return of Joseph Pope and Samuel Green, two of the more vocal critics of Cooper's policies in the 13th Assembly, gave anti-escheat forces a strong voice.

The composition of the 14th Assembly was substantially different from that of the 13th; slightly fewer than half the members were incumbents. In the weeks before the legislature met, rural residents in Kings County worked to ensure that the new assembly would address the escheat issue. On New Year's Day, Cooper chaired a meeting of the inhabitants of eastern Kings County at Dingwell's shipyard. Those attending drew up an escheat petition to submit to the assembly. At the same meeting a series of resolutions were passed that laid the basis for this subsequent petition.[16] Like earlier appeals, the petition argued that Island lands had been forfeited for non-fulfilment of the original terms of the grants and that the key issue was control over the value of the labour the tenantry were investing in the land. Short leases and high rents, the petition contended, gave landlords the power to harvest the labour of others and to repossess improvements they had done nothing to create. Responding to Lord Goderich's assertion that even with an escheat, tenants should not expect to obtain the lands they occupied as freeholds, the petition of 1835 indicated that tenants would be willing to become the king's tenants and to pay rent to the Crown, if need be. In early February, a few days after the assembly convened, Daniel Brenan presented the product of the Escheators' organizational labours – a massive petition, fourteen feet in length and bearing fourteen hundred names.[17] Joseph Pope's immediate attack on the petition was indicative of shifts in strategy and attitudes among leading members of the Island's mercantile community. By mid-decade more conservative members of the assembly had ceased giving such presentations a polite hearing.[18]

The Kings County petition provided its supporters in the new assembly with the leverage to once again place the escheat issue at the centre of political debate. With Cooper's backing, Brenan moved that a select committee be established to investigate the land question and that it be authorized – like the committee of 1832 – to send for the people, papers, and records it required for its investigations.[19] The committee ultimately reported back to the assembly, and its proceedings, along with the reactions of members of the assembly to the escheat issue, were published in the *Royal Gazette*.[20] The committee included four members of the previous house: William Cooper, Charles Binns, Daniel Brenan, and John Small Macdonald. There were also three new members – Thomas MacNutt, William Clark, and John Ramsay – all of whom would support the Escheat cause in the 14th Assembly. It was composed, then, predominantly of members who warmly supported the Kings County initiative.

The report the committee submitted to the assembly laid out the case for a general escheat. It was to become the central text in the renewed struggle for land reform in the second half of the 1830s. Beginning with a copy of one of the original grants, the report worked its way through the twists and turns of the land question across six decades, thus providing a comprehensive account of the political history of land relations on the Island. Pertinent documents dealing with the proceedings of the assembly and the policies adopted by the Colonial Office were incorporated into the history, as were census data and a skewed but nonetheless telling analysis of the relative value of the investments of landlords and tenants in improved lands. This step-by-step presentation of the case for escheat probably reflected the legal training of Charles Binns. Besides being noteworthy for its detailed account of the escheat issue, the report clarified the legal grounds on which a broad escheat could be sustained. By insisting that the legal meaning of 'settler' was an adult male, it set the population necessary to meet settlement requirements roughly four times higher than it would have been had the term included a settler's entire household. This was, in essence, a fall-back position for those desiring an extensive escheat, because the report asserted as well that Goderich's settlement indulgences permitting proprietors until 1826 to populate their lands and dropping the requirement that the settlers be foreign Protestants were in fact unconstitutional. The king's prerogative could not, the committee argued, be exercised in a fashion that infringed on the rights of third parties. Granting indulgences, the report maintained, did precisely that, for it gave landlords who had forfeited their land grants because of non-fulfilment of their conditions a claim on Island settlers and their improvements that they would not otherwise have had. Viewed another way, the report contended, the indulgences that permitted landlords to retain their claims – and thus the returns they might gain from rents and land sales – were in effect a tax on Island inhabitants for the benefit of proprietors, imposed without the authorization of the colony's legislature. This, the report insisted, violated policies on colonial taxation that had been established by Westminster in the late eighteenth century. This echoed an argument made in the Upper and Lower Canadian assemblies in the 1830s, when members there questioned the legality of Crown transfer of vast tracts of property to private land companies without local legislative approval.[21]

The petition and report led the new house to consider the appropriate responses to the demands for escheat proceedings. In March, Daniel Brenan presented a motion calling on the assembly to draft a statement of grievances and to send two delegates to Britain to bring Island complaints concerning escheat, and other matters, to the attention of the current ministry and in particular to Members of Parliament.[22] This was the action that Cooper had urged unsuccessfully two years earlier, and it echoed the successful strategy that Island leaders had adopted in the campaign to remove Lieutenant-Governor Smith. Although Brenan's motion combined the escheat question with other grievances, the discussion that followed left little question as to what was at issue: whether delegates representing the assembly would travel to Britain to press for land reform. The debate of 1835 revealed that support for more vigorous treatment of the escheat issue was growing in the assembly. Having been modified to stipulate the dispatch of one rather than two delegates, Brenan's resolution passed by a vote of ten to seven.[23] The following month, when it came time to appropriate money for sending the delegate, the house split evenly on the issue, and the casting vote of the speaker, George Dalrymple, denied the necessary funding.[24] Once again, action on escheat demands was to be restricted to an address composed by the assembly and sent to the lieutenant-governor for dispatch to the Colonial Office.

Besides raising the question of whether the house was going to support calls for an escheat, the report also prompted a debate over what members meant when they advocated an escheat. In so doing it forced a clarification of positions that had been obscured in the proceedings of the previous house. In explicitly laying out the grounds for a broad escheat that would affect the tenantry on settled lots, the report provoked a hostile reaction from those who had been willing to entertain the idea only of a minimal escheat to appropriate a handful of townships with few or no settlers. In the 13th Assembly, it was possible to overlook the divisions on the escheat issue that existed and to believe that – except for the votes of two resident landlords – there was a consensus on the land question. Then, assembly members had been voting on whether to establish an escheat court, not on what it should do, and the Colonial Office had conveniently said no to any type of escheat. The proceedings of the first session of the 14th Assembly, by contrast, exposed the lack of consensus on the escheat issue; even though support for vigorous agitation of the escheat issue was growing, so was vocal opposition to the cause. The position that a court of escheat should be able to go beyond assessing whether proprietors had fulfilled the new settlement terms laid out in Lord Goderich's dispatch of 1818 was denounced sharply by some of those who had supported the escheat bill of 1832. Joseph Pope described it as 'nothing short of downright robbery,' and Samuel Nelson, a Charlottetown merchant, shipbuilder, and land agent with a long involvement in Island politics, avowed that he would be 'ashamed' to ever sit in the house again if it advocated such a course.[25] Samuel Green and William Douse echoed this position. Those advocating a broader escheat, though, welcomed the words of the lawyer Charles Binns – one of the Charlottetown members – whose insistence that Islanders had every right to demand that an escheat go beyond Goderich's terms of settlement carried the imprimatur of professionally informed legal opinion.[26] Binns had studied law in England and had served as solicitor general and later as the attorney general during the Smith administration.[27] Although he later turned decisively against the Escheat movement, he initially occupied a more ambiguous position.

The proceedings of the first session of the 14th Assembly revealed a growing polarization and realignment around the escheat issue. Brenan and Binns, while not embracing Cooper's position in its entirety, supported escheat politics more vigorously than they previously had. They were joined by newer voices such as those of John Le Lacheur and Peter McCallum of Kings County, John Ramsay of Prince County, and the two Princetown members, Thomas MacNutt and William Clark. While there were substantial differences of opinion in this group concerning the extent of an escheat they were willing to support and the appropriate mode of agitating for it, Cooper was no longer isolated in his advocacy of a general escheat. He was opposed, however, by a core of anti-Escheat members, most of whom would nonetheless publicly declaim their willingness to entertain a partial escheat. Joseph Pope, perhaps the most articulate and able of this camp, was joined by incumbents such as Samuel Green and Samuel Nelson and by new members such as William Douse and Edward Palmer, son of J.B. Palmer and the other representative from Charlottetown, as well as by the two Georgetown representatives, John W. James and Edward Thornton. The latter, among other things, was a land agent for two descendants of Captain John Macdonald of Glenaladale.[28] The report of the escheat committee reflected the support within the committee of members leaning towards Cooper's position on the land question. When the issues were debated in the whole house, the committee's position was substantially modified. The address the house ultimately submitted to Lieutenant-Governor Aretas Young, like those of the previous assembly, spoke in generalities about the need to establish a court of escheat and to deal with other outstanding political grievances.[29]

Evidence of the effectiveness of the proprietors' lobby that had swung into action earlier in the decade was revealed to the house shortly after it began its 1835 sitting, when Young provided it with copies of Lord Stanley's dispatch of the previous May rejecting the civil establishment act.[30] Further indication of the proprietors' handiwork came in April, when dispatches arrived announcing that the Privy Council had disallowed the escheat act of 1832, as well as the land title act that had been passed that same year. Joseph Pope's hopes to channel political energies into obtaining greater autonomy and revenues did not appear to be leading anywhere either, in part because his initiatives, too, were encountering effective opposition mounted by proprietors. Pope would claim victory in an assembly/council dispute over appropriations in the spring of 1835, but on matters of importance the reality was that the politics of development, like escheat, had stalled.[31] Measures to raise additional revenues through land taxes, beyond those earmarked for government buildings by the 1832 legislation, had been rejected by the Legislative Council and the Colonial Office, and the revenues available to the Island government had fallen short of expenditures already committed or expected. Adding to the difficulties were directives from the Treasury Board disapproving of the amount of treasury bills in circulation in the colony and instructing the lieutenant-governor to deny any further issues and to ensure that the amount in circulation was reduced.[32]

There were signs as well that proprietors' exertions were achieving success outside the political arena. Events in Naufrage at the beginning of 1835 suggested that rural resistance to the enforcement of laws sustaining landlord interests was still vigorous; even so, it soon became clear that this resistance was the closing act in the series of conflicts that had been set in motion in the spring of 1832. In January 1835 a sheriff and a posse of twelve men again sought to apprehend the five tenants who had resisted Donald McVarish in September 1833, and once again armed tenants repulsed them.[33] Hugh Macdonald, who besides being an important merchant and a landlord served as sheriff at this time, reported that roughly thirty men and twelve women armed with guns, pitchforks, sticks, and a broadaxe had resisted his party, saying that they had taken up weapons to protect their persons and their property and 'that they would lose their blood before they would part with either.'[34] They told him they could double their numbers in a matter of hours and that they could and would resist any military force sent against them. For his part, Macdonald assured them that when he returned it would be with a much stronger force and that 'neither man, woman, or child would be spared.' Lieutenant-Governor Young was present on the Island at the time of this incident at Naufrage, and he questioned the sheriff closely when the latter returned with a request for troops to aid the civil power. Young learned in this way that most of the posse in fact had stopped half a mile short of Naufrage and that only three officers and John Macintosh, a local tenant sympathizer who would in time become one of Cooper's closest allies in the House of Assembly, had actually proceeded to the community. Given that no serious attempt had really been made to execute the warrants and that the tenantry had not physically resisted the officers, Young turned down the request for troops and instructed Macdonald to pursue his job more effectively.[35] Knowing that the absentee proprietors' view of events would be shaped by what they read in the *Royal Gazette* and that they would use evidence of tenant resistance to make a case for more vigorous law enforcement, Young persuaded the editor of the *Royal Gazette* to issue a new, revised version of the incident and kept the Colonial Office closely informed of events.[36] When Macdonald returned to Naufrage a week later, two of the men he was seeking had already turned themselves in. Forcing open the door of Allan Macdonald's house before daylight, he found Allan and Isabella and a four-month-old child all sick in bed. He arrested Allan and brought him back to Charlottetown along with his sister Nancy; he allowed Isabella to remain behind temporarily. Except that he had been denied entry into Allan Macdonald's household, the sheriff had met no resistance.[37]

The trial of those accused of resisting Flora Townshend's bailiff in 1833 was the first in the new courthouse that the Island government had erected at Georgetown with the monies raised by land taxes. Thus the conflict between tenants who had failed to obtain relief from the burdens of rents, and the proprietors who had been pressed to maximize the returns from their estates so that they might meet added tax burdens, was played out in one of the new structures erected by the colonial advocates of development politics. Chief Justice Edward Jarvis acquitted Allan and Nancy but convicted the remaining three of common assault, sentencing them to a month in the new Georgetown jail.[38] Under the heading 'Suppression of the Naufrage Rebellion,' the *Royal Gazette* noted with regret that it would not be issuing a special edition with tales of the 'hangings, drawings, and quarterings which generally signalize the suppression of such civil convulsions in countries less happily situate than this.'[39] The paper's treatment of the issue, and of Young and Jarvis's handling of the incident and the case respectively, carried the message that the threat of civil unrest and rebellion had been greatly exaggerated and was no longer an issue.[40]

David and Robert Stewart – and one would imagine other landlords who were following Island events through the *Royal Gazette* and correspondence with agents and friends in the colony – had initially been shocked to learn that physical resistance was persisting on the Island. As reports of the arrests and trial filtered back, they were relieved.[41] News of the proceedings of the first session of the 14th Assembly gave them grounds for optimism, too, as they read of the defeats of the Escheat cause in the house and of the attacks on agrarian positions by Pope, Green, and others. The Stewarts appear to have attributed these favourable changes to their lobbying efforts both with the Colonial Office and with potential allies on the Island. Writing to William Waller in June 1835 after receiving the latest papers and three letters from John Lawson, Robert Stewart heralded the victory he felt they were gaining: 'I think our long guns are beginning to make an impression in the Island.'[42] In subsequent weeks the Stewarts made a point of writing to their contacts on the Island assuring them that the assembly's continuing flirtation with escheat was a pointless and unthreatening initiative, as the proprietors who had negotiated with the Colonial Office on quit rents would be buying out the Crown's claims and gaining new grants as soon as the current land assessment act expired.[43] Indeed, correspondence was continuing, and as a result of the prodding of proprietors, the Colonial Office was drawing up and putting in place the procedures whereby landlords might commute quit rents and obtain new grants.[44]

For the Stewarts, the summer of 1835 was a time for pursuing developmental schemes and for re-establishing control over wayward tenants on their estate. As the assembly's proceedings earlier in the year had not led to objectionable legislation on the homeward-bound packet, they were able to turn their attention to other matters. Tensions had developed in the management of the New Brunswick and Nova Scotia Land Company. A key Prince Edward Island player in the group, John

MacGregor, had withdrawn from the scheme along with a number of Liverpool entrepreneurs. Having given up hope of becoming the company's chairman, MacGregor departed for Paris.[45] The Stewarts, though they remained active in the company, increasingly directed their attention to the newly coalescing North American Colonial Association. They and George Seymour exerted themselves to obtain passage of the company's act of incorporation, and in anticipation of this, the Stewarts were lobbying those involved to include Island lands in their portfolio and to think twice about the dangers of investing in the politically turbulent Canadas.[46] The idea of including Island lands in the project appears to have met with a favourable reception, and the Stewarts were involved with plans for including the Hill and Cambridge estates in the scheme.[47] As well, the Prince Edward Island Association (PEIA) was exploring banking and trade initiatives for the Island.[48] The colony, the Stewarts believed, was on the verge of great changes; massive injections of British capital and labour occasioned by the movements of large numbers of immigrants would lead to the rapid development of agriculture and manufacturing on the Island. Robert Stewart wrote to their agent William Prendergast in the fall of 1835, assuring him that the lightly populated region about his residence on Lot 10 would in five years be as busy as Charlottetown.[49]

Like other landlords who had encountered difficulties collecting rents in the aftermath of the 1832 excitement, the Stewarts were anxious to ensure that payments became regular and that arrears were settled. With Island affairs once again on a more normal footing, they wanted their accounts set straight. As it was, they were having to meet the new costs that the assembly had assessed through remittances from Britain.[50] Their irritation was compounded by their belief that other landlords were faring much better in this regard. They instructed William Morpeth to visit each of their tenants on Lot 47 personally and, refusing any further appeals for indulgences, to let them know that 'proceedings will be taken against the whole lot of them' if their rents and arrears since 1830 were not paid up.[51] Tenants were having a hard time meeting these demands. Rents were always a heavy burden for many rural Islanders, and a series of crop failures and difficult weather conditions in 1833 and 1834 had further reduced rural incomes. Although crops were better in 1835, once again there was bad news for some: rust and the Hessian fly had damaged the Island's wheat crop, and rot had taken much of the potato crop.[52]

For many rural residents the harvests of the mid-1830s were short on foodstuffs and long on bills and rent collectors. Constables, reported Ronald Macdonald from East Point, were 'skipping along the high and bye-ways' leaving ruin in their wake.[53] In 1835, as the Stewarts moved to force the collection of arrears from wayward residents in Kings County, they learned that their tenants were planning to sell the improvements they had made and leave.[54] Robert Stewart made it clear that he would insist on all his arrears being paid out of the proceeds of such sales. Similar reports of settlers planning to go elsewhere emerged from the Belfast district of Queens County the following spring; there it was reported that freeholders and tenants alike were raising a fund to send agents to the newly opened territory of Texas where they might escape 'the oppressions of nominal Township proprietors, and their law and land agents.'[55] The residents of southern Kings County, John Le Lacheur reported early in 1836, lived in dread of the constables who were moving among them.[56] An Island paper reported in the spring of 1836 that many of the Acadian inhabitants around Rustico were 'on the brink of ruin, on account of proceedings lately taken for the recovery of back rents.'[57]

Among those feeling the pressure of rent collectors were squatters. Before the 1830s it had been possible for some of the rural poor to occupy lands that were not being actively managed and scratch out a livelihood without paying much attention to the circumstances of their tenure. By the mid-1830s this was no longer so easily done. Land taxes and road assessments had made the sort of neglectful proprietorial land speculation that favoured squatting less viable, and had forced landlords to pay more attention to their holdings and to do what they could to ensure a flow of rents from their estates. Many who had squatted for years without being disturbed found in the 1830s that agents bearing leases and constables carrying legal papers were confronting them with demands for rent.[58]

These pressures on the rural population, arising from reinvigorated landlordism as well as from natural forces, and played out against the unrealized hopes of 1832, set the stage for resurgent agrarian activism in 1836. Much as had happened in 1835, a mass meeting in Kings County and a petition drawn up there succeeded in bringing the matter before the assembly in 1836 and in setting the initial terms of debate. On 12 January a public gathering was held in a field near Rollo Bay.[59] It was to be an information session on the current state of the escheat issue and an occasion for planning future initiatives. Around noon a sleigh was 'erected as a hustings' and the county's representatives were called upon to preside. Cooper and Le Lacheur began the meeting, which was said to have been 'numerously attended.' Their addresses used the recent report of the assembly's escheat committee to hammer home arguments about the justice of the tenants' cause, 'the rights of the people,' the need for a general escheat, and the tenor of the times. If they pressed on with their fight to gain the rights they were 'entitled to by the British Constitution,' Cooper assured the gathering, 'the poet's prediction' would be realized by Island developments:

> Truth shall pervade th' unfathomed darkness here,
> To light the features of desponding fear;
> Even now their eyes with fire of freedom burns;
> And as the slave departs the man returns.[60]

Peter McCallum and John Macintosh, the other two Kings County representatives, arrived late on account of soft roads, like many others, and they joined Cooper and Le Lacheur as the meeting moved from addresses to the development and presentation of resolutions. Macintosh, who had replaced Brenan when the latter stepped down to take one of the new government jobs that had been created by development legislation, was from the Naufrage district; he was the local notable whom the sheriff had recruited to act as an intermediary in his confrontation with angry tenants in January, as he was said 'to have influence upon them.'[61] The hustings had been equipped with writing materials, and William Dingwell acted as chairman, recording the eleven resolutions proposed by the audience and noting the names of those who made and seconded the motions. The language and message of the resolutions were now familiar. The inhabitants of the Island were, they claimed, being made to endure an unjust land system that deprived them of their political and economic rights. Immediate governmental action was required to halt the unjust workings of current structures pending a permanent solution. The meeting resolved that a petition detailing their grievances and their suggested solutions be drawn up for presentation to the assembly and the Executive Council. Having begun at noon, the meeting continued until dusk, with people still arriving after dark. After Dingwell recorded the last of the resolutions, including the decision to order the printing of six hundred escheat pamphlets that would include the land question report of the previous assembly, the gathering dispersed, with some, he noted, tarrying 'to refresh themselves with an extra glass on the occasion.'[62]

Underlying the petition that ultimately made its way to the assembly chambers was the public drama of farmers from dispersed and isolated settlements gathering to hear speeches, swap tales, and share in the excitement of the day. Some took a part in the ensuing public discussions and played a role in presenting and seconding resolutions, coming later to see their names in print as people who were advancing the agrarian cause in the colony. On this occasion the resolutions of Macdonalds, Macintoshes, McInnises, and McIntires were mingled with those of Doyles, Jalottas, Fallas, Leslies, Douglases, and Aitkens. Large escheat meetings such as the one at Rollo Bay reached beyond the isolated clusterings of daily rural life. They bridged localisms and ethnic divisions and brought together people with shared experiences and common grievances. Underlying the resolutions that the assemblymen laid before the house were a growing democratization of the political process and entry-level lessons in the ways of political discourse and leadership. Building as well was a growing sense of the shared plight of those who worked the land for a living.

Lieutenant-Governor Young died in December. When the 14th Assembly convened once again in February 1836, the members learned that he had not forwarded the assembly's address of the previous year to the Colonial Office.[63] As the current executive contended, his decision was probably rooted in the arrival of a dispatch indicating that Imperial authorities had denied royal assent to the escheat bill; even so, the discovery gave rise to new conspiracy theories.[64] Most importantly, though, the news ended expectations of new responses from the Colonial Office on the possibilities of an escheat. The Kings County petition that Cooper presented to the house provided, among other things, a rebuttal of the arguments the Colonial Office had made the previous spring to justify rejecting of the escheat act of 1832. Citing arguments that the assembly had developed in committee during the previous session, it explicitly laid out tenant demands for a general escheat. The 'industrious classes' of the Island, it asserted, needed to have their rights protected as they were suffering from the improper 'influence' that landlords were exercising over the ministers who were setting colonial policy as well as over 'the Courts of Judicature, the barristers and officers of Government' locally. Agreeing to become the king's tenants, the petitioners requested that George Wright – the temporary Island executive who drew an income from public office, business investments, land agencies, and small-scale landlordism and who was the son-in-law of John Cambridge – issue an 'injunction' on their behalf staying further land proceedings pending an investigation of the issue.[65] As well, they demanded that a deputation from the assembly be sent to Britain with a copy of the escheat committee report of 1835 and with instructions to lay their grievances before Parliament. This, they said, responding to the decision of the previous session not to allocate money for the cause, would be a worthy project for their tax monies.[66]

The petition, and Cooper's motion to establish a seven-man committee to deal with it, gave rise to a long and bitter discussion of the escheat issue. Joseph Pope's opening comments set the tone for the debates that followed. Many of the petitioners, he declared, 'were the very scum of society.' They were, he argued, advocating a general escheat rather than a partial one, 'least [*sic*] they should not come in for a share of the spoil.'[67] Stripped of the pejorative commentary, Pope's class analysis was not incorrect. The idea of a general escheat had great appeal among the squatters and tenants interested in gaining a secure hold over their improvements. Together, these two groups constituted the majority of Islanders, and it was they whom people of Pope's stature usually referred to as 'the lower classes' or the 'poorer class of colonists.' Pope was attempting to characterize a general escheat as something no reputable person would embrace, so he neglected to note that it drew many adherents from among small freeholders as well, and that its leadership included shipbuilders and small-scale rural merchants. The idea of a partial escheat drew support from a different cross-section of the Island population. The debate over the escheat issue in the 1836 session continued to sharpen the distinction that had always existed between these two positions. At one end of the spectrum was Cooper, who continued to advocate a general escheat, maintaining, among other things, that an equitable policy had to restructure the circumstances of all the Island tenantry, not just a fortunate few. He now had allies in the house who agreed with him on this. At the other end, Joseph Pope served as the spearhead for those who, while publicly claiming that they supported a partial escheat, were, as Pope himself put it, 'sick and tired of the question.'[68]

Pope and others were disgusted with the escheat question in part because it was pushing other issues away from the centre of political debate. In terms of both public attention and house procedural wrangles, escheat was shoving aside matters such as the fiscal relationship between the upper and lower houses, the civil list question, and opportunities for an expanded role for government in economic development. When in February 1836 Pope moved that the house begin crafting a bill to continue the land tax that had generated funds to construct government buildings, Cooper immediately opposed him, arguing that the assembly could not credibly argue that it was serious about the forfeiture of lands and an escheat while at the same time indirectly acknowledging these titles by taxing those who held them.[69] John Willock had advanced the same argument years earlier. If it gained support, it would make the development program, which was to be based on the land tax, contingent on an escheat of proprietorial lands. Until a general escheat had occurred, the two would be irreconcilable. Cooper lost on this issue by one vote; however, another division later in the session prevented progress on Pope's land tax plans.[70] Escheat did not displace all other discussion – or even as much of the legislative activity as Cooper and Le Lacheur and some of the other agrarians would have liked. It did, however, dominate the proceedings of the house in 1836, and in turn was the focus of public discussion.

The agrarian dreams embodied in the call for an escheat could not easily be deflected or ignored in the second half of the 1830s. According to Cooper, Escheators were winning the war of words in Island discourse; an effective rebuttal of their assertions concerning the land question had yet to be made.[71] Cooper's claim found indirect confirmation in the house when Pope complained that, though he 'had no turn for scribbling himself,' it was much to be regretted that statements originating with the Escheators were going unchallenged in the press.[72] The growing sense that agrarian radicalism was spreading, abetted by the silence of Islanders who should have been speaking out on these issues, led to a vigorous counter-attack against Escheat ideas early in 1836. Whatever else it did, the assault further highlighted the land question, as major speeches on the topic dominated the pages of the *Royal Gazette*. John Lawson, who was permitted to appear at the bar of the house on behalf of the Stewarts and Sir Thomas Sorell, devoted three hours to rebutting the arguments made by the Kings County petitioners.[73] Pope and Green then pitched in with strong anti-Escheat speeches. Cooper responded on behalf of the petitioners.[74]

Lawson opened his declamation by declaring that an 'epidemic of the worst kind' was 'raging in King's County.' Queens County too, he had learned had 'caught the infection.' He noted, not incorrectly, that 'before another week we shall hear of its having reached Prince County.' Unless it 'be timely checked,' he could but 'dread the consequences.' Pressing beyond proprietors' earlier arguments, Lawson contended that, among other things, the original conditions of the grants had been unconstitutional. As well, he maintained that tenants were foolish to think that a parliament of landlords would endorse an escheat as it might open the door to British inquiries into fulfilment of the terms of grants derived from William the Conqueror. In his response, Cooper did not deny that Escheat might run against the grain of landlord sentiments, but he noted that comparable transformations – such as the end of feudal relations in France and the termination of slavery in the West Indies – had been brought about despite the wishes of nobles and slave owners and that they were, when necessary, being realized not just by argument but by force – 'the Guillotine' and coercive legislation. As well, Cooper argued that 'the inhabitants of this Island are as much affected in their rights, by the original grants of land, as they are by the original grants of the great charter.' In response to those who argued that the king might alter the terms of the original grants by royal prerogative, Cooper contended that 'the next wonder we shall hear of is, that the King, by proclamation has cancelled the magna carta.'[75]

Lawson coupled his argument about the dangers of tampering with private property and tenant/landlord relations with the contention that petitioning the king for an escheat was something no 'honest man' would do. The equation of Escheat politics with immorality was a theme that would be played again and again in the attack against the agrarian position. Samuel Green would refer to the escheat question as the 'cheat' question, the product of those advocating a 'sweeping system of robbery and plunder.' Joseph Pope, too, had referred to escheat as 'robbery' and Samuel Nelson had talked of being 'ashamed' to sit in an assembly that could even propose such a thing.[76] The Stewarts as well were coming to see the problems they were encountering on the Island in moral terms. They were not, they felt, dealing with people who conducted themselves 'like honest men.'[77] The Stewarts' belief that many of the problems in the colony were rooted in the unprincipled attitudes that were developing among Islanders may have been linked with their increasing interest in proprietors' schemes for building schoolhouses and promoting education. In this regard the PEIA promised to support the educational plans being advanced by Captain R.C. Macdonald, son of Captain John Macdonald of Glenaladale.[78]

On moral and educational issues, as with policies directly bearing on economic development, the proprietors and the Island's leading business and professional men were promoting similar projects and shared a concern with social control. They differed, however, in their approaches to these matters. The development program that members of the assembly promoted in the 1820s linked state involvement in promoting industry and trade with state investments in jails and schools. All of these things were part of a broad vision of 'improvement.' Together they would, as one of the candidates in the 1824 election phrased it, 'prevent idleness, immorality and vice, by giving constant employment to the labouring classes of the community, and by rendering them sober, diligent and industrious, afford them the most certain means of becoming virtuous, prosperous and happy.'[79] But while colonial business leaders conceived their programs in terms of taxation and local state structures, proprietors were more interested in private initiatives. They differed, too, in their perceptions of social problems on the Island. Unlike Samuel Green and Joseph Pope, the Stewarts believed that leaders of the Island's professional and commercial community were adversely shaping the moral climate of the colony with their own behaviour towards the property of landlords. In their opinion, the local norms that sustained tenants when they made free with the lands of proprietors were intimately related to the local morality that permitted land agents to fleece proprietors and that allowed the mercantile community to profit from stripping landlords' property of its timber. Consider the case of James Yeo, a carter who began his life on the Island supervising lumber gangs and became an expert at extracting money from other people's assets and labour. He ultimately became a member of the assembly, a landlord, and one of the colony's great shipbuilders. The Stewarts calculated that he was stealing stumpage worth perhaps £750 per year, yet he had gained respect in Island society and was not shunned as a thief. This suggested to them that a broader moral turpitude existed among the merchant and professional communities of the Island and was radiating downwards to the lower classes.[80]

Opponents of Escheat not only challenged the logic and morality of those demanding sweeping land reforms, but also adopted a harder and more confrontational rhetoric. Pope's characterization of Escheat as a project of the 'scum of society' was the opening salvo in an analysis that cast those associated with Cooper's position as outside acceptable bounds of discourse. Pope spoke of the desirability of shipping off the 'mal-contents' to Van Diemen's Land, where, he claimed, they were likely ultimately to wind up anyway.[81] Samuel Green responded to Cooper's contention that without land reform rent collection would have to be sustained at the taxpayers' expense with military force, by accusing him of 'approaching as near to treason as may be' and pointing to the possibility of armed clashes, which he believed were in the making. The residents of Kings County, he said, 'have some little experience in the use of the bayonet' (here he was referring to the murder of Lord Townshend's land agent in 1819), and in the days to come 'no doubt will make a noble resistance with that weapon, or one fully as good, the pike, one easily procured in this country.' He was glad, he said, that plans that had been afoot earlier in the decade to provide the militia units with arms had not been realized as this dangerous gift would have armed people with an interest in challenging rather than defending the laws of the country. It was time, he declared, for 'those who have property to defend' to unite and 'provide themselves with the means of mutual defense' even as they prayed yet that the government might 'nip the evil in the bud' and avert the approaching calamity.[82]

The harsh rhetoric emerging in the assembly reflected, in part, the tensions of ongoing social and political challenges in the countryside – tensions that threatened to alter local power relations. As the debate unfolded over the Kings County petition, which had originated with a meeting at Rollo Bay, Escheat meetings continued to be held throughout the Island and yet more petitions supporting the cause flowed into the assembly (see map 7.1) In February, residents of Queens County submitted a replica of the Kings County petition to the assembly, and March brought new petitions crafted at meetings in Prince and Queens counties.[83] In early April, Kings County residents submitted yet another petition.[84] Treatment of the escheat issue in the house provoked this flurry of rural political activity, as it was conducted early enough in the session to generate a dialogue between open-air politics in the countryside and debate in the assembly. Escheat proponents in Kings County had suffered a setback at the end of February when a resolution calling for an address to the king and Parliament on the basis of the original Kings County petition, and the dispatch of a delegation to communicate it, was defeated by amendments proposed by Pope.[85] In the course of debate some assemblymen suggested that escheat was primarily a Kings County phenomenon, with little support in the countryside as a whole.[86] The meetings and petitions were responses to this claim. The growing rancour of the anti-escheat rhetoric in the assembly over the course of the session reflected, in part, sharp local conflicts that erupted when grassroots Escheat organizing spread onto the home turf of those opposed to the cause and challenged their leadership and position in local society.

In Prince County, Joseph Pope and Samuel Green, whose mercantile operations embraced shipbuilding and the timber trade in and about

Map 7.1. Escheat meetings, January to June 1836 (partial list)

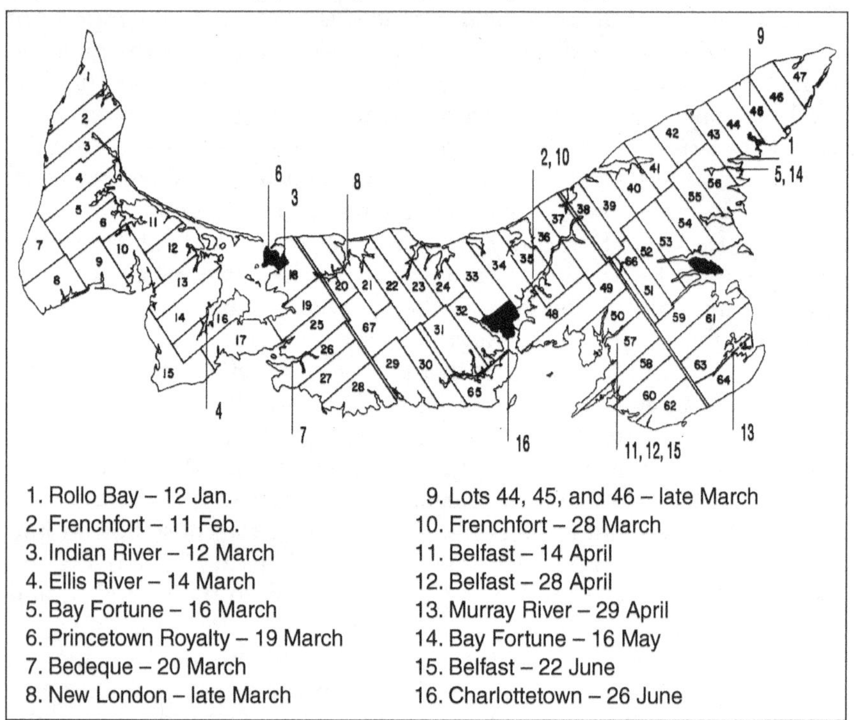

Source: *Royal Gazette*; *Prince Edward Island Times*

Bedeque and St Eleanors respectively, were outraged to discover that Escheators were organizing residents in their districts while the 1836 session was under way.[87] They complained bitterly that these Escheat gatherings in Prince County were being organized in a 'clandestine and private manner' and that they were not being notified of the meetings and, thus, could not attend and contradict the versions of the colony's land history that Escheators were articulating.[88] As well, they denounced the 'emissaries of escheat, or panderers for plunder' who were organizing these meetings, for turning local people against them by saying that Green and Pope were working to undermine the possibility of an escheat.[89] It seems that by mid-decade any public position short of advocacy of a general escheat was unacceptable in the countryside; support for a partial escheat was, in the eyes of most rural Islanders, tantamount to betrayal. Escheat accusations against men like Pope and Green had the potential to drive a wedge between these local bosses and their clients. On one occasion, having heard indirectly that there was to be an Escheat meeting in Bedeque, Pope attended and, working with the notion that advocacy of a general escheat was immoral, confronted the organizers by asking those present to indicate by a show of hands who in the room supported such a position. It seems that the assemblyman John Ramsay was the only one there willing to publicly oppose Pope and that the latter successfully used the issue, and his own personal authority, to undermine Ramsay and the other Escheators.[90] Such, of course, was one of the reasons why Escheators organized 'hole and corner meetings.'[91] Until the cause was firmly organized and some leadership established, the presence of men such as Green and Pope posed a threat. But as both these men knew, their hold even over immediate clients was precarious. Samuel Green had recently had a lesson in this when he gathered a group of Acadians – presumably his employees – to accompany him to a public meeting on the civil establishment act only to be left isolated, and humiliated, when they 'ratted on him' and voted with the majority.[92]

The climax in the assembly's 1836 escheat debate came in April with the tabling of the draft escheat address that the assembly would be presenting to the Crown. This was two months after the assembly had received the original Kings County escheat petition and after rural residents had held numerous meetings supporting escheat and forwarded petitions to the assembly. The draft address claimed that all Island lands had been forfeited for non-fulfilment of the terms of the original grants, provided a long history of the land question, and asked that a court of escheat be established so that the rights of the Island's tenantry might be examined before an 'impartial tribunal.'[93] In place of this draft, Joseph Pope introduced, by way of amendment, an alternative address that spoke of the need to allay the excitement that was 'increasing to an alarming extent' among 'a numerous class of the inhabitants' and that was 'preventing men of capital from settling in the country, and retarding the transaction of public business in the Legislature.' The Crown, Pope's address asserted, should establish a court of escheat to deal with the issue of lands liable to forfeiture and either expropriate these lands or confirm the grants 'in such cases where, after a full investigation, the Grantees may be found deserving of your Majesty's most gracious consideration under the indulgences granted by your Majesty's Royal predecessors.'[94] While Pope's petition could be billed as a call for an escheat, it was in fact a call for Imperial action to put an end to agrarian agitation for sweeping land reform. Pope managed to carry his substitute address by a narrow eight-to-seven vote. Thus, for the first time, the assembly had given its imprimatur to the use of the royal prerogative to alter the terms of the original grants – a procedure that Escheat advocates had said was unconstitutional for lack of such approval. Standing against Pope were all the Kings County members, the two representatives from Princetown, and John Ramsay from Prince County. The two loose fish who had given Pope his majority were John Small Macdonald of Queens County, who, though a member of the extended Macdonald of Glenaladale family and a small-scale landlord himself, had sometimes voted against Pope on land issues, and Charles Binns, who had in the past stood a good deal closer than Macdonald to the Escheat cause. The position of the Speaker of the House, George Dalrymple, who had cast the deciding vote against allocating money for an escheat delegate, remained unclear. At Pope's suggestion, the address was to be entrusted to Henry Labouchere, the Member of Parliament for Taunton.[95] Labouchere was an advocate of moderate reforms in British North America, and his brother John was a crony of the Stewarts and the acting director of the New Brunswick Land Company.[96]

The victory that Pope and his supporters achieved in the assembly touched off a wave of protest meetings in the countryside. The polarization that had led to a victory for anti-Escheat forces in the assembly found its echo outside the house in a powerful movement to dissolve the assembly on the grounds that its actions were not representative of Islander's wishes. There were a number of parallels between the rural excitement which developed in 1836 and that of 1832. In both cases, discussion of the escheat issue in the house stimulated events outside the chamber, and in both cases, rural residents expressed their sentiments through public meetings and, ultimately, through rent resistance. There were, however, important differences. In 1832 the meetings that were held around the Island were designed to lend support to initiatives that had begun in the assembly; they were based on the idea that the people's representatives were providing leadership and would, especially if they received encouragement from countrypeople, address their needs. In 1836, by contrast, the escheat meetings that were held around the Island were informed by the perception that most members of the assembly were opposed to rural desires and that no leadership could be expected from that quarter. This perception raised the question of the legitimacy of the power of those who claimed to be speaking on behalf of the Island's people – thus the call for a dissolution of the assembly. As well, it led to the founding of an alternative body to provide leadership for promoting the Escheat cause and to speak on behalf of those rural people who felt that their voices were not being reflected in the positions and statements emerging from the 14th Assembly. Under these circumstances, rent resistance and the use of force to repel law officers attempting to enforce landlords' claims were potentially of far greater significance than they had been earlier.

In mid-March, after the house had rejected the idea of sending an escheat delegation to Britain and had provided an early sense of how they were going to treat the Kings County petition, a public meeting in Bay Fortune, convened in response to these developments, indicated the contours of the rural reaction. The resolutions emerging from this meeting justified and outlined a new strategy. Those attending the Bay Fortune meeting argued that they had petitioned the assembly the previous year and that their address had not been forwarded to the Imperial authorities. In the current year they had petitioned again and their wishes had again been denied. They had appealed to the executive and had received no answer, so they had no faith that their case was ever going to be heard at the highest echelons of the Imperial government. In the meantime the tenantry continued to be subjected to 'all the horrors of distress, oppression, and Law without justice.' Citing Blackstone that 'when justice is denied to the people, they are at liberty to defend themselves,' they publicly declared themselves justified in defending themselves and their property, pending a proper hearing of their case by the Imperial government. They intended, they declared, to send Cooper to Britain to voice their complaints as soon as plans for raising the necessary monies could be coordinated with the other committees in the colony. Publication of the meeting's resolutions made it clear to those elsewhere who did not already know by other means that Bay Fortune's Escheators were again advocating rent resistance and attempting to coordinate committees to dispatch a delegate.[97]

Within days of the assembly's vote to sustain Pope's debilitating amendment, voices were heard demanding that the current assembly be terminated. A 'Reformer' in St Peters Bay called for the dissolution of the house on the grounds that the assembly had betrayed the people's interest by substituting a 'Milk-and-Water' escheat address for a real statement of their grievances. This same person noted that local developments were 'turning the attachment of a hitherto loyal and affectionate people from the parent state.'[98] Resolutions passed at a public meeting in Belfast, the central community on the Selkirk estate, made the same point concerning tenants and small freeholders having to choose between their loyalty to the Crown and the acceptance of oppression. Under the circumstances, they asserted, they were having to suppress their feelings of attachment to the king and, among other things, explore the possibilities of emigration beyond the British Empire. They, too, challenged the legitimacy of an assembly composed of men who '*pretend* to be *Representatives* of the people' even while blocking popular initiatives for obtaining an escheat, and they asserted their outrage at the 'unprecedented and unlawful proceedings' that were being conducted in order to recover rents on the Selkirk estate.[99] The local poet 'Momus' was more blunt about the relationship between patriotic allegiance and the exploitation of countrypeople: 'They rest, and feed, and bray out 'loyalty;' / Perverted word – the sons of men / Are only loyal to their gain. / But loyalty's a Cuckoo song / Used to delude the vulgar throng.'[100]

Gatherings, noted William Rankin, editor of the *Prince Edward Island Times,* at the end of April, were being 'held in all directions' so that 'the People may have opportunities of expressing their sentiments' on the escheat issue.[101] The frequency and broad distribution of meetings (see Map 7.1) confirm Rankin's comment. In March alone at least eight Escheat meetings were held in various locales in Prince, Queens, and Kings counties. A somewhat panicky George Wright, the acting executive, reported to the Colonial Office that a 'very great excitement' was prevailing 'throughout the Island' and that it was 'gaining ground.' He urged quick action to deal with the issue.[102] The meetings continued even during the busy months of April and May, with rural residents railing against the policies of the existing lower house, calling for the dissolution of the assembly, and drawing up of petitions to this effect for submission to the Island's new lieutenant-governor, John Harvey, when he arrived. As well, some meetings continued to demand that an Escheat delegate be sent to the Imperial government.[103]

As the spring progressed, the Bay Fortune Committee acted as a clearing house for the resolutions and communications on the escheat issue that were originating throughout the Island. In mid-May it held a local meeting to discuss the correspondence and to attempt to formulate a common plan of action. In a published letter and series of resolutions, the Bay Fortune group suggested that committees elsewhere, and Island inhabitants in general, should petition the Island government to stay ongoing land law proceedings. Such proceedings were, they believed, illegal, since the land had been forfeited; and without an Island court that would hear such a plea, tenants were suffering a wrong for which there was no legal remedy. Committees, they suggested, should try to maintain the peace and to keep their protests within constitutional bounds. But if despite their petitions the government chose to 'suffer the Grantees, or their Hirelings, to goad the people on by acts of oppression, to disturbance and bloodshed,' then, warned the Bay Fortune Committee, 'let the guilty be answerable for their conduct.'[104]

The Bay Fortune advice had a sharp ring to it. Unlike many of the effusions of the Escheat excitement of 1832, it carried the notion that realizing agrarian objectives would take time and effective organization. Responding, perhaps, to the worries expressed by committees elsewhere concerning the effect of the address that Pope had steered through the house, the Bay Fortune group contended that it did not pose an immediate danger and that Escheat activists should not let this provocation induce them to 'hurry matters, before the country is sufficiently prepared.' The watchwords of Escheat committees should be 'patience and perseverance.' Noting that some committees were calling for a 'General Meeting of Delegates,' it left it to one of the Queens County committees, which seemed to have originated the notion,[105] to 'name time and place, when the throng of planting is nearly over.' Regarding the issues of sending a delegate to Britain and agitating for dissolution of the assembly, it suggested that energies should be directed towards preparing dissolution petitions for presentation to the new lieutenant-governor and that the delegate idea could be reserved pending Harvey's arrival and his decision on the matter. The thinking of the Bay Fortune group was probably grounded in the hope that Harvey might call a new election and that the Escheat majority it anticipated would then be able to dispatch emissaries who would carry the authority of the will of the assembly and could be paid for out of the public purse.[106] Indications of the tactics that might be employed if Harvey chose not to dissolve the assembly appeared in a letter sent to the *Prince Edward Island Times* in the final days before the Island-wide meeting of delegates. Its author reported that 'a large proportion of the tenantry have mutually agreed to withhold their rents' if the present house was allowed to remain as the Island's representatives.[107]

Besides providing evidence of the new profile that Escheat had gained in Island affairs and the level of organization it had achieved, the meeting of Escheat delegates in Charlottetown at the end of June also revealed something of the tensions that existed among the ranks of those who claimed to be advancing the agrarian cause. Hints of the divisions that were to emerge when the delegates assembled are found in letters submitted to the *Prince Edward Island Times* from the days preceding the gathering. John Macdonald warned that an emissary supposedly acting on behalf of the Escheat cause was moving around the countryside with a petition that was 'at variance with our views and interests.' He wanted, he said, to advise other Escheat advocates not to sign the conciliatory document that Alexander Rae was circulating or to place trust in the leadership of those who were not 'our well tried and known friends.'[108] A similar report came from China Point in Queens County, where the unnamed Rae was said to be disseminating petitions and preaching 'passive obedience to the Proprietors.'[109] Rae's petition was a matter of complaint at a Belfast Escheat meeting where it was alleged, as in the China Point report, that he was working for the proprietors' interests.[110] It is not clear whether these reports were independent of one another, but certainly Rae, who attended the Charlottetown meeting as a Prince County delegate, faced strong opposition within Escheat circles from some who considered him too conservative. Rae later acknowledged that he had had to relinquish some of his early ideas and adopt a much more militant stand on the land question in order to maintain the support of his constituents.[111]

With the rapid growth of Escheat in the second half of the decade, the movement attracted leadership from a variety of quarters. Some may have been acting as much out of an interest in containing and controlling rural agitation as in promoting the objectives of agrarian dissatisfaction. Others, such as Coun Douly Rankin and Abercrombie Willock, who had been defeated in the 1834 Queens County election, may have joined the movement as a means to revive their political fortunes. One can imagine, too, that some of the movement's leaders were individuals who had long been leaders in their communities and who had (as so often happens) been pressed from below to participate in a challenge that went well beyond their own sentiments.[112] In other places more radical leaders had emerged. It is probably no fluke that the most militant voices, such as those of John Le Lacheur and Anthony Dougan, came from districts in Kings and Queens counties where there was a long history of Escheat politics. The differences of opinion that had come to light before the Charlottetown meeting and that were sharply expressed during the gathering reflect the omnibus nature of the Escheat movement and, it would seem, the uneven development of agrarian activism.

Despite such differences, the delegates attending the Charlottetown meeting at the Commercial Inn at the end of June 1836 succeeded in hammering out a series of resolutions on which they could concur. Most importantly, they agreed that the existing majority in the House of Assembly did not represent the interests of Islanders. Pointing to the illegitimacy of that assembly, Anthony Dougan asserted that the Charlottetown meeting expressed the real voice of 'the people.' The 'proceedings of the people' he claimed, were an unstoppable force. Answering his own question, 'Who are the people?' he went on to assert that 'we are the people, at the present time we the Delegates are the people.'[113] The extra-constitutional implications of this sort of language were strained out of the final resolutions, which, in keeping with Dougan's own sentiments, stayed well within the bounds of legality both in order to ensure consensus and 'so that the laws cannot lay hold of the actions of the people or those of their delegates.' The meeting resolved that committees be established in all the counties to petition for the dissolution of the assembly when the new lieutenant-governor arrived. It compiled a list of twenty-two committeemen who would do the organizational work in the three counties. The delegates also resolved to draft a petition countering the one being sent to Britain by the House of Assembly. Beyond this, they tentatively established an electoral strategy for the contest they believed would soon take place. The Escheat committees that were being established under the leadership of the twenty-two designated regional representatives were, when the time came, to hold nomination meetings so that appropriate people might in the future be chosen to represent the rural population in the house.[114]

The political strategy adopted by the Escheat movement straddled the ambiguous line between creating full-blown alternative institutions and creating a modern political party with its own platform, leadership, and riding associations. Like those who were challenging the status quo elsewhere in the British realm at this time, Escheators had no choice but to explore the grey zones between constitutional tactics and physical force.[115] And, like other movements elsewhere, there were diverse opinions on how best to achieve change.[116] Some, such as Alexander Rae, wanted to substantially modify Escheat objectives so that they would pose less of a threat to the existing order and thus could be more easily gained. Others, such as Cooper, were willing to entertain, if necessary, extra-constitutional means to achieve Escheat's original goals.

By the summer of 1836 Escheat forces had gathered considerable momentum. Their growing strength was aided by the absence of a lieutenant-governor to represent the Crown and give credibility to those on the Island who claimed to be speaking for the establishment. Harvey was detained in Britain for months and the Island was without a lieutenant-governor from Young's death in December 1835 until Harvey's arrival at the end of August the following year. As well, the significant challenges to the status quo elsewhere in the Atlantic world lent energy and a sense of legitimacy to those advocating the Escheat cause. Although Joseph Pope might contend that Escheators were isolated malcontents deserving penal exile, Escheat activists were able to see their cause as a locally grown facet of broader progressive transformations. Cooper spoke of the connection between Island events and what the French Revolution had accomplished for that country's peasantry, and land reformers repeatedly drew parallels between the initiatives that had resulted in British emancipation legislation in 1833 and the unshackling of fettered tenants that needed to take place on the Island.[117] Like the leaders of the labour movement in the United States, tenant leaders employed the imagery of slavery to convey their condemnation of existing social relations.[118] Cooper's resort to Romantic poetry in his speech at a large Escheat meeting at Rollo Bay and in an Escheat pamphlet indicated ways in which the movement might be understood as part of a broader transnational struggle for freedom.[119] Escheat advocates also regularly used the ongoing peasant unrest and political struggles in Ireland as examples for the edification and inspiration of rural Islanders, who, Escheators argued, were dealing with similar problems.[120] Though they did not often mention it in their speeches and writings, Escheat's leaders must have been following the growing tensions in other British North American colonies as well. The relationship that Escheat might have with the *Patriote* challenge in Lower Canada was brought to the attention of the assembly in the spring of 1836 when a letter from Papineau calling for all British North American assemblies to support Lower Canada's struggle for constitutional reform was laid before the house. By a narrow party vote during which the two loose fish, Binns and Macdonald, joined with Escheators, the assembly chose to enter it into their journals.[121] Le Lacheur described Papineau as 'not only a genuine patriot, but one of the very best subjects the King of England has in North America.'[122]

Besides deriving confidence and inspiration from the broader patterns of challenge and change developing within the British Empire, and beyond, Escheat drew strength from developments within the colony. The struggle to bring about fundamental changes in agrarian life through formal politics was sustained by broader social and cultural changes. As Escheat assemblymen gained power in the house, the voices they represented outside the assembly became bolder and ideas and perceptions that had previously enjoyed a more subterranean existence began coming to the fore. The report from an Escheat meeting in Belfast described participants who 'declared their sentiments fearlessly and freely,' and noted that '*all* of *them* resolved to unite their energies to obtain Redress of their grievances.' The language is a reminder of the distinction between public and private levels of discourse, between understandings that could be shared openly and those that had to be sustained more surreptitiously, and provides evidence of a broader phenomenon that was occurring.[123] The 1830s was a time when sentiments that might once have been expressed in conversation with a neighbour, or by a shared glance in the presence of one's superiors or, when challenged, by intimidating law officers or posting threatening notices, were becoming more public.[124] Rural people were finding their voice. Leaders like Cooper and Le Lacheur assisted this by combining popular perceptions concerning how the countryside of the Island should be organized with the ideas of thinkers like Locke, Blackstone, Chitty, and others they were less willing to name. As a result a vibrant agrarian ideology was staking a claim to legitimacy in public discourse.[125]

This ideological challenge to the status quo was supported by the emergence of a language of class that articulated the new self-confidence and understandings that were growing among the rural population. As the Escheat movement gathered strength, those associated with it replaced older, upper-class terms for the movement's constituency – the 'peasantry,' 'lower orders,' 'the vulgar,' the 'lower classes' – with a different vocabulary. Escheators spoke in terms of 'the productive classes' or the 'labourious classes.' And they employed a different vocabulary for the other end of the social spectrum as well. In place of the 'more respectable portion of the community' or those 'of higher attainments and respectability,' they began to speak of 'that class which draw their subsistence from the labour of others' and to talk publicly about Island history as a struggle between the productive and the parasitical, between 'worker bees' and 'drones.' This new vocabulary supported a radical social analysis. To describe the current ordering of society in this fashion was not just to suggest the possibility of change, but to call for it. If society was to be healthy, the creativity of 'the productive classes' needed to be freed from the burden of the parasitical, who by definition were unnecessary. As well, the new vocabulary sustained Escheat's demands for political change. To call for the state to uphold the interests of 'the vulgar' or the 'lowest classes' was problematic. Although such a demand could be integrated into a paternalistic framework – and to some extent was during the early years of the Escheat movement – doing so undermined demands that the state be controlled or guided by the lower classes. To speak in terms of 'the productive classes,' however, was to use a vocabulary that sustained claims for political power (and permitted a broad alliance) and that also supported demands for the state to protect labouring people's interests. Moreover, the vocabulary of productivity expressed the sense of class pride that was emerging in tandem with the growth of the Escheat movement.[126]

As far as the printed word was concerned, the possibilities for public expression were enlarged enormously when the *Prince Edward Island Times* opened shop in March 1836. Before this, one could read Escheat sentiments in the columns of the *Royal Gazette* and in committee reports published in the journals of the House of Assembly, but these venues were limited in terms of the types of material that could be published and the tone that was permissible. The new paper's editor, William Rankin, was a newcomer who had arrived on the Island in the early 1830s from Demerara. It seems that he was related to a leading player in the Belfast Escheat movement, Coun Douly Rankin. William Rankin made the columns of his paper available for a variety of anti-establishment materials. In this way he promoted the development of an Escheat literature and enabled cultural expressions to flower that previously might have reached only local audiences.[127] His publication of 'A.B.''s 'Irregular Stanzas. On a late and Important event,' for instance, allowed Island residents well beyond Pinnette, on the Selkirk estate, to savour the charivari for the land agent William Douse after the conclusion of the 1836 session of the assembly and to share in that community's poetic ridicule of the three-hundred-pound rent collector:[128]

As Cursty black and Blubberhead
Snugly in their bed were laid,
They awoke and began for to wonder,
Thought the devil was come
To take them there from
For the house it rattled like thunder.
Blubby jump'd from the bed
Cursty lay as if dead
Blubberhead stood amazed on the floor,

Bawling and roaring
As if there was pouring
Grape shot and bombshells at the door
...
O that I had
Not been so bad
In pursuing my selfish view,
But now too late
For to repent
I must bid them all adieu.
When daylight came
He took his flight
And ran in consternation,
To tell his friends
In Charlottetown,
That Pinette was in agitation.[129]

Rankin's new paper served to amplify the traditional rites of an offended community dealing with those who had violated local norms, just as the *Royal Gazette* had served to disseminate the elite's discourse to a broader audience.[130] And it did so in ways that reinforced popular sentiments and popular ways of expressing them. The significance of such a paper to agrarian radicalism on the Island was not lost on local observers with more conservative views. 'Satiricus' argued that the main body of people on the Island were 'ripe' for insurrection and that 'every number of such a paper will do the work of a hundred incendiary "swings"' – a reference to contemporaneous rural unrest in England.[131]

The satirical lines that the *Prince Edward Island Times* published in issue after issue point to a broader phenomenon sustaining the Escheat challenge both before and after the brief career of the paper. Most of the poetry, ballads, and spoofs that reinforced lower-class perspectives surely never made it into print; instead they would have moved in a more intimate fashion from house to house and tavern to tavern. A bitter critique of Samuel Cunard and his land agent, Samuel Peters, composed by a MacLean from Raasay, was maintained in this manner for more than half a century before being committed to print in Cape Breton's Gaelic newspaper *MacTalla*.[132] The poetry and ballads that are extant point to the relationship between this popular culture and the appeal of the Escheat movement. This literature reveals recurrent themes that were central to the Escheat struggle. MacLean of Raasay's ballad

'Complaint About America' speaks to the fear of eviction – 'and, if he doesn't die / we must leave this place' – as well as to the immorality of landlord behaviour – 'He will ultimately receive retribution / where he will not be able to use it [rent monies].' Similarly, the central lines of A.B.'s 'Irregular stanzas' alluded to the ethical vacuity of land agent's behaviour: 'Oh that I had / Not been so bad / In pursuing my selfish view, / But now too late / For to repent / I must bid them all adieu.' Momus's 'The Fox and the Bear' phrased it more bitterly: 'A few that suck the paps of power / In various ways their kind devour, / And hold the snouts of half a nation / Unto the grindstone of starvation.'[133] The popular notion that the existing structure and use of power was immoral – a theme strongly sustained in the folk culture – was central to virtually all Escheat petitions; the fear of losing a hard-won toehold on the land was also a common one.

The decline of paternalism was yet another recurrent theme and often informed considerations of immoral upper-class behaviour. Many would have brought this leitmotif with them from the Old World. Rory Roy MacKenzie's 'The Emigration' captures both the bitterness felt towards Highland overlords who had failed to abide by their social obligations, who 'reject us completely,' and the hope cherished at the time of sailing for Prince Edward Island in the first decade of the nineteenth century, for new relationships on the other side of the sea: 'If it be the benign Selkirk / who will grant us a place, / with my children I am eager / to sail without delay.'[134] 'Tit-for-Tat's 'His Lordship's S[hoes]' picks up on the immigrant's experience on Prince Edward Island by exploring what had become of relations on the Selkirk estate thirty years later. The promise of benevolent paternalism in MacKenzie's lines has led to a pathetic and immoral betrayal in those of Tit-for-Tat's:

Beware my Lord of the disgrace
That hirelings bring upon your name,
It ill suits one of noble race
To sanction deeds of sin and shame,
To represent you, is it fit
You should an ignoramus choose.
For 'muckle head and little wit'
Is standing in your lordship's shoes,
...

'Twas argued once that negroes were
Like brutes, and should be bought and sold;
Tis here affirmed that farmers are
Filth, scum, and fiends in human mould.
Oppression makes a wise man mad,
'Twould make a Job his patience lose.
Few petty tyrants are so bad
As he who fills your Lordship's shoes.

The 'scum' reference is to Pope's assembly speech denouncing Escheators; 'muckle head' is William Douse, Selkirk's agent.

Escheat pamphlets were yet another means to maintain and disseminate an agrarian literature. In one of these, printed in the summer of 1836, William Cooper picked up on the themes of morality and changing social relations, the appropriate relationship between people and the land, and the relationship between what had happened in the Old World and the hopes that rural people entertained for the New:

> In the old fashioned times the lands were considered to be for the use of the people, to give them employment and subsistence, to raise and maintain a hardy race for the support and defense of the country – but, according to the improved system, the land is not for the use of the people, but for the proprietor – and as the lands will yield more if cultivated by a few useful hands, without women or children, the supernumeraries are turned off to the manufacturing towns and the colonies, and villages are turned into sheep pastures and pleasure grounds; we have a right to expect from the improved method that as soon as the lands are cleared, the present inhabitants will be turned off to make room for large farms, which will either sell or let at a greater advantage; and when the present inhabitants are removed there will be no more complaints against proprietors, because the people who were deceived and deprived of the lands they have taken out of the wilderness will be either buried or removed.[135]

Cooper's analysis of the threat that 'yield more' and 'greater advantage' posed to those who had hoped to build anew on the western rim of the Atlantic was rooted in a popular rural understanding. The argument that the land should be used to sustain a hardy populace that would support and defend the nation echoes these words of Rory Roy MacKenzie: 'If it be sheep-walks / which will replace men, / Scotland will then / become a wasteland for France. / When the arrogant Bonaparte comes / with his heavy hand, / the shepherds will be badly off, / and we will not grieve for them.'[136] And Cooper's concern that Old World patterns were about to be repeated in the New echoes, of course, the worries of men like MacLean of Raasay, who were afraid they were about to be cleared from the lands yet again. Here can be found both a lament for the decline of the paternal order and a critique of the capitalist agriculture that was emerging in its stead. Both positions underlined the need to act to secure a new order that would protect the interests of small producers.

The literature that began to blossom in the *Prince Edward Island Times,* in pamphlets, and occasionally in the *Royal Gazette* in the mid-1830s injected a popular agrarian perspective into the world of print and in so doing both reflected and helped propel the ongoing Escheat challenge. An account of the immigrant experience by 'Philanthropist,' written in a style somewhat similar to Thomas McCulloch's *The Stepsure Letters* and Thomas Chandler Haliburton's *The Clockmaker,* speaks to the alternative vision that was being constructed and to its divergence from views that had previously held sway.[137] The Emigrant, having been passed from Mr Crimp (an attorney and land agent for 'the Lord in England)' onto Squire Clod (Crimp's factotum in the countryside), encounters difficulties in reconciling what he has learned of the Island from promotional literature with what he observes in person. Over time, he is enlightened and comes to recognize something of Island realities. The dark people dressed in rags who directed him to Squire Clod's were neither blacks nor Native Americans but new settlers experiencing the joys of burning and clearing. The vacant holding the Emigrant was to let turns out to be occupied. Sandy Ban, whose farm he is to have, is an old settler who has endured the ordeals of land breaking and of cutting ice two feet thick so that his family might survive hungry winters by digging clams. Through unending labour and sacrifice he has succeeded in creating a holding capable of supporting his family; unfortunately, he is incapable of supporting a landlord as well. After a lifetime of work, he must give up his holding for arrears. Why, the immigrant asks the squire, had he not learned about *this* reality from what he had been able to read in England? And how could it be that Sandy had had it so hard when it was widely understood in Britain that landlords had been at great expense to see to their tenants' needs? 'Bookmakers,' he is told, 'must tell good stories, that people may buy them; and as the books written about this Island are to please the landlords in England and to induce emigrants to clear land for them, the more that are deceived by them the better they will be paid.' The Emigrant's response, that 'a historian' who conceals what 'ought to be made known' is helping build something 'equally dangerous as a lie,' captured a central aspect of the agrarian critique of the status quo and of the version of Island reality that sustained it – that fundamental truths about rural life were being left unsaid. The Emigrant's physical and psychological journey from the world view reproduced in landlord literature to the truth as represented in Sandy Ban's concrete circumstances reiterated a recurrent theme in Escheat writings and in the Escheat challenge itself: that to combat exploitation and build a new order required an account of Island history that was true to the experiences of the rural population.

By the summer of 1836, Escheat had become more than the quietly shared hope of countrypeople and more than an issue for petitions; it had become a social movement of considerable force rooted in an alternative construction of the Island's past, present, and possible future. The Island-wide meeting of delegates held in the end of June demonstrated the growing strength and organizational maturity of the agrarian challenge.

8 Harvey and the Escheators, 1836–1837

Many in the ranks of the Escheators hoped that Lieutenant-Governor John Harvey's arrival in the colony would be a watershed. They firmly believed that he would see the merits of their request for new elections and, once a majority that reflected rural sentiments assumed leadership in the assembly, that he would help them make their case known at the highest echelons of the British government. To this end, prior to his arrival they began to prepare massive petitions setting forth agrarian grievances and asking that the governor dissolve the House of Assembly. These hopes proved to be misplaced. Indeed, Harvey would work strenuously to help sustain those who were opposed to the Escheators and to suppress the Escheat movement. Nonetheless, Escheat continued to gather strength over the short course of his administration.

Harvey came from a relatively humble background. After a successful military career, he had been able to rise to the position of colonial governor. He was not unacquainted with tenant unrest and New World land questions: in the mid-1820s he had been a member of the five-person commission appointed to determine the price at which wilderness lands in Upper Canada were to be sold to the Canada Company. In the years prior to his appointment as lieutenant-governor of Prince Edward Island, he was inspector general of police in Leinster, Ireland, which was the heartland of the agrarian disturbances associated with the tithe war. There he distinguished himself as a conciliator who gained support from partisans on both sides of the conflict and who sought compromises that would avoid violence. He would try to play a similar role on Prince Edward Island.[1]

Soon after taking up residence in Charlottetown in August 1836, Harvey embarked on journeys to the western and eastern sections of the Island, partly in order to investigate reports of serious crop failures. The trip was an opportunity to see the countryside and meet Island notables. While in the west he stayed with the Popes; in the east he was entertained in Georgetown by a delegation headed by Thomas Owen and Angus Macdonald, prominent merchants and shipbuilders who owned and/or managed local estates. Although Harvey had intended to venture more broadly about the Island, weather and the road conditions limited his travels. Others, claiming to be speaking on behalf of rural Islanders, who had as yet had little occasion to gain the governor's ear, soon came to Charlottetown to see him. On 13 October 1836 a deputation of Escheators from Kings County presented Harvey with a petition with 1,300 signatures, and on 24 October a Queens County deputation submitted a petition with 1,870 signatures. Both petitions complained that the assembly was not representing their views on the land question and asked that he call new elections.[2] Together, these two petitions represented the appeals of more than half the adult male population of the two counties – a remarkable testament to the extent of Escheat support and to the movement's organizing ability.[3] Harvey informed the Kings County deputation that he could not in fairness assent to their request that he dissolve the assembly, as the petition was that of only a portion of a much broader community. As well, he pleaded that he needed time to acquire an understanding of Island circumstances before responding to their ex parte statement concerning the history of the land question and Island politics. At the same time, he indicated that he did not believe an escheat would be of much benefit. In any case, a 'Royal decision' on the matter was expected soon, and he trusted they would all abide by it, whatever it might be.[4]

The posture Harvey assumed, much to his own surprise, did not appear to make him unpopular with Escheators, although they were disappointed with it.[5] Had they known the governor's real sentiments and intentions, his initial policies would have received a much chillier reception. Whatever his claims about the need for time to learn about Island questions, Harvey had charted his course on the question of escheat before he ever set foot on the Island. Prior to leaving Britain he had familiarized himself with Island affairs by reading over correspondence and records at the Colonial Office.[6] He had sought and gained the advice of Colonel John Ready concerning Island issues and individuals in the colony he could rely upon. Most importantly, he had spent a good deal of time meeting with those associated with the Prince Edward Island Association (PEIA).[7] Robert Stewart thoughtfully provided him with an index to much of the material in the Colonial Office and with Island papers dealing with the revival of Escheat activism in the colony.[8] While familiarizing Harvey with the land company's plans and their potential significance to Island development, the Stewarts and their associates drew his attention to the threat of Escheat agitation.[9] They assured Harvey that if he acted to ensure that the Imperial government vigorously upheld proprietorial claims to Island properties, they in turn would guarantee the colony's rapid economic development. Harvey was thus persuaded that the possibility of escheat action was the central question in Island affairs and that the issue needed to be exorcised from Island politics. He believed he would enhance his career by doing so and made this his primary object. In keeping with the advice of the Stewarts and others, before he left Britain he attempted to obtain an unambiguous Imperial dispatch that would say no to escheat for once and for all. He sought as well to induce the Colonial Office to provide proprietors with fee simple titles that could not be challenged.[10] Within days of his arrival he penned a dispatch reiterating his arguments: the 'slight degree of excitement upon the question of escheat' he had discovered would be permanently set to rest with an appropriate declaration of final British policy.[11] It was this repeatedly requested decisive no that he was referring to when he told Kings County Escheators that they needed to abide by the royal decision whenever it was announced and whatever it would be.

The new colonial secretary, Lord Glenelg, responding to the contentious escheat address the assembly had forwarded in April and to the appeals of Harvey and the proprietors, drafted a vigorous denial of escheat at the end of August, days before the governor wrote his first dispatch from the colony. To the governor's delight, it arrived before he needed to respond to the Queens County delegation.[12] Harvey had it published in the *Royal Gazette* so that it would be available for the public immediately.[13] In the dispatch, Glenelg argued that the settlement terms of the original grants – which were in some fashion to form the basis of any escheat – were impractical and thus the requirement had always been 'to all useful purposes, nugatory.' Beyond this, following the lines of earlier dispatches on the matter, he contended that there was no way to prove that lots without adequate numbers of settlers had not once been sufficiently peopled by their proprietors. Picking up on the developmental arguments that had informed the partial escheat position since it first emerged in the assembly in 1832, Glenelg defined the issue in the following terms: The 'evil' the assembly's escheat measures were concerned about rectifying was 'the uncultivated state of the Island by reason of want of settlers.' While escheat was out of the question, this fundamental problem could be handled by introducing a land tax that would penalize speculation. To this end, he passed on an Upper Canadian act that might serve as a model and promised that the Colonial Office would support fair legislation tailored to ensure that speculators gave up their lands to those willing to develop them.

Drawing the Queens County petitioners' attention to Glenelg's dispatch, Harvey announced that this represented a '*final* decision' on the escheat question and that they needed to turn their attention to their 'individual interests' and 'abstain from any further efforts' to gain an escheat.[14] Reiterating his refusal to dissolve the assembly, he indicated that he was optimistic that the current representatives would serve the colony well by passing useful measures in the coming session. His remarks no doubt reflected conversations he had had with leading members of the house. Before receiving Glenelg's dispatch, Harvey had written to the colonial secretary about the need for a land tax to sustain government expenditures for internal improvements and to force the sale or settlement of unimproved lands. He knew these matters were dear to the interests of the mercantile community, and the road now seemed open for legislative initiatives in this regard.[15] From his communications with Ready, and with government officials and members of the assembly such as Joseph Pope and George Dalrymple, Harvey had good reason to believe that if he could help the assembly gain greater revenues and expand their patronage and power, they in turn would support his leadership. Harvey's intention, following in Ready's path, was to support developmental policies, and the taxation strategies that went with them, and in so doing to develop a coalition of business leaders responsive to his needs.[16] He believed that by placing greater revenues in the hands of the assembly and allowing it a central role in promoting economic growth, he would be establishing a middle way that would enhance the political power of the colony's developmentally oriented merchants. This would weaken the Escheat movement and at the same time draw to his side those enlightened proprietors who recognized that a moderate land tax would help them secure their property rights.[17]

From the tenantry's perspective, the autumn of 1836 brought a harvest of disappointments. The governor had refused to dissolve the assembly, and Glenelg's dispatch had reiterated that the British would refuse to permit the establishment of a court of escheat; in the heels of all this came devastating frosts that cut deeply into the potato and grain harvests. One farm diary entry dated 9 September described the circumstances succinctly: 'Last night a very heavy frost which killed the potatoe [*sic*] tops and all the late grain, the two succeeding nights were just the same which entirely compleated the job.'[18] David Ross, a farmer on Lot 34, reported an earlier loss of some potatoes to a 21 July frost. Like the unidentified author of the first farm diary, he also noted the extraordinary severity of the 'hard frost' of 7–8 September, which killed his potato tops and those all across the Island.[19] Much of the potato crop around New London was said to have been destroyed by the July frost, but the destruction that came in September was Island-wide and unprecedented in its scope, in that it took both the potato and grain crops.[20] Particularly hard hit were newer and poorer settlers, who had little or no livestock and whose farm operations revolved almost entirely around grains and potatoes. With the failure of the crops, the prices for provisions soared in local markets. Some in the merchant community moved to import flour to take advantage of the scarcity of provisions. By early October there were concerns that unless an embargo was placed on the export of produce there would be a crisis of subsistence for many on the Island come spring.[21]

The assembly responded to the short-term needs of settlers by providing £1,500 for the emergency provision of seed potatoes and seed grain for spring planting, as well as £250 for emergency food supplies for the needy – costs that came close to the amounts usually spent on the entire roads budget.[22] As well, the assembly prohibited the export of foodstuffs.[23] Many rural Islanders, though, had come to believe that the government could and should address the fundamental long-term difficulties they faced. Besides the emergency help, which they welcomed, they wanted effective action on the land question.

In the weeks between the Island-wide meeting of Escheat delegates in late June and the presentation of the Kings and Queens County petitions to Harvey in October 1836, extensive organizational work had been done in the countryside. Behind the more than three thousand signatures lay numerous meetings organized by those who had been assigned this task by the central Escheat committee. As one critic complained, the countryside was crawling with 'certain persons ... that have assumed the name of Delegates, who, as well as their deputies, are strolling from settlement to settlement, prejudicing the hitherto peaceable and honest tenantry against their landlords' and against

Map 8.1. Escheat meetings, July 1836 to June 1837

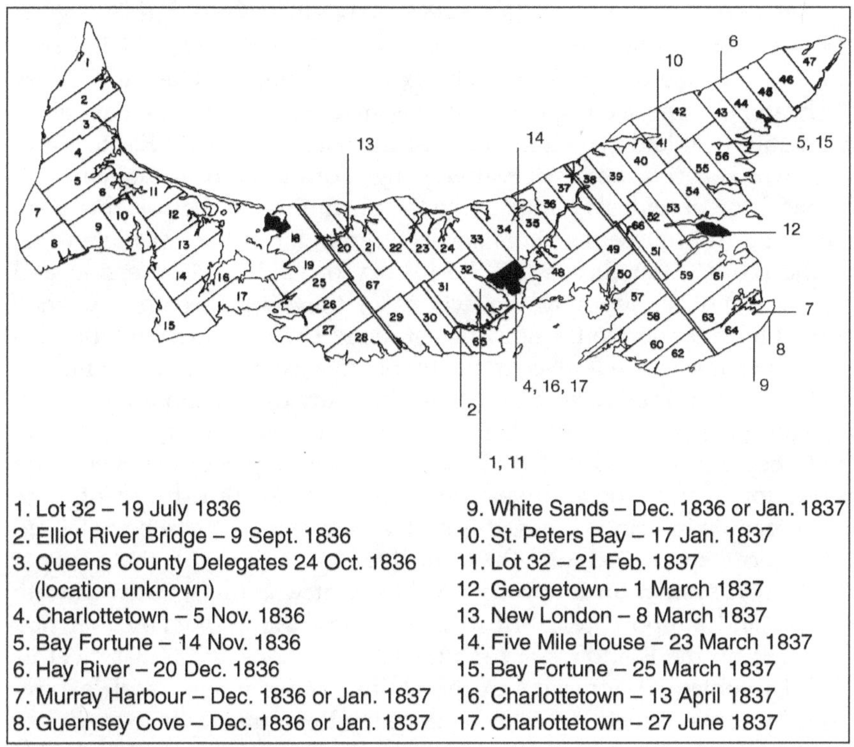

Source: *Royal Gazette*; *Prince Edward Island Times*

the assembly.[24] They were, this critic charged, convening small meetings all around the countryside to collect signatures and telling those who came that with a new House of Assembly in place they 'should all have king's land before the end of twelve months.' Some of these meetings were individually reported in Island papers, but many were not (see map 8.1). While the claims concerning promises made at these meetings should not be taken at face value, the general description of the political activity in the countryside was certainly correct.

A report from a large petition-signing gathering at Elliot River Bridge in Queens County reveals the importance of these meetings not only for generating documents that could be used at Government House or the Colonial Office but also as forums for building collective understandings and engaging in political debate. The assemblyman John Small

Macdonald attended the Elliot River meeting. The *Royal Gazette* reported that 'an animated discussion' took place as he attempted to defend – with what seems to have been minimal success – his conduct in the house against the charges of prominent Queens County Escheators.[25] The lead speaker at this meeting was James Bagnall, a moderate who had been a member of the Society of Loyal Electors and who was now on the conservative fringes of the Escheat movement.[26] His address provides a glimpse into the positions and rhetoric that were emerging from these meetings and is a reminder of the volatile temper of the times. After discussing the history of landlord oppression and injustice and condemning the actions of the 14th Assembly, Bagnall turned his attention to the activities of the PEIA. He contended that this 'new Directory' – a reference to the five-man executive body that named and controlled ministers in France in the years of reaction after the fall of Robespierre – had established itself as yet another governmental body beyond the tripartite division of legislative power between commons, lords, and king and was thus perverting the British constitution. Rural people in Prince Edward Island, he contended, were being asked by government officials and the local elite to submit to rule that was not the British system 'in its purity.' Although it was the settlers' duty to 'revere and support' real British institutions, the perversion that had emerged on the Island deserved no such allegiance and 'must meet its fall.' Discontented agrarians in the United States framed their aspirations in terms of their rights as heirs of the Revolution; those on Prince Edward Island based similar arguments on their due as the king's subjects.[27] Bagnall believed that Escheat forces would prevail by petition and the dispatch of a delegation, and he certainly had no intention of provoking a revolt against the Crown, but his remarks show the extent to which the public language, even of conservative voices within Escheat ranks, was edging towards militancy.

Harvey's actions and Glenelg's dispatch momentarily checked the momentum of the Escheat movement. The governor's refusal to dissolve the assembly undercut the excitement and organizational energies that Escheators were directing towards an expected election. Indeed, after reading Glenelg's dispatch some came to believe that the Escheat cause was altogether lost. For others it confirmed their concerns about the impact of the contentious address authored by Joseph Pope, which had been sent during the 1836 session of the assembly. Instead of taking it as proof that the Escheat cause was hopeless, they instead saw that dispatch as further evidence that they needed to carry their message to

Britain directly by delegation and to organize in the colony more effectively to ensure that politicians subversive to the Escheat cause did not dominate the assembly and mislead the Imperial government.[28] Both responses, however, postponed the day of reckoning until such time as a delegation could be dispatched or a new election was called.

Harvey was able to deliver these blows to the agrarian movement without damaging his image among Escheat forces in part because he effectively hid the role he had played in constructing the anti-Escheat policies emanating from the Colonial Office. He assumed instead the appearance of a conciliator anxious to learn the real circumstances and to help construct solutions. Also, he was able to capitalize on his position as representative of the Crown. As he and others repeatedly noted, the Island's people were in general 'most affectionably attached to the King.'[29] For this reason the royal representative on the Island, so long as he played his part skilfully, could exercise a good deal of leadership. The Escheat movement was built in large part on notions of loyalty and constitutionality, and many of its leaders repeatedly spoke of the struggle in terms of British justice. Loyalty, though, was a two-edged sword. It could inspire revolt, as in Bagnall's and Cooper's suggestions that loyal subjects had a right to struggle against a perversion of the real order; and, alternatively, it could subdue it when a credible figure such as Harvey appealed for loyalty and submission. Because the meaning of the idea of loyalty itself was in dispute, at least insofar as it applied to Island affairs, rapid shifts in the allegiance of consistently 'loyal' Island subjects were possible. Although Harvey initially invoked loyalty rhetoric to his advantage, he soon realized that it was easier to gain influence over popular opinion, than to retain it, and easier to define appropriate behaviour, than to enforce it.

In the late fall of 1836, Escheat activists were forced to reconsider their position and chart their course in the context of Glenelg's dispatch, the disastrous harvest, and Harvey's refusal to dissolve the assembly. These developments had generated a good deal of discouragement – indeed, they were the occasion for some of the movement's leaders to give up the cause. For tenants faced with mounting arrears and the immediate and urgent problems arising from a ruinous harvest, the hope of relief from their difficulties must have seemed ever more distant. Cooper later spoke of the discontent born of these discouragements and of having, as a leader, to respond to this and attempt to channel these feelings along what he believed to be constructive lines.[30] It seems that the Escheat leaders faced a dual challenge: they needed to contain manifestations of frustration and bitterness even while sustaining faith in the ultimate success of the primarily constitutional means the Escheat movement had adopted to bring about land reform.

County meetings to chart Escheat strategy were held in November in Queens County and a week later in Kings. According to the published report of the Kings County meeting, the Escheators absolved Harvey of responsibility for the unfavourable turn of affairs. Instead, Glenelg's dispatch was held up as another indication that greater organizational work was needed in order to educate Imperial policy makers. To get the Escheat movement rolling again, they resolved to hold a mass meeting at Hay River in northern Kings County at the end of December to consider a draft – which a committee would frame – of a major petition to be taken to Great Britain by a delegation. Once approved by the residents of northern Kings County, the petition would be taken to other districts for refinement and ratification.[31]

Although it was not noted in the published report of the proceedings of this meeting, those present also discussed rent resistance. The idea of using rent resistance to respond to a refusal to dissolve the assembly had gained currency in the summer months before Harvey arrived and before the disastrous harvest undercut the ability of tenants to pay their rents. Moreover, the Bay Fortune committee had been arguing since spring that rent resistance was an appropriate response to the British government's failure to permit the establishment of a court of escheat. Cooper would later argue, at a time when he was under intense official scrutiny, that he had been prompted to include resolutions calling for rent resistance in the petition he helped draft for Hay River by pressure from below that had emerged in the Escheat meeting of mid-November.[32] Macintosh made this same argument.[33] It is possible that their contentions were defensive and self-serving; even so, they are consistent with later attempts on their part to keep Escheat activists from charting too radical and confrontational a course.[34] Moreover, having been made publicly, their statements could have been refuted by anyone else present at the meeting. They were not. Members of the elite tended to view rent resistance as the work of dangerous individuals who were misleading a gullible tenantry; however, a close reading of the evidence suggests that Escheat leaders in the second half of the decade had to scramble to contain and keep ahead of more militant popular initiatives.[35]

Radical demands had their roots in the desperate economic circumstances facing much of the tenantry at this time. Even those who lacked sympathy for the Escheat cause were in agreement that many rural Islanders had no means to meet their rent payments in the aftermath of the harvest failures of the 1830s.[36] Cooper estimated that perhaps one in five could afford to cover their rents and/or arrears.[37] Under these circumstances, collective rent refusal and collective resistance to legal proceedings made sense not only in political terms – as a way to pressure the government to act – but also as an immediate strategy by which those tenants who were in financial difficulties might gain time and preserve a livelihood for their families. Without a collective refusal, those least able to pay rents and arrears were liable to lose their livestock and supplies, and perhaps their farms, one by one and at any time. By acting together they could impede the legal process by intimidating law officers and moving livestock and valuables away from farms where distress proceedings were to take place. The more broadly tenants resisted, the greater the immediate security they might gain, since the overtaxed legal and law enforcement system would be unable to respond effectively to their obstructions. Cooper's task, and that of other Escheat leaders, was in part to find words and arguments to justify the strategy of broad rent resistance – a strategy that their rural supporters wanted to follow for practical as well as political reasons.

Because the public meeting at Hay River on 20 December was intended as the first of a series of gatherings focusing on a new petition, Escheat delegates from across the Island attended it, along with residents from northeastern Kings County. Having participated in discussions of the draft of the new petition, delegates from elsewhere were then to take it home with them and present it to local meetings for confirmation and refinement.[38] Some who had come from a distance seem to have arrived the night before the meeting and to have joined local Escheators in reviewing and discussing the documents to be presented the following day.[39] The petition covered familiar ground concerning the history of the land question and the Escheat position. Among other things, it noted that most tenants were 'greatly in arrear' for rents and that if their collection were fully enforced it 'would absorb the whole stock and improvements' of many who had laboured for decades to carve out farms. The resolutions of the day called for the formation of two committees: one to work with Escheat committees in Queens and Prince counties to refine and ratify the petition, the other to oversee a subscription fund to subsidize the dispatch of an Escheat delegation to Britain.

More controversially, the resolutions accompanying the petition called for rent resistance. Turning the arguments of Pope and Green and the proprietors on their heads, the Hay River resolutions argued that landlords and their government allies had subverted the British system and violated all standards of justice. A true understanding of Island history revealed that the machinations of landlords and their proxies were 'wickedness in the sight of God, derogatory to the honour and dignity of the King and the British Nation, and subversive of the sacred right of property.' To 'pay rent to such landlords, under such circumstances,' was 'to foster oppression and to reward crime.' Those attending the meeting resolved that 'by the sacred obligations of religion – by the honour and dignity of the King and British nation – by the rights of men to the fruits of their labour,' and 'by justice and equity' they would 'preserve from the distress of such landlords the fruits of our industry.' Like those who collected rents, Escheat resisters laid claim to patriotism, religious integrity, adherence to justice, and the right to defend their own sacred claims of property.

Behind the shared language were, of course, different meanings. While landlords and their supporters conceptualized property in terms of state-derived title, Escheat leaders viewed property as the product of labour. And while the one found justice in court rulings, the other found it in local understandings concerning the distribution of resources. Escheators were not seeking an end to private property or to state involvement in securing it; rather, they wanted to bring the state on side. They wanted it to uphold the property rights in land derived from labour – rights that in rural communities were understood as legitimate. And they maintained that the British system in its purity promised this. The parallels between the thinking that emerged on Prince Edward Island and that informing land protests in the United States in the late eighteenth and nineteenth centuries are striking. Although the political culture in which agrarian protest was expressed on Prince Edward Island was different from that in the United States, and although the patriotic references were divergent, the fundamental propositions animating rural unrest on both sides of the border were of a kind: that labour created property; that those who created productive farms from the wilderness therefore had property rights in them; that the existing political system, properly understood, secured this natural right; and that justice lay in resisting those who said otherwise. Agrarian protest, then, raised fundamental questions about the meaning of citizenship, about the nature of property and of laws, and, significantly, about how states maintained their legitimacy.[40]

Although the resolutions that Cooper and other members of the Bay Fortune committee drafted for the Hay River meeting were in part tailored to meet the wishes of the tenantry of Kings County, and appear to have gained their support, they clearly were not in accord with the desires of some of the Escheat leaders who had journeyed from other districts. At the end of the meeting, local Escheators held a dinner for the members of distant committees. As Donald Macdonald's official report noted pointedly, 'several went away without notice' and others excused themselves and did not stay. Even among the twenty-seven who remained, he noted, the meal 'was hurried over, as if they had been travellers, who desired to be at home.' Policy disagreements among Escheat committeemen had been resolved in Charlottetown in June by the adoption of a moderate line. The Hay River resolutions represented a more militant, confrontational policy. Cooper, Le Lacheur, and Macintosh were willing to chair a meeting openly calling for rent resistance and obstruction of land proceedings, and were supported in this by a number of prominent Kings County Escheators; but there were others involved in the movement who would not do so. It remained to be seen who spoke for the sentiments of the tenantry as a whole and whether there were significant regional differences in tenant radicalism.

The Hay River resolutions quickly gained support elsewhere in Kings County. Meetings in Murray Harbour, Guernsey Cove, and White Sands in the southern part of the county endorsed the Hay River position and submitted their proceedings to the *Royal Gazette*. They were not, however, published. Instead, on the instigation of Governor Harvey, the editor, James Haszard, submitted an apology for printing the 'seditious' resolutions of the Hay River meeting.[41] Having seen the rent resistance resolutions in Haszard's paper, Harvey threatened to revoke Haszard's contracts with the Crown if he did not mend his ways.[42] The apology and subsequent refusals to print other radical Escheat documents followed. Escheators held yet another meeting to consider the Hay River petition and resolutions, at St Peters in northwestern Kings County, in mid-January. Peter McCallum, the fourth Kings County representative, was present and publicly opposed the two resolutions that called for rent resistance. While he understood that 'people could not pay their rent,' he nonetheless felt that they should pay whatever they could. As for the call to resist the enforcement of landlord's claims, he asserted that it was 'unconstitutional' and would 'end in bloodshed.' Cooper opposed him in debate, and except for Thomas Irwin, who supported McCallum, the two to three hundred people present endorsed the Hay River position.[43] That McCallum, who lived in St Peters and represented that area of the county in the assembly, could be overridden in a meeting on his home turf suggested that more moderate leaders elsewhere might also be out of step with rank-and-file sentiment in the Escheat movement.

The radical Hay River initiative had hardly gotten under way before Harvey threw his considerable power against it. The *Prince Edward Island Times* had folded with William Rankin's departure from the colony, leaving the *Royal Gazette* as the Island's only paper, so Harvey's threats to Haszard blocked unrestrained expressions of the radical Escheat perspective in an important public forum. Harvey then moved to deal with those who had articulated it. The governor'office sent letters to the three Kings County assemblymen who had chaired the Hay River meeting demanding an explanation for resolutions that called on tenants, in Harvey's words, 'to resist, by an illegal combination, the Law of the land' and that had a 'tendency to encourage similar combinations in other parts of the Island.'[44] Their responses, the letter said, would determine the measures the governor would adopt to 'vindicate and uphold the supremacy of the Laws.' When the assembly convened again in late January, Harvey submitted this correspondence along with a request that it deal with the miscreants. Included in his message was a lengthy denunciation of continuing escheat agitation in general and a pointed condemnation of William Cooper, John Le Lacheur, and John Macintosh. They were guilty, he said, of acting to 'inculcate sentiments inconsistent alike with law and with common honesty,' and their conduct was 'utterly at variance with the well-being of society within the Colony.'[45]

The assembly readily followed Harvey's lead. Not surprisingly, those who had been part of the majority who sustained Pope's substitute escheat address to the Imperial government the previous year eagerly took up the governor's charge. The three members who had presided at Hay River protested that they had not knowingly stepped across the line into illegal actions and apologized for appearing to have done so, but the majority of the assembly would have none of their contrition.[46] Thomas MacNutt, William Clark, John Ramsay, and Peter McCallum, who had in the past voted with Cooper, Le Lacheur, and Macintosh, advocated adoption of a relatively mild condemnation and apology, but the majority, led by Pope, condemned them in the strongest terms. They stood accused not only of disloyalty and inciting rent resistance but also of 'false and scandalous libel on this House' for having suggested, among other things, that the anti-escheat position assumed by the 1836 session was related to the land agencies held by members such as Pope, Thornton, and Douse.[47] The apology the majority demanded of them required admissions that, as McCallum put it, the assembly could 'never expect any independent honest man to submit to.'[48] When the three refused the apology, as expected, the assembly found them in contempt and committed them to the care of the sergeant-at-arms for the duration of the session, which meant that they lost their salaries, their right to be part of the proceedings, and their freedom of movement during the period the assembly was in session.

Harvey had given much thought to the appropriate way of dealing with Cooper, Le Lacheur, and Macintosh. Although he was not entirely pleased with the harshness of the apology the assembly demanded from them, events had unfolded as he wanted. He had considered having them expelled from the assembly and had been approached on the idea, but had decided against it, realizing that despite the official condemnations, the three would probably be re-elected and thus vindicated.[49] Although Harvey believed that their actions had been unconstitutional and perhaps 'treasonable,' he hesitated to put them on trial, both because he feared that a jury might find them innocent and because he realized that such a trial would provide a focus for continuing agitation. Whatever the outcome, he feared that the Escheat movement was likely to emerge the stronger for it.[50] As well, at some point he was advised by law officers that he might be wrong about what constituted an illegal act.[51]

Harvey's aggressive policy took the three assemblymen by surprise. At least initially, it also undermined their confidence and isolated them, thus widening earlier divisions within the Escheat movement. Their surprise at the governor's response to the Hay River resolutions was understandable, as tenant meetings had passed similar resolutions at a local level in the past and published them without provoking such actions.[52] That their opponents in the assembly would seize the opportunity to condemn and punish them was to be expected, but the compliance of McCallum, MacNutt, Clark, and Ramsay – all fellow escheat advocates – clearly was disorienting. Defending his position before the assembly's Committee of Privileges and Elections, Cooper stood by the justice underlying his actions but indicated that he had come to doubt the wisdom of the resolutions. Having been opposed on the matter by Harvey and the assembly and 'many whom he thought his friends,' and having found that 'they were viewed in a different light' by people 'whose opinion he respected,' he seemed unsure about his judgment.[53] Macintosh's remark that even if the Escheat leaders had not 'at all times been so discreet as they ought to have been,' he did not understand the extent of the attacks on the movement, points in this same direction.[54] Having an avowed advocate of a general escheat like Ramsay join Pope and Green and other anti-Escheat members in asserting 'disapprobation of the sentiments contained in the Hay River resolutions' caused the three Kings County members uneasiness about the wisdom of their own judgments and leadership.[55] They later acknowledged that had they had a better sense of the extent to which rural opinion supported them, they would have stood firmer in this confrontation.[56]

Developments in the assembly produced what Harvey wanted, no doubt in part because he took a hand in orchestrating them. With the most militant Escheators condemned, even by their allies in the assembly, and with the Island's only paper closed to their more radical statements, the movement had, he believed, been checked. To lend additional weight to his position, Harvey also dismissed Cooper and Joseph Coffin, another prominent King's County Escheator who had been involved in the Hay River proceedings, from various minor government appointments that they held.[57] At the time he initiated his actions, Harvey had hoped they would cause Cooper's supporters to 'desert *him* for *me*' and would allow him to assume leadership of the course of Island affairs.[58] Writing to a friend in early February, he noted that the response to the message he had delivered to the assembly had been beyond his 'utmost hopes,' and that it had brought about a profound 'moral revolution.' The question 'by which the prosperity of this fair Island has been so long obstructed (that of "Escheat") is settled *forever*.'[59] With the three Kings County representatives languishing in the custody of the sergeant-at-arms, the assembly, with Harvey's hearty approval, took up Glenelg's suggestion that they institute a land tax both as a means of securing revenues for government-led improvements and as an alternative to escheat. Clark's admission that he no longer saw any chance of effecting an escheat and, given Glenelg's latest dispatch, that the only workable policy was a land tax, demonstrated the extent of renewed support in the assembly for developmental politics. In complementary comments on the impossibility of the escheat option and on the desirability of new initiatives, George Dalrymple sketched out a line of argument that he and others would use to justify turning away from escheat. The 'whole scheme,' he argued, had been ruined by the 'imprudent means resorted to by those who warmly advocated the cause.'[60] A 'moderate and constitutional' course would have led to success, but general escheators, with their claim that the 'whole land on the Island was liable to confiscation,' and with their confrontational tactics and methods, had irreparably damaged the initiative.[61] With escheat banished from assembly discussion, the house took up and passed legislation instituting a differential land tax of four shillings per hundred acres on uncultivated lands and half that on properties under cultivation.[62] As well, it brought in a bill requested by entrepreneurs who wanted to establish a branch of the Bank of British North America in the colony, as well as legislation tailored to meet the needs of James Peake, one of Charlottetown's most prominent merchants, and others who were attempting to launch a joint stock steam-powered sawmill and gristmill.[63]

The developmental program that once again dominated the affairs of the legislature, and that the governor vigorously promoted, did not, however, address the concerns of many rural Islanders, who continued to believe in the justice of their claim to the land resources they needed to provide a livelihood for their families. Dismantling the Escheat movement required dealing with these beliefs and with the contention that the state had a role to play in protecting the tenantry. Harvey attempted to deal with these issues in his published correspondence condemning the Hay River proceedings. Noting that tenants needed to heed those offering 'sounder and kinder advice' and to withdraw their support for the policies of Escheators, the governor sketched out an alternative line of action for those currently sustaining the Escheat agitation. Central to Harvey's interpretation was the assertion that the problems faced by tenants were essentially private ones, concerning inviolable contracts between individuals and their respective landlords, and that these were not matters for state intervention.[64] Tenants, he contended, should not be looking to the government to restructure these relations, but to their proprietors for mercy. They should, he counselled, throw 'themselves upon the consideration of their landlords' and hope that their arrears might be reduced. Failing this, they should acknowledge their landlord's property rights and give up their farms. At this point they might then turn to the government and apply for a grant of Crown land on Prince Edward Island or in other colonies. There was, of course, little Crown land on the Island, and what there was had, through the lobbying efforts of landlords, been prohibitively priced at a minimum of £1 per acre. As most would need to move their families elsewhere and lacked the resources to pay for the move and to support themselves while they set about farm making yet again, Harvey suggested that they might petition the Crown for financial help 'to enable them to remove their families, and to establish themselves' again.[65] In short, unless landlords chose voluntarily to forgo exercise of some of their powers, the economic relationship between tenants and proprietors had to be allowed to run its course unimpeded, even if it led to the ruin of much of the Island's tenantry. It was not appropriate for government to intervene in these property relations. The resultant rural distress could be ameliorated by providing households with new lands from Crown reserves, if possible, and by charity or loans to assist emigration, if necessary.

When 'sounder and kinder' advice produced alternatives as unappealing and unlikely as these, it is little wonder that Escheat continued to find committed adherents among those who actually lived the consequences of the proprietorial system. At the heart of Cooper's political credo, and that of those who followed him, was the more attractive contention that the unfolding plight of the tenantry was not a private but a public question. They believed that the state had a paternal role to play in ensuring the welfare of the general populace. Cooper placed the social sphere over the economic in his priorities, repeatedly arguing that if existing property rights and exchange relations led to concentrations of wealth that denied the citizenry at large the chance to derive a living for themselves from the nation's resources and to be secure in the livelihoods their labour might provide, then the appropriate and just response of the state was intervention and restriction. Arguments concerning the validity of proprietorial titles were important not because there was intrinsic merit in adhering to the letter of the original grants, but because these details served to provide an opening by which the government might move to assert itself on behalf of the needs of the citizenry.[66]

The agricultural and economic crises of the mid-1830s highlighted the difference between this perspective and the articulation of a laissez-faire liberal perspective concerning the role of government in Island affairs. Harvey's public contentions that the plight of a distressed tenantry was a private, contractual matter found its echo in the assembly. Edward Thornton, for instance, while acknowledging that 'a great deal of distress existed in the country,' contended that the government 'had not the power to relieve it' and that 'there was little use in offering our sympathy and pity.'[67] Charles Binns argued similarly that it was 'quite out of the question' for the government to 'provide a general remedy for distress occasioned by arrears of rent, or for misfortune or poverty.'[68] Edward Jarvis, the chief justice and a member of the combined Legislative and Executive Council, expanded on the private nature of poverty. The roots of rural distress, he observed in the hungry spring of 1837, were found in the habits of individuals. The blasted crops of 1836 could, he suggested, 'prove a real blessing, by inducing small farmers and others, many of whom had hitherto been thriftless and improvident, to husband their resources.'[69] In a dispatch received and published on the Island in June 1837, Lord Glenelg made similar assertions concerning the demarcation between public and private issues and the appropriate role of the state. It 'would be impossible,' he noted, for the government to intervene in the human disaster besetting much of the tenantry 'otherwise than as a mediator between them and their landlords.'[70]

Despite such public expressions of liberal thought, prescient government officials recognized that they could not let events on the Island unfold in accordance with economic forces and existing property laws. Much as they may have disagreed with the ideology Cooper and other Escheators expounded, the alternative to accepting their position was even less palatable. Cooper's observation in 1833 that objection to the existing land system was becoming so great, and social distress so grievous, that soon the state's laws would be enforceable only with bullet and bayonet, was becoming increasingly true as the decade unfolded. Faced with growing threats to the state's hegemony over the interpretation of justice and the use of force, Imperial policy makers were compelled to move towards the positions the Escheators had articulated earlier in the decade.

Glenelg's admission that the government had a part to play as a mediator between the colony's tenantry and their landlords, small as it was, represented the beginning of a more profound shift away from the view that landlord/tenant relations were a private contractual matter and towards the Escheators' position on the issue. Writing to Glenelg at the end of January, Harvey noted the need for a stronger Imperial stance on the land question. In his public utterances to date he had suggested that the tenants themselves appeal to landlords for better terms; privately, though, in keeping with Glenelg's dispatch, he argued that the *government* should appeal to landlords on behalf of the tenantry. Indeed, Harvey moved beyond notions of a neutral role and advocated coercion. If landlords did not respond to the new terms suggested by the government, the latter should, he contended, demand the 'payment of all *their* arrears of quit rents.'[71] Besides acknowledging that the difficulties that agrarian activism was highlighting required some sort of state intervention, as Escheators maintained, Harvey's suggestions also picked up on a familiar Escheat complaint about the one-sidedness of the government's past enforcement of contractual obligations.

The proposal assumed concrete form in mid-February 1837, with Harvey drafting a circular to send to all the colony's landlords. He called on them to make tenants more secure in their holdings either by granting longer leases or by promising to compensate them for their improvements when they were dispossessed. As well, he asked them to accept the payment of rents in kind. Most importantly, he requested that they deal with the issue of unpayable arrears, suggesting that this could be done either by writing them off entirely – his preferred method – or by agreeing to accept payment of the interest on them rather than demanding the principal. For tenants, this would mean that their goods and improvements would be liable only for proceedings to collect current rents and for annual interest payments on arrears, though the whole of the arrears would remain as a liability.[72]

Driving these initiatives and shifts in Imperial policy was the continuing pressure of agrarian activism. Escheat had been effectively silenced in the house, but developments in the countryside soon indicated the limits of that success. Harvey's appeals for an end to any talk of an escheat, and his association of Escheat with disloyalty, had failed to influence opinion as widely as he had hoped. Despite the assembly's punishment of the most prominent Escheat leaders and Harvey's dissemination of pamphlets containing his correspondence with the assembly and the many condemnations of Cooper and Macintosh and Le Lacheur, the Escheat movement continued unabated.[73] At least four public meetings had ratified the Hay River proceedings in the short interval before the assembly condemned them. And other meetings continued, as initially planned, despite the anti-Escheat campaign. On 21 February the residents of Lot 32 in Queens County met to declare their adherence to the claims of the Hay River petition and to call for a further 'District County Meeting' followed by a 'General Meeting of Delegates for the County' to prepare the final Escheat petition that would be submitted to the Imperial government by delegation. More immediately, they also prepared another petition to the governor notifying him that they opposed the new land assessment legislation. Indeed, they asked him not to confirm it and informed him that they intended to carry on with their demands for an escheat.[74] Drawing the governor's attention to the reality that many were without the means to pay their rents, they asked him to stay landlords' rent collection proceedings pending the results obtained from carrying their appeal to Britain. To accomplish their ends, they established committees to correspond with Escheat groups elsewhere and to continue raising funds. As for the controversial resolutions accompanying the Hay River petition, those attending the meeting declared that though they did not 'entirely approve of some of the expressions' in it, they nonetheless were offended by the persecution to which the three Kings representatives had been subjected, and backed their sentiments with a collection to defray the costs the three were incurring.[75]

Thus, while the Island's elite perceived Cooper, Le Lacheur, and Macintosh as miscreants deserving of exemplary punishment, many in the countryside perceived them as martyrs suffering for their principled advocacy of agrarian objectives. The popular vision of history that had flowered over the course of the Escheat movement had an explanation for the treatment the three were receiving – not that they were traitors to the Crown or had committed errors and made misjudgments, but rather that they had dared to confront those who oppressed the tenantry. Although Harvey had hoped to discredit the Escheat leaders, the actions of the governor and assembly served to validate them among much of the rural population. Peter McCallum had astutely noted during the assembly's debate on punitive measures against the three Kings County members that the course it was adopting was not going to be interpreted outside the house in the way that the majority supposed. They were, he warned, fostering what they sought to repress.[76] Yet the popular support that coalesced around Cooper, Le Lacheur, and Macintosh in the aftermath of their persecution by the assembly surprised the three themselves.

Further meetings followed in the wake of the Queens County gathering. Acting in tandem with the Lot 32 committee, other committees prepared petitions to the governor and selected delegates for county and colony-wide Escheat meetings. A Lot 32 delegation presented an Escheat petition to the governor at the end of February. Yet another Queens County delegation delivered a similar petition the following month, asking the governor to stay land proceedings pending the results of the Escheat delegation to Britain, and asking him not to give his assent to the land assessment legislation that was just passed, as they felt it confirmed the proprietors' titles and went against the wishes of most Islanders.[77] A few weeks later a Kings County deputation presented a still stronger address condemning the 'coercive measures' adopted by the house and asking the governor to withhold assent to its land legislation and stay rent proceedings. In addition, it bitterly condemned statements that Chief Justice Jarvis had made at the opening of the March session of the Supreme Court in Kings County. Besides equating economic distress with improvidence and vice, he had condemned the Escheat movement as the work of 'artful demagogues' and had argued that those possessed of 'true loyalty' would not be involved in the agitation.[78] Though they probably did not realize it, the complaint was delivered to the appropriate person, as Harvey would appear to have requested Jarvis's statement in the first place and certainly approved of it.[79]

As winter gave way to spring, it became clear that Escheat remained well organized and robust. As intended, Hay River was the first step in a new campaign, and outside Government House, the legislative chambers, and the courthouses the anti-Escheat initiative failed to find a visible following. An attempt by some of the Georgetown elite to hold a public meeting to condemn the Hay River resolutions proved an embarrassment when four hundred Escheat advocates attended and voted otherwise.[80] In mid-April a Charlottetown meeting of 'District Delegates' assembled to continue work on the Hay River Escheat petition; they, too, sent a petition and delegation to Harvey informing him of their intentions and grievances and asking that he forward this preliminary petition to Britain. Their petition pointedly noted the difference between the objectives of those who had advocated a partial escheat as a facet of developmental politics and the wishes of the majority of the agrarian population. The claims made by these politicians and by the governor and the Colonial Office that a land tax was in any way a substitute for an escheat were, they argued, nonsense. Their complaints were not about the economic development of the colony and underutilized wilderness lands, as these parties contended, but about existing social relations. They were not protesting because there were 'not a sufficient number of inhabitants under the yoke of tenancy,' but because those already resident on the Island were suffering from landlord 'oppression.'[81] The assembly claimed to be representing the interests of the populace but the majority of its members did not, they argued, have the confidence of the people. Once again they asked Harvey to dissolve this assembly so that the popular voice might be heard. This petition was delivered to government house by William Clark and Peter

McCallum, two of the assembly members whom Harvey had hoped had permanently broken with Escheat. Their actions were evidence of the failure of Harvey's initiatives and the continuing momentum of agrarian mobilization. Once again, those who sought popular support had little choice but to identify with the Escheat cause. That William Clark had acted as chairman of the committee that drafted the petition further underlined the point.[82]

As Escheat organizing built towards a planned June convention of delegates from across the Island, Harvey was preparing for a May departure to assume the governorship of New Brunswick. His final communications to the Colonial Office urged two projects. First, to meet the desires of the business leaders who had rallied around his leadership, he vigorously called upon the Colonial Office to provide support for the land assessment bill and the act to facilitate the establishment of a branch of the Bank of British North America in the colony. Second, acknowledging the position Cooper had first asserted on the hustings in 1830, he informed the colonial secretary that the populace's only grievance lay with the refusal of the Imperial government to establish a court of escheat. It was time, he urged, to respond to this by giving the colony's governor authorization to convene such a court. Nothing short of this, he contended, would have the effect of 'tranquillizing the minds of the people.'[83] Given that Harvey's intention was to force an escheat only of lots that had not been adequately settled as of 1826, it is highly unlikely that it would have had the effect he wanted. It was, nevertheless, a major step away from the position he had initially attempted to maintain and can only be understood in light of his increasing recognition of the realities of agrarian power.

Harvey had assumed that if he could obtain the support of the Island's leading commercial and professional men, their sentiments would in turn inform the activities of others, and that working with them he would be able to wrest the leadership of the rural underclasses away from Escheators such as Cooper. This had not worked, nor had his attempts to directly bring tenants behind his leadership. Promises to act on behalf of the tenantry won him initial popularity, but over the short course of his administration his ability to strengthen his influence – and that of subsequent governors – with the tenantry declined as he proved unable to effect any real changes in their condition. At the beginning of his administration he had gained a following when he told rural audiences that in 'the King they had a father' and that he 'stood before them' as a representative of the sovereign wanting only to hear their needs and act in accordance with them.[84] This vision was fully in keeping with that of Escheat rhetoric, and it would have served him well had he been able to produce some ameliorative results. As Harvey discovered, however, the governor was essentially impotent as long as landlord/tenant relations were viewed as a private matter in which the Imperial government could not interfere. When he wrote requesting that the governor be given the power to constitute a court of escheat, he was seeking to enlarge the executive power so that the governor might be able to gain more credibility among a populace overwhelmingly concerned with land issues. He had begun his Island education and policies under the tutelage of proprietors and had continued to rely on local government officers and members of the mercantile community. His final dispatch, however, revealed that he was beginning to learn something about the limits of their understandings and about the force and appeal of the agrarian challenge.

9 Agrarian Institutions and the March to Power, 1837–1838

The Island's legislative assembly, which typically met from late January until April, was in recess when Governor Harvey's replacement, Charles FitzRoy, arrived, but its unofficial agrarian shadow was at work. FitzRoy had not been on the Island long before he found his agenda being set by the Escheat movement. Agrarian activism had moved into a particularly dynamic phase, and it rapidly swept the governor along with its momentum. Because of this, FitzRoy was drawn into making important statements on the land question soon after his arrival. Initially the lieutenant-governor's actions helped sustain the movement; later he would become a vociferous opponent. FitzRoy could and did exercise his power in various ways; what he could not do, although he tried, was change the subject of the central political debate. Escheators, FitzRoy discovered, held the initiative in political affairs.

During the period between the arrival of Lieutenant-Governor FitzRoy in the summer of 1837 and the colonial elections sixteen months later, Escheators extended and more firmly established the organizational structures necessary to sustain their growing challenge to the status quo. They held further Island-wide Escheat conventions like that of 1836, and they created a smaller, central managing committee that convened regularly to deal with the day-to-day affairs of the agrarian movement. The conventions and the monthly meetings of the managing committee enabled Escheat to clarify its program and allowed greater coordination in the activities of Escheat supporters across the Island. Formal Escheat committees assumed an ever greater profile in Island affairs and took on responsibility for matters ranging from setting standards for appropriate behaviour in rural communities when landlords used the state to enforce their claims, to the dispatch of delegates to represent Escheat interests in London and Quebec. The primary strategy of Escheat was to use constitutional tactics to achieve a political settlement of rural grievances, but its advocates explored additional tactics as well. Rent resistance and other forms of direct action provided ways to maintain political pressure and to assert alternative conceptions of justice and morality that upheld property rights rooted in labour. As well, they provided ways of dealing with the immediate problems of landlord demands. In some ways the new Escheat organizations that coordinated these activities assumed the role of a modern political party, in others that of a union bargaining for tenants' rights. They also held the potential to provide the core of an agrarian alternative to existing state structures. In the event, Escheators emphasized the first two facets of their mobilization and did not mount a revolutionary challenge. Having maintaining a constitutional stance after rebellions broke out in Upper and Lower Canada, Escheators were in a position to contest and decisively win the elections of 1838.

The Island-wide convention of Escheat delegates that met in Charlottetown at the end of June 1837 decided not to press ahead with plans to send a delegation to Britain. Because of the economic distress in the colony, subscriptions had not raised adequate funds. They resigned themselves to abandoning the plan for the year unless additional money could be raised by the end of July. The arrival of Harvey's replacement, Charles FitzRoy, two days before this meeting must have shaped their strategy as well. At the time of the Hay River meeting, Escheators had not known that Harvey's appointment was to be so brief and that come summer there might be an opportunity to gain the ear of a new governor.[1] They could not have known what to expect of the new governor, as his public career prior to arriving on Prince Edward Island had primarily been in the military, except for a brief and undistinguished term in the British Parliament.[2] Privately, he described himself as a 'liberal Whig.'[3] Unlike Harvey, FitzRoy was a member of the aristocracy by birth. Whether this would provide him with the stature to resist proprietors' pressures on Government House or make him sympathetic to their cause remained to be seen. Under the circumstances, the 1837 colony-wide Escheat convention resolved – as had the meeting the summer before – to mount a campaign to petition the governor to dissolve the assembly. It also called on him to intervene in tenant/landlord relations on their behalf. Once again, the convention struck a committee to carry out these objectives.[4]

Escheators intended to have these petitions ready for the governor on his arrival, but their preparations unfolded more slowly than anticipated. County meetings dealing with these and other issues were finally held in New London and St Margarets in late August. The documents the Escheators intended to submit to FitzRoy when he first took up residence in Government House were not ready for presentation until September. By then, other developments had already brought the land question to the new governor's attention. In mid-July, clashes over the enforcement of landlords' claims broke out again in northern Kings County. The first sign of trouble came when the county sheriff, Thomas Owen, and two constables were assaulted while arresting a rent resister, Angus Macdougald; they were forced to release their prisoner. A later attempt by law officers netted Macdougald along with one of the men who had helped free him. Both received jail terms during the July sitting of the Supreme Court. More resistance soon followed.[5]

In late August and early September the sheriff moved to execute a series of court orders that Thomas Sorell's land agent, H.D. Morpeth, had obtained against some of his tenantry. Owen succeeded in arresting one of Sorell's tenants. Sorell, an absentee landlord, claimed that the man owed him roughly £50, having resided on his property for ten years without paying rent. But the sheriff encountered stiff resistance when he attempted to execute the other court orders.[6] A serious confrontation occurred when Owen sought to proceed against John Robertson, an older settler who had begun farm making on Lot 42 at the turn of the century. Robertson had been disputing his landlord's claims in court for years, without success. Sorell wanted £160 in back rents from Robertson, which the latter refused to pay, in part because even after paying this large sum he still would not have secure possession of his holding.[7] Sorell was one of a number of proprietors who refused to grant leases, or would grant them only on short terms.[8] When in early September a sheriff's party arrived in the district to enforce a court order permitting Sorell to seize more than £60 worth of Robertson's goods and a smaller sum from John MacDonald (another of Sorell's tenants), an angry mob of men and women armed with sticks and stones drove the men off Robertson's farm and out of the district.[9] Sorell could win his case in court; however, his claims offended popular notions of justice and were for the moment unenforceable. Returning to their horses, which they had left at a distance from the farm, the sheriff and his assistant found that each had been mutilated by the removal of an ear.[10] The law officers were being sent a message, in a time-honoured fashion, concerning local sentiments about their behaviour.[11]

FitzRoy's first major statement on agrarian problems followed in the wake of these confrontations. Motivated in part by a desire to observe the power of Escheat in the countryside and understand its roots, FitzRoy, like Harvey before him, embarked on an extensive tour of the Island.[12] His travels took him to northeastern Kings County, the site of these clashes as well as many earlier ones, only days after Owen had been repulsed. On his arrival, Escheators presented him with a petition detailing their grievances. The residents of that district were not, they told him, a 'contented and happy people.' Three of them were currently in jail for resisting the imposition of laws they considered unjust and that they had been struggling to change for years. They argued in part that British land policy amounted to taxation without representation and was in violation of the Declaratory Act of 1778. They also pointed out that this act had been promulgated to put a stop to the obnoxious policies that had 'produced the successful resistance of the greater portion of the American colonies.' The petitioners called on FitzRoy to intervene to release their fellows from jail and to deal with the long-standing problems that were agitating the region.[13]

Hundreds of residents had assembled to present the petition to FitzRoy, and he used the occasion to make a public statement about Escheat. Reiterating the policy laid down in the most recent Imperial statement on the matter – a May 1837 dispatch from Lord Glenelg – he insisted that there was to be no escheat, as such a policy would threaten 'the security of all property.' He also denied that the Declaratory Act had any bearing on Crown land policy. As well, he contested Escheat contentions that the issue was a public matter, insisting instead that rural complaints were of a private nature and concerned 'voluntary contracts' that tenants had made with their landlords – contracts that they, 'as honest men,' were obliged to fulfil. Following the path Harvey had prepared, he offered to act as a mediator for them and to attempt to obtain better terms for the tenantry from their landlords. But he would not, he informed them, comply with requests that he stay land proceedings; nor, pending an investigation, would he pardon or release those being held in jail for resistance. As well, he took the occasion to condemn the most recent violence that had flared at John Robertson's farm.[14]

FitzRoy's first public statements, which had been forced on him by rapidly unfolding events in the land struggle, were in keeping with existing Imperial policy on the issue and with his responsibilities as chief executive. Yet his private thoughts reveal that on many points he agreed with the position of the Escheat advocates. Central to his decisions over the next few months was the perception that to permit landlords to exact what they legally might from their tenantry was both unjust and impolitic. This was, of course, the Escheat position as well. Indeed, to a striking degree FitzRoy's first major dispatch concerning what he had discovered after inspecting the colony echoes the perspective that Escheators had been building and defending over the past decade. Noting that escheat was the central issue in the colony and that despite repeated rejections by the government it still had the support of a 'considerable portion of the inhabitants,' FitzRoy acknowledged the reasonableness of the fundamental claims underpinning the agitation. In a passage that might just as easily have appeared in one of Cooper's speeches, FitzRoy argued that it was 'the labour alone of the settler which renders wilderness land of any value.' He noted that rents had to be paid against large holdings even as settlers were bringing them into production at the rate of two cleared acres or less per year. As a result, he argued, tenants were being forced to pay enormous rents for the few acres they had under production – rents much greater, he felt, than those demanded of tenants in Great Britain. These demands, FitzRoy argued, were unreasonable and often led to cases where (as in Robertson's situation or that of 'Sandy Ban' in the Emigrant's voyage of discovery) settlers lost the 'farms they had spent the best years of their lives in reclaiming from the wilderness.' These circumstances, he explained, lay at the root of agrarian unrest. It is ironic that while FitzRoy thought little of Cooper – 'a person of no education' – and believed that the bulk of the people following his lead were 'an extremely ignorant race of men,' he was nonetheless articulating arguments they had refined and pushed into the political arena.[15]

Like Harvey, FitzRoy faced this dilemma: How was he to reconcile a liberal, contractual definition of the land question and the appropriate role of the state with his recognition that there were fundamental injustices in landlord/tenant relations on the Island? As chief executive, he had to uphold Sorell's use of the legal system to take away John Robertson's livestock and farming equipment, and perhaps as well the farm he had spent thirty years creating. Indeed, as governor it was his duty to ensure that the sheriff had sufficient force to overcome resistance such as had arisen in Kings County. Yet at the same time, having acquainted himself with rural circumstances, FitzRoy understood the distinction that agrarians were drawing between what was just and what was legal, and he understood why they viewed landlord/tenant relations as an unresolved political question. In public he made the case for the rights of property stemming from titles and contracts; privately, however, he perceived the weakness and injustice of such a position insofar as Island land issues were concerned. Importantly as well, he understood that despite appeals to 'loyalty' and 'honesty,' in the existing circumstances alternative visions of justice were too strong to be overcome by anything short of force.[16]

FitzRoy, like Harvey, initially tried to address the problem by appealing to the landlords to change the terms of their contracts. The government was to act as a mediator. In the weeks following his Island tour he drafted a letter to be sent to all of the Island's proprietors. In it, besides upbraiding them for failing to respond to Harvey's appeal, he tried to set them straight concerning existing conditions on the Island. He informed them that contrary to Harvey's reports, escheat was still the cause of general excitement among rural Islanders and that this excitement included armed resistance to the sheriff. He had, he indicated, done what he could to uphold the law, and he hoped he had convinced 'some of the more moderate' Escheators to call a halt to physical resistance. The quid pro quo was his negotiations with landlords on the tenants' behalf, but this would only be effective if proprietors made significant concessions, quickly. FitzRoy reiterated Harvey's recommendations with one significant change. Dropping the idea of allowing arrears to stand and collecting only interest on them, FitzRoy recommended that arrears be entirely written off in cases where they could not be paid.

A central weakness in the governor's strategy was that it rested on the voluntary compliance of proprietors. To overcome this, FitzRoy, like Harvey, appealed confidentially to the colonial secretary for his 'interference and influence' with the British proprietors.[17] As well, he sought to bring a different sort of pressure to bear on those proprietors whom he believed were the most resistant to the changes he favoured. Driving a wedge into the proprietors' ranks, FitzRoy suggested in his circular that fair and honourable landlords were not having trouble with their tenantry and that the problems arising on the Island were rooted in the improper behaviour of a minority of landlords, who were 'bringing odium' upon the entire body. These bad landlords were, he claimed, rendering 'all property' in the colony insecure, and he cited a few cases of flagrant injustices to support his claim that the tenantry had cause for complaint. In private notes accompanying the printed circular that he mailed to all landlords, FitzRoy informed proprietors such as the Earl of Selkirk and the Earl of Westmorland that his criticisms did not apply to the management of their estates. Similar notes did not accompany the letters to landlords such as the Stewarts and the Worrells. FitzRoy's distinction between good and bad landlords fell, to a large extent, along a class cleavage in landlord ranks; it also fell between the key members and participants in the Prince Edward Island Association (PEIA) and its better heeled, less active fellow travellers. Thus his initiative opened the possibility of bringing social pressure to bear on the most recalcitrant proprietors and/or weakening their ability to recruit the prominent to support their position and sustain their lobbying power. As well, FitzRoy issued an important warning to proprietors: if they did not make concessions, the enforcement of their property claims would become even more difficult. The way things stood, he did not see how they could collect rents, as resistance made it possible for tenants to carry off and hide all the valuables on farms that were being subjected to distress proceedings. He warned landlords that if they thought they could stand by their private rights and count on government intervention to overcome popular resistance to their legal proceedings, they were operating on mistaken assumptions. They should not expect that 'the Government is to be at the expense of collecting your Rents' by backing up their land agents with 'an armed force.'[18]

While waiting for the proprietors to respond to his attempt at mediation, FitzRoy worked to quiet the volatile situation in northern Kings County. In late September he sent the head of the Island's militia, Ambrose Lane, who was also a member of the council and the mayor of Charlottetown, on a tour of the district. Lane's mission was to conspicuously make arrangements for housing a military force in the region and, more quietly, to take the pulse of the residents and report on what sort of reception further law proceedings would receive. Lane reported that although many tenants in the township were in the same vulnerable circumstances as Robertson, if Owen returned they would refrain from violence and take part only in passive resistance, such as hiding all valuables. On learning this, FitzRoy, acting through the attorney general, instructed the sheriff to return to the district with his writs. His orders were carefully framed. Owen was not in any way to provoke an incident, nor was he to let any of the men he took with him attempt to settle personal scores. Indeed, they were not to use force or violence in any way except to protect their own lives if attacked. If the people of the district confined themselves to passive resistance and hid all the goods Owen sought, he was simply 'to go there and return again.' The correspondence strongly suggests that a deal, or understanding, had been reached during Lane's visit and that the governor's primary concern, besides maintaining the appearance of law enforcement, was to keep local officers such as Owen and his assistant the constable John Collings in check and prevent them from fomenting a more serious conflict. In an interesting reversal of the observations that Chief Justice Jarvis had often made in the past concerning conflicts over the enforcement of landlords' claims, the attorney general's letter pointedly warned Owen that if a tenant were killed in one of these incidents, the law officers themselves would be liable for murder, if it turned out that they had not followed due procedure in executing their duties.[19]

Faced with Escheat demands and rent resistance, in the fall of 1837 FitzRoy sought breathing space during which he might induce the Island's landlords to make some significant concessions. Having read earlier Colonial Office correspondence on the land question before leaving Britain, and having spoken to some of the Island's proprietors about Harvey's earlier appeals, he believed he would be able to meet some of the tenantry's needs. During his fall tour of the colony, FitzRoy had publicly pledged that if tenants abstained from violence he would do everything he could to persuade the proprietors to ameliorate their condition and 'take away all just cause of complaint.'[20] In more intimate exchanges, FitzRoy discussed what would constitute removal of all 'just' causes of complaint, and in particular why it was he believed, after speaking to Robert Stewart and others before he left Britain, that he would be able to achieve a compromise.[21] Perhaps it was because FitzRoy had come to embrace the idea of a partial escheat.[22] There is no way of knowing what the governor said in these local conversations with rural residents. On the one hand, he needed to hold out sufficient grounds for hope to convince his listeners that the route he proposed was viable so that he might persuade them to trust his leadership and set escheat and rent resistance aside. On the other hand, it was not in his interest to encourage high hopes. Regardless of what he actually said, reports of conversations with the governor were rooted in what people thought he said, and/or wanted him to have said. Not surprisingly, in the wake of his travels, rumours were soon circulating throughout the countryside concerning the nature and contours of a deal that the governor might be able to obtain from the colony's proprietors.

Unbeknownst to the governor, a chain letter concerning his private conversations while visiting northern Kings County circulated throughout the colony in the fall and early winter of 1837. According to this letter, the compromise the governor was trying to reach – indeed, was offering – would see tenants released from all back rents and secured in long leases at half their current rents, with half the rent to be payable in produce. Cooper was the author of the letter, and it was soon being copied and circulated in all three counties, 'for the encouragement of those in distress and despondency.' Besides seeking to inspire hope among those associated with the agrarian cause, Cooper's letter included a call for a great mass meeting in November, where it would be decided whether they should continue to press for an escheat or whether they should accept compromise terms that would simply reduce the burden of proprietors' land tenure. The enumerated concessions, Cooper claimed, represented a great victory for the tenantry, amounting to a savings of roughly a quarter of a million pounds for the colony as a whole; though less than what they wanted, the offer deserved serious consideration. With the support of the 'Clans of the North on our right, and the Radicals of the South on our left,' Cooper wrote, some fifteen hundred to two thousand would muster 'in good order, and with good will to all men' for the mass meeting scheduled for November.[23]

The public was soon able to see the terms that FitzRoy was actually trying to obtain from the Island's landlords. The editor of the *Royal Gazette*, who had been commissioned by the governor to print fifty copies of the circular he was sending to proprietors, decided, despite being sworn to secrecy, to print a copy of it – which he falsely claimed to have gotten from a landlord – in his paper.[24] The greatest discrepancy between the terms advanced by rumour and those contained in the actual circular concerned the 50 per cent reduction in rents. Beyond that, they were not widely different, except that FitzRoy's circular made it evident that no deal had been struck and that the governor's role was simply that of appealing for better terms – something he had no certainty of achieving. On both points, publication of the circular raised serious questions about Cooper's letter – for those, that is, who had seen it or had had it read to them. Was it intentionally misleading to create an expectation that FitzRoy would then have to meet, or was it the product of rumour and bad judgment? Or had the governor been involved in the discussion of a 50 per cent rent reduction?[25] In all likelihood, discussions concerning what would be minimally acceptable to the tenantry had included the notion of halving the rents. Given that FitzRoy believed rents were too high, there is no reason to think he would have rejected the proposal out of hand. FitzRoy's response at the time is unknown, but the idea was not included in the proposal the governor drafted early the following month.

Perhaps the publication of FitzRoy's letter raised, or deepened, doubts about Cooper's leadership among some on the inside of the Escheat movement. In the event, ongoing developments marginalized the issue.[26] The published circular that gave rise to these questions also gave great momentum to an already vibrant movement. Besides the details of the compromise FitzRoy was attempting to obtain, the governor's circular provided exhilarating reinforcement for key claims that Escheat had been attempting to legitimize since the beginning of the decade. In his letter, FitzRoy revealed private perceptions that had remained unsaid in his public pronouncements. Islanders now knew that the governor believed, as did Escheators, that it was 'the hard wrought labour' of the tenant 'which alone stamps a value on the land he improves.'[27] As well, there was his assertion that it was not unreasonable for a tenant to resist being 'deprived of the hard earned fruits of the labour of the earliest and best years of his manhood,' whether through arrears brought on by unsustainable rents or through poor leases. The drive for a general escheat, the letter contended, was rooted in real grievances, and while they did not 'justify the extreme measure they seek to obtain, [they] go a long way to account for, if not to palliate the line of conduct pursued by them.' The governor also challenged a key plank in proprietors' claims – that the issue was strictly private – by arguing that the contracts determining landlord/tenant relations were not in general entered into by consenting parties, but instead that they were often rooted in fraud and deceit; new settlers not knowledgeable about Island conditions had been duped into accepting impossible terms. Is it any wonder that the governor's letter was read in English and translated and read in Irish Gaelic, Scots Gaelic, and no doubt French at Escheat meetings in the final months of 1837?[28] FitzRoy was reiterating many of the things the Escheat movement had been arguing for years, and furthermore, the underlying terms of reference were those of the agrarians: the theme of the letter was justice and oppression, not settlement and economic development.

The fall of 1837 was a time of rising rural expectations and excitement. The combined Kings and Queens County Escheat meeting held on the outskirts of Georgetown on 8 November proved the biggest public meeting the Island had ever seen, and was a manifestation of the enormous enthusiasm that had grown around the Escheat cause. In mid-September, as John Le Lacheur, John Dalziel, and Daniel Campbell pored over their almanac to select a sunny day for the gathering, the meeting's planners hoped that between fifteen hundred and two thousand would attend.[29] It appears that even more than this came. Donald Macdonald estimated that the square in front of Sentiner's tavern was packed fifty people deep and forty wide, and that 'hundreds more' were in 'detached groups around the fires in the woods, in the houses and fields, on the roof of the forge, & c.' Organized by committee and marching in district contingents, those who came participated in the public drama of the day. The Escheators from Three Rivers and Murray Harbour, dubbed 'the radicals of the south,' had gathered at Sentiner's first and served as hosts for the others. When discharges of musketry signaled the arrival of the Escheators of northern Kings County, known as 'the clans of the north,' a piper struck up 'the clans are coming' and local Escheators hoisted a St George's Ensign on a thirty–foot pole. They provided a similar welcome for the Queens County Escheators when they arrived later in the day marching in a long procession bearing a Union flag and headed by a piper. The symbols brought to the gathering and the speeches that followed reflected Escheat's claims to represent a genuinely loyal and constitutional position.[30]

The three Escheat assemblymen from Kings County chaired the meeting when it began around noon. The business of the day was the proposal and passage of resolutions reflecting the current position of the Escheat movement. Final organization of the proceedings was arranged by the leaders of the local Escheat committees, who squeezed into Sentiner's for a quick conference before the mass meeting was opened. Key Escheat figures from the two counties submitted five resolutions to the assembled crowd. The resolutions were cautiously phrased and defended. One speaker, John Thomson of Georgetown, apologized for having to disagree with the governor whom he respected, but opinions, he contended, had to be considered 'separate and distinct from persons.' Nonetheless, the resolutions were clear in their intent. Two main arguments and objectives emerged that were to guide continuing agrarian activism: first, that the assembly, which did not represent the wishes of the people, should be dissolved; and second, that the struggle for a general escheat, rather than a lesser settlement, must be maintained. One of the resolutions held, as had those passed at Hay River, that rent claims were illegal, though it did not go on to specify the appropriate response to illegal claims.[31]

The mass meeting at Sentiner's was an occasion for defining the ongoing objectives of the Escheat movement and for demonstrating its strength; discussion of how to actually achieve those ends fell to a smaller meeting of thirty-five delegates who had been appointed by local Escheat committees in Kings and Queens counties. Assembling in Charlottetown the week after the meeting at Sentiner's, these delegates adopted resolutions of considerable significance to the movement. Ideally, Escheators wanted a majority in the assembly that reflected their sentiments and that could negotiate the land question during the critical phase it had now entered. Lacking this, the Charlottetown meeting fashioned policies to deal with both aspects of this dilemma – their weakness in the assembly, and the need to coordinate responses to the major new developments. So far as assembly politics were concerned, the delegates moved beyond indicating their desire that the house be dissolved, and set about establishing organizational structures for an election so that they would be prepared to participate effectively whenever it was held. They divided each county into four districts and decided that Escheators in each district would appoint a twelve–person Committee of Election and Grievances. These committees, composed altogether of nearly 150 individuals, were to remain in force until after the next election. Each of these committees was, in turn, to appoint three of its members as delegates to Island-wide meetings, which would be held in Charlottetown. Escheat candidates for the next election would be proposed at the district level, but would also have to gain the approval of the Island-wide assembly before they could run. Once candidates had been selected, anyone who voted for someone other than those chosen in this fashion would, they declared, be henceforth 'deemed unworthy of trust or confidence.'[32]

Besides addressing electoral organization, the meeting dealt with the problem of responding to ongoing developments pending the creation of a reconstructed house with an Escheat majority. The delegates resolved to establish a committee of fourteen, who would be responsible 'for managing the Escheat question, until the new House of Assembly came into existence.' Henceforth, no Escheat meetings were to take place unless local committees had the Managing Committee's consent in writing, no reports were to be submitted to papers without first having been vetted by the central committee, and no deals or negotiations bearing on the land question were to be undertaken without similar authorization. The committee was to appoint a secretary, who would handle all correspondence 'in all official matters touching the

Escheat question.' If there were disagreements within the managing committee, a minimum of seven signatures would be required to authorize an action. The organization that was being hammered into shape in the last months of 1837 was a multifaceted achievement in popular democracy. It was a tenant union for collective bargaining, a highly developed political party, and a rudimentary alternative agrarian assembly – one that claimed a legitimacy that the official house lacked among much of the rural population.

With the Sentiner's rally, the subsequent delegates' meeting, and the creation of a more formal Island-wide agrarian assembly, Escheat entered a particularly active and creative phase of its existence. In the wake of the mid-November Charlottetown gathering, Escheators organized more than a dozen local meetings across the colony between mid-December and mid-March (see map 9.1). These gatherings produced a number of important proposals and innovations, with various local groups discussing the land question and exchanging ideas. In Prince County, a series of meetings running from mid-December to mid-January gave rise to a cluster of new policies and strategies. The relationship between the rights of freeholders and the impact of a possible escheat had been a matter of concern to the movement for years, and Escheators had noted the need to ensure that the rights of small freeholders were undisturbed. The appropriate division between freeholder and landlord/speculator, though, had remained unspecified in these discussions. The Prince County meetings recommended a ceiling of five hundred acres, beyond which holdings were to be subject to escheat action. As well, they passed a series of resolutions bearing on rural behaviour and distinguishing between friends of the people and their enemies. They resolved that it was appropriate to withhold 'all the courtesies of life' from those involved in persecuting the oppressed, and that those voluntarily acting as bailiffs in land cases or bidding at distraint auctions 'unless requested by the Tenant to buy the same in at a very reduced value' would be considered Escheat enemies and dealt with as such. In addition they decided to compile 'lists of those who oppose Escheat in their respective districts.'[33] In a similar vein and at roughly the same time, the Acadian inhabitants of the Rustico region resolved to organize a boycott (though the word had not been coined yet) against those in the mercantile community who were opposing Escheat policies. Their suggestions were in turn supported by Escheat meetings elsewhere.[34]

Electoral and financial strategies were a matter of debate in the local

Map 9.1. Escheat meetings, July 1837 to September 1838

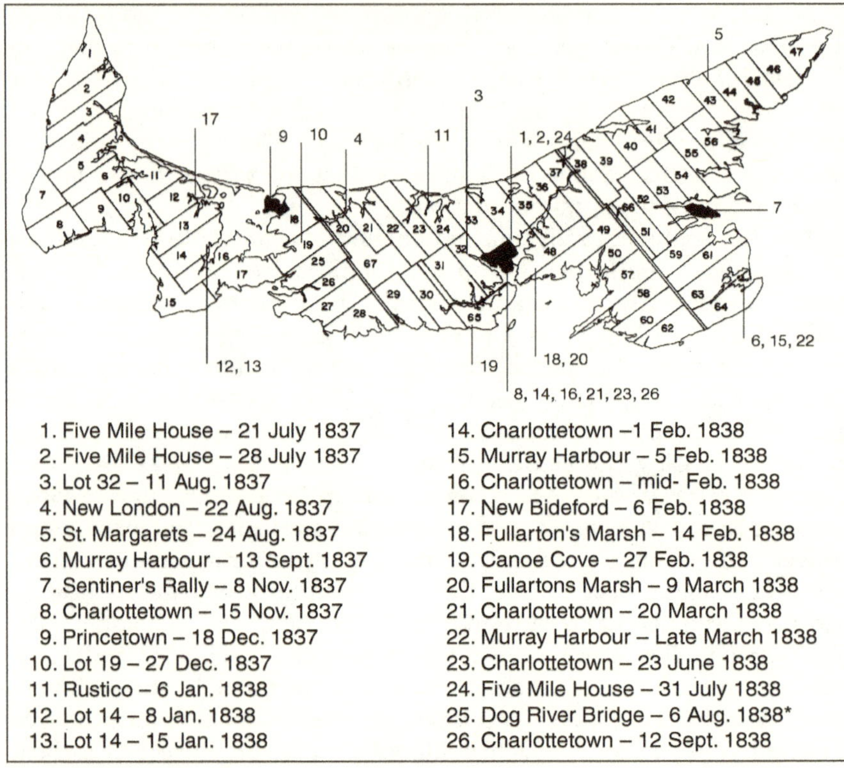

* Location unknown
Source: *Royal Gazette*, *Colonial Herald*, NAC, CO 226

meetings as well. The Prince County gatherings resolved that all candidates, besides having to be nominated and approved by Escheat committees, should have to sign a pledge committing themselves to support the cause in the assembly.[35] The Acadians of Rustico proposed a further innovation arguing that electoral laws should be rewritten to permit constituent recall of members who violated their wishes.[36] As far as financial affairs and the organization of the land struggle were concerned, the residents of Murray Harbour decided to form 'bonds of union and cooperation' to protect their property from rent proceedings (physically one assumes) and to provide financial support to those suffering for their role in rent resistance or for advocating Escheat politics. As well, they suggested that the colony's tenantry should combine to obtain off-Island counsel to represent tenant interests.[37] In March yet another new proposal emerged: a local meeting in Queens County suggested that it was time to establish an alliance with sympathetic residents of Charlottetown and Royalty, and called on them to form an urban committee that might be incorporated into the movement's organizational structure.[38]

The discussions and resolutions that emerged in local meetings held around the Island in the months after the Sentiner's meeting provided the backdrop for the policy initiatives the Escheat Managing Committee developed as delegates from the various districts brought these ideas to their meetings in Charlottetown. The notion of forming 'bonds' and obtaining legal counsel, for instance, re-emerged in a March Committee of Management resolution calling on tenants across the colony to 'join in a constitutional and legal obligation' to pay a sum into a collective fund, which would be used to retain counsel and otherwise sustain the ongoing land struggle.[39] Electoral initiatives proposed at local-level meetings were consolidated in a statement of Island-wide policy in June.[40] The Managing Committee also initiated policies beyond those appearing in the resolutions of local meetings; for example, in March it decided to explore the possibility of organizing its own newspaper.[41] Most importantly, the Managing Committee addressed the task of hammering together a bargaining position that would reflect ongoing Escheat thinking on the land question. Although the resolutions passed at Sentiner's called for a continuation of the struggle for a general escheat and denied the justice of accepting the partial amelioration of grievances proposed by Harvey and FitzRoy, the movement's leaders were open to a compromise settlement. Believing that such a settlement might indeed be possible, the Escheat Managing Committee moved to clarify its position in the months after Sentiner's. By mid-February it had produced a document stating its position and was able to publish an up-to-date account of it in the *Colonial Herald*. As well, the committee ordered a printing of three hundred copies, fifty of which were to be sent to members of the British Parliament.[42]

The Managing Committee's statement provided a detailed blueprint for a possible final land settlement. The Escheat position hinged on two key points. One was the old contention that the landlords' estates were open to reclamation by the Crown; that is, they were liable to escheat. This claim was particularly important because it provided a means for overcoming landlord resistance to bringing about some sort of settlement. Because they insisted on the legal vulnerability of the landlords' titles, the Managing Committee's proposals for resolving the land question were potentially enforceable, should landlords refuse to become involved in a negotiated settlement. The proposals made by Harvey and FitzRoy, in contrast, were rooted in the voluntary compliance of proprietors. In addition, the Managing Committee's position did not leave the door open for a continuation of the proprietorial system under revised terms. The other key aspect of the committee's policy was the admission that despite the weakness in their titles, some landlords might have just claims for compensation in a final land settlement. Landlords, it contended, had a right to be reimbursed for the costs of introducing immigrants, for the value of any land improvements that they had made, and for the value of any provisions or stock they might have provided settlers. As well, it acknowledged that a fair settlement would see landlords compensated for the wilderness value of their lands, assessed without the value added by settler improvements, either on the property itself or on adjacent lands. Set against this figure would be the rents and land sales payments landlords had received.

The new policy also provided guidelines for how various classes of rural dwellers might equitably be settled on their lands. Existing freeholders were simply to be secured in the possession of their farms. Tenants were to be able to purchase freeholds of their farms by paying for the value of their land at its wilderness rate. Those who had paid their rents were to have interest-free loans to do this, and those who had not were to pay the interest charges on the fee simple price. Squatters were to be allowed to purchase fee simple rights to their farms on the same terms. Whether or not the sums raised from the sale of lands at a wilderness rate would match the sums that would prove to be due to proprietors was not of course clear, but the policy statement pointed towards a settlement that would include some compensation for some proprietors. A court of escheat, having been established, would provide a forum in which these claims could be adjudicated.

Over the fall and winter of 1837–8, Escheat activism gathered strength in two interrelated spheres. First, there were policies and strategies designed to achieve political power and/or to persuade those who had it to listen to demands for a negotiated settlement of the land question. Second, there were strategies for dealing with the land system as it currently existed. These were formulated with an eye towards protecting tenants from its exploitative effects pending a settlement. They also aimed to undercut the position of proprietors and their agents and their will to hold out by depriving them of income and the power of the rent roll. Making the system unworkable was both a policy in itself and a step towards achieving a more permanent resolution of the land conflict. The sophisticated organizational structures that Echeators had developed by the fall of 1837 played a central role in both facets of the struggle. Evidence bearing on their role in rent resistance is thinner than that concerning political activities. The experiences of those involved with the Hay River resolutions no doubt had something to do with this. Details of plans for physical resistance to law officers were unlikely to be committed to the written record in any case. While the recorded resolutions of local Escheat meetings tell us something about the strategies that were to be used once land resistance cases found their way to the courts and/or resulted in distraint auctions, evidence concerning organized physical resistance to land law proceedings comes not from these records but from descriptions of actual confrontations.

In the late summer and early fall of 1837, northern Kings County had been the scene of land conflicts, Thomas Sorell's land agent, H.D. Morpeth, had attempted to assert proprietorial rights in that region. Following the Sentiner's rally, the focus of tensions shifted to southern Queens County and the Selkirk estate. As with the events in northern Kings County earlier in the fall, the timing and locus of confrontations was in large part determined by landlords and their agents. Tenants throughout the Island were in arrears and vulnerable to legal actions, and it seems that tenants across much of the Island were involved in organized rent strikes and in plans for resisting legal process.[43] Whether circumstances would result in physical conflict depended on whether proprietors and their agents chose to confront their tenantry head on. The incidents in southern Queens County took place because Selkirk's agent, William Douse, chose to take action.

In the aftermath of developments in the fall of 1837, tenants organized rent resistance on the Selkirk estate. Their collective action emerged in November as a labour strike. On the Selkirk estate, as on a number of others, rents could be redeemed by labour. Given the extent of existing arrears, land agents wishing to collect rents through labour had a vast workforce at their command that could be mobilized by the simple expedient of threatening distraint or ejection if workers from tenant households were not forthcoming when summoned. On the Selkirk estate, the land agent used tenant labour to save the Earl of Selkirk the costs of some of the state-organized highway and boundary work and also to prepare wilderness sections of the estate for new immigrants.[44]

In the winter of 1837, Selkirk's agent, William Douse, sought to dispatch crews to aid the surveyor's boundary work and to continue construction projects on the estate, but found himself unable to recruit any workers.[45] Faced with a rent/labour strike, Douse informed Selkirk's tenants that he would initiate distraint proceedings unless they ceased their work stoppage. What happened next is not altogether clear, but it appears that tenants responded with threats of their own, for Douse soon fled the estate under the cover of darkness, supposedly in fear for his life.[46] Convinced that FitzRoy's circular was largely to blame for the developments on the Selkirk property, Douse unsuccessfully sought the governor's intervention in the matter.[47]

According to Douse, the tenantry were not worried about threats of distraint because they were organized to resist any attempts at legal process. Events soon proved that this indeed was the case. In late January a party of Charlottetown notables, including the rector, travelling across the Selkirk estate towards Wood Islands on a baptismal mission, was mistaken for law officers and confronted by an armed party of local men and women. Residents used conch shells to sound the alarm and mobilize resistance. The surprised Charlottetowners found themselves surrounded by an armed and hostile crowd, some of whom fired shots over their heads to intimidate them.[48] Reports from elsewhere indicated that the state of affairs they had discovered on Selkirk's lands was much more general. Donald Macdonald of Glenaladale reported that he had been threatened by his tenants and warned not to try to collect rents.[49] In January a group of resident Island proprietors, including Macdonald, drafted a memorial claiming they could no longer collect rents and that their 'lives and property alike' had become 'insecure.'[50] Their memorial, addressed to the PEIA, was an appeal for help. What they wanted most urgently was the dispatch of more troops to the Island and firm government backing for the enforcement of landlords' claims. It was, of course, in their interest to paint matters as starkly as possible – as the governor pointed out in his own dispatch concerning the memorial. But even FitzRoy, although he disputed the claims of personal danger that proprietors and agents were making, acknowledged the presence of highly organized rent resistance across much of the Island.[51]

By late January, FitzRoy believed that a physical showdown was looming and that tenant resistance needed to be suppressed. Proprietors' forces would have been relieved had they known his position on the matter. The government, though, faced a problem, as FitzRoy had noted in a dispatch following the incidents of the previous fall. The governor lacked the military force necessary to ensure victory in a physical confrontation. Extra troops that had been stationed on the Island earlier in the decade had been removed from the colony to meet the threat of revolt in the Canadas in the fall of 1837, and the score or so of soldiers remaining were, FitzRoy believed, insufficient to deal with any 'serious tumult.'[52] Nor did the government have a reliable alternative armed force. Given the popularity and power of Escheat and rent resistance, FitzRoy did not believe that civil forces and the militia could be relied on to suppress tenant resistance. Faced with a mounting crisis early in 1838, and no doubt troubled by the news of serious battles in the Canadas, FitzRoy urgently requested the dispatch of at least two full companies of the line to the colony as soon as possible after the ice went out.[53] As proprietors' pressure had been mounting, both in the colony and in Britain, for firm action to suppress tenant activism, the Colonial Office's initial response to the governor's request – besides agreeing to send troops – was to draft a letter to the PEIA notifying them of developments. Ultimately, though, the communication was cancelled for fear that news of events in the colony would further damage the Imperial government's reputation by highlighting the existence of yet another disaffected colonial population that could be kept quiet only by the deployment of troops.[54]

When distraint actions proceeded on the Selkirk estate early in February 1838, events unfolded as had been expected. Douse targeted four prominent Escheat activists for legal action. As law officers moved in and attempted to seize goods from their farms, crowds summoned by horns descended on the constables. They prevented the distraints and in one case rescued cattle the law officers had seized, even though some of the constables involved drew pistols in an attempt to maintain their possession of the animals.[55] Douse used these incidents as proof of the impotence of civil authorities in the countryside and called on the governor to send troops in with his bailiffs to permit the execution of the distraints and the arrest of those who had been involved in the initial resistance.[56] Given the extent to which Escheat had undermined the legitimacy of rent claims and the degree to which it aided the coordination of rent resistance, proprietors and land agents desperately wanted a show of force, and Douse's actions provided useful evidence to strengthen landlord demands for military support.[57]

Escheat leaders were not unaware of the risks of pressing resistance too far and playing into the hands of proprietorial interests. What they sought to establish, pending a political settlement, was a strategy that would impede landlords from enforcing their claims on tenants but in such a way as to deny them a chance to respond effectively with force. FitzRoy's earlier published warning to proprietors that they could not expect the state to sustain rent collection with troops, coupled with the limited garrison present during the winter of 1837–8, had no doubt encouraged the organization of physical resistance to landlordism. Escheators were exploring other long-term tactics as well, including more creative use of the courts. While legal proceedings usually vindicated proprietors' claims, the process was expensive for landlords as well as for tenants. Proprietors tended to turn to the courts as a last resort, typically targeting those whom they believed to be leading resistance.[58] The decisions taken by Escheat organizations to provide a fund for legal costs arising from rent resistance and to provide compensation for those suffering from such actions were aimed at undercutting the effectiveness of this tactic by proprietors. Lose they might, but by equitably sharing the burdens imposed on those who were prosecuted as an example for others, tenants could make the courts an arena for a costly war of attrition that would deplete landlords' resources as well.

Tenants explored a wide variety of tactics, rooted in the broadly shared anti-landlord sentiments of the rural community, to ensure that landlord victories, when gained, were dearly bought. They shifted goods from farm to farm to deny distraining constables a chance to seize them. They assumed collective control of distraint auctions and ensured that seized goods sold for only a fraction of their real price and were returned once again to their owners.[59] William Douse's description of the stubborn legal resistance of Joseph Atkinson, an Escheat advocate on the Selkirk estate, points to a broader set of tactics of attrition. Owing £33 in back rents in 1836, Atkinson abandoned his farm but refused to surrender his lease despite promises of payment for it from Douse. This tied up the property and prevented Douse from obtaining a new tenant who might pay rent. Douse was forced to sue Atkinson for the back rent, and Atkinson was sent to jail for his debts. To avoid surrendering his claim on Douse's terms, Atkinson transferred his lease to an ally, who was then in a position to carry on with the original policy of holding the farm without paying rents or occupying it. For his pains, Atkinson lost his farm and spent at least twelve months in prison, but he was supported there by fellow Escheators. As FitzRoy noted with disgust, jail discipline was lax and the agrarian agitators who were thrown into prison were often moving into 'positive places of luxury' by comparison with their own dwellings.[60] Atkinson, nonetheless, paid a heavy price for his resistance. Lord Selkirk, though, could not afford many victories such as this. Having spent more than £16 on legal expenses and lost £33 in rents, the landlord was no closer to having control of the farm in dispute than when it began legal proceedings.[61]

Escheators explored yet another fruitful area of non-violent resistance in the winter of 1837–8 by challenging proprietors' claims to the shoreline. Although most township deeds reserved the first five hundred feet of shoreline above the high-water mark for the Crown, landlords laid out lots for their tenantry without regard to these fishery reserves and had over the years pocketed rents for them. Roughly two-thirds of the original grants included fishery reserves. The majority of these grants retained the soil of the reserves for the Crown. In some, the fisheries reserve was more like an easement. Given that Island settlement remained concentrated along the shores of the colony in the 1830s and that land clearing typically proceeded from the front of the lot to the back, the first five hundred feet of land on shorefront farms was both a significant area of farmland and one of particular value. As well, where it existed, coastal marshland was among the most coveted assets of early Island farmers.[62] For the Island as a whole, if the word 'shore' in the original grants was defined as all land bordering on tidally influenced water, the Crown land originally retained in fishery reserves might have been defined as including as much as fifty thousand acres, and the area where the Crown retained an easement for the public an additional fifteen thousand acres. With a more restricted definition of 'coast,' the area contained in the reserves would be less.[63]

Like the settlement terms of the original grants, the fishery reserves represented a weakness in proprietors' deeds. Given sufficient effort and creativity, they offered a possible opening for forcing proprietorial concessions. John Lawson, who besides being solicitor general also handled proprietorial business, thought it a potentially more damaging legal weakness than the settlement terms of the original grants. In drawing developing tenant strategy in this regard to the Stewarts' attention in 1836, he noted that it wore 'a more serious face than the silly cry of Escheat and will perhaps be more difficult to be got over.'[64] In January 1838, FitzRoy wrote to the Colonial Office that he was being flooded with tenant requests for the lease of fishery reserves and that he suspected that this soon would be as important an issue as claims for an escheat in the ongoing land struggle.[65] The governor postponed a decision on the requests, pending instructions from the Imperial government, but he counselled strongly against resolving the matter by relinquishing the fishery reserves to the proprietors.[66] Such a move, he warned, would seriously weaken the colonists' attachment to the Crown.

In the period between the great rally at Sentiner's in the late fall of 1837 and the Managing Committee meetings early in 1838, those challenging the status quo in Upper and Lower Canada had become involved in open armed rebellions. The course of Escheat continued remarkably undistracted by these events. Elite organizers of loyalty meetings staged in the wake of the risings had worried that local countrypeople might disrupt their meetings, but political divisions in the Canadas did not come to intersect with Island politics in this fashion. A potentially contentious Charlottetown loyalty meeting unfolded without hitch, with the only tension of the night emerging when the Speaker of the House of Assembly, George Dalrymple, drew the disapprobation of the chair by suggesting that rebellion grew out of legitimate grievances.[67] Instead of being drawn into these issues, Escheat leaders continued on course, holding meetings as planned. When the legislature convened again at the end of January, the Legislative Council submitted an address to the governor that attempted to discredit the Escheat movement by linking it with the rebellions in the Canadas. The 'tragical occurrences' there were the result of the actions of 'a few factious and designing demagogues,' and they trusted that the events in the Canadas would serve as a warning to the citizenry of other colonies not 'to lend themselves to the designs of restless and unprincipled men.' The assembly followed suit, speaking of their regret at the 'revolutionary spirit' that had emerged in the Canadas and of their determination to suppress 'any attempt which may be made by designing or disaffected persons' to subvert the constitution and foster 'insubordination' on Prince Edward Island.[68] The attempts to discredit agrarian protest in this fashion were not particularly effective.

Other issues quickly dominated the legislative agenda after the 1838 session began. The Hay River affair was the first issue of the day for the house, as a decision had to be taken concerning whether the three Kings County representatives should remain in the custody of the sergeant-at-arms. Joseph Pope again successfully led the yes faction in an unchanged division on the question. He argued that despite rumours of the 'evil consequences' that would befall the assembly if it continued to punish the three, the house needed to stand firm and not appear to be conceding to the seditious pressure that was building in the countryside.[69] Within days of this vote, the behaviour of the Kings County

Escheat leaders was again before the assembly. FitzRoy had just obtained a copy of the chain letter concerning the promises he had supposedly made as an mediator, and he now requested that the assembly give publicity to his denial of Cooper's claims and publish correspondence that he had had with Cooper on the matter.[70] That numerous copies of Cooper's September letter – which, among other things, was a call for attendance at the massive Sentiner's rally – could be the talk of rural regions for four months before FitzRoy was aware of it speaks volumes about the distance between Government House and the countryside.[71] Cooper subsequently petitioned, from his exile in the custody of the sergeant-at-arms, for the opportunity to respond and to put on the record documents that he believed would substantiate to the assembly his side of the dispute. This gave occasion, once again, as with the Hay River debate the previous year, for the assembly to discuss the behaviour of Escheat's leader. As with the previous year's deliberations, moderate Escheat voices in the house distanced themselves from Cooper, even as they provided unsuccessful support for his attempts to gain a hearing.[72]

The renewed incarceration and silencing of the three Kings County members drew strong protests from their supporters in the countryside. The persecution enhanced their popularity and gave them greater credibility in rural eyes.[73] Interestingly, they used their power to appeal for moderation from their backers. When Pope had talked in terms of a cabal to intimidate the house, Cooper had been quick to his feet both to deny its existence and to say that he would be the first to help suppress any such thing.[74] And after the three Kings County assemblymen were consigned to the custody of the sergeant-at-arms, they published an advertisement in the *Colonial Herald* thanking their supporters for expressions of sympathy, but calling on them to be patient under the circumstances.[75] As far as rent resistance was concerned, they counselled Escheators to fight their battles in the courts on the basis of the settlement terms of the original grants, and the fishery reserves where relevant, but to exercise caution and not to press beyond the law. If, after all legal resistance had been offered, law officers came for their possessions and farms, they advised their followers to surrender them and appeal to the Imperial government for redress from oppression. The three repeated this point with even greater emphasis later in the spring, warning their followers not to let themselves be driven to 'open insurrection.' Instead, they asked that they 'bear all with patience' and 'suffer themselves to be stripped of every article they possess, rather than attempt any resistance, which would have no other effect than to expose their dwellings to desolation and themselves to all the horrors of military execution.'[76] Sobering news from the Canadas of the harsh repression of the rebellions there reinforced Escheat leaders' fears of what could happen on Prince Edward Island. The admonition to be patient is yet another reminder that a central challenge facing the Escheat leader was that of channelling and containing popular forces that might employ more radical means to vent their dissatisfaction with the status quo. To maintain the pressure and public excitement necessary to sustain activism and propel changes, all the while avoiding actions that would justify crippling repression, was a difficult balancing act. Having been made martyrs to the cause by the actions of the assembly, the Kings County members had the stature necessary to call for discipline and sacrifice, and they thought it necessary to do so repeatedly.

Two of the primary concerns of the assembly during the 1838 session were land taxes and electoral legislation. Passage of the land assessment bill in the previous session had, not surprisingly, occasioned enormous outcry on the part of the landlords. The PEIA had followed developments in the legislature through Island newspapers, and its secretary remained in touch with the Colonial Office as the bill made its way east across the Atlantic. The association brought pressure to bear on the colonial secretary when it arrived, and in response to its pleas, operation of the act was suspended for six months.[77] Having received an account of the proprietors' case against the bill and promised them the opportunity of a hearing on the matter before the Privy Council, the Colonial Office requested that the Island's legislature submit a brief defending its original actions.[78] Legislation supporting development, such as the land assessment bill, found vigorous support not only in the assembly but in the Legislative Council as well, and the two bodies combined forces in this instance to construct a long and detailed point-by-point rebuttal of the proprietors' arguments.[79]

With an election due to be held in 1838, the possibility that the Escheat movement might translate its power into control of the next assembly was a matter of concern to the governor, the current house, and the Island's upper classes in general. William Douse, who could feel the rural pulse better than many of his fellows in government, believed an Escheat victory to be inevitable; he thought that the best response would be for the assembly to vote a revenue bill for three years rather than one, thus permitting the governor to avoid calling the new house.[80] FitzRoy and his closest advisers, he believed, were operating under the foolish and mistaken notion that the Escheat leaders did not speak for most rural Islanders.[81] The actions of the governor and the legislature suggest that they, too, were keenly aware Escheat's popularity and the threat of an Escheat majority in the lower house. To guard against this, the majority in the assembly drafted new electoral legislation during the 1838 session to undercut the Escheators' strength, and FitzRoy hurried it off to Britain for royal assent. Under the new act, counties were divided into districts, with two members per district and three districts per county. Besides giving each county two extra members, this put an end to voting at large. The intent of the legislation was to defeat the strategy of cooperative regional voting that Escheat had pioneered in the previous election. It would also, its designers hoped, keep the most militant Escheat regions from having a broader impact over electoral results. Escheators, as the attorney general argued in the opinion he submitted to the Colonial Office with the bill, would be prevented from extending 'their influence over a whole county by a concentration of that influence at one fixed place.'[82] Believing that the electoral power of Escheat would to a large extent 'be destroyed' by it, FitzRoy supported the bill energetically and succeeded in persuading the Colonial Office that it required royal assent in time for the 1838 election.[83]

By the spring of 1838, FitzRoy had retreated from his early espousal of the agrarian position and become a solid ally of the most influential figures in the politics of development and an active partisan in their struggle to maintain political power and contain agrarian radicalism. His initiatives to obtain moderate land reform had brought torrents of criticism upon him from the proprietorial lobby, deepening his earlier distaste for many of its members. By 1838 this antipathy was matched by a loathing for the Escheat leaders, who had played a part in luring him into a confrontation with landlords. Furthermore, Cooper's chain letter had infuriated him. In the fall of 1837, FitzRoy's public denunciations of Escheat activists had lacked commitment, but by the following spring he was a dedicated player in the anti-Escheat cause. FitzRoy took the occasion of the closing of the assembly in early April to deliver a hard-hitting speech condemning any continuing calls for an escheat and warning tenants that he would not be timid about suppressing attempts to interfere with 'the undoubted rights of private property.'[84] Believing that in the past Escheators had intentionally mistranslated statements of government policy at public meetings, the governor had his speech printed in French and Gaelic and distributed throughout the colony.[85] Among its other accomplishments, the Escheat movement was forcing the government to recognize the multilingual realities of the Island's countryside.

FitzRoy hoped he would be able to help his allies discredit and subdue the Escheat movement before the next election and lent his energies to the effort in a number of ways. For example, he appealed to the new Island bishop to steer his flock away from the Escheators. Bishop Bernard Donald Macdonald, an Island-born relation of the proprietorial Macdonald of Glenaladale family, assured the governor that he would do what he could to influence Roman Catholics who 'may have been deceitfully led to believe' that there was 'a possibility of obtaining lands free from the payment of rent.'[86] Macdonald warned him, though, that many Acadian tenants would never be able to pay their arrears and that 'Cooper's emissaries' were working among them in an attempt to gain their participation in illegal combinations. But for the energetic efforts of Harvey and the British Colonial and Foreign Offices, FitzRoy might not have been ensured of such a cooperative response from the Catholic hierarchy. Following the death of the previous bishop, Angus MacEachern, Harvey had exerted himself to prevent the Vatican from appointing a French or Irish bishop in his place. In the spring of 1837, writing to Upper Canada's Bishop Alexander McDonell (a man with a solid reputation for using the church to combat radicalism), Harvey requested his assistance and intervention with Rome lest the church see a 'political tool of the Papineau placed in so influential a situation.'[87] The British government, too, exerted great efforts to ensure that a French or Irish appointment did not occur, letting it be known that in the case of the first it would lodge an objection.[88] Although the Vatican appears to have initially appointed a man of Irish birth to the post, the lobbying ultimately paid off in the appointment of Macdonald.[89] While Harvey had claimed that a French or Irish appointment was objectionable because priests of such backgrounds tended to mix politics with religion, it was precisely such interference, on the side of the government, that made Macdonald valuable to the subsequent governor.[90]

FitzRoy also played a role in defeating Escheat efforts to block electoral changes. After the close of the legislature, the Managing Committee prepared a memorial to the Colonial Office protesting the new legislation. FitzRoy moved to discredit its petition before it even arrived. The memorial, he instructed his superiors, was not 'entitled to the slightest consideration.' Those signing it were by and large 'extremely ignorant and illiterate farmers of the poorer class who are duped and led away by Cooper.'[91] Such arguments, coupled with his own vigorous promotion of the electoral initiatives, helped ensure that the legislation received early Privy Council approval. Lord Glenelg had intended to wait for the memorial and to read its arguments before passing judgment on the act, but he was persuaded to change his mind.[92] Although the land assessment bill was held up for six months so that the arguments of proprietors might be heard against it, the new elections bill was hurried on before Escheat complaints had even reached the colonial secretary.

The memorial against the elections bill was one of a number of initiatives undertaken by the Escheat Managing Committee in the months following the close of the assembly. More ambitious was the decision its members took in mid-April to send William Cooper to Britain to bring their case before the Colonial Office and Parliament.[93] It was, of course, a project that Escheators had been advocating for years, and an unrealized plan of agrarian reformers decades earlier. In 1837 it had been postponed in part because of the shortage of funds occasioned by the disastrous harvest of the previous fall. In part, too, there were grounds to hope that the new governor would act in a fashion that might relieve the tenantry from the expense of this line of action. By the following year there had been a good harvest, and any hope Escheators might have had that FitzRoy might assist them had seriously diminished. Before leaving, Cooper applied to the governor – who on his arrival had promised to help the tenantry bring their grievances to the attention of the colonial authorities – for a letter of introduction. FitzRoy complied with his request twice over, first by penning a letter that he gave Cooper, and second by sending a confidential alternative introduction on to the Colonial Office. In the latter he condemned the man, the project, and its supporters in unstinting terms. Cooper, he warned, was an 'illiterate' and an 'extremely artful person and possessed of much low cunning.'[94] The claims he intented to submit on arrival saying that he had been 'delegated' by a 'large majority of the inhabitants,' FitzRoy informed Lord Glenelg, were 'entirely without foundation.' Cooper's influence, the governor contended, was collapsing, and he had the support only of 'the most ignorant of the Tenantry.' The cause had never been 'upheld by a single person of respectability or property in the Colony.'[95] Unbeknownst to Cooper, this letter was in Glenelg's hands by the time of his first meeting with the secretary at the Colonial Office.[96] Whether the governor knew how much he was stretching the truth in this dispatch is not clear; what *is* apparent is the degree to which FitzRoy had become an active and 'cunning' player in partisan politics.

Cooper arrived in London at the end of June and began talks with officials in the Colonial Office in the beginning of July.[97] Over the next two months he submitted a ream of petitions and documents and engaged in a series of conversations and interviews with Lord Glenelg and others in the Colonial Office. The central document he brought to these meetings was the Escheat petition constructed in the wake of the Sentiner's meeting. It bore nearly three thousand signatures. Also included in the papers Cooper carried with him and submitted to the Colonial Office was a petition from the Island Mi'kmaq, drawn up with the assistance of members of the Escheat Managing Committee, concerning Native claims for land and justice.[98] Cooper's ability to present effectively the grievances of Island residents, however, had been seriously undermined by FitzRoy's previous communications as well as by past reports of others, who had portrayed Cooper as a troublemaker who had incited the tenantry to insubordination. James Stephen noted on Cooper's first request for an interview that the reply should state that the Colonial Office was informed that the governor had granted him a letter of introduction with reluctance and that they understood that he represented 'a comparatively small and unimportant body of persons of whom he is the leader agst. the local gov. and house of assembly.'[99] Island voters would demonstrate the inaccuracy of this statement in a matter of months, but when Cooper attempted to present the tenants' case in the summer of 1838, he had to work against these preconceptions. As well, he was handicapped by his unfamiliarity with the customs and manners of those with whom he was dealing. His first request for an interview, for instance, included an apology for any mistakes in procedure he may have made, for, as Cooper admitted, he was 'unacquainted with the rules to be observed at the Colonial Office.'[100]

The results were predictable. With FitzRoy exerting himself to defeat Cooper's project, the majority of the assembly standing against him, and the proprietors' lobby adamantly opposed to his plans, Cooper's mission was doomed from the start. Under the circumstances, he could have gained the profile necessary to gain a hearing for his arguments only by arguing effectively that the Escheat case he was presenting was backed by the majority of Islanders. FitzRoy was claiming otherwise, and there was no reason for Colonial Office officials to doubt his contentions. Furthermore, those Cooper was dealing with at the Colonial Office had reason to believe that the mediation efforts begun by Harvey and continued by FitzRoy had resulted in new policies among the proprietors that would allay the grievances of much of the tenantry. These new policies, they reasoned, would solve the problems Cooper was concerned with and also undercut whatever limited political support he had.

In January 1838, George Rennie Young, acting as counsel for the proprietors associated with the PEIA, had submitted a land settlement proposal to Lord Glenelg. It would, he claimed, remove every ground for complaint and put an end to the escheat agitation.'[101] Glenelg, who had discussed the terms with Robert Stewart and Andrew Colvile as well as George Young, gave it his stamp of approval.[102] The proposal was in turn submitted to FitzRoy with the colonial secretary's imprimatur.[103] Cooper had left before Young's terms arrived on the Island, so he saw the proposal for the first time when Glenelg gave it to him.[104] He was not impressed. Except for promising clearer contracts and uniform terms for the purchase and lease of land – and the opportunity to pay rents in produce – it conceded nothing.[105] Even Young's contention that it met with the minimal terms suggested by Harvey and FitzRoy was false. There was no mention of the pressing issue of arrears, which threatened much of the tenantry, nor any proposal to reduce annual rents. Indeed, the terms offered were harsher than those which already existed on many of the Island estates. Tenants interested in purchasing wilderness lands could do so at rates between 6/3 and £1 per acre. The Stewarts had paid on average 1s/acre for their lands in the 1830s, and Selkirk roughly 3.5d. at the turn of the century.[106] Even at 6/3 per acre the Stewarts and Lord Selkirk were selling at prices between 600 and 1,800 per cent above their costs of purchase. Most other landlords had paid comparable amounts and stood to make similar profits from land sales at this rate. Rents were to be one shilling *sterling*[107] per acre when they became full as of the sixth year of a tenant's lease – an annual levy higher than the total per acre price many landlords had paid to acquire their land in the first place – and leases were to be for between sixty-six and ninety-nine years. At the end of that time, tenants would of course lose all the improvements they had made to wilderness lands and/or have to renegotiate at rents reflecting the value of their own improvements. There was no mention of any greater security for tenants, or of compensation for the value they had added to the proprietors' lands.

Cooper, not surprisingly, rejected this proposal, pointing out how far short it fell of tenants' expectations. However, the Colonial Office argued for time to see how the Islanders responded to Young's terms.[108]

Here again, Cooper's negotiations with officials at the Colonial Office were seriously undermined by communications from FitzRoy. Standing against whatever Cooper said about the weaknesses of the proposal was the support given it by members of the proprietors' lobby, who had already discussed the matter with the colonial secretary and had convinced him of the merits of their position. Nonetheless, Cooper might have succeeded in providing an Island counterpoint to this perspective had not FitzRoy already pre-empted him. In a dispatch that arrived at the Colonial Office at the beginning of July, the governor assured his superiors that if Young's terms were 'acted upon in good faith, they will be satisfactory to the great majority of the Inhabitants of the Colony.'[109] It is hard to believe that FitzRoy believed what he said, for he recognized that the key issue of arrears had been omitted. Nor did he think that Young or the proprietors associated with the PEIA were acting in good faith or that Glenelg had shown good judgment in his assessment and handling of Young.[110] Certainly too, he knew that one shilling sterling per acre was a staggering – perhaps impossible – rent for many and that the 'long' leases the proposal promised were for one-tenth or less of the period more liberal proprietors had always provided. Whether FitzRoy was intentionally responding in a way that would undermine Cooper, or whether he had determined that he was no longer going to suffer the consequences of communicating the realities of tenant life to the Colonial Office – particularly after the colonial secretary had taken a position on the matter – the effect was to yet again reduce whatever persuasiveness Cooper might have had.

Cooper returned to the colony with very little to show for his efforts. At the end of his negotiations the Colonial Office had once again said no to a court of escheat and, as well, had informed him that it would not interfere with the new changes in the electoral laws. Establishing a court of escheat, he was told, would 'unsettle the minds of the inhabitants' and 'shake the rights of property.'[111] Beyond this, the Colonial Office told Cooper that it would not negotiate the land question with any 'third party' until Glenelg had had a chance to hear tenants' responses to the proposal being put forward by Young. At least he had gotten a hearing; when Charles Duncombe sought to see Glenelg concerning Upper Canadian grievances in the fall of 1836, Glenelg opted not to deal with him.[112] It is not clear how Cooper fared in his efforts to gain allies in Parliament. He saw Joseph Hume, and in so doing began an important relationship between Escheators and this radical member of the House of Commons. It appears that Cooper tried and failed to get

Daniel O'Connell's support for Escheat's legal position on the land question, though here again he seems to have gained a political ally.[113]

Although the responses to Cooper's efforts had, in general, been discouraging, there were grounds for Escheators to believe that they would yet have a chance to alter Imperial policy. For one thing, the policy of saying no to further negotiations pending the tenants' possible acceptance of Young's proposals was rooted in a wild misreading of Island circumstances and the terms of the offer, and guaranteed that there would be a need for further discussions. Also, the belief that the claims of Cooper and the Escheat Managing Committee could be dismissed as those of a minority who were losing influence in Island politics was soon to be put to a public test. There were some grounds for hope, too, in the dispatch Glenelg had sent to FitzRoy with Young's terms. Central to the case being made by Escheat was that the land question was a public issue requiring government intervention. The proprietors, by contrast, insisted on its private nature and that it was inappropriate for the government to infringe on their rights of property. Much as the Colonial Office wanted to sustain a reading of the issue as a private, contractual matter, events – as their latest communication revealed – continued to tug them towards Escheat's position on the nature of the problem. Glenelg's dispatch represented yet another public acknowledgment of the government's shift away from a laissez-faire position. Although landlord/tenant relations were, 'correctly speaking, an affair of private concern, in which the Government have no power to exercise any authority,' Glenelg stated that there were 'circumstances in this case which seem to me to require, if not to justify, its interposition.' The three reasons he then cited all had their roots in Escheat activism. There were, he noted, the repeated appeals to the government for redress of tenant grievances. There was the reality that if the government did not take action to deal with these, they would have to take action to suppress resistance to the law. And, as well, there were the precedents established by Harvey's and FitzRoy's attempts to take on the role of mediator and thereby undercut the power of the Escheat movement. Glenelg's instructions to the governor reveal his discomfort at being drawn away from a 'correct' reading of the issue. Acknowledging that it was difficult to 'define the limits' of what the government's role should be, he asked FitzRoy to continue acting as a mediator without forgetting that the parties were 'free agents.' While this provided no ground for optimism, there was some in the admission that landlord/tenant relations were a public issue requiring government intervention. The challenge for Escheators remained the same: to demonstrate that the government would not be able to deal effectively with its public responsibilities in the matter until it showed some willingness – as it had in the case of slave emancipation – to infringe upon the rights of private property.

During the same period that Cooper was visiting London and new proposals for settling the land conflict were being discussed on the Island, Lord Durham was in the Canadas holding, in the wake of the rebellions there, discussions on the future of British North America. In the summer of 1838, hoping to find a sympathetic audience for Islanders' grievances in the new forum for political discussion that was being opened in the interior of the continent, the Escheat Managing Committee sent John Le Lacheur to Quebec as a delegate to represent its interests. The committee was not alone in recognizing the importance of this forum and in moving to gain a voice within it. Proprietors and the mercantile community clustered around Government House also attempted to shape the story that Durham and his associates heard and the policies that would emerge. Given the power that others were able to exert in this regard, the opportunities available to the Escheat Managing Committee were highly circumscribed.

Realizing the significance that Durham's report might hold for their plans and investments, those associated with land company developments in the Atlantic provinces used their connections to ensure that their interests would be protected. The new Maritime participants in these joint ventures involving British and colonial capital appear to have been most sensitive to the possible threats. Samuel Cunard approached the matter by attempting to control both the tellers and the listeners associated with the Durham Commission. In the first regard, he wrote to FitzRoy before the governor left for Quebec City and pressed on him the importance the new land company schemes held for the Island's economic development. He argued that by acting to 'meet the views of the Company' he 'would be serving the best interests of the Island.' In addition, Cunard, as he explained it to Colvile, 'wrote to a particular friend of mine who is secretary to Lord Durham and one of the Special Council and who will interest himself to see that no injustice is done to us.'[114] As well, he adopted a conciliatory policy towards those who were criticizing land speculators for retarding colonial improvements and who were agitating for land taxes. Cunard was one of the Nova Scotians whom the Durham Commission interviewed on land issues in British North America. In his testimony, he stressed the need for more state expenditures on transportation to cure the region's ills; he also conceded that it was fair to place moderate taxes on the holdings of large proprietors.[115] Having come to realize the extent of official support for such policies, and having grave concerns about more radical challenges to proprietors' investments, he thought it wisest to concede the inevitable and thereby gain allies in the struggle against more dangerous forces. Land taxes, he argued to Colvile, represented 'a pledge on the part of the government that there shall be no escheat.'[116] George Rennie Young and his father-in-law Thomas Brooking were substantial partners in the new land company that was being formed by Colvile, Cunard, the Stewarts, and others. They worked to ensure that the Durham Commission would hold no surprises for that venture.[117] Young wrote to FitzRoy about proprietors' concerns and played a part in getting Nova Scotia's governor Sir Colin Campbell to explain 'our view' to FitzRoy and to gain FitzRoy's 'friendly interference on behalf of the proprietors in the event of the Escheat Question being moved on by Lord Durham.'[118] Moreover, Campbell's aide-de-camp, Young informed Colvile, was an intimate friend and a 'master of the pamphlet' and had at his request 'promised to protect us.'[119] George Young's brother and legal partner, William, was also a member of the Nova Scotia delegation, and Cunard's son was its secretary.[120]

The proprietors' group need not have worried about FitzRoy's position on escheat. He, too, was anxious that nothing occur in Quebec that would give any credence or stimulus to the initiatives that Escheators were pursuing. On becoming aware of Le Lacheur's mission on behalf of the Escheat Managing Committee, FitzRoy immediately wrote to Lord Durham – as he had to Lord Glenelg prior to Cooper's mission – to discredit the man and his project before he arrived, and to request that Le Lacheur not be allowed to raise the escheat issue with the Durham Commission. Le Lacheur, he informed him, represented an insignificant faction in Island affairs.[121] The voices to listen to were his own and those of the leading figures among the mercantile community, who dominated the House of Assembly and who were allied with Government House. They represented, as one of those associated with this group phrased it in a pamphlet published in the summer of 1838, a 'third class,' a middle class with interests distinct from those of proprietors and tenants.[122] Travelling to Quebec as part of the official delegation representing the Executive Council and the legislature were FitzRoy, Robert Hodgson, T.H. Haviland, Joseph Pope, and George Dalrymple. While these particular men certainly were distinct from the tenantry, they were intimately related to proprietors' interests. All these Islanders were land agents, and some would in time become substantial landlords themselves. Nonetheless, their interests were – as their pamphlet suggested – different from those of the big proprietors. They shared those men's desire to extinguish tenant activism, but at the same time, they had a developmental agenda that many proprietors found repugnant. They, and the others sharing their interests who later testified before Charles Buller's Crown land committee as it travelled to the Maritimes, argued in favour of a moderate tax on wilderness holdings as a stimulus for economic development and as a solution to the Island's land question.[123] As well, many of them advocated long leases and more liberal terms for the Island's tenantry.[124]

Le Lacheur left on his mission in early July and returned in September.[125] Island tenants and their allies raised money to pay his passage and to permit him to buy a suit so that he might appear before the commissioners. In his recorded testimony before the land commission, Le Lacheur insisted that the Island's proprietors had never lived up to the terms of their grants and that none had ever attempted to: 'Not one foreign Protestant was introduced by any of the grantees.'[126] As well, he argued that despite repeated efforts to gain an escheat of these grants, proprietors had succeeded in defeating the course of justice by 'false representations.' During his time in Quebec, Le Lacheur dealt on an official basis with Buller's assistant, Richard Davies Hanson, and had, it would appear, extensive discussions with him.[127] As well, he was able to obtain an invitation to a dinner that Lord Durham was attending and to discuss Island affairs with him, receiving an assurance that Island grievances would not be overlooked in his considerations.[128] Le Lacheur no doubt took the occasion to assure Durham that Escheators supported the political changes he was proposing. Federal union and the abolition of the unelected upper houses in British North America found warm support in Escheat circles, for land reformers had much to gain from a greater democratization of political institutions and from the transfer of the legislative review functions from the Privy Council in London, where they were all too easily influenced by landlords' lobbying, to a new federal assembly in British North America.[129]

As with Cooper's mission, the managing committee's Quebec initiative produced little in the way of immediate tangible results. Le Lacheur had been only one among many Islanders making presentations to Durham's commission; the others told different tales and highlighted different issues. In the long term, Le Lacheur and those he represented must have derived some satisfaction from seeing that despite the many obstacles thrown in his way, the voice of the impecunious delegate dispatched by the Escheat Managing Committee that had gathered at a Charlottetown tavern had a significant influence on Durham's report. Le Lacheur's evidence on the weakness of proprietors' land claims and on the history of the land question went unchallenged in the recorded testimony of other Islanders and was cited as definitive in the final report.[130] As well, it played a part in leading Charles Buller to suggest in his summary of the land question in British North America that, though an escheat approach to breaking the grip of land speculators in the colonies would in general be unfair as provincial assemblies had failed to maintain the Crown's settlement claims in early land grants, Prince Edward Island was perhaps an exception.[131] Buller's report ultimately backed the mercantile community's land tax program; nonetheless, it left the escheat door ajar.

Shortly after his return, Le Lacheur became embroiled in a controversy with FitzRoy and Hodgson concerning what he had accomplished and what he had been told. On their arrival in Quebec, Hodgson and FitzRoy had made a point of inquiring into Le Lacheur's activities; they requested and got copies of his testimony. They sought as well – and supposedly received – assurances that the commissioners had not discussed the possibility of an escheat with the managing committee's delegate and that he had been told that the idea of a court of escheat was out of the question.[132] Le Lacheur, for his part, contended that he had been able to raise the issue while in Quebec and that he had been told that a court of escheat should be established. Behind the details of this disagreement lay the colonial election scheduled for November. The governor and the party associated with him wanted to portray escheat as an impossible dream not worthy of voter support; Le Lacheur and other Escheat leaders wanted to put the best face possible on their efforts and their chances of success. The *Colonial Herald* and the *Royal Gazette* published letters from Hodgson and FitzRoy contesting Le Lacheur's claims.[133] As well, FitzRoy obtained a letter from Lord Durham himself denying that he had promised LeLacheur that a court of escheat would be established.[134] Le Lacheur, though, had never claimed that *Durham* was the one who said that it should be, and he responded by publishing letters he had sent to Durham and Hanson detailing what had passed between them and asking that they vindicate his contentions.[135] And so it remained at the time of the election.

Cooper did not return until days before the first polling got under way. As with Le Lacheur's mission, Escheators highlighted Cooper's accomplishments, announcing shortly before he returned that they had received letters from him containing good news.[136] Working with these letters – which included copies of Cooper's correspondence with the Colonial Office – Le Lacheur hammered together a summary of Escheat's electoral policy.[137] Central to the Escheators' appeal was the claim that with proposals from the proprietors now on the table, the assembly would need to provide a forum for discussing those terms and would be called upon to speak for tenants' interests on the matter. Escheators argued that the assembly's statements would carry great weight with the Imperial authorities and that those demanding land reform needed to make sure that their representatives guided this discussion. Escheators drew the attention of rural voters to Glenelg's statement that he was waiting to be informed of the tenantry's reaction to Young's proposal before involving the Colonial Office in any further mediation attempts.

Escheators did their best to sustain faith in political action as a method for dealing with the land question; their critics argued that such faith was misguided and that rank-and-file Escheators were being duped into supporting a costly agrarian organization that would never be able to provide the results they wanted. Countrypeople were, they argued, being gulled into providing the means whereby Escheat leaders could travel and pontificate at their expense.[138] A series of satirical letters in the *Royal Gazette* purporting to be intercepted correspondence between Cornelius Little, who owned the Charlottetown tavern where the Escheat Managing Committee met, and William Cooper – 'C. Littletodo' and 'W. Barrelmaker' – captured the gist of much of this attack, portraying the managing committee squabbling among themselves over policy as they sought to cope with the lack of success emerging from the costly dispatch of delegates.[139] These and other anti-Escheat letters certainly were correct in noting that Escheat leaders were straining to find hope in developments that in fact provided minimal grounds for optimism. They also correctly assessed the Managing Committee as an internally divided and uneasy coalition. But the election results indicated that Escheators were not in as much disarray and despair as the critics suggested. Despite the forces that had been assembled to defeat them, Escheators prevailed in the 1838 election. Indeed, they achieved a massive victory, reducing anti-Escheat voices to but six of the twenty-four seats in the new assembly.

Most of those who were elected to the house in 1838 had been Escheat delegates or local Escheat leaders during the years when the central committee provided rural Islanders with an alternative voice. Alexander Rae, Mungo Macfarlane, Malcolm Forbes, Charles MacNeil, Vere Beck, John Dalziel, Donald Macdonald, John Arbuckle, William Clark, William Dingwell, Joseph Dingwell, Thomas Gorman, Allan Fraser, John Thomson, and of course Cooper, Le Lacheur, and Macintosh, had all been members of the central committee and/or office holders with local Escheat committees. The Dingwells had been continuously involved in Escheat politics since providing crucial backing to Cooper in his first election bid of 1830. Vere Beck's involvement in the cause too went back to the beginning of the decade. Donald Macdonald, among other things, had been the recording secretary at the great Sentiner's rally. John Thomson was the man who had risen at Sentiner's to politely but firmly take on the new governor's policy by introducing a resolution denying the legality of existing land laws. Joseph Dingwell and Vere Beck as well had been among the half-dozen figures who introduced resolutions at Sentiner's. Mungo Macfarlane, like Vere Beck, had served a term as the corresponding secretary of the central committee. Malcolm Forbes, besides being a member of the central committee, had repeatedly led Queens County Escheators in bringing petitions before Government House. John Dalziel, like Beck, Thomson, Forbes, Macintosh, Le Lacheur, and Cooper, had been part of the Escheat committee that formulated the new land settlement policies that emerged in the aftermath of the Sentiner's rally. Alexander Rae had been involved in the first Island-wide committee debate in the summer of 1836. John Arbuckle was the local corresponding secretary for the highly active Belfast Escheat committee. For most of the new Escheat members, assuming office was a matter of moving their deliberations from Cornelius Little's tavern – where the central committee had been meeting in the fall of 1838 – to the assembly chambers.

Escheat achieved its greatest success in Kings County. There the movement took all the seats for the county as well as those for the royalty of Georgetown. In the latter, John Lewellin, Laurence Sulivan's land agent and a member of the 12th General Assembly, and Edward Thornton, an incumbent and the land agent for R.C. Macdonald, son of Captain John Macdonald of Glenaladale, went down to defeat. Thomas Owen, who seems to have considered attempting a return to the assembly, wisely chose otherwise, as Escheators in Kings County won either by acclamation or by big majorities. In Queens County, John Small Macdonald was the only incumbent who managed to retain a seat after a hard-fought election.[140] George Dalrymple, one-time champion of a partial escheat, speaker of the previous house, and a member of the official delegation that had journeyed to Quebec, was trounced in southern Queens County, losing by a ratio of one to seven to the winning candidates, John Le Lacheur and John Arbuckle. In the first district of Queens, Escheators won by acclamation. Except for John Small Macdonald's seat, the only victories for the anti-Escheat forces were in Prince County and Charlottetown. In the latter, James Bagnall and Abercrombie Willock were easily defeated by Francis Longworth and Edward Palmer. Longworth was a member of a prominent entrepreneurial family that was involved in tanning and shipbuilding and, like Palmer, was a second-generation Charlottetown notable.[141] In Prince County the return of Joseph Pope and the election of James Yeo and Richard Hudson meant that half the seats there were taken by anti-Escheat members. The other three went to Escheat supporters.[142]

Despite the redistricting brought about by the majority of the 14th assembly, and despite the rebuffs that FitzRoy and others had engineered for Escheat initiatives and scathing criticism of their cause in the assembly, in the press, and from Government House, Escheat had achieved an impressive victory at the polls in the fall of 1838. Behind their success lay the tremendous organizational work that had facilitated the growth of Escheat as a coordinated movement in the years prior to the electoral contest. In effect, the election officially transferred legitimacy from the mercantile leaders advocating developmental politics, who had met in government chambers, to the agrarian representatives who had constituted themselves as an alternative assembly two years earlier and who had persistently argued that they, and not the members of the 14th General Assembly, were the real voice of the people. Now the newly elected Escheators faced the difficult challenge of translating success at the polls into tangible gains for rural Islanders. Having chosen to adhere to constitutional means in their struggle, and having gained overwhelming control of the popular house, it remained to be seen whether their faith in the political process would prove well founded.

10 The Limits of Democratic Power, 1838–1842

The tactical choices Escheators made in the 1830s were predicated on the notion that the British constitution provided opportunities for them to realize their goals within existing government structures. They were not unaware of the powers of non-elected officials, but Escheators believed that state claims to legitimacy rested on wielding power in accordance with the needs of the people at large: ultimately the power of the non-elected rested on the consent of the governed. Adherence to such notions of 'contractualism,' as John Belchem has noted, was 'a cornerstone of popular constitutionalism.'[1] The years at the turn of the decade provided a test of Escheat beliefs in this regard. Having mobilized vast numbers around the Escheat program and achieved overwhelming control of the House of Assembly, Escheators had, in their opinion, incontrovertibly demonstrated that they spoke for the people.

Escheat's years of power in the lower house were a bitter lesson in the limited power of democracy within existing structures. Having won control of the assembly, they soon discovered that power lay, or had receded, elsewhere. Their legislative initiatives were blocked, and their petitions for a redress of agrarian grievances went unheeded. Concurrently, the weight of the legal system was brought to bear on tenants contesting landlords' claims in the countryside. Using their control over the non-elective organs of government, proprietors and leading elements of the Island's mercantile community vigorously resisted the upsurge of agrarian democracy. Believing, or hoping, that alterations in their program might reduce this opposition and permit its passage, Escheators displayed a good deal of flexibility concerning the means by which land reform might be realized. Their manoeuvres, though, proved unsuccessful. Escheat's achievements in the political arena had altered the issues at stake, and the primary points of contention did not so much concern land reform as the control of state power. What the movement's opponents sought was to suppress independent agrarian political mobilization, and to achieve this they had to deny Escheat any gains.

Escheat's central objective remained to resolve the land question in favour of the tenantry, the majority of the population. Thus soon after electing William Cooper as the new Speaker of the House, the Escheat-dominated 15th Assembly created a Committee of Grievances to investigate the land question and propose legislative solutions for the problems faced by rural Islanders. The committee's research included investigation of the means by which landlordism had been eliminated elsewhere. Realizing that they were tackling a local facet of a broader historical challenge, and drawing inspiration from the malleability of rural social structures in other settings, Escheators proposed remedies that were firmly grounded in the particularities of Island circumstances. The committee's solutions were embodied in two pieces of legislation: one of these defined the regulations that were to govern the fishery reserves specified in the original grants; the other arranged for the forfeiture of proprietory lands and the settlement of the rural population on freehold lands.

In keeping with earlier Escheat attempts to make use of this limitation of the 1767 grants, the assembly's fishery reserves bill sought to secure the Crown's coastal reserves for the benefit of freeholders and tenants. In the debate over the issue in previous years, the Imperial government had become persuaded that the reserves should not be alienated to proprietors – indeed, perhaps they could not legally be assigned to them. Continuing with their own ongoing initiatives to define these as public lands, and acting as well on the basis of recent correspondence from the Colonial Office indicating that the assembly might need to enact laws governing use of the reserves, the Escheat majority passed a bill clarifying the extent of the lands and the rules that were to govern their use.[2] The bill addressed many practical issues concerning how to reconcile use of the land for the fishery with other pre-existent uses. It also defined the scope of the reserves. The original reserves applied to land five hundred feet above the 'High Water Mark' on the 'coast' of lots. The assembly's bill defined 'coast' as including 'any or all of the Bays or narrow arms of the Sea, as far as sea or salt water runs at highwater.' As well, it barred proprietors from collecting rents or land payments for land within all the reserves, regardless of how they had been defined in the original grants that contained fishery reserve clauses. This provision in the act addressed the legal obstacles that tenants would otherwise face in challenging the terms of existing leases and that buyers would face in challenging earlier sales agreements. Importantly, the act also allowed tenants and small freeholders to deduct payments they had already made for lands within the fishery reserves from claims proprietors might seek to make for the recovery of rents or land payments.[3]

The implications of the act, were it to become law, were huge, as it would relieve tenants and small freeholders from rents and land payments on tens of thousands of acres of valuable land and, importantly, allow them to deduct payments they had made for this land in the past from any future debts owing to proprietors. The second provision was likely to halt rent collection on front land farms for many years. As the Island's solicitor general had noted earlier in the 1830s, the fishery reserve clauses of the grants posed a serious legal problem for proprietors. They posed a major problem for Islanders working as land agents, too, since, by the terms of the act they stood to lose an important source of revenue. The assembly's definition of the meaning of 'coast' in the grants was consistent with legal advice that the Colonial Office would receive when it began considering the fishery reserves issue in light of Escheat activism. And the provisions concerning rent and land payments, at least insofar as they applied to grants where the Crown retained the soil in the fishery reserves, were in keeping with the property rights that should always have applied to the fishery reserves.[4]

The land forfeiture and settlement bill was also a legislative embodiment of earlier Escheat initiatives. Drawing from the proposals that the Escheat Managing Committee had made in the months following the Sentiner's rally of 1837, it provided for the appointment of one or more Commissioners of Escheats and Forfeitures, who would be empowered to investigate fulfilment of the settlement conditions by summoning a jury and holding a public inquest. The legislation defined a settler as a fee simple holder of one hundred acres or more of land, exclusive of fishery reserve lands, and it accepted Lord Goderich's indulgence of 1818 granting proprietors until the beginning of 1827 to fulfil their settlement terms and eliminating the requirement that those settlers be foreign Protestants. This definition, and the act's provisions concerning suitable evidence for proving settlement, addressed earlier Colonial Office complaints that escheat proceedings were unacceptable because they would be too complex and that determining who had or had not met the settlement terms in the eighteenth century was too difficult. As with the proposals the managing committee had framed earlier in 1838, the bill provided procedures for determining the compensation due to proprietors for monies they might have spent on the settlement and improvement of their lands and for their losses from forfeiture. As well, in keeping with the land settlement policies established after the mass meeting at Sentiner's, the bill stipulated the different costs and terms whereby freeholders, rent-paying and non-rent-paying tenants, and squatters might gain freeholds of the lands they worked. Should cases arise where lands proved to be exempt from escheat proceedings, it provided a mechanism whereby tenants might be ensured compensation for the value of their improvements, thus pioneering tenant compensation legislation on the Island.[5]

The land forfeiture and settlement bill was an extraordinary piece of legislation. Unlike the 1832 escheat bill, which was thin on detail and (at approximately four hundred words) less complex than the bill passed that same year to prevent swine from running at large in Princetown, the 1839 act anticipated each step of the process that would be involved in investigating the original grants and facilitating a new order. In this new order, proprietors who had met settlement requirements would get new fee simple grants, those who had not would be compensated for the costs of improvements, occupiers would be secured in their possession of land and enabled to buy or acquire fee simple title, and the Crown would regain unsettled lands. The 1839 act was roughly twenty times the length of the 1832 act and included four schedules to serve as templates for the procedures required to bring the legislation into effect.

The Legislative Council blocked both bills. It amended the fishery reserve bill so as to completely change its significance; the assembly subsequently rejected it. And the council threw the land settlement and forfeiture bill out entirely.[6] These actions were indicative of the patterns that would prevail between the upper house and the popular house throughout the Escheators' dominance of the assembly. The council that took these steps was newly constructed weeks after the 15th Assembly convened. In the years prior to 1839, the Island's Executive Council and Legislative Council had been composed of the same individuals, and unlike the assembly, it had not had a great deal of credibility in the colony at large, being composed almost entirely of Charlottetown residents and by and large of men with little profile in the community beyond their government positions.[7] In 1838 FitzRoy temporarily delayed separating and restructuring the two councils – a plan that had been in the works earlier in the 1830s – as he thought Lord Durham might recommend abolition of the upper house altogether. When Durham subsequently changed his mind, FitzRoy submitted a list of candidates to the Colonial Office that he and John Harvey had selected for the new councils.[8] Knowing that changes were impending, the Escheat majority in the assembly petitioned early in the 1839 session for a stay in proceedings so that they might bring their views to the attention of the Colonial Office. They failed in this, and shortly after the assembly convened, FitzRoy received confirmation of his list of appointments and prorogued the house for a week so that he could construct two new, separate councils.

The Legislative Council that FitzRoy established in 1839 was overwhelmingly composed of Escheat's Island opponents – indeed, many of its members had recently been driven out of electoral politics by the movement's rise.[9] T.H. Haviland, besides being colonial treasurer and a close confidant of FitzRoy, was a land agent who had played a significant role in confronting rent resistance. Rumour – which proved to be accurate in the long term – had it that he would be the new owner of the township that included Bay Fortune, Lord Townshend's Lot 56.[10] Robert Hodgson, the attorney general, also served as a lawyer for proprietors and as a land agent.[11] John Brecken, once a member of the assembly, lived on an income derived from extensive properties and also served as a private banker for many in the mercantile community.[12] George Goodman was the collector of customs and the surveyor of shipping. Charles Worrell and Donald Macdonald were resident landlords who had played prominent roles in combating the rise of agrarian activism; both had been rejected at the polls early in the 1830s.[13] FitzRoy appointed Samuel Green and George Dalrymple[14] as well; both were members of the mercantile community and had weathered the early years of the Escheat movement, maintaining positions in the assembly in the second half of the decade. In 1838, both lost their seats in the house – and Dalrymple the speaker's chair as well – when rural voters rejected incumbents who had fought against Escheat in the 14th Assembly. They were, then, victims of growing democratization and radicalism – a tide that saw an earlier antipathy to proprietors come to include a rejection of the political leadership of many in the professional and mercantile communities as well. Yet another of the new members, Peter Stewart MacNutt, had been in the assembly and had played a role in condemning the more radical wing of the Escheat movement, though he had at times supported some of its measures. These men were joined by William McIntosh, a relative newcomer to the colony and said to be an 'independent agriculturalist,' by John Levitt, also a newcomer with an 'independent income,' and by John MacGowan.[15] Those representing proprietors and merchants' interests had been marginalized in the lower house over the course of the 1830s; now, with the help of governors Harvey and FitzRoy, they had secure control of the non-elected upper house.

The new Executive Council, too, was strongly weighted against the political orientation of the 15th Assembly. Besides Haviland, Hodgson, Brecken, and Goodman, it included John Cambridge's son-in-law, George Wright, who was the surveyor general and owner of a small estate, and James Peake, one of the leading merchants of the colony and John Brecken's brother-in-law. As well, in keeping with instructions from the Colonial Office that the new Executive Council include members of the assembly who might facilitate cooperation between the two branches of government, FitzRoy appointed Joseph Pope and John Small Macdonald, two of the half-dozen anti-Escheat voices who had been able to retain a place in the house. Besides holding many government offices and taking an active hand in his family's mercantile and shipping businesses, Pope was a land agent. Macdonald was a cousin of the resident landlord Donald Macdonald of Glenaladale, who had just been appointed to the Legislative Council. FitzRoy had seen to it that the executive and Legislative Councils would be bastions of mercantile and proprietorial power. With Escheators possessing overwhelming control of the popular house but lacking any representation in the Executive and Legislative Councils, a clash was inevitable.[16]

Conflict came first in the relationship between the Legislative Council and the House of Assembly. Although there had been troubles between the two houses before, they had not previously been as profound, nor had they carried the importance beyond the chambers of the legislature that the deadlock between Escheators and their opponents soon would. Before this, the two had been more alike in class composition, and any tensions had been over status and prerogatives more than over substantive disagreements on colonial issues. In the past, legislation bearing on crucial issues concerning the land question had found backing from leaders of the Island's business community and prominent government officials and had in consequence received majority support in both houses. The strongest opposition to the assembly's land initiatives had emerged as a result of proprietors' intervention at the Colonial Office and before the Privy Council.[17] When the fundamental political cleavage was between professional and commercial interests on one hand, and big landed interests on the other, it had been articulated in geographical terms as well: Islanders versus absentees, though the reality was often more complex. With the rise of popular forces in the colony over the course of the 1830s and the demand for more radical treatment of the land question, the most important cleavage shifted. As the rural underclasses struggled to articulate their own objectives over and above the proprietors' interests and those of leading mercantile and professional men alike, the struggle for power in the colony assumed fundamental importance. Following the election of 1838 and the reconstruction of the Legislative Council, this crucial division of interests fell between the two levels of the legislature.

To sustain their position in colonial politics, those being challenged by the agrarian upsurge depended on Imperial support. Fortunately for them, FitzRoy, like Harvey and Ready before him – and to a lesser extent Young – believed that colonial policy should reflect and sustain the interests of the Island's mercantile and professional community. The governors shared the view that these men's interests needed to be sustained against more broadly based democratic demands as well as against the reactionary appeals of a narrow proprietorial community. The positions these Island governors suggested had in general found support within the Colonial Office, but Imperial policies had not always been in keeping with gubernatorial advice, especially when the issues to be decided pitted the plans of the Island's leading commercial men against the proprietors' lobby. Although the scuttling of developmental legislation in the Privy Council earlier in the decade had embittered some members of the Island's business community, the dispute between the assembly and the Legislative Council in 1839 provided proof of the continuing importance of the Imperial connection to their political interests.

By the end of April 1839, as the 15th Assembly finished its first year's proceedings, it was clear that the lower and upper houses were going to remain at odds on the most important legislative initiatives and that there was little or no room for compromise. While the governor and his allies on the councils could and would suffer disappointments as a result of the assembly's refusals to initiate policies they sought – the assembly, for instance, refused to back their call for a promise of military support in the growing Maine–New Brunswick border dispute – it was the Escheators who had the most to lose from the political deadlock.[18] Their rise had been predicated on the assertion that political power could be translated into tangible ameliorative changes in the daily lives of their rural constituents. Given the existing power relations, however, Escheators had little chance of fulfilling the hopes that had brought them to power. The results of the 1839 session suggested that some minor victories notwithstanding, there would be little to show for all the sacrifices that had been made to obtain an Escheat majority in the assembly. The 15th Assembly reopened the previous house's treatment of the Hay River affair, for instance, and passed resolutions exculpating the behaviour of the three Kings County representatives, expunging from the official record the charges brought against them for their presence at the Escheat meeting and reimbursing them for the pay they had been denied while in the custody of the sergeant-at-arms.[19] As well, tenants gained an official condemnation of the inadequacy of George Young's offer on behalf of the proprietors as the assembly recorded its rejection of the terms of his proposals.[20] Since Lord Glenelg had previously declared that the imperial government would suspend further consideration of the land question pending the tenantry's responses to what he considered an equitable proposal, this at least kept the Colonial Office from easily closing the door on the issue.

On substantial matters, though, the Escheators' initiatives had been stymied. Their two key bills bearing on the land question had both been defeated, and furthermore, Escheators were unable to get legislation dealing with public education through the upper house. Early in the term a schools committee recommended changes in existing laws governing state-funded education in the colony, to more equitably distribute funds, to decentralize governmental control, and to give greater power to small rural communities. As well, the committee sought to reduce the manipulation of educational policy by conservative forces in Island society, by calling for an end to annual competency tests that permitted the central Board of Education to dismiss teachers for their political opinions. Similarly, the committee recommended that communities, rather than the central board, be entitled to determine whether schoolhouses would be made available for political meetings. The same committee also recommended provisions that would permit teachers (such as Alexander Rae and John Arbuckle) to appoint substitutes in their stead so that they could participate in political life and represent their communities as members of the assembly.[21]

At the end of the 1839 session, faced with the rejection of their most important legislative initiatives and with structural obstacles that precluded any realization of popular political demands, the Escheators once again dispatched Cooper as a delegate to Britain to bring their grievances to the attention of the Imperial government. This time Cooper travelled with the backing of the House of Assembly. Although the Escheat Managing Committee had claimed to represent majority opinion in 1838, the Colonial Office had, on the advice of FitzRoy, regarded him as the representative of only a small segment of Island opinion. With the Escheat landslide at the polls in the fall of 1838 and a seventeen-to-five vote in the assembly supporting Cooper's mission and sustaining an address calling for a redress of rural grievances, the fiction that the Escheat position was not that of the majority was no longer sustainable. George Young's proposal on behalf of the proprietors had also by this time been rejected by the tenantry, which removed yet another excuse for delaying further consideration of the land question. With two of the crucial Escheat contentions that had been challenged in 1838 – that Young's offer would not be acceptable, and that Cooper represented the interests of a majority – now confirmed, agrarians had grounds to believe that their delegate would be more successful on his return visit.[22]

Once more, though, FitzRoy undermined Cooper before he arrived. In a long dispatch concerning Cooper's impending visit, he again provided the Colonial Office with a reading of events that cast Cooper in a highly unfavourable light and that provided continuing justification for the Imperial authorities to reject his appeals. Escheators, he contended, had swept the election of 1838 because the Colonial Office had left Cooper and his supporters too much room for optimism following his first mission and because proprietors had failed to abide by the proposals Young had put forward. Besides supplying an explanation regarding the errors in his own claims about the adequacy of the proprietors' solution to the land question and in his predictions concerning the decline of Escheat in 1838, FitzRoy's arguments provided justification for an even stronger rejection of Cooper's mission in 1839, despite the election victory and despite Cooper's ability to present his case as Speaker of the house. Escheat's position, FitzRoy argued, was grounded in deception and voter stupidity. Because of the 'extreme ignorance' of most rural Islanders, they were 'entirely at the mercy of agitators' such as Cooper and the other Escheat leaders, who had led them to believe that an Escheat electoral victory would result in radical land reform. As well, he contended, their continuing popularity was grounded in 'the more respectable portion of the [Island] Community' not bothering to seriously contest the election, as they felt that their initiatives were not receiving adequate support from the Imperial government. The bitter election contests suggest otherwise, but FitzRoy was attempting to shape policy, not to reflect impartially on Island realities. The dispatch was a plea for policies to sustain the advocates of developmental politics over and against the rival claims of Escheators and proprietors. FitzRoy, like his immediate predecessors, saw his role as that of building a government party out of 'respectable' elements of colonial society. To do this he needed to be able to reward his allies with Colonial Office support and to ensure the defeat of their competitors' initiatives.[23]

Cooper arrived in London in July bearing documents substantiating his case for a solution to the land question and for redress of the constitutional problems that had developed on the Island. Unfortunately for him, the Imperial government was in turmoil at the time of his arrival; with colonial affairs a central issue in opposition attacks on the Whigs, the energies of Secretary of State Lord Normanby were directed towards the pressing issues in Parliament, so he had little time to see the delegate from Prince Edward Island.[24] Although Normanby entered into preliminary discussions with Cooper concerning his deputation and promised early treatment of his appeals, week after week passed without a response indicating what Cooper could expect concerning Colonial Office policy.[25] In early September, Lord Russell superseded Normanby as colonial secretary and Cooper began anew with Normanby's replacement, providing him with an account of Island history and tenant grievances and asking for a speedy answer so that he could lay the assembly's grievances before Parliament if necessary.[26] While Russell intended, ultimately, to respond to Cooper's requests through the governor alone, he had initially hoped to provide Cooper with a chance to present his case in person. In the event, though, he was unable to find the time to meet with him.[27] While the letter the Colonial Office sent to Cooper suggested that Russell would not see him because it would be improper for the colonial secretary to discuss these issues with the Speaker of the House, time constraints appear to have been central to the refusal.[28]

Russell's decision not to tell Cooper of the Colonial Office's response to his mission, coupled with the long delays in even indicating this much, seriously impeded Cooper's ability to bring the issue before Parliament, should he have chosen to do so while he was in London.[29] Parliament had been prorogued while he was still waiting to hear back from Normanby, and Lord Russell's dispatch did not make it to the Island until November. Cooper was later criticized for not having brought Island grievances to the attention of Parliament while he was waiting for a reply from the Colonial Office, but Cooper appears to have believed that it was best to await the results of these overtures before carrying the case beyond the Colonial Office. It seems, too, that Cooper's actions reflected the advice he received from Joseph Hume, who had agreed to present the Escheat case to Parliament, and from friends among a Nova Scotian delegation who were in London at the time to discuss colonial grievances with officials at Downing Street.[30] The thinking here appears to have been that because the parliamentary card was likely to be a weak one, particularly given the negligible preparation for its use, it was best held in reserve and not played prematurely. The advice of Hume, who had spent years using parliamentry tools to try to being about change and who was a key spokesman in the commons for the cause of reform in the Canadas, must surely have had a significant impact on Cooper's decisions.[31]

Russell's response to Cooper's mission arrived on the Island in late November and was published in Island newspapers.[32] To their surprise, Islanders learned that the Colonial Office had been considering new propositions for resolving the land question beyond those which had been proposed by the assembly and advanced by Cooper's mission to London. FitzRoy's earlier confidential dispatch notifying the Colonial Office of Cooper's visit had included a plea for action to settle agrarian unrest. Arguing that 'the time has arrived when some remedy is absolutely necessary,' FitzRoy contended that there were three possible approaches: a court of escheat, repurchase of proprietary grants by the Crown, or a heavy penal tax on wilderness land. He vehemently opposed the first option for a variety of reasons, including past Imperial policies on escheat and his own earlier statements on the matter, not to mention his fervent desire that nothing be conceded which might enhance the credibility of Escheators. Nor did the idea of a penal tax receive his strong support as a solution to agrarian unrest. To have any utility, the rate of taxation would have to be raised far beyond that imposed by the tax bill passed by the assembly in 1837 and it would be best to use taxes in conjunction with other means. The strategy FitzRoy advocated was a repurchase scheme under which the Crown would resume ownership of the proprietors' grants. To ensure that proprietors would choose to sell, FitzRoy recommended that the offer be linked with the threat of implementation of a severe punitive land tax. Landlords should be offered an option: sell their lands to the government at between two to four shillings per acre, or face the consequences of a massive increase in land taxes.

Although FitzRoy's proposal was described as an alternative to the policies being advocated by Escheators and was intended to wrest the lead in land reform away from them, it owed much to the ideas publicized by the Escheat movement. Indeed, it is possible that plans submitted to FitzRoy by a renegade Escheat assemblyman, John Thomson, formed the basis of his proposals.[33] In keeping with Escheat contentions, FitzRoy argued that the land question required state intervention and that the government needed 'to interfere and insist on providing some remedy.'[34] As well, the governor's proposals, like those promulgated by the Escheat Managing Committee in 1838, sought to link land sales to existing and future settlers with the provision of a fund for compensating proprietors for the property losses they would suffer in a land settlement. Where they differed was in the amount of compensation to be given landlords and in the modes by which they would be induced to participate in the settlement. While Escheators clung to the notion of a continuing right of the Crown to reclaim proprietors' forfeited grants, and to the fishery reserves, as the only sure basis for effecting a settlement, FitzRoy believed that the threat of massive penal taxation would effectively serve the same purpose.[35]

Russell's response to Cooper's and FitzRoy's proposals alike was negative. In keeping with FitzRoy's advice and with past Colonial Office policy, he rejected out of hand a land settlement based on escheat. As for the repurchase scheme, he had no objection in principle but was unwilling to commit the British government to the £200,000 outlay that FitzRoy said it would require. As well, Russell doubted whether proprietors would sell at the rates FitzRoy proposed and whether, even if they did, the Island government would succeed in collecting the monies it expected from the sale of lands. But the idea of a further penal tax – which was in keeping with the recommendations of the Durham Report – received Russell's tentative approval as a policy for the future. The controversial penal land tax passed by the 14th Assembly had finally received royal assent late in 1838, and Russell argued that the best policy was to wait and see the effects of its operation before considering a further tax. It was his hope that it would cause proprietors to develop their properties or sell them, and to accede to the plans laid out by George Young. Once again, the grievances of the tenantry were being conflated with the growth-oriented concerns of the

Island's commercial community. One of the faulty assumptions behind this policy – an assumption FitzRoy had helped foster – was that adherence to Young's proposals or to more active estate management would redress the grievances underlying tenant unrest.[36]

FitzRoy's characterization of Island circumstances shaped Russell's responses in other ways as well. The governor had described the Escheat electoral victory of 1838 as a sleight of hand: a declining cluster of agitators had duped ignorant rural voters into electing them solely on the grounds that this would automatically result in Imperial acceptance of schemes for massive land reform. This is why Russell believed that the negative response he gave Cooper would ensure Escheat's immediate collapse and resolve the constitutional deadlock on the Island. FitzRoy had described the situation in this manner in order to justify his earlier descriptions of Escheat as a movement on the verge of collapse and to ensure that Cooper was rebuffed at the Colonial Office; but he was not prepared to follow Russell when on the basis of this analysis the colonial secretary suggested that the governor consider dissolving the assembly and calling a new election.[37] Acknowledging that Escheat's electoral success was rooted in years of agitation and organization, FitzRoy suggested that its decline would be gradual and that agrarian activism would not be 'suddenly allayed.' Arguing that dissolution would see the return of another Escheat majority – a contention seemingly at odds with his earlier analysis of the movement's 1838 victory – FitzRoy suggested that the Colonial Office simply let Escheators hold the popular branch while providing support for the upper house, which was sure to continue blocking agrarian legislation.[38]

Escheators spent the months following publication of Russell's dispatch and the return of Cooper attempting to reformulate their policies and organizational strategies in light of the developments of 1839. At a chilly outdoor public meeting held at Sentiner's early in January 1840, Cooper reported on his mission to Britain and Escheators considered how they might respond to the events of the previous year. The November 1837 Sentiner's rally had attracted more than two thousand people; this time four or five hundred attended. The turnout, no doubt, reflected the season, but probably as well it reflected declining enthusiasm and hope. Cooper highlighted the narrow grounds for optimism that could be discerned in Russell's dispatch, noting that while Russell was against escheat as a means for obtaining a settlement, he was not against government action to bring about change. He observed that in principle Russell posed no objection to penal taxes and state purchases of proprietors' land. As well, Cooper and others effectively pointed out the flaws in Russell's argument that a land tax alone might solve the tenants' complaints. Indeed, Cooper noted, the reverse was likely to happen, as such a tax would induce landlords to be yet more aggressive in collecting the rents they needed to meet these new costs.

Given that Russell's immediate strategy was doomed, Cooper suggested that Escheators should formulate legislation that would provide an alternative and at the same time meet some of the objections raised by Russell to the legislation of 1839. To this end he suggested – as had FitzRoy in his confidential memo to the Colonial Office – that the assembly combine a buy-back scheme with a heavy penal tax that would force landlords to sell their lands to the government. As well, in keeping with advice he had received from Joseph Hume and the Nova Scotian barrister Scott Tremain, Cooper argued that tenants should continue to press their challenge concerning the legitimacy of proprietors' titles in Island courts and if necessary carry their suits on to British courts and to Parliament. The anomaly that Prince Edward Island had no court of escheat even though the neighbouring province of Nova Scotia did – it had dealt with more than thirty claims over the part two decades and was hearing cases at the time of Cooper's appeals – seemed to all concerned to be a matter of legal grievance.[39] To deal with these matters, Cooper proposed establishing a new legal fund that might be used to retain good lawyers. John Le Lacheur and John Macintosh, for their part, noted the need to broaden the application of such funds so that ongoing tenant/landlord disputes that were to be considered in the next sitting of the Supreme Court would receive the attention and backing of the Escheat committee overseeing legal affairs. Others noted the need, too, for a legislative inquiry into the Island's judicial system. The meeting thus produced the rough outline of a strategy for continuing the struggle through legislative initiatives to effect a government buyout of proprietorial grants and through legislative and court challenges focused on the operations of the colony's legal system.[40]

When the legislature convened again in 1840, Cooper's mission was debated in the house. He faced criticism from Escheat opponents and also from some members of his own party for his performance as a delegate. Within Escheat ranks the great disappointment many felt concerning the failure of their delegate's mission was coupled with a sense that Cooper had not pursued the cause vigorously enough while he was in Britain. To varying degrees, Clark, Arbuckle, Thomson, and

Rae all joined with anti-Escheat voices in condemning Cooper's handling of his task. Feeling the barbs of friends and foes alike, Cooper lashed out at two of his most vociferous antagonists, the representatives from Charlottetown, Palmer and Longworth; in so doing he inadvertently prolonged the destructive haggling by raising the question of a breach of privilege. Rae, like a number of other Escheat lieutenants questioning Cooper's leadership, was looking to assume a greater profile within the movement, and he tailored his remarks to this end. Nonetheless, he was probably correct in suggesting that Cooper had growing doubts about the possibility of success and in contending that Cooper's seemingly lacklustre performance in Britain was connected with the discouragement he must have felt as hope waned for a modicum of support at the Colonial Office. Though it was rooted in substantive questions concerning Cooper's behaviour, the debate over his actions in Britain and in the assembly, which dragged on for nearly a month, was the by-product of a broader malaise. Escheat was losing both its momentum and its sense of direction.[41]

While it debated Cooper's mission, the assembly also considered the appropriate legislative strategies to pursue in light of it. Here, too, the dissolution that was occurring within Escheat ranks was apparent, and Escheat's opponents energetically pressed their advantage, doing what they could to widen the divisions that were developing among the movement's leaders. All the Escheat assemblymen who spoke in debate agreed that there must be a shift in strategy and that a buy-back policy should be central to the new approach; they differed, however, in their ideas concerning how far they needed to go towards conciliating landlords. Escheat had always embraced an amalgam of positions, and the crisis brought about by the events of 1839 emboldened the more conservative voices within the movement. Some argued that a strategy of confiscation had been wrong and that it was time to shear the movement of its radicalism and its challenges to the rights of property. In this vein, Thomson and Clark condemned earlier Escheat policies and argued in favour of establishing commissions of five men in each of the counties – two appointed by the legislature, two by the proprietors, and one by the governor – to pave the way for a settlement by providing an impartial assessment of the value of proprietors' lands.

Others objected that this approach would leave tenants in a minority position when it came to determining the costs they would have to face to gain secure control of their lands. They criticized as well the statements of foes and former allies alike that past Escheat policies had been false promises and delusions because as of 1839 they had failed. In addition, they resisted their more conservative colleagues' willingness to embrace the proprietors' own definitions of property rights. Rae, for one, defended earlier Escheat policies even as he sought to play a leading role in developing a middle ground between the more radical positions assumed by Cooper and his closest followers and the more conservative views that others in Escheat ranks were articulating. Russell's response to Cooper's mission was not, he argued, final proof that Escheators 'had led the people astray' by suggesting that they might gain what was in fact impossible. Ministers, he contended, were not infallible, and justice was often repeatedly denied. That the oppressed lost a battle did not mean that they were wrong to have taken up the cause in the first place. Furthermore, he was not willing to accept that they had not changed the Island for the better.[42]

The proceedings of the first month of the assembly's 1840 session revealed serious divisions in Escheat's ranks and produced repeated challenges to Cooper's leadership. Even so, by the end of the session Escheat's divisions had begun to heal. Votes on issues concerning Cooper's behaviour as a delegate repeatedly split substantial numbers of Escheators from the core of the party, but Cooper's supporters managed ultimately to quell the debate. Significantly, Cooper and Le Lacheur were able to find majorities for their resolutions even when they clashed with Rae and Thomson and others regarding the best procedures for formulating new legislative policies.[43] John Arbuckle, a liability for Escheators both within their ranks and as a breakaway opponent, was expelled from the house for unparliamentary behaviour in March and replaced by the far more useful Charles Young, who easily defeated William Douse in a by-election.[44] When, towards the end of the session, Escheators had developed new initiatives they could report out of committee, they once again presented the appearance of a more unified party. The central land legislation of the session gained a sixteen-to-four victory, reminiscent of those at the beginning of the first session in 1839.[45]

Yet the results of the assembly's legislative efforts in 1840 were quite similar to those of the previous year. Discussions of educational policy in the house led to a report that was submitted for public debate over the summer/fall recess; thus there was no upper and lower house division on this issue. But in other regards, the pattern established in 1839 persisted. For the second time, the assembly passed legislation to ban the circulation of private bank notes issued by the Cunards' New

Brunswick operation; once again, it was rejected by the upper house.[46] The same happened with the assembly's new fishery reserves bill. And yet again, Escheat's land policy was embodied in a major piece of legislation that did not get past the Legislative Council.[47] In keeping with the policies proposed at Sentiner's after Cooper's return from his second delegation to the Colonial Office, the assembly passed a bill that combined penal taxation with Crown repurchase of proprietors' grants.[48] By the terms of the act, monies raised by land taxes – including those derived from the recently approved assessment bill of 1837 – were to be earmarked not for new government buildings but for land purchases to meet the needs of the Island's tenantry. Tenants were to be allowed ten years to meet the four to six shilling per acre costs that would be required for freehold deeds to the lands they occupied. Arguing that it was 'inexpedient' to pass such measures without first getting the approval of the Crown and the proprietors for the policies proposed, the Legislative Council blocked the legislation.[49]

Once again the assembly appealed to the imperial government for support in its efforts to obtain a land settlement and to overcome the resistance of the upper house. Once again FitzRoy succeeded in undercutting their appeals and sustaining his allies on the Island. Choosing the cheaper method of petition (rather than delegation), the assembly appealed to the Queen and to parliament concerning their grievances, asking that both councils – executive and legislative – be reconstructed so that they reflected popular opinion, and also asking the Imperial government to support their land settlement initiatives.[50] The Escheators' new land legislation reflected some of the ideas confidentially proposed by FitzRoy to the Colonial Office in 1839; despite this, the governor argued vigorously against them and in favour of continuing Imperial support for those who were blocking the agrarian legislation. The central issue now at stake was not the policy that Escheators were adopting so much as their political leadership. FitzRoy and his allies hoped to crush the Escheators for good by denying them any tangible victories whatsoever. This strategy, which Russell had supported since becoming colonial secretary, was working, FitzRoy assured his superiors. Dissatisfaction with Escheat's performance in office was growing, and if the Imperial government would only stand by its allies on the Executive and Legislative Councils and resist all Escheat demands, disillusioned Island voters would soon be petitioning for new elections so that they could defeat the scoundrels who had not delivered on their promises.[51]

Yet at the same time, both FitzRoy and officials at the Colonial Office recognized that they would have to couple their denial of Escheat initiatives with ameliorative policies originating elsewhere. In the spring of 1840, FitzRoy again complained that the Island's proprietors had not met even the minimal promises contained in George Young's proposal. In addition, both he and Harvey had asked for remissions of arrears and there had not even been a hint of such developments. Russell, he suggested, needed to pressure the landlords to act on these matters.[52] The colonial secretary, in keeping with his initial response to Cooper's and FitzRoy's land settlement proposals of 1838, continued to show an interest in greater penal land taxes, as suggested by Lord Durham. In a dispatch responding to the assembly's demands that the land question receive ministerial attention, Russell refused to support the land purchase bill or to reconstruct the councils to break the deadlock in Island government; he did, however, promise that the British government would again press the proprietors for some solution to the impasse on the land question.

Importantly, Russell acknowledged that though the land question originated in 'motives of private interest' it had assumed 'the character of a public question, and as such must be treated.'[53] This was and had always been Escheat's position on the matter, though Escheators would have added as well that the solutions to public questions required consultation with the general public concerned – in this case with the popular house in Prince Edward Island. Indeed, it was their own policy not to proceed with important legislation without first submitting it to their Island constituents for review.[54] This was not, however, the philosophy that informed Russell's thinking. Instead, the Colonial Office contacted the PEIA and a number of the most important proprietors concerning appropriate policy initiatives. The Colonial Office told the Island's landlords that George Young's proposal had been rejected by the Island assembly, speaking on behalf of the tenantry, and was a dead issue. Russell wanted to bring about 'an immediate and final' settlement of the land question, and unless they came forth with something better, he intended to move towards a heavy tax with confiscation of land for non-payment.[55]

Proprietors, not surprisingly, were appalled by the Colonial Office's suggestions concerning the need for government intervention. Robert Stewart penned a quick response condemning the injustice of the suggestions and asking for time for the many proprietors currently out of town to assemble and make their position known to Lord Russell.[56]

Over the remainder of the fall and winter, Samuel Cunard, George Seymour, and Charles Worrell also wrote and/or saw Russell on the issue. Many of the most important landlords met at the Stewarts' residence the following spring, and once again the organizational structures hammered together earlier in the decade served to coordinate proprietors' resistance to potentially damaging state policies.[57] Present at the meeting were the Earl of Selkirk, Viscount Melville, the Stewarts, Colvile, Cunard, Seymour, Sulivan, Hemsworth, and an agent for the Fanning/Wood properties.[58] Collectively their opposition carried some weight at the Colonial Office. Seymour, who had just returned from visiting his Island estate, was, like Cunard, able to defend proprietors' policies using information drawn from his own direct observations of Island affairs. Melville knew of Island affairs from correspondence with his son Henry, who had visited the colony while he was posted to the region with the military and who had later been involved in suppressing the rebellions in the Canadas.[59] What they wanted, they informed the government, was resolute action to curb agrarian challenges to their property rights in the colony and an end to government consideration of the broader issues that were prompting these challenges. Law enforcement was a public issue, but landlord/tenant relations were a private matter. Despite their well-organized efforts and their profile, their demands would not have been as favourably received had they not received the backing of the mercantile and professional group clustered around government House in Charlottetown. FitzRoy, who had been kept abreast of the correspondence by the Colonial Office, provided the telling contribution to the discussion.

FitzRoy's response to the considerations at the Colonial Office was conditioned by political developments on Prince Edward Island. News that the Colonial Office was responding to continuing Escheat pressure and considering new measures reached the Island in the summer of 1840 and continued to trickle in over the remainder of the year. Again the news raised hopes that agrarian political activism was at last going to produce substantial results. In July there was news that Joseph Hume's activities in parliament on behalf of the Escheat cause had drawn a promise of action from the colonial secretary. In a parliamentary exchange concerning circumstances on Prince Edward Island, Russell asserted that the Island's proprietors had failed to fulfil the terms of their original grants and that his government was moving to resolve the issue. He hoped to have something more to say on the policy his government was going to adopt by the time parliament met again.[60]

This news touched off speculation on the Island that the Imperial government was going to accede to the general terms of the bill passed by the assembly during the previous session.[61] Later in the year, reports of the Colonial Office's letter to the PEIA, with its threat of penal taxes and land expropriation, touched off rumours that a court of escheat was about to be established.[62] Hope once again flared in rural communities.

Prior to this news there had been few grounds for optimism. The difficult early years of Escheat dominance of the assembly had also been a period of frustrating and embittering defeats for Escheat in the courts and in the countryside. While Escheat's legislative program was being checked in the political arena, its opponents were using the judicial system to crush agrarian resistance to landlords' claims in the countryside. These actions demonstrated the continuing vulnerability and powerlessness of tenants in the courts. In January 1839, Chief Justice Edward Jarvis sentenced two of those involved in rent resistance on Lord Selkirk's estate the previous winter to jail terms of six months and four months respectively. Neither had used any violence against bailiffs attempting to distrain on neighbouring farms, and one had simply been among the crowd that had gathered. Jarvis justified their sentences on the basis that a deterrent was needed to bring an end to the continuing resistance to the numerous ongoing land proceedings.[63] The sentences were a warning that even being present during a potentially confrontational gathering could be legally dangerous; indeed, it could draw a four-month jail sentence. In July, Hugh MacLeod and his wife fought a losing battle to resist seizure of goods from their French River farm in northern Queens County. They successfully turned back the bailiff and constable who first came to execute writs; later, a sheriff's party led by John Small Macdonald broke down the door of their house and overcame them as they and their children attempted to resist with gun, pike, and household implements. Bail was set at a staggering £400.[64] In this case, tenants ultimately could find some grounds for cheer, for despite remonstrances from Jarvis concerning the need to crush rent resistance, the jury returned a verdict of not guilty.[65] On other matters, though, where the judge's opinion could not be challenged, decisions were less favourable. For instance, Jarvis dismissed attempts to dispute Lord Selkirk's claimed right to collect rents from fishery reserve lands, once again on the grounds that tenants had no right to challenge the titles of those from whom they had taken a lease.[66]

The most significant and widely publicized incident of legal process and resistance in this period happened in Kings County, and involved

James Douglas's struggle to uphold his rights against the demands of his landlord, Flora Townshend. Douglas and his neighbour Alexander Dingwell, who was also involved in the challenge, were older settlers who had taken up their farms shortly after the turn of the century. These two, along with their neighbour William Cooper, were community leaders and had been pioneers in the resistance to proprietors that emerged in the late 1820s. They occupied shorefront farms, and both had over time cleared large tracts of land and turned them into valuable holdings. Their legal problems began in 1829 when they challenged the right of their landlord to collect rents for more land than was contained in their holdings. Douglas was being billed for a 150–acre lot; after paying the cost of a survey, he demonstrated that it contained only two-thirds of the stipulated acreage. Dingwell was being billed for 200 acres even though his lot contained only 130. Years of legal appeals had seen the case go from the Supreme Court to Chancery and had exhausted the funds of both tenants. Dingwell's farm was sold at the suit of the proprietor in the winter of 1839–40. In December 1839 Douglas lost his case in Chancery and was assessed ruinous costs. The community these men had lived in for more than thirty years, not surprisingly, strongly resisted attempts to enforce the court's decisions.[67]

Tensions came to a head in January 1840 when the Kings County sheriff, Peter McCallum, put Douglas's livestock up for auction. Sympathizers came to attend. McCallum, who had parted ways with Escheators in the aftermath of the Hay River affair and had been denounced as a traitor in the press and at public meetings, was not given a friendly reception. It did not help matters that many believed that his appointment to the position of sheriff was a reward for renouncing Escheat and cooperating with its opponents. When the crowd bid on the goods at a fraction of their value in an attempt to recover Douglas's property, McCallum refused to relinquish the goods. What occurred after he terminated the auction became a matter of dispute. Despite the animosity of those present, McCallum lingered at Douglas's farm. The sheriff later claimed that except for the angry crowd he would have removed the cattle from the premises and that while he and his assistants were considering this step they were endangered by having hard objects hurled at them. Local residents argued that McCallum had no right to remove animals that had already been sold at auction. As well, they contended that the sheriff and his men acted provocatively: McCallum had clubbed an innocent young bystander with his brass-knobbed whip handle, and one of his assistants had harassed people by riding his horse through their midst. The local people acknowledged that members of the crowd had hurled objects at the law officers, but contended that these had been only snowballs and frozen dung and that McCallum's party had acted in a manner that provoked this response. In the wake of the incident, McCallum applied to the Executive Council and was given permission to incur the costs of assembling a large civil force to assist him with further proceedings on the Douglas farm and elsewhere in the region. A party of eight or nine heavily armed men – some carrying three pistols each – returned to seize stock at the Douglas farm. They held James Douglas at gunpoint as they broke into his barn. Similar heavy-handed incidents took place elsewhere as McCallum seized stock, arrested people he believed had been involved in resisting him, and asserted his power in the community.[68]

Seven men were brought to trial in July for their part in the Douglas farm affair. The jury, in keeping with Island law, was selected by the sheriff.[69] The accused had delayed a March trial in the belief that, as was normal, a new officer would be appointed to replace McCallum before the court's summer term.[70] In an unusual move, though, Island authorities reappointed McCallum, leaving him in a position to select the jury in his own case. The jury's foreman was William MacGowan, brother of one of FitzRoy's new appointees to the Legislative Council. Before the term's cases were heard, Chief Justice Jarvis instructed the jury concerning the duties that lay before them. Drawing their attention to the matters of rent resistance that they would be called on to consider, he advised them that this was 'a crime which the strong arm of the law must nip in the bud.' Those who were 'so hardy and reckless as to resist' law officers carrying out their duties 'must be after conviction, punished with some severity, so as to show the country that the laws must be upheld.' In the past, he was pleased to observe, Kings County juries had always done their duty and refused to protect 'those who were evidently guilty.'[71] After the evidence in this case had been presented at trial, Jarvis reminded the jury that simple presence in a crowd intending to impede the sheriff's auction was a criminal offence and that it did not have to be proven that the defendants had in any way assaulted McCallum. This would constitute an additional offence. Not surprisingly, all but one of the accused were found guilty of riot and/or assault. Jarvis thanked the jury for having 'placed a barrier against the further progress of that pernicious course' which agrarian activists had been following for years. He then sentenced all who had been found guilty to jail terms ranging from four to ten months.[72] Some were given £20 fines as well.

The proceedings outraged the people of the district; for them, it proved that 'there was no justice in the Country.'[73] Despite Jarvis's statement that mere presence at the auction constituted an indictable offence in this case, twenty-five people who had been there signed an affidavit saying that they had witnessed the day's events and that the testimony presented on behalf of McCallum was falsely given. This affidavit and a petition with nearly one thousand signatures were presented to the governor, appealing to him to intervene in the case. This he refused to do through either investigation or pardon.[74] As well, he denied a request from the assembly that Douglas's legal challenge be considered a matter of public interest to be pursued at government expense.[75] The Escheat majority in the house would attempt to use its power over the purse to prevent publicly subsidized deputations from suppressing tenant resistance and would attempt as well to alter the rules governing judicial procedures that permitted the manipulation of juries; it would be checked in these initiatives as well. The hard fact was that proprietors and their allies could use the courts to reach into the heartland of Escheat and crush its supporters. In their eyes, these were necessary steps in the education of the tenantry and part of the process of bringing countrypeople 'to their senses.'

In this context, supporters of Escheat eagerly embraced the snippets of hope provided by Lord Russell. Had Escheators known that both Worrell and Seymour had approached the Colonial Office concerning the possibility of selling their claims to Island property to the state, and that William Douse had previously advised Colvile to arrange the sale of his estate to the government, the movement might have picked up yet more momentum.[76] Acting on the basis of Russell's dispatch and other signs that the Imperial government intended to address the land question on Prince Edward Island, the assembly gave the issue renewed attention during the 1841 session. It took Russell's assertion that agrarian grievances were a public question requiring government intervention as a favourable concession.[77] In the belief that Russell's appeals to the proprietors would not produce acceptable responses, the assembly resurrected its land settlement bill of the previous session and once again passed it, arguing that it was still the best option available.[78] Once more as well, it passed the fishery reserves bill.[79] The Legislative Council, adhering to its previous arguments, again killed both pieces of legislation.[80]

The dispute between the assembly on one hand and the councils, governor, and other appointed government officers on the other became increasingly entrenched and embittered over the course of the

1841 session. Besides throwing out the lower house's two land bills again, the upper house rejected bills that would have made proprietors pay the costs of ensuring rights of way to their tenants on backland properties, stopped landlords from passing their tax burdens onto tenants, and provided for the relief of Loyalist land claimants. In addition, it rejected the assembly's appropriations bill because it would have provided a salary for employing Joseph Hume as the colony's agent in London.[81] The assembly, for its part, refused to act on or pass a number of measures proposed and/or initiated by the governor, the Legislative Council, and the chief justice. Among other things, these would have provided a salary to hire an assistant chief justice, altered the modes of jury selection, and coerced reluctant constables to enforce the law. As well, despite the unanimous support of the Legislative Council, the assembly refused a request made by the Colonial Office on behalf of FitzRoy that the colony supplement his salary with an additional £1,000. FitzRoy for his part refused to provide the assembly with papers bearing on the unusual costs that law enforcement officers had incurred in suppressing rent resistance in 1840. He refused as well to heed the assembly's plea that McCallum not be reappointed as Kings County sheriff.

The 1841 session of the legislature ended in late April with appointed officials and democratically elected representatives locked in acrimonious dispute. Once again the assembly appealed to the Colonial Office and to Parliament for redress of their grievances. The assembly's petition to Parliament declared that what they wanted was action to end landlordism in the colony. Citing the historical experiences of 'Carolina, Pennsylvania, Maryland and all other proprietory colonies,' they argued that Prince Edward Island, too, needed to be delivered from the evils of this system of land tenure.[82] Significantly, the assembly argued that if this problem could be resolved, the constitutional problem highlighted by the struggle between the assembly and the councils would not be a matter of pressing grievance. To further its case, the assembly prepared five hundred copies of a documentary history of the land question and posted them to Hume for use on their behalf. Its petition to the Queen noted the unfairness of the Imperial government's refusal to authorize a loan for the repurchase of proprietors' grants when Imperial refusal to sanction escheats made such an expedient necessary. Given that the cost, rather than the principle, of the approach appeared to be the sticking point, it suggested that the Imperial government might get around this by permitting colonists to reimburse landlords for the purchases over time, thus forcing proprietors to carry the financing for the scheme.

The Legislative Council responded to developments over the course of the session by appointing its own committee of correspondence to present its case to the colonial secretary and, if necessary, to Parliament.[83] Rejecting the assembly's charges that council members were a family compact intimately associated with proprietors' concerns and at odds with the wishes of most Islanders, it contended that the council stood for the 'true interests' of the residents. It rejected lower house legislation only when it 'invaded the prerogative of the Crown' and entailed 'wild and unconstitutional measures which attacked the sacred rights of property.' This was the case with the land settlement bill because it had fixed the prices that proprietors were to receive for their lands. The council's role in Island politics had been to put a stop to these sorts of initiatives and to attempt to 'awaken the Tenantry' from the 'fatal delusion' they had been lured into by the present majority of the assembly, who had come to power by persuading tenants that with political power the assembly could put an end to landlordism and relieve tenants of the burden of rents. Those advancing these schemes in the assembly and petitioning the Colonial Office and Parliament were, the Legislative Council contended, 'ignorant and illiterate men, having but a trifling stake in the country' and possessed of 'no influence in society, beyond that based on their advocacy of Escheat.' Indeed, the greater portion, it claimed, were tenants themselves, many of whom were in arrears for rent. Such men and projects did not, the council contended, deserve the serious attention of the Imperial government.[84]

The council's position, and that more generally of the anti-Escheat coalition around FitzRoy, hinged on the notion that its members represented the 'true interests' of the colony, pursuing what was possible, and that Escheators were frauds who had gained a majority by 'deluding' the populace into thinking that alternative structures could be established. Having challenged Escheat's claims concerning the breadth of political and social choices available and concerning the ability of rural people to achieve what they sought, they had to ensure that events bore out the inevitability they claimed for their vision. Perceiving the peril the governor's party might be placed in should Russell take significant steps towards resolving the land question at this juncture, FitzRoy argued vigorously against any new Imperial initiatives on agrarian grievances in the colony. Russell had, he argued, already given tenants too much hope and thereby strengthened the position of

Escheators by saying that agrarian concerns were a public question and by indicating to Parliament that he intended to redress their grievances.[85] What Russell needed to do, FitzRoy argued, was tell Escheators in 'most unequivocal language' that the home government had resolved 'no longer to entertain any further complaint or representation from the Assembly on the subject of the tenure of land in this colony.'[86] This, he claimed, would terminate the hold that Escheat agitators had gained over the agrarian population. James Stephen, reviewing this claim at the Colonial Office, doubted the governor's predictive wisdom, curtly noting that 'men do not usually cease to agitate public questions mere[ly] because they are told that the govt. is resolved to concede nothing beyond a certain point.'[87]

The governor and his allies, though, had their eye not on the long-term issue of rural unrest that Stephen was considering but on the election that by law had to take place in 1842. Besides requesting policies that would deny the hope for change that was the foundation of Escheat power, FitzRoy called on the colonial secretary to continue providing support for the councils and the governor's other allies in Island politics and to turn a deaf ear to the assembly's complaints. Again, he suggested the expediency of once more substantially altering the rules that governed electoral politics in the colony. As things stood, 'persons of property' and 'of higher attainments and respectability' were unable to be elected in sufficient numbers to dominate the assembly. In 'nine cases out of ten the ignorant settler will think that his own interests, or what he is worked upon to believe such, will be best represented by one of his own class, and occupying the same position in society as himself.' As a consequence, 'the general good of the colony and the encouragement or development of its resources was being entirely lost sight of, or rather not being thought of.' With the breakdown of paternalism and the growth of class politics on the Island – a process FitzRoy believed had started with the 1830 election – democratic forces had nudged developmental politics aside. Tenants speaking on behalf of tenants had insisted on giving their own concerns priority. The governor believed that denying the existence of the possibility of achieving the tenants' goals through politics was a useful line of defence. As well, he urged the Colonial Office to advise the assembly to 'turn its attention to the development of the great natural resources of the colony and to local improvements instead of wasting time in fruitless attempts to infringe upon the rights of private property.' He had little faith, though, that this would prove sufficient. Also needed were changes in the property qualifications of assemblymen and in the provisions that permitted assemblymen to be paid for their time in the house. As things stood, those possessing a freehold or leasehold property worth £50 currency could assume a seat on the assembly and be compensated for their efforts. The property qualification for the house, he argued, should be altered before the next election. Membership in the assembly should be restricted to those possessing property worth £200 to £500. In addition, he contended that assemblymen should be denied all pay, or at the very least be forced to accept less than their current salaries of roughly £30 per term.[88] In short, qualifications should be designed so that no member of the rural underclasses would be allowed to sit in the popular chambers. In keeping with this line of thinking, the Legislative Council served notice in a newspaper proclamation at the end of the session that it intended to block future appropriation bills if they included significant salary provisions for assemblymen.[89]

FitzRoy and the allies gathered about him gained crucial support from the Imperial government, but on some issues their thinking was out of touch with the shifts in political sensibilities that had been occurring in Britain. The notion that the members of the house should not be allowed to vote salaries for themselves did not get very far at the Colonial Office.[90] Indeed, on the broader issue of the role of the upper house in controlling appropriations, Imperial sentiment was not in keeping with the position of power that the Island's Legislative Council was attempting to retain.[91] Nor, on a separate but related appeal, was FitzRoy able to get permission to circumvent the assembly's refusal to vote him a salary by dipping into the permanent revenue that was technically still at the disposal of the governor in council.[92] As well, although the governor had temporarily secured his allies' anti-Escheat position by giving them a dominant voice on the councils, this too was out of step with current thinking, which held that the executive at least needed to be constructed so that it operated cooperatively with the house and contained assemblymen who had the confidence of the majority. Although he managed to postpone the day of reckoning until after yet another election, FitzRoy's assembly appointees on the Executive Council – Joseph Pope and John Small Macdonald – were not congruent with a construction designed to achieve harmonious relations.

On other matters, though, the line of conduct advocated by the governor and his party had the support of the Imperial government. While there were doubts about the long-term success of the land policy FitzRoy advocated, it had, as James Stephen noted, the merit of being simple and easily done.[93] As well, it was fully in accordance with the demands the proprietors' lobby was making. With Escheators on one side and the proprietors, the governor, leading government officers, and commercial interests apparently on the other, Russell was willing to shelve plans for decisive treatment of the land question and to repeat a simple no to any further consideration of the issue.[94] In a dispatch drafted at the end of June and published in Island papers one month later, Russell informed Islanders that an escheat and/or repurchase of proprietor lands by the Crown was out of the question. Having been informed that the great majority of proprietors had acceded to the proposal put forward by George Young, the Imperial government intended to do nothing more on the matter. There was, he asserted 'no sound footing for direct legislation' to deal with agrarian grievances. It was time, the dispatch continued (as FitzRoy had advised), for Islanders to stop considering these issues and 'turn their attention to improvement of the resources, and the encouragement of the growing wealth of Prince Edward Island.'[95] The discussions that Escheators had opened needed to be ended so that developmental politics could resume. Proprietors and the Island's leading commercial and professional men might disagree on how to pursue these goals, but they shared an interest in returning politics to these more limited confines. Although the internal memos of the Colonial Office suggest that the arguments FitzRoy put forward on behalf of the members of the colonial bourgeoisie associated with the government party were the most telling influence on Imperial policy, the proprietors were also delighted with the line that was adopted. Russell's dispatch was, Cunard wrote, 'everything I could ask.'[96]

The new Colonial Office policy was a critical setback for Escheators. This discouraging turn of events was soon compounded by unfavourable political developments in Britain. Escheat leaders were flabbergasted by the abrupt shift in Imperial policy indicated by Russell's latest communication and discouraged by what it appeared to augur for the immediate future. They had not, however, limited their appeals to this avenue alone; they were also attempting to bring pressure on the Imperial government through Parliament. In this regard, Hume put the assembly's petition before the House of Commons in June.[97] Parliament, though, was dissolved shortly thereafter, and the pamphlets the assembly was printing for use in its campaign to petition Parliament did not leave the Island until late in the year. By the time they arrived, Escheat's advocate had lost his seat in the election and the Whigs had been turned out of office. Dr Bowring, co-founder of the *Westminster*

Review with Jeremy Bentham, and a vigorous voice in the cause of reform, agreed to make Escheat's case in Parliament when it resumed sitting in February 1842, but with the change of ministries and with British politics in turmoil over the corn laws, the chances of gaining a hearing in that quarter in the near future were not promising.[98] As the natural term of the Island assembly was nearing its close, there were few if any grounds for Escheators to believe that they might have something tangible to show for their efforts to achieve land reform while in office. FitzRoy left for Antigua in late September to become lieutenant-governor of the Leeward Islands. His replacement, Henry Vere Huntley, most recently the lieutenant-governor of Gambia, provided no reason for optimism; indeed, Huntley initially became more closely allied with the Island's landed interests than FitzRoy had ever been.[99]

Finding a way forward in these circumstances posed enormous difficulties to Escheators. Events appeared to be bearing out all that their opponents had been saying about the 'delusions' that Escheators had been practising on gullible country people foolish enough to believe that political activism could result in changes in land tenure. Realizing that they would have little to hold up on the hustings to their rural constituents, for whom the main issue was property rights, some within Escheat ranks advocated adopting vigorous developmental initiatives – policies that might be more easily pursued and that could garner the support of a more affluent constituency. Alexander Rae, for instance, suggested that the assembly turn its attention to promoting manufacturing on the Island, by introducing measures to foster import substitution and to encourage Islanders to produce textiles and wood products suitable for export.[100] As for the land question, he suggested that little could be done beyond continuing to petition for redress of Islanders' grievances and that such initiatives required only a day or two of the assembly's time.

In the event, Escheators continued to pursue new initiatives on the land question in the final session of the 15th Assembly even while seeking, in keeping with the suggestions of Rae and others, to appeal for voter support on other grounds. In the first regard, they adopted a more conciliatory line towards the Legislative Council and arranged to cooperate with it in some issues of common concern.[101] Huntley reported early in the session that the assembly, was working more cooperatively with the executive and the upper house and had 'less disposition to embarrass and more to be of real service than formerly.'[102]

Escheators were nonetheless continuing to consider the land question in committee and preparing new resolutions, which they presented at the end of the session. Escheat's position had always been grounded in a number of economic propositions concerning the production of value and the equitable distribution of wealth. Some were not directly amenable to quantification and proof, but others were, and a special committee collected and assembled data bearing on some of these matters, such as the relationship between rents and Island revenues, and the relative value of proprietors' and tenants' contributions to rural capital formation. Using the 1841 census, land registry books, and various other records, as well as their own knowledge of rural circumstances, they established the price that many of the proprietors had paid for their lands and constructed estimates of what they had received from rents and from land sales and what they had paid out in taxes and road costs.[103] As well, they established figures for the total value of rural capital and the total level of colonial expenditures, so that colony-wide rental demands could be understood in the context of the Island's economic circumstances. Some of the figures told a compelling story. Data from the nearly 200,000-acre Selkirk estate, often held up as a model of liberality and humanitarian concern, indicated that land that Selkirk was selling at £1 per acre and leasing for 1 shilling per acre or more had originally been purchased for £3,000 – roughly 3.5 pence per acre. *Annual* rents were three times the cost per acre that Selkirk had paid for title for the lands, and the sale price of land was more than sixty times the initial cost per acre. Data from other estates revealed a similar pattern.

Evidence collected in committee provided the underpinnings for renewed demands for Imperial action to alleviate inequities in the structure of land ownership. As the 1842 session drew to a close in mid-April, the house passed a series of resolutions that once again embodied its position on the land question. There was, Escheators argued, no reason for them to depart from their position in the previous three sessions. The value of rural property was rooted in rural labour, and those who were creating wealth on the land needed to be secured in the products of their work. As things stood, rents undercut the ability of the industrious to enjoy the fruits of their exertions, and the state needed to act to change this. Proprietors might have a claim to some compensation for the wilderness value of Island lands, but it was unfair to permit them, through government indulgences, to maintain the broader grip on Island property that they currently held. Indeed, so far as the fishery reserves were concerned, the government had a right to recover the rents that proprietors had been collecting from these lands.

Adopting yet another new tack – perhaps inspired by suggestions from Hume – the assembly asked Parliament to appoint commissioners from New Brunswick and Nova Scotia to determine the fee simple value of the land in its wilderness state so that a settlement might be achieved.[104] The assembly's own calculations would, it no doubt hoped, help provide a framework for such considerations. In conjunction with this, the assembly maintained, as it had often in the past, that the best way to ensure that proprietors would ultimately accede to the recommendations for settlement terms made by such a commission would be to assert the right of the Crown to commence escheat proceedings should landlords resist its recommendations. Despite earlier fractures in Escheat ranks, these final resolutions of the 15th Assembly, which continued to assert the central tenets of the agrarian cause, passed by votes of fifteen to seven and sixteen to six – margins reminiscent of those which had prevailed in the first months of their years in power in the assembly.[105] While there is no doubt that Imperial policy – framed in large part in accordance with the advice of the governor's party – had abetted conflicts within the agrarian leadership and had led to much discouragement among Escheators, the party had managed to maintain a good deal of cohesion throughout its years in power.

The assembly was dissolved after the session was terminated in April, and elections were held in July 1842. The new governor, like FitzRoy before him, took a prominent role in abetting anti-Escheat forces. Although the Colonial Office had advised an early dissolution of the house as a means to test the strength of Escheat backing when the assembly and council became deadlocked in 1839, both governors had chosen not to follow this advice for fear that the party they were attempting to lead to power would not succeed.[106] Escheators had expected an election in the second half of 1841 after Huntley arrived on the Island. He, too, was eager to alter the membership of the assembly, but he decided the timing was not right.[107] As he noted later, it would 'have been very premature for no plans had been organized tending to ensure a more suitable representation.'[108] Huntley personally applied himself to the task of recruiting appropriate candidates for the 1842 election.[109] As well, it seems that he, like the previous governor, used his control over appointments to remove some of those from Escheat ranks who could be lured away. FitzRoy had appointed Charles Young to the Legislative Council shortly after he won a seat in the house in order, he said, 'to deprive the majority of the Assembly of the only man of education amongst them,' and to prevent Young from aiding them in 'bringing forward measures hostile to the proprietors.'[110] The appointment of William Clark as sheriff of Prince County after he joined eleven other Escheat assemblymen in a call for continuing the battle for land reform may have been for the same purpose.[111] The governor also used his position as chief executive to discredit the political initiatives of Escheators. Huntley, like FitzRoy the previous year, closed the 1842 session with a pointed attack on the Escheat majority. They had, he claimed, adopted policies that were 'injurious to this Colony.' Islanders would, he was sure, not 'disregard their true interests, for the visionary propositions and disquietude' propagated by Escheators.[112] Besides telling Islanders how to vote, Huntley was corroborating the more general line of attack employed by those attempting to unseat Escheators. Holding up the agrarians' inability to prevail in achieving land reform as evidence of the foolhardiness of their project, opponents of Escheat characterized the movement as a delusion that had been propagated by Cooper and his allies for their own aggrandizement. The most vicious attackers claimed that the Escheat leaders were out primarily to enrich themselves at the public's expense, dangling the impossible dream of radical land reform before ignorant countrypeople so that the latter would vote them into office, where they might gain salaries as assemblymen.[113]

In a perceptive analysis presented as an open letter to the electors of the colony in the spring of 1842, Cooper closely examined the forces behind the evidence sustaining the thesis that radical land reform was impossible. Voters, he argued, needed to understand how dispatches such as the latest inconsistent and discouraging one from Lord Russell were created and how decisions such as those concerning treatment of the representations of the Escheat assembly to the Colonial Office were generated. They did not reflect unalterable verities, nor indeed were they primarily the creations of either the Colonial Office or its representative in the colony, the governor, although, because 'few of the people can trace the evil to its proper source, the odium generally falls too often on the Imperial government.'[114] Behind the statements emanating from the Colonial Office lay information fed to it by the governor, and shaping the position adopted by the governor was a coterie of prominent Islanders. Those associated with the governor – and here he particularly singled out the members of the Executive Council – were using the Imperial connection to control Island politics. Working through the governor, they sent 'representations to the Home Government as would bring out Dispatches from Ministers to suit their views and interests.' They, rather than the elected assembly, were the main voice behind gubernatorial and Imperial policy. Believing that Huntley was required to bring the Executive Council in line with the wishes of the assembly following the 1842 election and to move towards responsible government, Cooper appealed to electors to maintain an Escheat majority that might insist on a place on the Executive Council and through it alter the shape of Imperial policy on the land question. Their opponents, he contended, were turning constitutional principles on their head by attempting to use the power of the executive to create a popular house that would reflect the interests of those on the Island's councils. The promise of reform, heralded in policies laid down by Durham and Russell, was for power to flow in the opposite direction, but this would not happen, Cooper argued, if Island voters did not recognize what was being attempted by those in the governor's party and how it might affect their lives.

Escheat appeals to hold fast in the face of these challenges did not prove sufficient to give them the election. In the immediate aftermath of the polling, James Haszard calculated that Conservatives had gained twelve seats and Escheators seven; the remaining five had gone to moderates and/or men whose politics were unknown.[115] By Huntley's calculations there were thirteen members opposed to Cooper, four of unknown principles, and seven Escheators.[116] Voting patterns in the 1843 session of the assembly indicate that these figures underestimated continuing Escheat popularity. The assembly member not included in Escheat ranks in Huntley's and Hazard's calculations, Duncan MacLean, proved initially – as he had promised during the campaign – to be a strong voice for the Escheat cause.[117] Opposing Escheat advocates were a dozen or so conservative voices, with a small cluster of loose fish voting against important Escheat initiatives but joining Escheators occasionally on other issues. On the county hustings, then, the election was basically a draw with Escheators gaining eight of the eighteen seats and the Conservatives, if George Coles is counted among them, gaining nine.[118] Dr MacGregor, who was elected with the support of Queens County Escheators, proved to be a loose fish in the first session of the new house.[119] Escheators retained all but one of their six Kings County seats and two of the three Prince County seats they had previously held. The most significant rural electoral changes occurred in the central region of the colony (see map 10.1 and table 10.2). In Queens County,

Map 10.1. County districts and the elections of 1838 and 1842

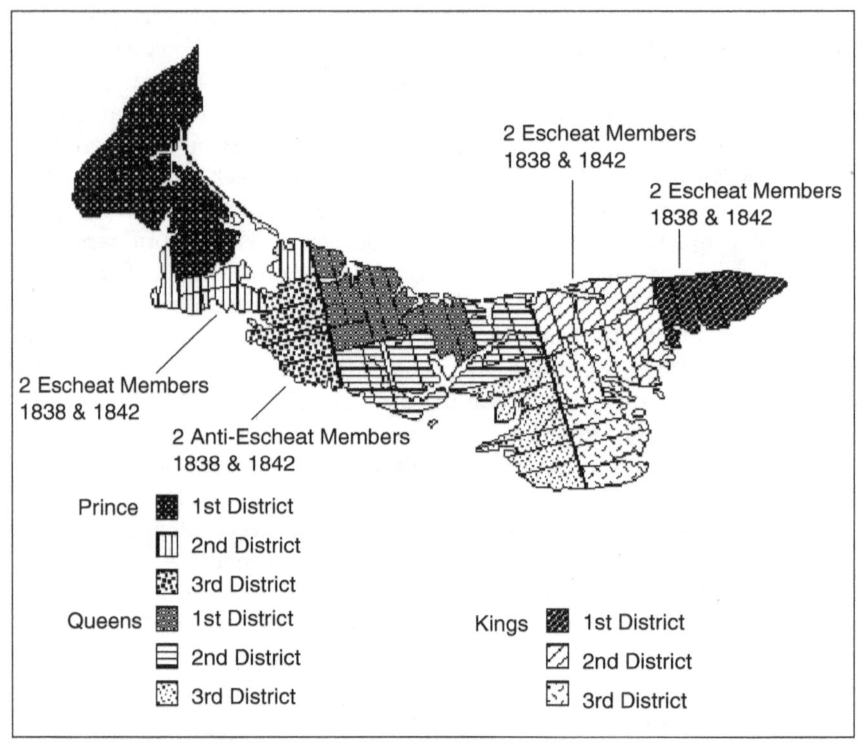

Source: *Royal Gazette*, 20 Nov. 1838; *Colonial Herald*, 23 July 1842

Escheators were trounced in the Belfast district and lost seats by narrow margins elsewhere.[120] A shift of sixty votes among the more than five thousand cast in Queens County would have given them two additional seats. The greatest change in Escheat's electoral fortunes came not in the rural regions but in the royalties and involved relatively few votes. Roughly two thousand votes were cast in the populous Queens County ridings to determine the district representatives; the Georgetown and Princetown seats, by contrast, were decided by fewer than 150 votes. The members from Princetown and Georgetown had added to the numbers in the Escheat majority of 1838. In 1842 the Escheators lost these seats.[121] Had they retained them, they would have remained the strongest party in the house.[122]

Noting with surprise that support for the Escheat party had remained unchanged in many of the rural districts, Huntley suggested to the Colonial Office that the exertions of capitalist farmers had been behind the limited number of shifts that had occurred. Where 'this higher class' of rural dweller had a significant profile, the Escheat tide had been pushed back, but in districts where an indebted tenantry predominated, Escheators had retained the support of the electorate.[123] Given the class appeal of Escheat and the arguments of its opponents, Huntley's analysis is not unreasonable, though it was being made as an appeal for policies to sustain the creation of a larger pool of wealthy farmers and a yet more hierarchical rural order. Data from the 1841 census, while too broad in its categories to provide a definitive test of his hypothesis, suggest a more complex reality (compare tables 10.1 and 10.2). One would expect, if this hypothesis were true, that districts with substantial numbers of freeholders would tend to support anti-Escheat candidates and that those with large numbers of tenants and squatters would be bastions of Escheat support. The pattern, though – if there is any discernible – seems to work in the other direction. The three ridings that returned Escheat slates were among the five districts that had the greatest percentage of freeholds; one had more than 50 per cent, another close to this. Fraser and Rae's riding in Prince County, which proved once again to be an Escheat stronghold, had by far the greatest amount of freehold land of any of the electoral districts in the colony. While it is true that Escheators lost in the Belfast district of Queens, which had the second-largest amount of freehold acreage, they also lost in the second district of Queens, which had the least, and in general did better in the ridings that had the greatest numbers of freeholders.

Prior to the election, the Escheat party feared that its constituents would lose the faith and enthusiasm necessary to sustain class politics against the countervailing forces of patron/client relations and the pull of employers' daybooks, merchants' ledgers, and the rent rolls of proprietors and their agents.[124] This concern was realistic. In 1838, rural voters feeling the tug of these forces might well have shrugged them off in the belief that rent rolls would soon be a thing of the past and that other ties of dependence also would be reduced as the burden of proprietorial relations was lifted from the rural districts. There were no grounds for such faith in 1842. Political dominance of all that was open to democratic control had not substantially changed the terms of rural life. Torn between the conflicting appeals of old power brokers and new ones who claimed that a popular assembly would have the tools to break the grip of the old patterns, many had bet on the possibility of

Table 10.1. District land characteristics, 1841

	Arable Land	Freehold Land	Leasehold*	Squatter Held
Prince				
1st District	21%	33%	23%	16%
2nd District	25%	67%	23%	4.5%
3rd District	24%	49%	41%	4%
Queens				
1st District	26%	29%	56%	4%
2nd District	21%	27%	52%	2%
3rd District	31%	57%	26%	4%
Kings				
1st District	21%	49%	14%	33%
2nd District	21%	47%	33%	8%
3rd District	16.5%	31%	23%	31%

* Written leases
Source: 1841 Census

Table 10.2. Electoral victors, 1838 and 1842

Elections	1838	1842
Prince		
1st District	Yeo & *Gorman**	Yeo & Cambridge
2nd District	*Fraser* & *Rae*	*Fraser* & *Rae*
3rd District	Pope & Hudson	Pope & Hudson
Queens		
1st District	*MacNeil* & *MacFarlane*	*D. MacLean* & Coles
2nd District	J.S. Macdonald & *Forbes*	J.S. Macdonald & MacGregor
3rd District	*LeLacheur* & *Arbuckle*	A. MacLean & Douse
Kings		
1st District	*MacIntosh* & *D. Macdonald*	*Macintosh* & *D. Macdonald*
2nd District	*Cooper* & *Dingwell*	*Cooper* & *Dingwell*
3rd District	*Beck* & *Dalziel*	Wightman & *Dalziel*
Royalties		
Prince	*William Clark* & *Montgomery*	Bearisto & Montgomery
Georgetown	*Thomson* & *Dingwell*	Thornton & Macaulay
Charlottetown	Palmer & Longworth	Palmer & Longworth

* Names in italics indicate members associated with Escheat.
Source: *Royal Gazette* 20 Nov. 1838 and *Colonial Herald* 23 July 1842

change in 1838, and had lost. In 1842, the chances of political success in the near future looked bleak. Cooper's acknowledgment in the spring of 1842 that he intended to leave the colony within the eighteen months suggested that even he had lost faith in Escheat's ability to prevail.[125] In Britain, the Tories were back in power and the trend in Colonial Office policy – as the suspension of Newfoundland's constitution proved – did not bode well for colonial reformers.[126] Perhaps as well the upturn in the Island's economy since the last election persuaded greater numbers of the possibility of accommodation within the existing system. The 1838 election was held in the wake of a series of ruinous harvests and economic slumps. That of 1842 followed a series of abundant harvests and a broader economic upsurge that saw vessel construction equal and finally surpass that of 1826 for the first time in a decade (see the tables in the appendix). By the following year it would be evident that hard times were once again the order of the day, but the election in July 1842 was held during an exceptionally buoyant economic period, one in which more and more tenants were gaining the income necessary to make annual rent payments and whittle away at arrears if they so chose.

Partial amelioration of rural distress occasioned by an economic upturn, and a loss of faith in political action, constituted the crucial backdrop for the defeat of Escheat at the polls in 1842. It is possible that a closer rural analysis that disaggregated the broad category of freeholder would provide more support for Huntley's belief that the move away from Escheat was brought about by the leadership of prosperous farmers; however, the limited evidence suggests that the key players in the anti-Escheat swing, besides the governmental appointees who helped shape the context of the battle, were merchants and land agents. With the exception of Dr MacGregor's victory, the Escheators who were thrown out of county seats – farmers all – were replaced by men of these callings. While merchants and land agents might well have been able to gain the support of wealthier members of rural communities who shared their class interests, such men also could call in the support of people whose indebtedness – whether for rent or for goods acquired on credit – made them vulnerable. In 1838, many voters when faced with such claims on their franchise had gambled that it was worth their while to resist them. The patterns suggest that fewer felt that way in 1842. Given the forces that were brought to bear on rural voters and the context of the election, perhaps the most surprising thing about the returns was that so many persisted in voting for Escheat despite the personal costs that many must have incurred for their choice, made publicly in front of their community at the open polls.[127] Notwithstanding the vigorous assault on its electoral position and the setbacks it had suffered, Escheat's profile in the 16th Assembly remained greater than that in any prior to its 1838 landslide victory.

Conclusion

Escheat's electoral defeat in the summer of 1842 was one of a number of setbacks marking the decline of the most dynamic rural protest movement in Prince Edward Island history. In the short run, its opponents on the Island and in Britain had succeeded in blocking the popular challenge it posed. But they had done so only after a prolonged and difficult struggle, requiring the exertions of leading members of the Island's commercial and professional community to shape the opinions and policies of Island governors and the Colonial Office, as well as the efforts of resident and absentee landlords. One of the consequences of their victory over Escheat was that it postponed resolution of the land question for another generation.

James Stephen of the Colonial Office was prescient, however, in dismissing Lieutenant-Governor FitzRoy's suggestion that the Imperial government could end rural protest simply by refusing to consider the land question further. As he noted at the time: 'Men do not usually cease to agitate public questions mere[ly] because they are told the govt. is resolved to concede nothing beyond a certain point.'[1] Certainly this was true on Prince Edward Island. A year after the defeat of Escheat at the polls, Lieutenant-Governor Huntley found it necessary to send troops into eastern Kings County to deal with tenant unrest. Chief Justice Edward Jarvis characterized the disturbances there as the work of 'about 2 thousand men armed with scythes, pitchforks, &c.' who 'threatened fire and destruction.'[2] It would not be the last time tenants dealt with their grievances through direct action, nor would it be the last time the Island government found it necessary to use troops to maintain its authority in the countryside and to uphold the claims of landlords.[3]

And that was the contradiction at the heart of the Island land question. In the long run, maintaining landlords' claims at the point of a bayonet was not a viable option. Neither the colonial state nor the Imperial state was willing to pay the cost of using the army to enforce property claims that would otherwise be unenforceable. Failing to act, though, when tenants and their allies resisted landlords' use of the courts and officers of the law to uphold their claims was not a viable option either, as such a course would undermine the state's authority. Ultimately something would have to give if the state was to maintain its hegemony over the use of force. The populace would have to bow to the definition of property rights upheld by the coercive power of judges, bailiffs, and sheriffs, backed when necessary by the military acting in aid of the civil power. Or the state would have to bring the property regime on the Island in line with popular perceptions of a just order. It was the latter that the Escheat movement sought to achieve in the 1830s, and in this it was defeated.

The Escheat movement shared much with other popular movements that took shape in the North Atlantic world in the late eighteenth and early nineteenth centuries. It insisted that the state had a duty to protect the rights and property of the labouring population and reflect their interests; it used mass public meetings and newspapers to construct state-wide solidarities; and it developed a popular organization capable of sustaining large-scale challenges to the status quo. Rural protest on Prince Edward Island was part of what Reeve Huston has characterized as 'a broad international trend, as rural people throughout the modern world translated ancient desires for land into the languages of republican, liberal or socialist revolution.'[4] The extraordinary popular mobilization of the Escheat movement drew strength from the belief that progressive change was possible and that working people could, if they acted together, build a better world, in part by gaining greater control over state power. In the context of the British Empire, this hope was propelled by Catholic emancipation, the Reform Bill, and the abolition of slavery, all of which provided evidence of progressive change as well as of the efficacy of popular agitation. As Dorothy Thompson notes in her study of Chartism, 'For a short period, thousands of working people considered that their problems could be solved by a change in the political organisation of the country. They believed this passionately.'[5] And because they believed change was possible, they were willing to make sacrifices and to struggle. For supporters of the Escheat movement, this faith was dented by the experience of gaining control of the House of Assembly in the late 1830s and discovering that political power at that level would not produce the ameliorative changes they sought.

Although the Escheat movement failed in its immediate goals, it advanced the interests of tenants and smallholders in a number of significant ways. One of its lasting achievements was to help construct a narrative of Island history – and of the role of tenants and smallholders within it – that made it difficult for others to dismiss the legitimacy of their concerns and their property claims. By the late 1830s even the lieutenant-governor was at times claiming that it was 'the hard wrought labour' of the tenant 'which alone stamps a value on the land he improves,' and that it was wrong for tenants to be 'deprived of the hard earned fruits of [their] labour.' These propositions concerning Island history and property rights and justice were at the core of Escheat's credo. It followed that tenants had legitimate property interests worthy of state protection. Years of continuing struggle lay between FitzRoy's inadvertent use of the language and thinking of the Escheat movement and state intervention to bring landlordism entirely to a close in the 1870s. That said, one of the most striking aspects of the historical record bearing on the land question over these years is the persistence of the ideas, language, and historical claims that Escheat made in the public arena in the 1830s and the early 1840s casting Island tenants as the victims of injustice. Escheat's vision of Island history became, in time, part of a body of broadly shared truths, articulated by Islanders from across the social spectrum. This was in part testament to the educational impact of a movement that drew thousands of Islanders into sustained political engagement with the land question. And it would be central to the ultimate defeat of landlordism on the Island.

Yet another of Escheat's contributions to checking landlordism, and in time bringing it to a close on the Island, was the movement's success in placing the land question at the centre of Island politics. It had not always been there. The Escheat movement elevated the profile of the issue; it '*made it a public question*,' and, continuing with Cooper's words (and emphasis), it did so through 'long continued agitation, disturbing the peace of the colony.'[6] This was an important achievement. The Escheat movement may have failed to bring about a solution to the land question, but it succeeded in persuading Islanders that property rights were a public issue requiring a political solution. Subsequently, the land question became a political problem that could not be dismissed. As Lieutenant-Governor Dundas noted in a dispatch he wrote in the late

1860s, the land question was 'the principal political test' on the Island. As well, he observed, it would 'continue to be agitated, so long as there are any considerable number of Rent payers to influence elections' – that is to say, until landlordism had been defeated.[7]

Yet another of Escheat's legacies is that it helped change how Colonial Office officials thought about the land question. At some point, across the years of managing controversy after controversy concerning the land question on Prince Edward Island, the officials charged with this task began to see the defence of landlordism as a lost cause for which they needed an exit strategy. It is impossible to date a watershed change in attitude, given the shifting Imperial personnel responding to the Prince Edward Island file, and their own disagreements on the matter as well as the sporadic nature of the crises that focused their attention, but it is clear that the Escheat challenge raised enduring questions about both the viability and the wisdom of sustaining proprietors' claims in the colony. Harvey's initiatives for brokering a compromise settlement of the land question were the beginning of a long series of discussions aimed at negotiating a solution that would relieve the state of the burden of defending proprietors' claims to ownership rights. FitzRoy's warning to proprietors – which became part of the Colonial Office record – that they should not expect the state to 'be at the expense of collecting your Rents' by sustaining their land agents with 'an armed force' was indicative of the shifts in thinking that Escheat was generating. It proved to be one of many steps by which the Imperial government, over time, began to distance itself from a defence of proprietors' interests in the colony and to increase the pressure on landlords to respond to tenants' demands.[8]

Escheat's impact is evident as well in the thinking of proprietors and their agents. Towards the end of the 1830s some of the more prominent proprietors begin to explore the possibility of extricating themselves from the problems of being a landlord on Prince Edward Island by selling their estates to the government.[9] These initiatives reflected Escheat's ability to limit the profitability of landlordism and, relatedly, to dampen the private market for Island estates. Lord Russell squelched the possibility of beginning to address the land question through state purchase of proprietors' estates by refusing to fund land purchases. This strategy would remain untried until 1853, when the Island legislature succeeded in passing legislation that received Imperial approval permitting the Island government to buy out landlords who were willing to sell to the state. In the 1850s and 1860s, voluntary land purchase, under this and other acts, allowed the Island government to chip away at the proprietors' control of the colony's land base, ultimately with significant success. The first steps towards these land purchase initiatives of mid-century – which required both that proprietors be willing to sell to the state and that the state have the resources and the will to buy – are found in the late 1830s, a time when the rise of Escheat activism led landlords, government officials, and agrarian leaders alike to explore an array of means for resolving the land question.

A central proposition of the Escheat movement was that resolution of land tensions on the Island would require a comprehensive solution. Its leaders insisted that the state retained the right to escheat grants for nonfulfilment of their terms long after the grants were made, and to recover rents that proprietors had collected from the state's fishery reserves. Both these contentions were grounded in large part in the need to assert claims that would give an enlightened state the tools it required to bring landlordism to a close, and at a cost that rural Islanders might reasonably sustain. Escheators were prescient in this. The final solution to landlord/tenant conflict on the Island only came when the state began using coercion to bring about a comprehensive solution by forcing the last of the landlords to sell their estates to the Island government. The Land Purchase Act of 1875, which made compulsory sale possible, bore many traces of the Escheat struggle. Landlords holding more than five hundred acres of land were subject to that act's terms, which compelled proprietors to surrender their estates to the Island government so that it might in turn make them available to landlords' tenants and other settlers. A tripartite commission comprising representatives selected by proprietors, the Island government, and the governor general was charged with determining the sum proprietors were to be paid for their estates. The commissioners were required, when assessing the value of estates, to consider the extent to which proprietors had fulfilled the terms of their conditional grants.

There is more than a little in the terms of the Land Purchase Act that would have sounded familiar to the men of the Escheat Managing Committee who gathered at Cornelius Little's tavern in Charlottetown in 1838 to hammer out policies and mechanisms for a possible solution of the land question, including the following: the overall plan of state purchase of landlords' holdings on behalf of tenants and others interested in purchasing small holdings; the need for coercion; attention to the flaws in landlord titles when valuing landlords' estates; a ceiling for the concentration of land ownership; the need for a forum to adjudicate the rival claims and interests of landlords and tenants; and the use of a tripartite commission to achieve a solution that reflected the conflicting interests of the parties. No doubt, however, most Escheat leaders would have been dismayed by the costs to Island taxpayers, and to settlers who later acquired land from the state, of purchasing landlords' estates under this and previous legislation. The resolution of the land question that ultimately unfolded saw a substantial transfer of cash into the hands of landlords. A significant number of these men were local entrepreneurs drawn from the ranks of Escheat's opponents, who purchased estates after the Escheat movement had been defeated and later sold them to an Island government they continued to effectively influence.

Landlordism's final defence crumbled only after the Supreme Court of Canada ruled on the constitutionality of the Land Purchase Act of 1875 and the validity of the proceedings of the land commissioners who had been appointed under its terms. In his judgment, which upheld the legislation and the work of the land commissioners, Chief Justice William Buell Richards spoke of the extended land struggle on Prince Edward Island and the need to bring it to a close. Converting 'leasehold tenures into freehold estates' was, he argued, 'a matter of very great importance, and one which, if not settled, would be likely to affect the peace as well as the prosperity of the province.' Under such circumstances it was not unreasonable, or unlawful, for 'private interests' to be 'made to yield to the public good.' This judgment embraced, and accepted as obvious truths, propositions concerning the evils of landlordism and the appropriate role of the state in regulating property relations and establishing a just order that Escheators, building on earlier traditions of rural protest, had struggled to uphold in the 1830s.[10]

Appendix

Timber exports from Prince Edward Island, 1823–32 (in £)

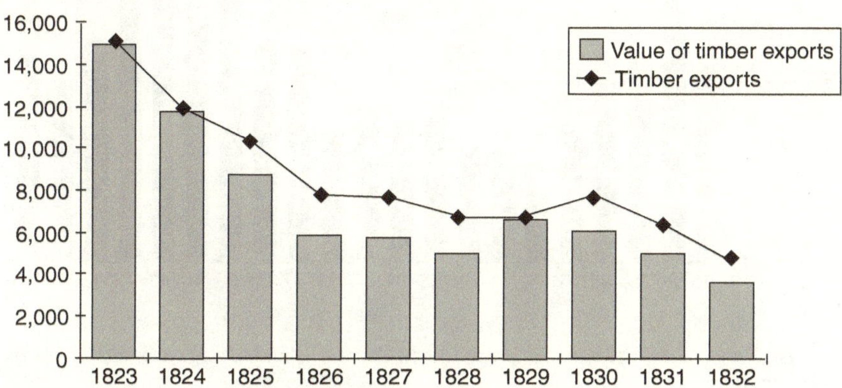

Source: NAC, CO 231 and the *Prince Edward Island Register*

Agricultural exports from Prince Edward Island, 1824–32 (in £)

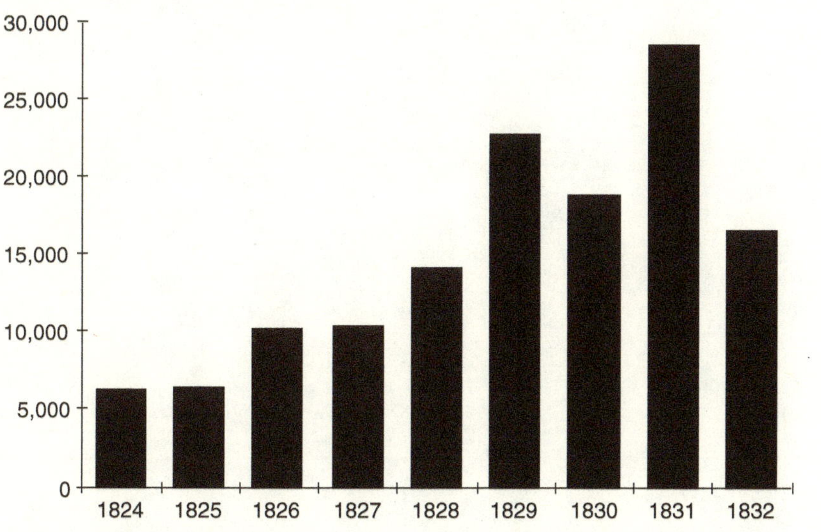

Source: NAC, CO 231 and the *Prince Edward Island Register*

Vessel construction, 1825–45

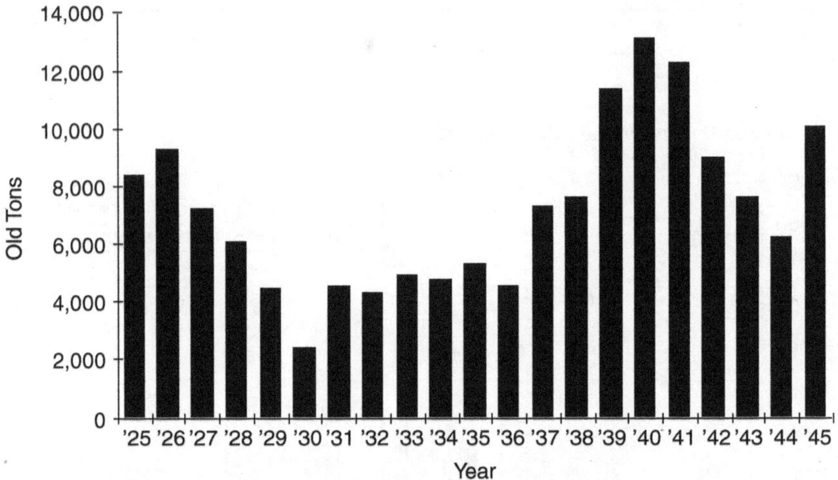

Source: *Prince Edward Island Register*, Prince Edward Island, *Journals of the House of Assembly*

Notes

Abbreviations

APCE	*Acts of the Privy Council of England*
BL	British Library
CHR	*Canadian Historical Review*
DCB	*Dictionary of Canadian Biography*
DNB	*Dictionary of National Biography*
JCTP	*Journal of the Commissioners of Trade and Plantations*
JEH	*Journal of Economic History*
JHA	*Journals of the House of Assembly*
JLC	*Journals of the Legislative Council*
LAO	Lincolnshire Archives Office
NAC	National Archives of Canada
NAS	National Archives of Scotland
NBM	New Brunswick Museum
NLI	National Library of Ireland
NRA	National Register of Archives (London)
OH	*Ontario History*
PANB	Public Archives of New Brunswick
PANS	Public Archives of Nova Scotia
PARO	Prince Edward Island Public Archives and Record Office
PEIC	Prince Edward Island Collection, Robertson Library, UPEI
SRO	Scottish Record Office
UPEI	University of Prince Edward Island
WCRO	Warwickshire County Record Office
WSRO	West Sussex Record Office

Introduction

1 *Colonial Herald*, 25 Nov. 1837, in CO 226/56/141–2, NAC
2 Bumsted, *Land, Settlement, and Politics*, 12–26; Lockerby, 'The Deportation of the Acadians from Ile St.-Jean, 1758'
3 Taylor, *Liberty Men and Great Proprietors*; Huston, *Land and Freedom*; McCurdy, *The Anti-Rent Era*; Kim, *Landlord and Tenant in Colonial New York*; Sakolski, *Land Tenure and Land Taxation in America*; Rink, *Holland on the Hudson*; Summerhill, 'The Farmers' Republic'
4 Ouellet, *Lower Canada, 1791–1840*, 293–7; Chabot, 'Cyrille-Hector-Octave Coté'
5 Read and Stagg, eds., *The Rebellion of 1837*, xix–c; Craig, *Upper Canada*, 226–51; Kilbourn, *The Firebrand*, 143–78
6 Read and Stagg, eds., *The Rebellion of 1837*, 95–103
7 Dorothy Thompson, *The Chartists*, ix

1. The Eighteenth-Century Roots of Rural Protest

1 To avoid confusion I refer to the colony as Prince Edward Island throughout this study.
2 Meinig, *The Shaping of America*, 1: 267–307; Bailyn, *Voyagers to the West*, 7–24; Bumsted, *Land, Settlement, and Politics*, 12–26
3 Tebeau, *A History of Florida*, 80; Abernethy, *Western Lands and the American Revolution*, 1–58; Matt Bushnell Jones, *Vermont in the Making*, 40–66
4 *APCE*, 26 Aug. 1767 (and 13 April), in *Colonial Series*, vol. 5, AD 1766–1783, 56–80
5 Copies of the grants can be found in the Nova Scotia Crown Lands Record Centre, Books 8 and 9, and in RG 16, Land Registry Records, 1769–1872, PARO.
6 *JCTP*, vol. 74 (1767), in *JCTP from January 1764 to December 1767*, reprint ed., 12: 393–4; *London Gazette*, 6–9 June 1767.
7 Bond, *The Quit-Rent System*, 219–438
8 Kulikoff, *From British Peasants to Colonial American Farmers*, 150–63; Weaver, *The Great Land Rush*, ch. 5; Sakolski, *Land Tenure and Land Taxation in America*, 18–58; Karr, *The Canada Land Company*; Saunders, 'The New Brunswick and Nova Scotia Land Company'; Little, *Nationalism, Capitalism, and Colonization*, 36–63; Martin, *Dominion Lands Policy*, 28–99
9 Riddell, 'A Study in the Land Policy of the Colonial Office,' 387–8
10 Martin, *Dominion Lands Policy*, 141. Women were denied access to 'free'

Crown land. See McCallum, 'Prairie Women and the Struggle for a Dower Law,' 19.

11 For a critique of this view of Imperial policy see Bumsted, *Land, Settlement, and Politics*, 12–26.

12 Bloch, *Feudal Society* , vol. 2, *Social Classes and Political Organization*, 443; Hilton, 'Feudal Society' in Bottomore, ed., *A Dictionary of Marxist Thought*, 166

13 Bond, *The Quit-Rent System in the American Colonies*, 25–34, 439

14 Harris, *Origin of the Land Tenure System*, 60

15 Ibid., 117–25; Lefler and Powell, *Colonial North Carolina*, 35

16 For an example of such an attempt, see the terms of Harry Compton's leases as printed in John Mollison, 'Prince County,' in D.A. MacKinnon and Warburton, eds., *Past and Present of Prince Edward Island*, 85.

17 Head, *Eighteenth-Century Newfoundland*, 146–7; Richard Colebrook Harris, *The Seigneurial System in Early Canada*; Greer, *Peasant, Lord, and Merchant*

18 Daigle and Leblanc, Plate 30, *Historical Atlas of Canada*, vol. 1

19 Ells, 'Clearing the Decks,' 50

20 Joshua Mauger Grant, Nova Scotia Land Grant Book, Old Book 6, p. 545, Reel 13036, PANS

21 Ells, 'Clearing the Decks'

22 Bumsted, *Land, Settlement, and Politics*, 40

23 Many townships were granted to two or more people. For a listing of grantees see Andrew Hill Clark, *Three Centuries and the Island*, appendix B.

24 Ibid., 55; Bumsted, 'Peter Stewart,' 777

25 Bumsted, 'Sir James Montgomery and Prince Edward Island,' 80, 86

26 Bumsted, *Land, Settlement, and Politics*, 55–60; MacLeod, 'The Glenaladale Pioneers'; Pigot, 'John MacDonald of Glenaladale'

27 Bumsted, *Land, Settlement, and Politics*, 62–4; Holman, 'John Cambridge'; *A Short Description of the Island of St John*, 25 June 1779, PARO, Acc. 4437

28 Bailyn, *Voyagers to the West*, 59–61, 400; Pigot, 'Thomas Desbrisay.' Royle and Laoire note that forty-two individuals from Ulster are listed on leases Desbrisay signed in 1771; see 'DesBrisay's Settlers.' As well, Royle and Laoire shed light on the subsequent exodus of some of these individuals: '"Do not send my dear babies here to starve,"' 15.

29 Harvey suggests a figure of no more than thirteen hundred, while Bumsted suggests fifteen hundred. See Harvey, ed., *Journeys to the Island of St. John*, 7; Bumsted, *Land, Settlement, and Politics*, 64. See too Harvey, 'Early Settlement and Social Conditions in Prince Edward Island.'

30 The first grants were issued in 1768. In some grants this clause is phrased

as 'shall thereupon become null and void & of none Effect.' Although the imperial instructions for issuing grants assumed that the grants would be issued immediately and, at one point, the Privy Council required proprietors to acquire their grants by May 1769 or lose them, the granting process stretched out across nearly three decades. In consequence, the deadline for meeting the settlement terms varied from grant to grant. *London Gazette*, 2–5 July 1768.

31 On the Nova Scotia and New Brunswick escheats see Ells, 'Clearing the Decks'; Neil MacKinnon, *This Unfriendly Soil*, 13–15; New Brunswick 'Escheat Book' and 'Escheats [1785], Surrenders, etc. 1785,' Department of Natural Resources: Crown Lands RS 107/RNA/C/9/3/3–4, PANB. For Cape Breton's situation see Morgan, 'Orphan Outpost.'

32 Bumsted, *Land, Settlement, and Politics*, 83–138; Bolger, 'The Beginnings of Independence, 1767–1787,' in Bolger, ed., *Canada's Smallest Province*, 55–65

33 Bumsted, *Land, Settlement, and Politics*, 101

34 Bock, 'Micmac'; McGee, 'The Micmac People'; Virginia Miller, 'The Micmac,' 326–31; 'Memorial of Abbé Calonne on behalf of a part of the Mikmac Indians,' [1806?], CO 226/21/194–5, NAC

35 As Griffiths has noted, even during the French regime the Acadian population of the Maritimes was 'more free-ranging in settlement than a strict seigneurial system would have permitted': Griffiths, *The Contexts of Acadian History*, 21.

36 Bumsted, *Land, Settlement, and Politics*, 50

37 John Macdonald to Nelly, 6 March 1784, Macdonald Papers, Acc. 2664/8/3–4, PARO; Hill Memorial, [n.d.], CO 226/17/143–4, NAC. Ada MacLeod, 'The Glenaladale Pioneers,' 319. Lord Selkirk's agent, James Williams, noted this propensity for shifting about when he attempted to settle Highlanders on Selkirk's estate in the first years of the nineteenth century. More than one-sixth of one group of settlers proved to be, as he dubbed them, 'changelings.' Williams to Fanning, 4 August 1805, Selkirk Papers, MG 19/E1/56/14899, NAC. A fragment of these shifts emerges in the founding of the rural community of Middle River in Cape Breton; see Bittermann, 'Economic Stratification and Agrarian Settlement.' For use of the threat of exodus as a bargaining ploy see Robert Urquhart's testimony, 14 December 1791, CO 226/14/259–61, NAC; House of Assembly petition to Fanning, 1797, CO 226/15/180, NAC; Hodgson to Knox, 5 Jan. 1803, CO 226/19/255–6, NAC.

38 CO 226/41/180, NAC

39 For an example of the continuing significance of squatting in the nineteenth century see Nicholas Conroy's testimony concerning settlement on

Lots 1 and 2, in Robertson, ed., *The Prince Edward Island Land Commission*, 69.

40 Frank MacKinnon, *The Government of Prince Edward Island*, 13–15

41 John Macdonald to sister, 26 June 1781, MacDonald Papers, Acc. 2664/5/2–3, PARO

42 Brown, 'Back Country Rebellions'; Countryman, 'Out of the Bounds of the Law'; Nobles, 'Breaking Into the Backcountry'

43 With imperial restructuring of the Maritime colonies after the Revolutionary War, the chief executive of the Island was demoted to the rank of lieutenant-governor, initially (1784–6) subordinate to the governor of Nova Scotia, but as of 1786 subordinate to the governor-in-chief of British North America, resident in Quebec; Frank MacKinnon, *The Government of Prince Edward Island*, 17–19.

44 Hill memorandum, [n.d.], CO 226/17/110 5, NAC

45 The printed manifesto was not the text that first circulated in the countryside, and observers claimed at the time that alterations were made to the manifesto – perhaps a toning down of its language – prior to its publication. Hill's biographical sketch of Joseph Robinson, CO 226/18/215, NAC.

46 For Joseph Robinson's career, see Bumsted, 'Joseph Robinson'; Cashin, *The King's Ranger*; John Hill's biographical sketch, CO 226/18/215, NAC.

47 Bumsted's contention that Robinson was not against tenancy and that what he sought was to have the Crown 'act directly as the landlord of the small holder on the Island' is misleading; Bumsted, 'The Origins of the Land Question,' 54. What Robinson called for was a distribution of freeholds in small tracts 'having quit-rents only to pay to his Majesty, in the same manner as the inhabitants of the neighbouring British Colonies.' In practice this meant being liable, perhaps, to a Crown demand for a 'rent' amounting to one-fiftieth of the average rents that proprietors demanded of their tenantry. In no place does his pamphlet indicate that Robinson approved of tenancy. By emphasizing the unique aspects of life on a northern agricultural frontier, Robinson was able to avoid a blanket condemnation of landlordism – what was inappropriate for Prince Edward Island need not be so in Great Britain – but his pamphlet did not endorse landlordism in any context, and he is quite clear in his rejection of it as a viable system on Prince Edward Island. On popular resistance to the possibility of landlordism in Loyalist New Brunswick see Bell, 'Sedition among the Loyalists,' 228–9.

48 'To the Farmers in the Island of St. John, in the Gulf of St. Lawrence,' Smith, Alley Collection, Acc. 2702/684, PARO

49 John Macdonald to Portland, enclosure, 24 Nov. 1798, CO 226/16/143, NAC

50 Bumsted, 'Robert Hodgson.' See too John Hill's contemporary biographical sketch of Hodgson in CO 226/18/215–16, NAC
51 The petition noted, among other things, that grants in New Brunswick issued at a similar time, and with conditions like those contained in the Prince Edward Island grants, had been escheated; House of Assembly petition, CO 226/15/272, NAC
52 John Hill's biographical sketch of Robinson, CO 226/18/215, NAC
53 On the rent resistance see Enclosure, John Macdonald to Portland, 24 Nov. 1798, CO 226/16/142–3, NAC; Hill's biographical sketch of Robinson, CO 226/18/215; Hill memorandum, CO 226/17/138. In the pull and tug of inter-elite rivalries, landlords too sometimes assumed the role of popular champions and took a hand in encouraging the purported tenants of others to resist rent claims. On the role of John Macdonald in some of the rent resistance, see John Webster's affidavit, 19 Oct. 1798, CO 226/15/381.
54 An error that appears to be a misprint in Bumsted's *Land, Settlement, and Politics*, 188, giving the date of the Princetown revolt as 1794, is particularly unfortunate as it reverses a critical chronology: the political initiative preceded militia resistance associated with land grievances.
55 Fanning to Portland, 30 Sept. 1797, CO 226/15/264–7, NAC; Joseph Robinson's report, 25 Aug. 1797, CO 226/15/268–9
56 Hill memorandum, [n.d.], CO 226/17/126–7, NAC. For Hill's career see Bumsted, 'John Hill.'
57 Macdonald to Fanning, 15 April 1797, CO 226/15/211, NAC
58 Fanning to Portland, 30 Sept. 1797, CO 226/15/267, NAC
59 Bumsted, 'The Origins of the Land Question,' 45
60 Warman has aptly compared the situation confronting the historian in these circumstances to the problems of following a play in which the most important actor says nothing. Warman has suggested, in the case of Mexico's development that the persistent influences of a silent peasantry have provided the essential continuities and determinants of national history. Landlords and the bourgeoisie may have had all the lines, but their behaviour reflected the position of the rural masses who physically dominated the stage; Warman, *'We Come to Object,'* 4. Scott has suggested a coral metaphor to make this same point. Like the millions of polyps whose actions go into the construction of reefs, peasant actions in aggregate create a political presence that make some routes possible and lead to the wreck of those attempting others. Scott, *Weapons of the Weak*, xvii. Allan Greer notes a similar dynamic occurring between a 'powerful, though largely underground, current of habitant belief' and Patriot rhetoric and policies; Greer, *The Patriots and the People*, 282.
61 David Bell makes a similar argument concerning the role of elites in

creating and controlling popular unrest in Saint John in the turbulent 1780s. Bell, *Early Loyalist Saint John*, 129–33.

62 Macdonald to Fanning, 15 April 1797, CO 226/15/215, NAC
63 Fanning to Portland, 30 Sept. 1797, CO 226/15/264–7, NAC
64 Bumsted, 'The Land Question,' 8
65 John Stewart, *An Account of Prince Edward Island*, 227–30. The concern to maintain proprietorial monopoly of island lands, and to control the cost of access to it, was not unreasonable from a landlord's perspective. See Bolland, 'Systems of Domination after Slavery.'
66 Bellot, *William Knox*, 210–12; Bumsted, 'The Land Question'
67 The terms of the original grants provided for forfeiture *only* in the case of failure to meet settlement requirements, and the deadline that mattered for forfeiture was the requirement to meet one-third of the settlement requirement within four years of the issue of the grant. The procedures for enforcing payment of quit rents were not specified in the grants issued in Nova Scotia. Most of those issued on Prince Edward Island included a clause indicating that the recovery of quit rents was to be in accordance with the 'Laws, Practice and Customs of Great Britain and of said Island,' provided the latter conformed with British law. Quit rents were to be recovered as any other debt: by the seizure and sale of sufficient property to cover the debt and costs.
68 Hobart to Fanning, 6 August 1802, CO 227/7/9–18, NAC
69 See Fiat Justitia to the editor and the editor's comments, *Royal Gazette*, 16 Oct. 1832, and Maria Fanning's response, 30 Oct. 1832.
70 Fanning to Townshend, 2 March 1804, Smith, Alley Collection, Acc. 2702/12/122, PARO; Fanning to Hobart, 3 May 1803, CO 226/19/128–9, NAC
71 Bumsted, 'The Land Question,' 19
72 PEI, *JHA*, 1805, 8–12
73 'Quit Rents of Prince Edward Island, General Account of Receipts and Disbursements,' CO 226/20/144, NAC
74 John Stewart, *An Account of Prince Edward Island*, 252; MacNutt, 'Fanning's Regime,' 53
75 Holman, 'John Cambridge'; Bumsted, 'John Hill'; M. Brook Taylor, 'Charles Worrell'; Webber, 'Robert Shuttleworth,' 9; Andrew Hill Clark, *Three Centuries and the Island*, 52, 67; Bumsted, 'Settlement by Chance'; John Morgan Gray, 'Thomas Douglas'; Macqueen, *Skye Pioneers and 'The Island'*

2. Land Issues in a Changing Context, 1800–1824

1 Lot 24 Rent Books, p. 2, 1530, Proprietors' rent books, Series 2, RG 15, PARO

2 Ibid.
3 Ibid., 3, 10, 28
4 Ibid., 9, 24
5 Wynn, *Timber Colony,* 29
6 Isabella Desbarres to Sir William Dolben, 21 March 1809, DesBarres Papers, MG 23/F1–5/14/2781–4, NAC
7 On the costs and difficulties of island farm making, see Bittermann, 'Farm Households and Wage Labour.'
8 Holman, 'James Bardin Palmer'
9 Proprietorial Memorial, CO 226/26/173, NAC
10 On Palmer's thinking in his early years on the island see 'Report by Major J.B. Palmer on Conditions in Prince Edward Island,' 20 Aug. 1805, DesBarres Papers, MG 23/F1–5/14/2708–17, NAC.
11 Testimony of William Haszard, 16 Aug. 1811, CO 226/27/80, NAC
12 Resident landlord memorial, 4 Dec. 1805, CO 226/20/108, NAC
13 Palmer deposition, 16 May 1811, CO 226/28/66, NAC. On the Dublin Society see Meeman and Clarke, eds., *The Royal Dublin Society*; Beckett, *The Making of Modern Ireland,* 175–6. On its influence on the formation of other comparable associations, see Ulrich Im Hof, 'German Associations and Politics,' 211.
14 J.C. Beckett, 'Introduction,' lix
15 J.B. Palmer memorandum, 4 March 1813, CO 226/27/81, NAC; John Macdonald to Selkirk, 23 April 1810, Selkirk Papers, MG 19/E1/56/14999, NAC; Bumsted, 'The Loyal Electors'; Holman, 'James Bardin Palmer'
16 Peter Magowan letter, 1807, PARO, Acc. 4082
17 For biographies of some of these men, see Bumsted, 'William Roubel'; Kenneth MacKinnon, 'Coun Douly Rankin'; Bumsted, 'Angus Macaulay'; Marianne G. Morrow, 'James Bagnall.'
18 Charles Wright deposition, 23 April 1812, CO 226/26/195–6, NAC
19 Macdonald to Selkirk, 23 April 1810, Selkirk Papers, MG 19/E1/56/15000, NAC
20 Holland to Smith, 21 Dec. 1815, CO 226/31/15, NAC
21 Macaulay deposition, 22 Aug. 1811, CO 226/28/73, NAC; John Macdonald to Selkirk, 23 April 1810, Selkirk Papers, MG 19/E1/56/15001, NAC; 'An Enemy to Party' to the editor, *Weekly Recorder* (Charlottetown) 23 Oct. 1810, 6–7
22 The argument here expands on Harvey's contention that a distinction needs to be made between the motives of the elites associated with the Society of Loyal Electors, which he argued were selfish, and the content of their policies, which he believed to be in the interests of the tenantry.

Harvey, 'The Loyal Electors.' It differs, however, from Bumsted's contention that the Society of Loyal Electors had no commitment to sweeping land reform and that those who have seen it in this light have read this 'back into the conflict.' The society may not have had an interest in land reform at the time of the 1806 election, but this was not the case in later years; Bumsted, 'The Loyal Electors,' 12.

23 Charles Stewart to Montgomery, 20 April 1812, CO 226/26/228, NAC; Colclough to Hill, 28 April 1812, CO 226/26/225–6

24 For an electoral breakdown see Colclough to Montgomery, 26 March 1812, CO 226/26/234, NAC

25 Bumsted, 'William Roubel'; Roubel deposition, 30 July 1813, CO 226/28/63, NAC; Judd, *Members of Parliament*, 106

26 Colclough response to Grand Jury, *Weekly Recorder*, 28 March 1812, 52–3; Hill and Montgomery, 'Statement Relative to Prince Edward Island,' [n.d.] CO 226/26/165, NAC; Cambridge to Richardson, 9 March 1818, CO 226/34/391

27 There were parallels here as well, though, with Jacobin precedents; see Kennedy, *The Jacobin Clubs*, 3–30.

28 In this regard, it is worth noting that the form J.B. Palmer proposed for the Island's first agricultural society explicitly drew on a Russian precedent; Palmer report, 20 Aug. 1805, DesBarres Papers, MG 23/F1–5/14/2712, NAC.

29 White, ed., *Lord Selkirk's Diary*, 5

30 Macdonald to Selkirk, 23 April 1810, Selkirk Papers, MG 19/E1/56/14986, NAC

31 Peter McAuslane advertisement, *Weekly Recorder* (Charlottetown), 27 June 1812

32 Charles Wright deposition, 23 April 1812, CO 226/26/195–6, NAC. For a general discussion of the history of Loyalist land grievances see Bumsted, 'The Loyalist Land Question.'

33 Colclough to Hill, 2 Dec. 1811, CO 226/26/200, NAC

34 Macdonald to Selkirk, 23 April 1810, Selkirk Papers, MG 19/E1/56/14997–15002, NAC

35 Roubel deposition, 17 Sept. 1811, CO 226/25/102, NAC

36 Tilly, 'Britain Creates the Social Movement'

37 For a consideration of the significance that a focus on the state held for the patterns of change in collective action, and for a chronology of the emergence of state-focused activism, see Tilly, *From Mobilization to Revolution*, 143–71.

38 LeSeuer to Attorney General Charles Stewart, 24 April 1812, CO 226/30/83–5, NAC

39 Colclough to Robert Montgomery, 26 March 1812, CO 226/26/235, NAC; Bumsted, 'Caesar Colclough,' 160
40 Macdonald to Selkirk, 23 April 1810, Selkirk Papers, MG 19/E1/56/14997, NAC; Charles Stewart to Montgomery, 20 April 1812, CO 226/26/228–31, NAC; Hill to Bathurst, 8 April 1816, CO 226/31/244
41 Goodwin, *The Friends of Liberty*; R.R. Palmer, *The Age of the Democratic Revolution*
42 Thorpe to Sullivan, CO 226/19/369, NAC
43 Buckner, 'Charles Douglass Smith,' 824
44 Smith to Bathurst, 29 July 1814, CO 226/29/67–70, NAC
45 William Haszard affidavit, 4 March 1813, CO 226/27/83; Smith to Bathurst, 29 July 1814, CO 226/29/72, NAC
46 Smith to Bathurst, 13 Sept. 1814, CO 226/29/82, NAC
47 25th George III, c. 4; 35th George III, c. 10
48 Smith to Bathurst, 13 Sept. 1814, CO 226/29/80–2, NAC; 29 July 1813, ibid., 67; 17 Sept. 1814, ibid., 82–3; 23 March 1815, ibid., 30/14–5, 13
49 Smith to Bathurst, 13 June 1815, CO 226/30/45, NAC; 15 July 1816; ibid., 31/86
50 Smith to Bathurst, 15 June 1816, CO 226/31/84–6, NAC; Smith to Bathurst, 28 June 1816, CO 226/31/88–9
51 Bolger, 'Land and Politics, 1787–1824,' in Bolger, ed., *Canada's Smallest Province*, 88
52 Memorial of P.D. Stewart, 22 Feb. 1816, Governor General's Office, Records from the Lieutenant-Governor's Offices, Prince Edward Island, RG 7, G 8 D/4/223–7, NAC
53 Smith to Bathurst, 31 Oct. 1816, CO 226/31/126–7, NAC; 1 Dec. 1816, ibid., 160, 24 March 1819, ibid., 35/105
54 *Prince Edward Island Gazette* (Charlottetown), 19 Jan., 14 March, and 18 April 1818
55 Robie to Johnson, 29 Nov. 1817, CO 226/34/9, NAC
56 'Spectator' to editor and Proclamation, *Prince Edward Island Gazette*, 16 February 1818
57 Smith to Bathurst, 15 Feb. 1818, CO 226/34/20–2, NAC; 15 March 1818, ibid., 31
58 'Spectator' to editor, *Prince Edward Island Gazette*, 16 Feb. 1818.
59 Scully [?] to Hill, 15 June 1818, CO 226/34/283, NAC
60 Petition of the Proprietors of Landed Estates in Prince Edward Island, [1818], CO 226/34/337, NAC
61 Public notice that the inhabitants of escheated lands were to be given

licences of occupation was advertised in March 1818; *Prince Edward Island Gazette*, 14 March 1818.

62 Seymour to Palmer, 8 June 1816, Prince Edward Island Letters, vol. 2, Seymour of Ragley Papers, CR 114A/563/2, WCRO. Bathurst solicited Smith's ideas on quit rent policy and warned him that changes were imminent in March 1815, and notice to this effect was posted on the Island in Oct. 1816; Bathurst to Smith, 18 March 1815, Governor General's Office, Records from the Lieutenant Governor's Offices, Prince Edward Island, RG 7, G 8 D/4/186–7, NAC; *Petitions from Prince Edward Island addressed to the King, Representing the Conduct of the Lieut. Governor Charles Douglass Smith*, 6.

63 Binns to [Street], 1 Aug. 1818, Langton Papers, 6/2, LAO; *Prince Edward Island Gazette*, 8 Aug. 1818

64 Memorial of the Proprietors of Lots in the Towns and Royalties of Charlotte Town, Prince Town, and George Town in Prince Edward Island, Aug. 1818, CO 226/34/342, NAC

65 Johnston to Selkirk, 28 Aug. 1819, Selkirk Papers, MG 19/E1/16/6461

66 Resolutions of Meeting, 29 Nov. 1817, CO 226/32/277, NAC

67 *Prince Edward Island Gazette*, 14 Oct. 1818

68 Smith to Bathurst, 15 March 1820, CO 226/36/11–13, NAC

69 Kenneth MacKinnon, 'Coun Douly Rankin,' 741

70 See 'Spectator' to the editor, *Prince Edward Island Gazette*, 31 Jan. 1818, 'An Old Observer' to the editor, 27 April 1818.

71 Lemuel Cambridge to John Cambridge, 1 May 1819, Governor General's Office, Records from the Lieutenant Governor's Offices, Prince Edward Island, RG 7, G 8 D/5/62, NAC

72 Requisition to Sheriff, CO 226/41/64–5, NAC

73 [?] to Cambridge, 21 March 1823, CO 226/39/422, NAC

74 *Prince Edward Island Register*, 4 and 11 Oct. 1823; [?] to Cambridge, 21 March 1823, CO 226/39/420, NAC

75 Smith to Bathurst, 3 Nov. 1823, CO 226/39/153–6, NAC

76 After his return to Britain, Smith prepared a lengthy point-by-point response to the charges brought by absentee proprietors and Islanders. He effectively rebutted many of them. After a full reading of Smith's responses to the original charges, James Stephen changed his position substantially. He no longer thought the governor guilty of anything worse than poverty, a quick temper, and misplaced confidence in the family members he appointed to office. He was, Stephens said, a 'martyr of calumny and falsehood'; Stephen to Horton, 6 Jan. 1826, CO 226/43/177–80, NAC.

77 Buckner, 'Charles Douglass Smith,' 827

3. The Limitations of Developmental Politics, 1824–1831

1 For consideration of the politics of development and escheat in this period, see Bittermann and McCallum, 'When Private Rights Become Public Wrongs.'
2 Vass, 'John Ready'
3 *Prince Edward Island Register*, 20 Nov., 27 Nov. and 4 Dec. 1824
4 On the 'party' spirit that he was attempting to dampen see Ready to Horton, 28 March 1825, CO 226/42/37–8, NAC; Ready to Murray, 7 June 1830, CO 226/47/72–3. On assembly/council tensions see Ready to Bathurst, 12 June 1827, CO 226/44/49–50; Ready to Huskinson, 9 May 1828, CO 226/45/42–3; Ready to Huskinson, 27 May 1828, CO 226/45/149–150. For a synthetic statement of much of the thinking on economic development that emerged from this alliance see the joint statement of the assembly and council contained in Ready's dispatch of 2 June 1829 with his letter of support. Ready to Hay, 2 June 1829, CO 226/46/85–90.
5 *Prince Edward Island Register*, 27 March 1824
6 William Johnston, John Stewart, and Thomas Owen were land agents, Robert Hodgson and William Johnston lawyers, and John Jardine and Angus Macaulay doctors. For the biographies of some of these men see Robertson, 'Sir Robert Hodgson'; Bumsted, 'Angus Macaulay'; F.C. Pigot, *John Stewart of Mount Stewart*; Pigot, 'John Stewart'; M. Brook Taylor, 'William Johnson.'
7 Included among the shipbuilders were Benjamin Coffin, Thomas Owen, Lemuel Cambridge, Ewen Cameron, Alexander Campbell, John McGregor, and George Bearistoe.
8 Holman, 'John Cambridge'
9 Owen, *Arthur Owen*, 8
10 Beck, *Politics of Nova Scotia*, vol. 1, *Nicholson-Fielding, 1710–1896*, 86–99; MacNutt, *New Brunswick*, 193–208; Creighton, *The Empire of the St. Lawrence*, 205–54. See too Acheson, 'The Great Merchant and Economic Development in Saint John.' While highlighting the divisions that emerged within the merchant community, towards mid-century, over appropriate strategies for development, Acheson describes areas of political consensus among Saint John's merchant community on issues such as infrastructure development.
11 See, for instance, Statutes of PEI, 5 Geo. IV, c. 11, 12, 14; 6 Geo. IV, c. 1, 2; 8 Geo. IV, c. 1, 5, 9, 10; 9 Geo. IV, c. 3; 10 Geo. IV, c. 3, 6, 7, 11.
12 Return of the Net Internal Revenue and Expenditure of Prince Edward Island for the Years 1824, 1825, and 1826, CO 226/44/98, NAC

13 Buckner, *The Transition to Responsible Government*, 65–6
14 Ready to Horton, 28 March 1825, CO 226/42/38, NAC; PEI, *JHA*, 1825, 20
15 Vindex to the Editor, *Royal Gazette*, 30 Nov. 1830, p. 3; J.L. Lewellin, *Emigration: Prince Edward Island*, 5; McGregor, *Historical and Descriptive Sketches of the Maritime Colonies*, 95
16 For an intelligent description of settlement patterns and the significance that investments in roads held for the Island's agricultural economy see Fade Goff to Hay, 15 July 1828, CO 226/45/332–8, NAC
17 On the importance that road construction held for broadening the region supplying John Hill's sawmill at Cascumpec see J.B. Palmer to George Seymour, 12 Aug. 1816, 'Prince Edward Island Letters,' vol. 2, Seymour of Ragley Papers, CR 114A/563/2, WCRO. On the relationship between the routing of new roads west of Three Rivers in Kings County and the demands for wood at the shipyards there see Thomas Irwin's comments in *Royal Gazette*, 13 Jan. 1835.
18 Ready to Horton, 28 March 1825, CO 226/42/38; Ready to Horton, 20 July 1826, CO 226/42/170; Fade Goff to Horton, 21 Feb. 1827, CO 226/44/169–70; Joint Address of the Council and Assembly, 2 June 1829, CO 226/46/87–90, NAC
19 *Prince Edward Island Register*, 31 Jan. 1826, 3, 10 April 1827, 3. The specific amounts indicated on the official export returns need to be treated with caution. Undecked vessels, for instance, were not required to report to the customs house in this period. The result is a substantial undervaluation of the value of agricultural exports. Contemporary observations suggest that timber exports from the colony may have been undervalued in the official returns as well. Despite these weaknesses, the overall patterns indicated by these figures are a useful indicator of the trends in the Island economy and the extent of the depression of the late 1820s. Cautionary comments on the accuracy of the export returns can be found in the *Prince Edward Island Register*, 31 Jan. 1826, 10 April 1827, 29 Jan. 1828.
20 See appendix, pages 277–8.
21 Exports, 1824–5, CO 231/7–8, NAC
22 *Prince Edward Island Register*, 31 Jan. 1826, 10 April 1827
23 Lewellin, *Emigration: Prince Edward Island*, 5–6; Bolger, 'The Demise of Quit Rents and Escheat, 1824–1842,' in *Canada's Smallest Province*, 95
24 Census 1827, PEI, *JHA*, 1928; 1833 Census, ibid., 1834, appendix C; Rusticus to the editor, *Prince Edward Island Register*, 23 Aug. 1825
25 Ready to Huskinson, 9 May 1828, CO 226/45/42–3, NAC; Ready to Murray, 7 Jan. 1829, CO 226/46/9
26 Ready to Horton, 28 March 1825, CO 226/42/38, NAC

27 Annual revenue bills that received approval include 5 Geo. IV, c. 19, 20; 6 Geo. IV, c. 10, 11; 8 Geo. IV, c. 12, 13; 9 Geo. IV, c. 10, 11; and 10 Geo. IV, c. 20, 21. 9 Geo. IV, c. 22 and 11 Geo. IV, c. 20 were disallowed.
28 5 Geo. IV, c. 18; 6 Geo. IV, c. 12; 9 Geo. IV, c.1; 11 Geo. IV, c. 16
29 Petition of the House of Assembly, 18 March 1825, CO 226/42/45–6, NAC
30 11 Geo. IV, c. 17
31 10 Geo. IV, c. 10
32 Statements of Ready's thinking on these issues can be found in Ready to Horton, 9 May 1825, CO 226/42/61–2, NAC; Ready to Murray, 7 Jan. 1829, CO 226/46/7–9. See too Vass, 'John Ready'; Vass, 'The Ready Touch.'
33 For an absentee landlord's argument against quit rents and in favour of greater investments in internal improvements in the colony, see Seymour to Hay, 20 May 1829, CO 226/46/195–7, NAC.
34 Regarding the development of similarly designed anti-absentee taxation policies on the American agricultural frontier see Gates, *The Farmer's Age*, 85–9.
35 These figures are drawn from a list of Island proprietors and their holdings submitted by Governor Ready in 1830. It shows these proprietors as owners of twenty-nine townships and part owners of seven more; CO 226/47/166–8, NAC.
36 Land tax books from 1835 showed that roughly half the eighty-two proprietors owning more than five hundred acres of land in the colony were residents; George Seymour's 'Journal of Tour of Canada and the United States' (1840), entry for 8 September, Seymour of Ragley Papers, CR 114A/380, WCRO. On escheat policy concerning the distinction between small freeholders and proprietors see chapter 9.
37 At the time of the 1841 census, small freeholders held roughly 250,000 acres.
38 The equivalents are derived from Lewellin, *Emigration: Prince Edward Island*, 16, 20.
39 See chapter 6.
40 James Stephen provided a preliminary assessment in 1824 and suggested that on the basis of the limited evidence, the escheat proceedings appeared to be legal. Looking over more complete evidence in 1831, when one of Smith's escheats was being challenged by a proprietorial claimant, he judged correctly that the challenge was unlikely to succeed. Stephen to Horton, 29 March 1824, CO 226/41/430–1, NAC; Stephen to Hay, 5 Feb. 1831, CO 226/48/201–5.
41 The sentiments of the lawyer and land agent Charles Binns were probably

broadly shared in the proprietorial community. In a letter written following publication of the new settlement terms, he suggested that they were of little importance: 'I rather suppose you will have nothing to fear from that regulation'; Binns to [Street] , 1 August 1818, Langton Papers, 6/2, LAO.

42 *Prince Edward Island Register*, 4 Dec. 1824
43 PEI, *JHA*, 1825, 1st Session, 3
44 PEI, *JHA*, 1825, 1st Session, 44, 59. The full petition is contained in CO 226/43/5–6, NAC.
45 The house decided that interference with imperial government policy on the escheat issue was 'at present premature': PEI, *JHA*, 1825, 2nd Session, 11.
46 For a consideration of settlement growth in the adjacent colonies of Cape Breton and Nova Scotia and the plight of latecomers see Hornsby, 'Scottish Emigration and Settlement'; Bittermann, 'Economic Stratification and Agrarian Settlement'; Bittermann, MacKinnon, and Wynn, 'Of Inequality and Interdependence.' For an insightful treatment of variations in leases and the burden of rents see Hatvany, 'The Proprietary Burden?'
47 The value of oats and sheep is derived from the export returns of 1826, *Prince Edward Island Register*, 10 April 1827. The rate for labour varied depending on the duration of the contract and the skills and resources brought to the job. A daily rate of from 2/6 to 3/ per day appears to have been typical for general labour in this period. See, for instance, the Alex McLellan Account Book, McLellan Family fonds, Acc. 2802/1, PARO.
48 'Rental of the Property of Sir James Montgomery,' 1833, GD 1/409/16, SRO
49 The equivalents are derived from the export returns of 1826, *Prince Edward Island Register*, 10 April 1827
50 Lot 24 Rent Books, pp. 46–9, 1526, RG 15, PARO
51 Ibid., 130
52 Lot 24 Rent Books, p. 15, 1521, RG 15, PARO
53 Stewart to Hency, 23 April 1835, Stewart Letterbooks, Stewart Family fonds, Acc. 2316/2/194–5, PARO
54 Lebergott, 'The Demand for Land.' New York's landlords came to similar conclusions concerning the relationship between the value of tenants' improvements and their arrears. See Countryman, *A People in Revolution*, 21; Kim, *Landlord and Tenant in Colonial New York*, 219.
55 Lemuel Cambridge to George Young, 28 Oct. 1838, George Young Papers, MG 2/725/F1/1237, PANS

56 In an election speech Charles Binns thought it necessary to articulate his disagreement with those who maintained that landlords would pass on any tax burdens to their tenantry; *Royal Gazette*, 5 Oct. 1830.
57 The literature dealing with the changes occurring in the countryside of the British Isles in the late eighteenth and early nineteenth centuries and bearing on the experiences of immigrants to British North America is vast. Useful works include Hunter, *The Making of the Crofting Community*; MacLean, *The People of Glengarry*; Elliott, *Irish Migrants in the Canadas*; Kirby Miller, *Emigrants and Exiles*; and Bailyn, *Voyagers to the West*.
58 On the significance of this motive in the behaviour of merchants elsewhere in the region see Acheson, 'The Great Merchant and Economic Development,' 12.
59 *Royal Gazette* (Charlottetown), 19 Oct. 1830; MacKinnon and Warburton, eds., *Past and Present of Prince Edward Island*, 114
60 Hobsbawm, *The Age of Revolution*, 138–40; Harry L. Watson, *Liberty and Power*
61 The issue occasioned sharp debate on the Island, and legislation enfranchising Catholics lost by close division. For examples of the discussion see 'A Protestant Catholic' to the editor, *Prince Edward Island Register*, 21 Feb. 1826; 'A Real Protestant' to the editor, ibid., 7 March 1826; 'A Protestant Catholic' to the editor, ibid., 14 March 1826; and 'P.P.' to the editor, ibid., 14 March 1826. Parts of the final debate in the house were reprinted in ibid., 3 April 1827. See too MacMillan, *The Early History of the Catholic Church*, 237–81.
62 See McNeill's speech, *Royal Gazette* 28 Sept. 1830; Little's speech, 5 October 1830.
63 My emphasis. *Royal Gazette*, 15 Feb. 1831
64 *Royal Gazette*, 14 Sept. 1830
65 *Royal Gazette*, 21 August 1832. See chapter 4. Unfortunately there is no record concerning who was nominated in September 1830 or what the criteria were for nominations.
66 John Willock's arrival on the island is noted in the *Prince Edward Island Register*, 8 Sept. 1829.
67 *Royal Gazette*, 19 Oct. 1830
68 *Royal Gazette*, 8 March 1831
69 Baglole, 'William Cooper'; Cooper, 'A Pioneer Family.' A discussion of Cooper's role in the anti-Smith meetings can be found in a letter he wrote to 'The Committee appointed to report upon Mr. Waller's Letters,' 16 Dec. 1837, CO 226/56/186–7, NAC.

4. Escheat Enters the Political Arena, 1831–1833

1 The sequence of events underlying the formation of the Escheat Movement raises questions about the universality of the model of democratic movement creation suggested by Lawrence Goodwyn. In the case of Escheat, politicization of the movement emerged not as a final stage of movement development, as Goodwyn has posited, but as a central aspect of its creation; Goodwyn, *The Populist Moment*, xviii.

2 For another view of this election see Bumsted, 'Parliamentary Privilege and Electoral Disputes.'

3 Women were disenfranchised by statute in 1836, but had, with few exceptions, been excluded from voting by other means prior to this; Garner, *The Franchise and Politics*, 155.

4 PEI, *JHA*, 1832, appendix A, 5–6

5 For details of the electoral law that was in place at this time see Garner, *The Franchise and Politics*, 44–5.

6 The other candidates were Dr John Jardine of Morell, a member of the previous house, and Thomas Irwin, a schoolteacher and surveyor living in Charlottetown; L.F.S. Upton, 'Thomas Irwin.'

7 PEI, *JHA*, 1832, appendix A, 6

8 *Royal Gazette*, 19 July 1831. Macdonald was in third place at this time, behind Jardine, who had forty votes.

9 PEI, *JHA*, 1832, appendix A, 10

10 PEI, *JHA*, 1832, appendix A, 4

11 *Royal Gazette*, 26 July 1831

12 *Royal Gazette*, 15 Feb. 1831; *Royal Gazette*, 12 Oct. 1830; Cooper, 'A Pioneer Family'

13 See 'A Sincere Roman Catholic' to the editor, *Royal Gazette*, 7 Sept. 1830; Philanthropos to the editor, *Royal Gazette*, 21 Sept. 1830

14 'A King's County Elector' to the editor, *Royal Gazette*, 22 Feb. 1831

15 See Robertson, 'Daniel Brenan.' Robertson's contention that Brenan acted 'as a staunch Tory' in the assembly opposing the machinations of radical Escheators, though, is incorrect. Although Brenan locked horns with Cooper and other Escheat leaders on a number of occasions in the 1830s, he was a Reformer and not a Tory and as such at times worked with Cooper, Le Lacheur, and the other advocates of sweeping land reform. For his 1830 election speech calling for *'radical reform'* see the *Royal Gazette*, 12 Oct. 1830. For his role as an ally of Escheators in the first session of the 13th Assembly see, for example, *Royal Gazette*, 10 Feb. 1835. See too

Brenan's publication of a letter describing his role in island politics as that of 'one of the staunchest Reformers in Prince Edward Island' as he sought to justify his decision to resign from the house; *Prince Edward Island Times*, 10 May 1836.

16 PEI, *JHA*, 1832, appendix A, 3

17 The incident is a reminder that ethnic solidarity and the cultural baggage that rural immigrants brought from the Old World could just as easily undercut tenant solidarity and agrarian collective action as contribute to it; Bittermann, 'Agrarian Protest and Cultural Transfer.'

18 The 1841 Census recorded place of birth. This is a flawed measure both because it neglects the ethnicity of Island-born residents and because it captures that of immigrants who were not present in July 1831. Despite these weaknesses, it does provide a rough indication of ethnic patterns of settlement. Among the foreign-born, Irish immigrants were more numerous than English and Scots in three of the four townships about St. Peters (Lots 39–42) and in four of the ten northern Kings County townships. The dominant profile of the Irish in the St Peters region was noted as well by travellers. See Census of the Population and Statistical Return of Prince Edward Island, taken in the year 1841; George Seymour's 'Journal of Tour of Canada and the United States' (1840), entry for 1 September, Seymour of Ragley Papers, CR 114A/380, WCRO.

19 Census of the Population and Statistical Return of Prince Edward Island, taken in the year 1841. See too Andrew Hill Clark's maps of ethnic settlement patterns using data from the 1848 census in *Three Centuries and the Island*, 85, 89–90.

20 Catholics constituted 41 per cent of the combined population of Townships 51–59, 61, 63–4, and 66; Census of the Population and Statistical Return of Prince Edward Island, taken in the year 1841.

21 Worrell's candidacy was sustained not so much by '*his* agents' leading '*his* tenants' (my emphasis) to the polls, as Brook Taylor has suggested, as by the organizing work of men such as Charles and John Stewart and James Williams, who rallied Highlanders who were tenants of others; M. Brook Taylor, 'Charles Worrell.' See Macaulay deposition, 22 Aug. 1811, CO 226/28/72–3, NAC.

22 PEI, *JHA*, 1832, appendix A, 7

23 PEI, *JHA*, 1832, appendix A, 2–3

24 For an account of Sims's behaviour see PEI, *JHA*, 1832, appendix A, 4–5. For a profile of Donald Macdonald see Robertson, 'Donald Macdonald.'

25 M. Brook Taylor, 'Charles Worrell'

26 Rudé, *The Crowd in History*, 267

27 Baglole, 'William Cooper,' 155

28 Ibid.; Baglole, 'William Cooper of Sailor's Hope'; Baglole, 'The Legacy of William Cooper'

29 Thorne, *The History of Parliament*, 405–6; Cooper, 'A Pioneer Family'

30 Cooper to 'the Committee appointed to report upon Mr. Waller's letters,' 16 Dec. 1837, CO 226/56/185, NAC

31 Marryat was an officer on board a frigate that Townshend commanded in British North American waters and provides an intriguing description of their encounter with an Irish immigrant ship out of Belfast headed for the United States. Townshend persuaded the seventeen or so Irish families on board to redirect themselves to his property on Prince Edward Island. With the permission of the admiral stationed in Halifax, he accompanied them there and set his crew to work clearing land, planting crops, and building houses for his new tenants. Marryat, *Frank Mildmay*, 161–6.

32 My description of Cooper's activities as a land agent is drawn primarily from the 'Report of a Select Committee of the Inhabitants of Lot or Township number 56 in Prince Edward Island. Submitted to the Inhabitants at a Public Meeting the 16th January 1838,' CO 226/56/177–88, NAC. The September 1837 statement of Archibald Steele et al., published in the *Colonial Herald*, is informative as well; CO 226/55/316.

33 Harry Baglole has argued that Cooper's behaviour as a leader of the Escheat Movement following his dismissal in 1829 was so different from his past behaviour that it was akin to a religious conversion as dramatic as that of Saint Paul. Cooper had shifted from forcing tenants to comply with Lord Townshend's difficult rental terms to becoming the tenant's advocate – a polar reversal. Such, perhaps, was Lord Townshend's view of the matter, and it developed firm roots in the rhetoric of Cooper's political opponents, who found it a useful characterization of his actions. This perception misses essential continuities in Cooper's behaviour and in the positions of those who continued to support Cooper after he ceased to be the land agent for Lot 56 and became an advocate of land reform in the political arena. See Baglole, 'William Cooper,' 156; Baglole, 'The Legacy of William Cooper,' 17.

34 *British American*, 13 April 1833

35 'Report of a Select Committee of the Inhabitants of Lot or Township number Fifty-Six in Prince Edward Island. Submitted to the Inhabitants at a Public Meeting the 16th January 1838,' CO 226/56/179, NAC

36 Cooper to 'The Committee appointed to report upon Mr. Waller's letters,' 16 Dec. 1837, CO 226/56/185, NAC

37 'Report of a Select Committee of the Inhabitants of Lot or Township number Fifty-Six,' CO 226/56/179, NAC

38 PEI, *JHA*, 1831, 36, 49

39 PEI, *JHA*, 1831, 71–2
40 *Royal Gazette*, 17 May 1831
41 PEI, *JHA*, 1832, 16
42 PEI, *JHA*, 1833, 9–10
43 PEI, *JHA*, 1832, 125
44 PEI, *JHA*, 1833, 44
45 Taylor, 'George Dalrymple' 8; Taylor, 'Charles Binns'; Owen, *Arthur Owen*, 8; Holman, 'John Brecken'
46 PEI, *JHA*, 1832, 80–2, 84, 102–3
47 This argument is made in Baglole, 'William Cooper,' 156.
48 *Royal Gazette*, 7 Feb. 1832
49 Ibid.
50 See chapter 3.
51 *Royal Gazette*, 7 Feb. 1832
52 Some certainly played a double game of appearing to stand for one thing for the sake of their rural constituents while working behind the scenes to block these initiatives; see Robert Stewart to John Lawson, 6 Aug. 1833, Stewart Letterbooks, Stewart Family fonds, Acc. 2316/1/277–84, PARO.
53 PEI, *JHA*, 1832, 102–3; *Royal Gazette*, 7 Feb. 1832. On the Comptons and Macdonalds see MacKinnon and Warburton, eds., *Past and Present of Prince Edward Island*, 83, 85, 327, 570–1; Leard, 'Political Relations'; Tuck, 'St. Eleanors'; *Prince Edward Island Register*, 18 March 1825, 15 August 1826, 9 Sept. 1828; *Royal Gazette*, 7 Sept. 1830. For proceedings in the house see *Royal Gazette*, 10 May 1831.
54 *Royal Gazette*, 7 Feb. 1832; *Royal Gazette*, 3 April 1832; *Royal Gazette*, 29 Jan. 1833. Note too the focus on productivity and 'improvement' in the discussions within the Escheat Committee, PEI, *JHA*, 1832, 80–1. Whig politicians in New York engaged in a similar reinterpretation of tenant grievances in the second quarter of the nineteenth century, recasting landlords as an obstacle to progress. See Huston, *Land and Freedom*, 99–100.
55 Edward Jarvis, Charles Binns, Thomas Owen, John Brecken, and Daniel Brenan to Bainbridge, 11 Oct. 1831, Appendix 'C,' PEI, *JHA*, 1832, 25. On the significance of this venture for Prince Edward Island see chapter 6.
56 Mr Cooper's Speech on the Escheat Question, *Royal Gazette*, 3 April 1832
57 *Royal Gazette*, 7 Feb. 1832
58 Mr Cooper's Speech on the Escheat Question, *Royal Gazette*, 3 April 1832
59 The count includes 'injustice' as well as 'justice.'
60 On the significance of classical precedents to agrarian radicalism during the French Revolution see Rose, 'The "Red Scare" of the 1790s.'
61 Greer, *The Patriots and the People*, 278; Huston, *Land and Freedom*, 112–14

62 *Royal Gazette*, 3 April 1832. On the importance of a labour theory of value to agrarian thought and agrarian protest in North America see Alfred F. Young, ed., *Beyond the American Revolution*, 319–20; Huston, *Land and Freedom*, 111–12; Summerhill, 'The Farmers' Republic,' 55, 127; Slaughter, *The Whiskey Rebellion*, 84; Alan Taylor, *Liberty Men and Great Proprietors*, 7, 101–3; Brown, 'Back Country Rebellions,' 78; Gates, 'The Decided Policy of William Lyon Mackenzie,' 186.

63 PEI, *JHA*, 1833, 36–9

64 W.H. Williams to the editor, *Royal Gazette*, 24 April 1832

65 James Beck, *The Descendants of Vere Beck*, ii-iv; V.B. to the editor, *Royal Gazette*, 1 May 1832

66 John Arbuckle to T.H. Haviland, 25 Jan. 1838, CO 226/55/297, NAC. Thompson notes that the 'readership' of Chartist papers was much greater than circulation figures would suggest as well, for similar reasons. *The Chartists*, 51–2.

67 V.B. to the editor, *Royal Gazette*, 1 May 1832

68 Mr Cooper's Speech on the Escheat Question, *Royal Gazette*, 3 April 1832

69 *Royal Gazette*, 24 April 1832

70 W.H. Williams to the editor, *Royal Gazette*, 29 May 1832

71 *Royal Gazette*, V.B. to the Editor, 1 May 1832; *Royal Gazette*, 29 May 1832

72 D. to the editor, *Royal Gazette*, 5 June 1832

73 *Royal Gazette*, 21 Aug. 1832

74 *Royal Gazette*, 6 July 1832; *Royal Gazette*, 4 Sept. 1832

75 *Royal Gazette*, 29 May 1832

76 See W.H. Williams to the 'Leaseholder,' *Royal Gazette*, 3 July 1832

77 W.H. Williams to the editor, *Royal Gazette*, 24 April 1832

78 See, for instance, *Legislative and Other Proceedings on the Expediency of Appointing a Court of Escheats in Prince Edward Island*, Ms 2334/18, PARO.

79 See the evidence of Mr Clements, *Abstract of the Proceedings of the Land Commissioner's Court Held During the Summer of 1860 to Inquire into the Differences Relative to the Rights of Landowners and Tenants in Prince Edward Island*, 154; 'Report of a Select Committee of the Inhabitants of Lot or Township Number Fifty-Six in Prince Edward Island Submitted to the Inhabitants at a Public Meeting the 16th of January 1838,' CO 226/56/180–1, NAC. It was reported that 'bonds' were formed in other communities too, but there is not, understandably, much evidence indicating the degree of formal organization underwriting rent resistance. See *British American*, 27 Oct. 1832.

80 *Colonial Patriot*, 6 October 1832; Beck, 'Jotham Blanchard.'

81 *Royal Gazette*, 11 Sept. 1832. In the second half of the 1820s imperial au-

thorities moved away from policies that had made land relatively cheap to obtain towards a land sales policy that restricted access to the soil and was expected to increase the revenues generated by Crown lands. Riddell, 'A Study in the Land Policy,' 385–405

82 Trevelyan, *England in the Age of Wycliffe*, 220, 225–7; Hobsbawm, *Primitive Rebels*, 119–21; Field, *Rebels in the Name of the Tsar*; Yves-Marie Bercé, 'Rural Unrest,' 135–6; J.F.C. Harrison, *The Common People*, 89–106; Hobsbawm, 'History from Below – Some Reflections,' 64; Blum, *The End of the Old Order*, 335

83 *Royal Gazette*, 4 Sept. 1832

84 'Fiat Justitia' to the editor, *Royal Gazette*, 16 Oct. 1832. The language of cabal and conspiracy draws from a broader transatlantic vocabulary of political criticism, but there was no shortage of substance giving rise to the critique on Prince Edward Island. See Bumsted's historical assessment of Fanning's character and his role in the land question at the turn of the century in 'Edmund Fanning.'

85 *Royal Gazette*, 16 Oct. 1832. On Haszard's career see Ian Ross Robertson, 'James Douglas Haszard.' It should be noted that Haszard's politics changed over the course of his life and that he was not always associated with the Tory elite.

86 Haszard modified his position to exclude Edmund Fanning from blame for the conspiratorial deeds of proprietors. *Royal Gazette*, 30 Oct. 1832

87 PEI, *JHA*, 1833, 36–9, 109–10

88 2 Wil. IV, c. 19

89 Robert Stewart noted seeing a letter sent to Britain by an assemblyman who argued that the escheat act and land registry act were unjust and should be opposed by proprietors and the Home Government, 'though he supported them through all their stages.' While one can wonder whether this protestation of principle should be given any more credence than those made while voting in the assembly, at the very least it shows how some played both sides of the proprietorial/tenant contest and helps to explain the absence of vigour in the 13th Assembly's pursuit of the escheat issue. See Robert Stewart to John Lawson, 6 Aug. 1833, Stewart Letterbooks, Stewart Family fonds, Acc. 2316/1/277–84, PARO.

90 *British American*, 13 April 1833

91 Marilyn Bell, 'Mr. Mann's Island'

92 Holman, 'Joseph Pope'

93 Buckner, *The Transition to Responsible Government*, 147–9, 218

94 PEI, *JHA*, 1833, 65

95 The salaries of the governor, the supreme court judge, the expected position of assistant judge, the colonial secretary, and the attorney general would be permanent, and the salaries of the other officers of the government would depend on annual appropriations. PEI, *JHA*, 1833, 93, 126–7; *Royal Gazette*, 21 May 1833
96 Goderich to Young, 27 Jan. 1833, CO 227/8/7–10; PEI, *JHA*, 1833, 122
97 *British American*, 13 April 1833
98 *Royal Gazette*, 9 April 1833
99 The designation 'urban' is used to draw a distinction between those who lived in centres such as Charlottetown and St Eleanors and those who lived in dispersed farm dwellings.
100 *Royal Gazette*, 24 April 1832

5. Resistance in the Countryside, 1832–1834

1 John Crisp to the editor, *Royal Gazette*, 21 Aug. 1832
2 For insightful consideration of the significance of such waves of enthusiasm to social movements see Hobsbawm, *Primitive Rebels*, 105–7.
3 Lefebvre, *The Great Fear*
4 Phillip Buckner, 'Sir Aretas William Young'
5 Young to Goderich, 18 Sept. 1832, CO 226/49/171–2, NAC
6 Extract of a letter to Edward Worrell, 15 June 1832, CO 226/49/188. This probably was from his brother Charles on the Island.
7 Robert Stewart to Goderich, 9 July 1832, CO 226/49/216, NAC
8 Extract of a letter from William Forgan to David Stewart, 11 June 1832, CO 226/49/286–7, NAC
9 See J.L. Lewellin's advertisement in *Royal Gazette*, 16 Oct. 1832.
10 'Report of a Select Committee of the Inhabitants of Lot or Township Number Fifty-Six,' CO 226/56/181, NAC
11 *Royal Gazette*, 24 April 1832
12 *Royal Gazette*, 29 May 1832
13 *British American*, 27 October 1832. There is evidence regarding rent resistance in the testimony given by Mr Clements before the Land Commission of 1860 as well. Although Clements discusses rent resistance that occurred 'shortly after' the escheat question was raised, he appears, judging from the personalities mentioned, to be referring to a period somewhat later in the 1830s. *Abstract of the Proceedings of the Land Commissioner's Court Held During the Summer of 1860*, 154.
14 Chief Justice Edward Jarvis's statements to the grand jury during the

Trinity Term session of the Supreme Court in 1833 suggested that he, for one considered such gatherings to be illegal. See below, p. 93.

15 H.D. Morpeth to David Stewart, 3 March 1833, CO 226/51/733, NAC
16 C. Worrell to Stanley, 11 Jan. 1834, CO 226/51/32, NAC; Hill to Under-Secretary of State, 28 Nov. 1833, CO 226/50/253. Evidence cited earlier sustains Morpeth's contentions concerning the Macdonald and Townshend estates.
17 See chapter 4.
18 *British American*, 27 October 1832
19 See, for instance, *Collings v. W. McKay*, Land Judgments and Indictments, Supreme Court Records, 1833, RG 6, PARO
20 *British American*, 27 October 1832
21 H.D. Morpeth to David Stewart, 3 March 1833, CO 226/51/733, NAC
22 *British American*, 27 Oct. 1832
23 *Royal Gazette*, 9 April 1833; *British American*, 13 April 1833
24 PEI, *JHA*, 1833, 121–2
25 *British American*, 13 April 1833
26 For the earlier escheat address see PEI, *JHA*, 1833, 109–10.
27 *British American*, 13 April 1833
28 On Samuel Green see Tuck, 'St. Eleanors,' 4. For responses to Cooper's speech see *Royal Gazette*, 9 April 1833.
29 *British American*, 13 April 1833
30 John Lawson to David Stewart, 20 May 1833, CO 226/51/734–5.
31 *King v. Archibald Campbell, et al.*, Land Judgments and Indictments, Supreme Court Records, 1833, RG 6, PARO
32 Acheson, *Saint John*, 51
33 Bumsted, 'Edward James Jarvis,' and Lawrence, *The Judges of New Brunswick*, 270–9
34 *Royal Gazette*, 2 July 1833. 'Hidden hand' explanations of revolt and resistance were, as George Rudé has noted, pervasive among those in authority in the eighteenth and nineteenth centuries and have in turn engendered a historiography – Prince Edward Island not excepted – that shares these assumptions. Rudé, *The Crowd in History*, 214–17. See also Huston, *Land and Freedom*, 137.
35 *Royal Gazette*, 2 July 1833
36 Holdsworth, *A History of English Law*, 3rd ed., 9: 160
37 Huston, *Land and Freedom*, 111; Ellis, *Landlords and Farmers*, 297–8
38 It would appear that the grants for six of the Island's townships were never recorded in Nova Scotia or Prince Edward Island: Nova Scotia

Crown Lands Record Centre, Books 8 and 9; RG 16, Land Registry Records, 1769–1872, PARO.

39 See Spencer Smith ad, *Royal Gazette*, 22 April 1834; *Royal Gazette*, 4 Feb. 1833; 'Petition of the Inhabitants of the Eastern District of King's County or Otherwise Naufrage,' CO 226/51/208–9.

40 *Abstract of the Proceedings of the Land Commissioners' Court*, 131

41 Petition of the Inhabitants of Prince County, Jan. 1832, Ms 2659/6, PARO; *Royal Gazette*, 31 January 1832; 1, Geo. IV, c. 12

42 MacGregor to Goderich, 24 July 1832, CO 226/49/179–80, NAC; *Royal Gazette*, 21 April 1835

43 See Resolution 7 of the public meeting at Rollo Bay, *Royal Gazette*, 12 Jan. 1836

44 *Royal Gazette*, 17 July 1832

45 On the cases of Alexander Dingwell and James Douglas see chapter 10.

46 One of the Bay Fortune Committee to the editor, *Royal Gazette*, 13 Nov. 1832. See too the plea for 'common justice' in 'Petition of the Inhabitants of the Eastern District of King's County or Otherwise Naufrage,' CO 226/51/208–9, NAC.

47 One of the Bay Fortune Committee to the editor, *Royal Gazette*, 13 Nov. 1832

48 On the significance of this grievance to the rebellions in Upper Canada see Romney, 'From the Types Riot to the Rebellion,' 113–44. On American parallels to Cooper's proposals see Ellis, *The Jeffersonian Crisis*, 113–14, 137–8; Szatmary, *Shay's Rebellion*, 42.

49 PEI, *JHA*, 1833, 23

50 *Royal Gazette*, 15 Jan. 1833

51 *King v. Archibald Campbell, et al.*, Land Judgements and Indictments, Supreme Court Records, 1833, RG 6, PARO

52 A statement of their defence is contained in 'Affidavit of Defendants,' *King v. Archibald Campbell, et al.*, Court Judgements and Cases, Supreme Court Records, 1833, RG 6, PARO.

53 See the testimony of William Cousins and Donald Montgomery before the Land Commission of 1861: *Abstract of the Proceedings of the Land Commissioners' Court*, 92–9.

54 *Royal Gazette*, 5 June 1832

55 'Affidavit of Defendants,' *King v. Archibald Campbell, et al.*, Court Judgements and Cases, Supreme Court Records, 1833, RG 6, PARO

56 Indictments were returned against Archibald Campbell, John Burke, Andrew Macpherson, George Stewart, and Thomas Lanigan. The crowd that gathered was larger than this and probably included some of the

others who were being served writs. As well as those named, these included William Mackay, John Murray, John Donally, Angus Mackenzie, David Smith, William Whitehead, John Mackay, James Mackay, George Sutherland, and George MacLeod.

57 *Royal Gazette*, 9 July 1833

58 Ibid.

59 *Royal Gazette*, 2 July 1833

60 *Alexander Smith v. Donald Macdonald*, Judgments, Supreme Court Records, 1833, RG 6, PARO

61 *Crown v. Malcolm Steel*, Indictments, Supreme Court Records, 1834, RG 6, PARO

62 Supreme Court Minutes, 18 Jan. 1834, RG 6, PARO

63 PEI, *JHA*, 1834, 8–9

64 'Report of a Select Committee of the Inhabitants of Lot or Township Number Fifty-Six,' CO 226/56/181, NAC

65 Robert Stewart to John Lawson, 6 August 1833 and 30 June 1834, Stewart Letterbooks, Stewart Family fonds, Acc. 2316/1/277–84 and 405–7, PARO

66 Billings to Cundall, 2 Feb. 1834, Ms 2518/2, PARO

67 PEI, *JHA*, 1834, 29

68 See the appendix.

69 See *British American*, 27 Oct. 1832; *Royal Gazette*, 2 July 1833, 21 Jan. 1834, 24 June 1834, 8 July 1834. See also *Donald MacDonald v. Alexander MacInnis and Angus MacPhee*, Land Judgments and Indictments, Supreme Court Records, 1833; *John Collings v. William MacKay*, Land Judgments and Indictments, Supreme Court Records, 1833; *James Allen and James Coughlan v. Matthew Connick, et al.*, Indictments, Supreme Court Records, 1834; *Crown v. John Renahau and Catherine Renahau*, Supreme Court Minutes, 1834; and *Crown v. John Renahau and Catherine Renahau*, Indictments, 1834.

70 There was a slight error in the reporting: *three* men and two women were in fact indicted. *Royal Gazette*, 21 Jan. 1834; Indictments, Supreme Court Records, 1834, RG 6, PARO

71 McVarish's account of his actions and his responses to examination at the time of the trial are found in 'Jarvis' Minutes of Naufrage Trial,' CO 226/52/46–8, NAC

72 'Jarvis' Minutes of Naufrage Trial,' CO 226/52/46, NAC

73 For a more detailed examination of this incident and of the roles women assumed within the Escheat Movement see Bittermann, 'Women and the Escheat Movement.'

74 'Jarvis' Minutes of Naufrage Trial,' CO 226/52/47, NAC

75 Two constables refused to serve the warrants, but whether this was sufficient to stop proceedings at this time is unclear; see note 86.
76 *Royal Gazette*, 17 June 1834
77 Among the names appearing on the petition of the 'Inhabitants of the Eastern District of King's County or Otherwise Naufrage' were MacDonald, Robertson, Campbell, MacIsaac, Laramore, O'Keefe, MacAulay, O'Henly, Darry, Schelly, McMullen, MacKinnon, and Ryan; CO 226/51/209, NAC
78 Jarvis to Young, 1 July 1834, CO 226/51/166, NAC
79 Stewart to Young, 29 July 1834, Stewart Letterbooks, Stewart Family fonds, Acc. 2316/1/409, PARO
80 Stewart to Coville, 17 April 1834, Stewart Letterbooks, Stewart Family fonds, Acc. 2316/1/393–4, PARO
81 Stewart to Rice, 1 Sept. 1834, CO 226/51/362–3
82 Stewart to Earl of Aberdeen, 22 Dec. 1834, CO 226/51/368–9
83 The problems with the traditional system of policing that confronted island authorities was of course more general to law enforcement in the Empire at this time. See Mather, *Public Order in the Age of the Chartists*; Broeker, *Rural Disorder and Police Reform*; Stanley H. Palmer, *Police and Protest*.
84 Stanley Palmer's term 'crime/protest' is apt for the challenges facing authorities on Prince Edward Island in the 1830s. Except for infractions rooted in resistance to landlords' use of the law, crime was not a problem for island authorities at this time; Palmer, *Police and Protest*, 520. See also Greer, 'The Birth of the Police in Canada.'
85 Two constables were charged with refusing to assist the deputy sheriff in the *Naufrage* case. See *King v. Hugh Logan* and *King v. Hector MacEachern*, Indictments, Supreme Court Records, 1834, RG 6, PARO.
86 *Royal Gazette*, 30 July 1833; *Royal Gazette*, 1 Oct. 1833
87 Others included Joseph Coffin, Cornelius Little, James Bagnall, and Coun Douly Rankin; *Royal Gazette*, 26 Nov. 1833.
88 'An Old Soldier' to the editor, *Royal Gazette*, 24 June 1834
89 *Royal Gazette*, 12 Aug. 1834
90 Young to Rice, 19 July 1834, CO 226/51/164–5, NAC
91 Young to High Sheriff, 9 July 1833, Governor's Letter Book, p. 111, vol. 5, Sub-Series 1, Series 4, RG 1, PARO
92 CO 226/51/210–1, NAC
93 Petition of the 'Inhabitants of the Eastern District of King's County or Otherwise Naufrage,' CO 226/51/208–9, NAC
94 'The petition of the Inhabitants of Part of Lot 44,' CO 226/51/211–2, NAC

95 Excerpts, David Stewart's Journal, Mr and Mrs Clinton Stewart Collection, Acc. 3209/28/7–9; David Stewart to John Lawson, 2 April 1833, Stewart Letterbooks, Stewart Family fonds, Acc. 2316/1/234–7, PARO
96 Excerpts, David Stewart's Journal, Mr and Mrs Clinton Stewart Collection, Acc. 3209/28/15, PARO
97 The Stewarts' recalcitrant Lot 47 tenants appear to have sued for peace late in 1834: Robert Stewart to John Lawson. 30 Dec. 1834, Stewart Letterbooks, Stewart Family fonds, Acc., 2316/2/66–73, PARO.

6. Organizing Proprietors, 1831–1834

1 David Stewart to Thomas Farrer, 2 May 1833, Stewart Letterbooks, Stewart Family fonds, Acc. 2316/1/250, PARO
2 Robert Stewart to William Waller, 23 May 1833, Stewart Letterbooks, Stewart Family fonds, Acc. 2316/1/254, PARO
3 Cambridge died in 1831 at the age of eighty-three; John Hill lived to be eighty-seven, dying in 1841. For their careers and the bankruptcies that overcame their estates see Bumsted, 'John Hill'; Holman, 'John Cambridge.' The Cambridge estate had a mortgage of more than £12,000 against it in 1832 to cover John Cambridge's business losses; Lemuel Cambridge to Thomas Owen, 1 Feb. 1832, Owen Family fonds, Acc. 3744/21, PARO.
4 Pigot, 'John Stewart'
5 M. Brook Taylor draws attention to both of these limitations on Worrell's influence in 'Charles Worrell.'
6 Circular of Mr Pleace and Mr Worrell, CO 226/47/177, NAC; William Waller to Secretary of State, 31 Dec. 1829, CO 226/46/237–8; Alex Mundell to Hay, 22 July 1830, CO 226/47/229–30
7 Robert Stewart to William Buchanan, 24 March 1834, Catherine St John Collection, Acc. 3023/1/a, PARO; 'Disposition of Deed and Settlement by Mrs Isabella Purdie or Stewart,' 27 June 1851, Catherine St John Collection, Acc. 3023/4; Explanation of Will, Catherine St John Collection, Acc. 3023/5, PARO; Deborah Stewart, 'Robert Bruce Stewart and the Land Question,' 3
8 Some London street directories list them as 'surveyors' (in the plural) and land agents. See *Post Office London Directory*, 1835; *Robson's London Directory*, 1835. Others, though, only list David Stewart as a surveyor, which is in keeping with the evidence from professional listings. See *Pigot's Directory*, 1836; E.G.R. Taylor, *Mathematical Practitioners*, 436; Eden, ed., *Dictionary of Land Surveyors*, 3. Certainly evidence from their letterbooks indicates that David was constantly on the move from estate to estate

about the British Isles while Robert handled business matters from Bloomsbury.

9 Reader, *Professional Men*

10 Robert Stewart to Lt. Col. Sorell, 21 April 1823, Robert Stewart Letterbooks, Stewart Family fonds, Acc. 2316/1/4, PARO. According to Deborah Stewart, 'Robert Bruce Stewart and the Land Question,' the Stewarts acquired their first island land in 1806.

11 Robert Stewart to D. Davidson, 14 July 1832, Stewart Letterbooks, Stewart Family fonds, Acc. 2316/1/150, PARO

12 David Stewart to Lt.-Col. Sorell, 9 Jan. 1832, Stewart Letterbooks, Stewart Family fonds, Acc. 2316/1/85, PARO

13 David Stewart to Lt.-Col. Sorell, 9 Jan. 1832, to Thomas Farrer, 5 April 1833, Stewart Letterbooks, Stewart Family fonds, Acc. 2316/1/1, and 86, PARO

14 Robert Stewart to John Stewart, 13 July 1830; Robert Stewart to Edward Worrell, 20 July 1830; David Stewart to John Lawson, 2 May 1833; Stewart Letterbooks, Stewart Family fonds, Acc. 2316/1/33–5, 135–6, and 245–8, PARO

15 David Stewart's Journal, Ms 3209/28/20–1, PARO; 'We the undersigned resident proprietors and Agents ... ,' CO 226/51/614–15, NAC

16 'We the undersigned Proprietors and Agents ... ,' July 1831, CO 226/51/312–13, NAC

17 David Stewart to the Earl of Selkirk, 20 Sept. 1831, Robert Stewart Letterbooks, Ms 2316/1/51, PARO. This is the 6th Lord Selkirk. The 5th Lord Selkirk, who had initiated settlement projects in Upper Canada, Prince Edward Island, and Red River, died in 1820.

18 Robert Stewart to William Waller, 3 July 1832, Stewart Letterbooks, Stewart Family fonds, Acc. 2316/1/139, PARO

19 Robert Stewart to John Lawson, 6 August 1833, Stewart Letterbooks, Stewart Family fonds, Acc. 2316/1/377–84, PARO

20 Lady Westmorland to Lord Melville, 25 June 1842, GD 235/10/18/18–20, NAS

21 Sorell was consul at Oporto in the early 1830s and then Consul-General in the Lombardo-Venetian States after 1834: Finding Aid, 12889, GC/SO/147–225, NRA.

22 C. Binns to [Rev. G. Street], 1 Aug. 1815, R. Lea to Rev. G. Street, 3 Aug. 1818, C.D. Rankin to Rev. G. Street of Langton, 13 Aug. 1825, Collins to Harrison, 25 April 1831, J.A. Street to Rev. G. Street of Langton, 22 Nov. 1831, Langton Papers, 6/2, LAO. On the position of the Langtons in Lincolnshire society see Olney, *Rural Society and County Government*.

23 David Stewart to John Stewart, July 1831, to A. Colvile, 6 Dec. 1831, Ms 2316/1, PARO; Wynn, *Timber Colony*; Bittermann, 'Economic Stratification and Agrarian Settlement,' 83
24 David Stewart to John Stewart, July 1831, to Lt.-Col. Sorell, 9 Jan. 1832, to John Stewart, 9 April 1832, Stewart Letterbooks, Stewart Family fonds, Acc. 2316/1/39, 79–88 and 104–6, PARO
25 David Stewart to John Lawson, 2 May 1833, Stewart Letterbooks, Stewart Family fonds, Acc. 2316/1/245–8, PARO
26 *APCE*, 1764, 654–9
27 *APCE*, 1767, 80–5
28 Hutchinson to Captain Seymour, 22 Oct. 1814, Correspondence, Seymour of Ragley Papers, CR 114 A/563/1, WCRO
29 For one such London meeting chaired by John Hill and attended by prominent islanders associated with the proprietorial cause see 'At a meeting of the Proprietors of Lands ...,' 5 March 1824, CO 226/41/268–70, NAC.
30 David Stewart to the Earl of Selkirk, 20 Sept. 1831, Robert Stewart Letterbooks, Stewart Family fonds, Acc. 2316/1/55, PARO
31 David Stewart to Charles Worrell, 2 Oct. 1831, Stewart Letterbooks, Stewart Family fonds, Acc. 2316/1, PARO
32 David Stewart to John Stewart, 3 Oct. 1831, to John Lawson, 3 Oct. 1831, Stewart Letterbooks, Stewart Family fonds, Acc. 2316/1/61–4, PARO
33 On the significance of the Reform Bill to the timing of their initiatives, see Robert Stewart to John Stewart, 7 June 1832, Stewart Letterbooks, Stewart Family fonds, Acc. 2316/1/136, PARO. David Stewart to the Earl of Selkirk, 20 Sept. 1831, to Lt.-Col. Sorell, 9 Jan. 1832, Stewart Letterbooks, Stewart Family fonds, Acc. 2316/1/50–6 and 79–88, PARO.
34 Robert Stewart to Andrew Colvile, 15 May 1832, Stewart Letterbooks, Stewart Family fonds, Acc. 2316/1/119, PARO
35 Robert Stewart to Edward Worrell, 15 May 1832, Stewart Letterbooks, Stewart Family fonds, Acc. 2316/1/120, PARO
36 Colvile to Goderich, 25 May 1832, CO 226/49/211–12, NAC
37 Andrew Colvile's (Wedderburn) family had been involved with the West Indies trade for three generations. During Colvile's years at the helm the business was merged with that of Graham and Simpson. A consummate businessman, Colvile recognized entrepreneurial skills in others and is credited with spotting the potential in the young George Simpson after he came as an apprentice to the business, directing him on to a career in the other firm in Colvile's life, the Hudson's Bay Company. Galbraith, *The Little Emperor*, 17.

38 Gray, *Lord Selkirk of Red River*, 342
39 Goderich to Young, 1 June 1832, CO 227/8/177, NAC
40 Covile to Goderich, 11 June 1832, CO 226/49/213–14, NAC
41 Young to Goderich, 14 July 1832, CO 226/49/165–6, NAC
42 Robert Stewart to Edward Worrell, 15 May 1832, to William Waller, 23 May 1832, Stewart Letterbooks, Stewart Family fonds, Acc. 2316/1/120 and 130, PARO
43 One wonders whether they submitted the escheat bill for legal judgment as well and decided not to pass this judgment on to the Colonial Office.
44 Memorial of the undersigned Proprietors, CO 226/49/274–83, NAC
45 'Case,' CO 226/49/182, NAC
46 Robert Stewart to William Waller, 9 Aug. 1832, Stewart Letterbooks, Stewart Family fonds, Acc. 2316/1/174, PARO
47 Deborah Stewart, 'Robert Bruce Stewart and the Land Question'
48 H.D. Morpeth to George Birnie, 23 Jan. 1835, George and Alexander Birnie business fonds, Acc. 3269/12, PARO
49 John MacGregor to Goderich, 24 July 1832, CO 226/49/179–80, NAC
50 Cowan, *British Emigration*, 85–143; Norman Macdonald, *Canada, 1763–1841*, 237–64
51 Karr, *The Canada Land Company*; Norman Macdonald, *Canada, 1763–1841*, 265–301; Little, *Nationalism, Capitalism, and Colonization*, 36–63
52 Saunders, 'The New Brunswick and Nova Scotia Land Company'; Norman Macdonald, *Canada, 1763–1841*, 302–11
53 See Samson, 'Industrial Colonization.'
54 David Frank has described Smith as a 'professional gentleman' involved in promoting the economic transformation of his era. One might aptly describe David Stewart in similar terms. Frank, 'Richard Smith.' On the GMA see Martell, 'Early Coal Mining in Nova Scotia,' and Gerriets, 'The Impact of the General Mining Association.'
55 David Stewart's Journal, Mr and Mrs Clinton Stewart Collection, Acc. 3209/28/26, PARO
56 David Stewart's Journal, Mr and Mrs Clinton Stewart Collection, Acc. 3209/28/31, PARO. Stewart's professional experience included canal as well as estate and wasteland surveys. Eden, ed., *Dictionary of Land Surveyors*, 473
57 David Stewart to Thomas Farrer, 17 Sept. 1831, Robert Stewart to G.V. Duval, 17 Sept. 1831, David Stewart to John Bainbridge, 8 Oct. 1831, Stewart Letterbooks, Stewart Family fonds, Acc. 2316/1/42–4, 44–7 and 65, PARO
58 David Stewart to Lt.-Col. Sorell, 9 Jan. 1832, to John Bainbridge, 18 April

1832, Stewart Letterbooks, Stewart Family fonds, Acc. 2316/1/87 and 109–10, PARO; 'Resolutions agreed to at a Meeting of the Provisional Committee of the New Brunswick Land Company,' 2 March 1832, CO 188/44/73–4, NAC

59 David Stewart to Thomas Farrer, 5 April 1833, Stewart Letterbooks, Stewart Family fonds, Acc. 2316/1/242, PARO

60 John McGregor to Goderich, 27 Aug. 1832, CO 226/49/284, Robert Stewart to Howick, 12 Dec. 1832, ibid., 301; Robert Stewart to John McGregor, 30 Aug. 1832, Stewart Letterbooks, Stewart Family fonds, Acc. 2316/1/175–8, PARO

61 Bainbridge to Goderich, 22 March 1832, CO 188/44/80. Although this letter went out over Bainbridge's signature it appears to have been a Stewart production. See their draft, 22 March 1832, Stewart Letterbooks, Stewart Family fonds, Acc. 2316/1/97–9, PARO.

62 Goderich to Young, 25 March 1833, CO 227/8/16

63 W. [?] and J. Campbell to Goderich, CO 226/50/194–5

64 Robert Stewart to John Hill, 20 Sept. 1833, Stewart Letterbooks, Stewart Family fonds, Acc. 2316/1/316–8, PARO

65 Robert Stewart to Howick, 22 March 1833, CO 226/50/278

66 Young to Stanley, 25 May 1833, CO 226/50/100–1

67 Stephen to Hay, 10 Sept. 1833, CO 226/50/199–200

68 PEI, *JHA*, 1833, 109–10

69 This was recognized by assemblymen and proprietors alike. See Joseph Pope's remarks on the issue, *Royal Gazette* 9 April 1833; Robert Stewart to William Forgan, 6 Aug. 1833, Stewart Letterbooks, Stewart Family fonds, Acc. 2316/1/287–8, PARO.

70 Robert Stewart to Andrew Covile, 31 May 1833, Stewart Letterbooks, Stewart Family fonds, Acc. 2316/1/255–6, PARO

71 Holman, 'John Cambridge,' 107. Henry Winchester was the oldest son of William Winchester, Cambridge's brother-in-law. As Ceasar Colclough noted earlier in the century, Cambridge's London address was the Winchester residence on the Strand. Colclough to O'Hara, 8 April 1813, O'Hara Papers, Ms 20287/5, NLI.

72 Beaven, *The Aldermen of the City of London*, 1:214; vol. 2:144; *Gentleman's Magazine*, June 1838, 662

73 Winchester drew the censure of Common Council in 1835 for refusing to permit political meetings in Common Hall 'during a most eventful period' and thereby denying Londoners the 'constitutional means of expressing their opinions on matters of great public importance.' See City of London, *Minutes of the Proceedings of the Court of Common Council*, 1835, 169.

74 Some insights into the man and his political activities, which included incurring 'great personal danger' to ensure the return of the government candidates in the election of 1818, is provided in Henry Winchester to the Earl of Liverpool, 15 April 1823, Liverpool Papers, 38293/f/349; BL.
75 'Sir George Francis Seymour,' *DNB* 17: 1259; Sobey, 'Prince Edward Island in 1840,' 26
76 In part this was because the escheat bill had no suspending clause. Lieutenant-Governor Young had not initially sent the bill but rather had written to learn what the Colonial Office wished of him on this matter. Young to Goderich, 25 May 1832, CO 226/49/211–12, NAC; Robert Stewart to William Waller, 9 Aug. 1832, Stewart Letterbooks, Stewart Family fonds, Acc. 2316/1/174, PARO. The escheat act was disallowed in December 1834: *Royal Gazette*, 21 April 1835.
77 Robert Stewart to William Waller, 23 May 1833, Stewart Letterbooks, Stewart Family fonds, Acc. 2316/1/254, PARO
78 Waller to Stanley, 23 May 1833, CO 226/50/30; 20 July 1833, ibid., 305–6; 30 Aug. 1833, ibid., 307
79 Robert Stuart to Andrew Colvile, 29 May 1833, Stewart Letterbooks, Stewart Family fonds, Acc. 2316/1/254–5, PARO
80 Robert Stewart to William Waller, 1 Aug. 1833, Stewart Letterbooks, Stewart Family fonds, Acc. 2316/1/276–7, PARO
81 George Seymour, Personal Diaries, entry for 28 Aug. 1833, Seymour of Ragley Papers, CR 114A/ 374/10, WCRO
82 Robert Stewart to John Bainbridge, 6 Aug. 1833, Stewart Letterbooks, Stewart Family fonds, Acc. 2316/1/287–8, PARO
83 Robert Stewart to William Waller, 24 Aug. 1833, Stewart Letterbooks, Stewart Family fonds, Acc. 2316/1/288–9, PARO
84 Robert Stewart to William Waller, 24 Aug. 1833, Stewart Letterbooks, Stewart Family fonds, Acc. 2316/1/288–9, PARO
85 'The humble memorial of the undersigned and others ...,' [14 Sept. 1833], CO 226/50/321–4
86 'John Fane,' *DNB* 6: 1040
87 Bourne, ed., *The Letters of the Third Viscount Palmerston*
88 John Hill to E.G. Stanley, 8 Sept. 1833, CO 226/50/249
89 Robert Stewart to Andrew Colvile, 31 Aug. 1833, Stewart Letterbooks, Stewart Family fonds, Acc. 2316/1/297–9, PARO; Robert Stewart to R.W. Hay, 19 Sept. 1833, Stewart Letterbooks, Stewart Family fonds, Acc. 2316/1/297–9 and 315, PARO; Robert Stewart to E.G. Stanley, 29 Aug. 1833, CO 226/50/286–90, NAC; George Seymour to [E.G. Stanley], 9 Sept. 1833, ibid., 291–2; George Seymour to Hay, 30 May 1833, ibid., 282–5

90 Buckner, 'The Colonial Office and British North America,' xxxii–xxxiii; Cowan, *British Emigration*, 97–8
91 Robert Stewart to Elliot, 1 Jan. 1833, CO 226/50/267, NAC; 3 Jan. 1833, ibid., 269; 29 Jan. 1833, ibid., 280; Robert Stewart to Elliot, 15 Feb. 1833, ibid., 273
92 Goderich to Young, 31 Jan. 1833, CO 227/8/14, NAC
93 David Stewart to Lt.-Col. Sorell, 9 Jan. 1832, to Alexander Baring, 20 April 1832, Stewart Letterbooks, Stewart Family fonds, Acc. 2316/1/87 and 110–12, PARO
94 Robert Stewart to Ms Fanning, 1 April 1834, to Andrew Colvile, 4 April 1834, to Edward Worrell, 11 April 1834, to William Waller, 12 April 1834, Stewart Letterbooks, Stewart Family fonds, Acc. 2316/1/371–2 and 379–82, PARO
95 Stewart Letterbooks, Stewart Family fonds, Acc. 2316/1/383–91, PARO
96 Robert Stewart to William Waller, 14 April 1834, Stewart Letterbooks, Stewart Family fonds, Acc. 2316/1/392, PARO
97 George Seymour, Personal Diaries, entries for 27 March 1834 and 14 April 1834, Seymour of Ragley Papers, CR 114A/ 374/11, WCRO
98 Stanley to Young, 28 May 1834, CO 227/8/23–6, NAC
99 Seymour to Colvile, 29 March, to Hay, 30 March, to Waller, 8 April 1834 and 13 May 1834, Private Letter Books, Seymour of Ragley Papers, 114A/ 508/1, WCRO; George Seymour, Private Diaries, entries for 29 March and 13 May 1834, Seymour of Ragley Papers, CR 114 A/374/11, WCRO
100 Memo of Conversation with Mr Stanley, 13 May 1834, Seymour of Ragley Papers, CR 114A/565, WCRO
101 Seymour to Waller, 13 May 1834, Private Letter Books, Seymour of Ragley Papers, 114A/508/1, WCRO
102 Robert Stewart to Andrew Colvile, 17 April 1834, Stewart Letterbooks, Stewart Family fonds, Acc. 2316/1/393–4, PARO
103 Seymour dined with Young at the Earl of Westmorland's on 18 July and presented him with a memorial from the proprietors on 8 Aug. George Seymour, Private Diaries, Entries for 18 July and 8 Aug. 1834, Seymour of Ragley Papers, CR 114 A/374/11, WCRO
104 Robert Stewart to William Waller, 20 Aug. 1834, Stewart Letterbooks, Stewart Family fonds, Acc. 2316/1/421–2, PARO
105 Robert Stewart to D. Rennie, 21 Aug. 1834, Stewart Letterbooks, Stewart Family fonds, Acc. 2316/1/422, PARO
106 The establishment of the association was noted in the *Royal Gazette*, 4 Nov. 1834. Resolutions and notes concerning the first meeting are in Stewart Letterbooks, Stewart Family fonds, Acc. 2316/2/10–12, PARO.

107 Robert Stewart to Lady Gabriel Wood, 13 Sept. 1834, Stewart Letterbooks, Stewart Family fonds, Acc. 2316/2/27–9, PARO

108 This would be one of the heirs to Isaac Todd's Lot 19 property.

109 Robert Stewart to Lady Gabriel Wood, 13 Sept. 1834, to John Bainbridge, 13 Sept. 1834, Stewart Letterbooks, Stewart Family fonds, Acc. 2316/2/27–9, PARO

110 Robert Stewart to William Waller, 7 Sept. 1834, Stewart Letterbooks, Stewart Family fonds, Acc. 2316/2/24, PARO

111 The Stewarts had been attempting to keep Hill at arm's length for some time. See Robert Bruce Stewart to John Hill, 29 Oct. 1832, Stewart Letterbooks, Stewart Family fonds, Acc. 2316/2/196–7, PARO

112 Robert Stewart to William Waller, 16 Sept. 1834, Stewart Letterbooks, Stewart Family fonds, Acc. 2316/2/31, PARO

113 Proceedings and Accounts of the Prince Edward Island Association, Seymour of Ragley Papers, CR 114A/566/5, WCRO

114 Seymour to Waller, 20 Sept. 1834, Private Letter Books, Seymour of Ragley Papers, 114A/508/1, WCRO

115 Lewellin, *Emigration;* Robert Stewart to John Hill, 10 March 1835, Stewart Letterbooks, Stewart Family fonds, Acc. 2316/2/149–51, PARO

116 Robert Stewart to John Lawson, 12 Nov. 1834, Robert Stewart Letterbooks, Ms 2316/2/45, PARO; Proceedings and Accounts of the Prince Edward Island Association, Seymour of Ragley Papers, CR 114A/566/5, WCRO

117 See, for instance, 'Plough Coulter' to the editor of the *Kentish Gazette,* 21 May 1832; 'Edwardiensis' to the editor of the *Times,* 17 Oct. 1833; 'A Nova Scotian' to the editor of the *Spectator,* 6 Jan. 1834; 'A Nova Scotian' to the editor of the *Spectator,* 7 Jan. 1834; 'Gracchus Colonus' to the editor of *Gardener's Magazine,* 16 Jan. 1834; 'A Nova Scotian' to the editor of the *Spectator,* 18 Feb. 1834; 'A Subscriber' to the editor of the *Morning Advertiser,* 19 Feb. 1834; Robert Stewart to Dr. J. Wishart (Dingwall, Rosshire), July and 17 Nov. 1832, to Neil MacLean (Rosshire), 13 Oct. 1832, and to John Pendergast (Kilkenny), 22 Feb. 1834; Robert Bruce Stewart to Joseph Todd (Weybridge), 2 Nov. 1832, all Stewart Letterbooks, Stewart Family fonds, Acc. 2316/1/126–9, 326, 345–58, 152–7, 208–9, 187–9, 360–3, and 199–201, 'An Old-Fashioned Farmer' to the *Times,* 22 Sept. 1836; Robert Stewart to John Duffles (Aberdeen), 10 Feb. 1835; Robert Stewart to Henry Gisby (Sandwich), 23 Feb. 1835, all in Stewart Letterbooks, Stewart Family fonds, Acc. 2316/2/314–15, 208–9 and 123–4, PARO.

118 Robert Stewart to William Forgan, 2 April 1834, Stewart Letterbooks, Stewart Family fonds, Acc.. 2316/1/276–8, PARO

119 Robert Stewart to G.R. Young, 3 Sept. 1834, Stewart Letterbooks, Stewart Family fonds, Acc. 2316/2/23, PARO
120 Robert Stewart to John Lawson, 30 June 1834, Stewart Letterbooks, Stewart Family fonds, Acc. 2316/2/405–7, PARO
121 It was commonly charged that this was the motivation behind commercial and professional men's involvement with these bills and with escheat. See Circular of Mr Pleace and Mr Worrell, CO 226/47/177, NAC; Douse to Colvile, 18 Nov. 1837, Selkirk Papers, MG 19 E1/73/19235, NAC.

7. Organizing Escheat, 1834–1836

1 Goodwyn, *The Populist Moment*
2 1833 Census, PEI, *JHA*, 1834, appendix C
3 *Royal Gazette*, 5 Oct. 1830
4 *Royal Gazette*, 5 April 1831
5 PEI, *JHA*, 1833, 66–7, 108; *Royal Gazette*, 12 Feb. 1833
6 *Royal Gazette*, 15 Jan. 1833
7 *Royal Gazette*, 5 Feb. 1833
8 *Royal Gazette*, 2 April 1833
9 See the remarks of Thomas Owen, Roderick Macdonald, Dr Jardine, and John Le Lacheur during the Kings County election and Samuel Nelson and John Small Macdonald on the hustings at Queens: *Royal Gazette*, 25 Nov. 1834 and 9 Dec. 1834
10 Thomas Irwin, 'To the Electors of King's County,' *Royal Gazette*, 13 Jan. 1835; Joseph Coffin to the editor, *Royal Gazette*, 3 Feb. 1835
11 *The History of Deleware County, Iowa*, 630. I am grateful to Robert Fraser of the *DCB* for this reference.
12 'Construction of the House of Assembly of Prince Edward Island,' 13 Aug. 1842, CO 226/64/31, NAC
13 *Royal Gazette*, 25 Nov. 1834
14 *Royal Gazette*, 9 Dec. 1834
15 Ibid., 9 Dec. 1834
16 *Royal Gazette*, 13 Jan. 1835
17 PEI, *JHA*, 1835, 25–6; *Royal Gazette*, 10 Feb. 1835
18 *Royal Gazette*, 10 Feb. 1835
19 PEI, *JHA*, 1835, 27
20 *Royal Gazette*, 14 March 1835
21 PEI, *JHA*, 1835, 77–88. On the significance of the Declaratory Act to anti-land company agitation in the Canadas see *The Vindicator* (Montreal), 20 Oct. 1835.

22 PEI, *JHA*, 1835, 120
23 *Royal Gazette*, 31 March 1835
24 *Royal Gazette*, 5 May 1835
25 For information on Samuel Nelson see the Island's shipping registers and *Prince Edward Island Register*, 4 and 11 Dec. 1824.
26 *Royal Gazette*, 31 March 1835
27 Taylor, 'Charles Binns'
28 *Royal Gazette*, 20 Dec. 1836
29 PEI, *JHA*, 1835, 146–7
30 PEI, *JHA*, 1835, 20–1
31 *Royal Gazette*, 5 May 1835
32 Glenelg to Young, 22 Sept. 1835, CO 227/8/55–6, NAC
33 *Royal Gazette*, 6 Jan. 1835
34 'Council Minutes,' 7 Jan. 1835, CO 226/52/30, NAC
35 Ibid., CO 226/52/31–2
36 *Royal Gazette*, 13 Jan. 1835; Young to Hay, 12 Jan. 1835, CO 226/52/27–9, NAC
37 'Sheriff's Report,' 20 Jan. 1835, CO 226/52/40–1, NAC
38 On reviewing the minutes of the trial, James Stephen noted that in 'point of law' the defendants were in fact innocent of any crime as the bailiff had failed to produce a warrant and under the circumstances they were well within their rights to repulse him. CO 226/52/50. On the issue see too Glenelg to Young, 20 July 1835, CO 227/8/50.
39 *Royal Gazette*, 17 March 1835
40 For the governor's concluding remarks on the Naufrage affair see Young to Hay, 20 March 1835, CO 226/52/45–6.
41 Robert Stewart to Hay, 19 Jan. 1835, CO 226/52/240–1; Robert Stewart to Morpeth, 1 April 1835, Stewart Letterbooks, Stewart Family fonds, Acc. 2316/2/171–4, PARO
42 Robert Stewart to William Waller, 20 June 1835, Stewart Letterbooks, Stewart Family fonds, Acc. 2316/2/214, PARO
43 Robert Stewart to Forgan and to Morpeth, 1 July 1835, to John Lawson, Stewart Letterbooks, Stewart Family fonds, Acc. 2316/2/222–36. PARO
44 See Sir C. Saxton to Hay, 10 July [1835] and 18 Nov. 1835, CO 226/52/250–1 and 258–9, NAC; George Wright to Glenelg, 2 May 1836, CO 226/53/63–4.
45 Robert Stewart to John Hill, 19 March 1835, Stewart Letterbooks, Stewart Family fonds, Acc. 2316/2/153–6. PARO
46 Robert Stewart to George Seymour, 9 July 1835, to John Angerstein, MP, 9 July 1835, to Lord James Townshend, 9 July 1835, to John Walter, MP,

10 July 1835, Stewart Letterbooks, Stewart Family fonds, Acc. 2316/2/237–39, PARO; George Seymour to Robert Stewart, 11 July 1835, Private Letter Books, Seymour of Ragley Papers, 114A/508/1, WCRO; Robert Stewart to Donatus Henchy, 12 March and 25 March 1835, Stewart Letterbooks, Stewart Family fonds, Acc. 2316/2/153 and 159–62, PARO

47 Robert Stewart to J. Woodman, 3 June 1835, Stewart Letterbooks, Stewart Family fonds, Acc. 2316/2/210–1, PARO. By the following year the Selkirk estate was being included in these plans as well: *Royal Gazette*, 22 March 1836.

48 Robert Stewart to John Lawson, 3 June 1835, Stewart Letterbooks, Stewart Family fonds, Acc. 2316/2/206–10, PARO; George Seymour to William Waller, 10 March 1835, to T.H. Haviland, 15 March 1835, Private Letter Books, Seymour of Ragley Papers, 114A/508/1, WCRO

49 Robert Stewart to John Prendergast, 7 Oct. 1835, Stewart Letterbooks, Stewart Family fonds, Acc. 2316/2/305, PARO

50 Robert Stewart to Spring Rice, 1 Sept. 1834, CO 226/51/362–3, NAC

51 Robert Stewart to Morpeth, 3 June 1835 and to John Lawson, 2 Sept. 1835, Stewart Letterbooks, Stewart Family fonds, Acc. 2316/2/206–10 and 263–8, PARO

52 *Royal Gazette*, 22 Sept. 1835 and 27 Oct. 1835

53 *Royal Gazette*, 11 March 1834

54 Robert Stewart to John Lawson, 2 Sept. 1835, Robert Stewart Letterbooks, Ms 2316/2/263–8, PARO

55 *Royal Gazette*, 19 April 1836

56 *Royal Gazette*, 2 Feb. 1836

57 *Prince Edward Island Times*, 24 May 1836

58 On the timing of these developments on Lots 2 and 27, see *Abstract of the Proceedings before the Land Commissioner's Court*, 49, 80.

59 *Royal Gazette*, 2 Feb. 1836

60 Mr Cooper's speech, ibid. The quotation was also used for the cover of an Escheat pamphlet published in 1836: *Legislative and Other Proceedings on the Expediency of Appointing a Court of Escheats in Prince Edward Island.*

61 'Council Minutes,' 7 Jan. 1835, CO 226/52/57, NAC

62 *Royal Gazette*, 2 Feb. 1836

63 PEI, *JHA*, 1836, 21

64 *Prince Edward Island Times*, 31 May 1836

65 Bumsted, 'George Wright'; *Prince Edward Island Register*, 29 May 1824

66 *Royal Gazette*, 16 Feb. 1836

67 Ibid.

68 Ibid.
69 *Royal Gazette*, 1 March 1836
70 PEI, *JHA*, 1836, 52
71 *Royal Gazette*, 2 Feb. 1836
72 *Royal Gazette*, 29 March 1836
73 Speech of the Solicitor General at the Bar of the House of Assembly, *Royal Gazette*, 29 March 1836
74 Mr Cooper's reply to the Solicitor General and others on the Escheat question, *Royal Gazette*, 8 March 1836
75 'Speech of the Solicitor General at the Bar of the House of Assembly,' *Royal Gazette*, 29 March 1836; 'Mr Cooper's reply to the Solicitor General and others on the Escheat question,' *Royal Gazette*, 8 March 1836.
76 *Royal Gazette*, 29 March 1836
77 Robert Stewart to John Lawson, 2 Dec. 1835, Robert Stewart Letterbooks, Ms 2316/2/234–41, PARO
78 Robert Stewart to R.C. Macdonald, 26 Dec. 1835 and 27 Jan. 1836, Robert Stewart Letterbooks, Ms 2316/2/355–7 and 377–80, PARO
79 *Prince Edward Island Register*, 4 Dec. 1824
80 Robert Stewart to William Forgan, 1 April 1835; Robert Stewart to John Lawson, 7 Oct. 1835, Robert Stewart Letterbooks, Ms 2316/2/174–6, PARO. Their view of Yeo is in keeping with that found in Greenhill and Giffard, *Westcountrymen in Prince Edward's Isle*, and Greenhill, 'James Yeo.'
81 *Royal Gazette*, 29 March 1836
82 Ibid.
83 PEI, *JHA*, 1836, 51, 72, 74
84 Ibid., 85
85 Ibid., 50
86 *Prince Edward Island Times*, 26 March 1836
87 Their backgrounds and operations are described in Mackinnon and Warburton, eds., *Past and Present of Prince Edward Island*, 86, 397a; Holman, 'Joseph Pope.'
88 *Royal Gazette*, 29 March 1836
89 Ibid.
90 Joseph Pope to the editor, *Royal Gazette*, 21 June 1836.
91 Ibid. On Pope's intentions to intimidate others, see John Ramsay to the editor, ibid., 17 May 1836.
92 *Royal Gazette*, 19 March 1833
93 PEI, *JHA*, 1836, 93–7
94 Ibid., 97

95 Judd, *Members of Parliament, 1734–1832*, 249
96 PEI, *JHA*, 1836, 120–1; Buckner, *The Transition to Responsible Government*, 141–2; 'Resolutions agreed to at a Meeting of the Provisional Committee of the New Brunswick Land Company,' 2 March 1832, CO 188/44/73–4, NAC
97 *Royal Gazette*, 29 March 1836
98 *Prince Edward Island Times*, 16 April 1836
99 *Royal Gazette*, 26 April 1836
100 The Fox and the Bear, *Prince Edward Island Times*, 10 May 1836
101 *Prince Edward Island Times*, 23 April 1836
102 George Wright to Glenelg, 5 May 1836, CO 226/53/85, NAC
103 *Royal Gazette*, 10 May 1836 ; *Prince Edward Island Times*, 10 May 1836; *Royal Gazette*, 26 April 1836
104 *Prince Edward Island Times*, 31 May 1836
105 The plans for this appear to have been made at a meeting at French Fort on 28 March 1836; *Prince Edward Island Times*, 7 June 1836.
106 *Prince Edward Island Times*, 31 May 1836
107 Pacificus to Rankin, *Prince Edward Island Times*, 28 June 1836
108 John Macdonald to Rankin, *Prince Edward Island Times*, 28 June 1836
109 *Prince Edward Island Times*, 28 June 1836
110 Ibid.
111 *Royal Gazette*, 16 Feb. 1841
112 On this dynamic between rural elites and common people on the Island, see Macaulay to Selkirk, 3 Oct. 1814, Selkirk Papers, MG 19/E1/73/19133, NAC. For considerations of the dynamic elsewhere, see Slaughter, *The Whiskey Rebellion*, 165; Alan Taylor, 'Agrarian Independence,' 230.
113 *Prince Edward Island Times*, 12 July 1836. Anti-rent tenants in New York made similar arguments concerning the meaning and scope of popular sovereignty during their struggles in the 1840s. See Huston, *Land and Freedom*, 132.
114 *Royal Gazette*, 5 July 1836
115 Tilly, 'Britain Creates the Social Movement,' 44–5; Belchem, *Industrialization and the Working Class*, 73–83, 104–11; Parssinen, 'Association, Convention and Anti-Parliament'
116 John Belchem, *'Orator' Hunt*, 6; Ward, *Chartism*, 111–42
117 See, for instance, Mr Cooper's reply to the Solicitor General and others on the Escheat question, *Royal Gazette*, 8 March 1836; Editorial, *Prince Edward Island Times*, 26 July 1836; *Royal Gazette*, 29 March 1836.
118 The notion of 'wage slavery' enters the language of politics in the United States in the 1830s. Foner, 'Abolitionism and the Labor Movement in

Antebellum America,' 255. The imagery of slavery has an older history in the vocabulary of Anglo-American political protest and was commonly employed to describe what the future held for a portion of the citizenry if action was not taken to halt the plots of others. In the case of rural protest in Prince Edward Island it was used to characterize existing circumstances. See Bailyn, *The Ideological Origins of the American Revolution;* Taylor, 'Agrarian Independence,' 222; Bell, *Early Loyalist Saint John*, 122–3.

119 Mr Cooper's speech, *Royal Gazette*, 2 February 1836; *Legislative and Other Proceedings on the Expediency of Appointing a Court of Escheats in Prince Edward Island*

120 Editorial, *Prince Edward Island Times*, 14 June 1836, 19 July 1836, 9 Aug. 1836; Mr Cooper's reply to the Solicitor General and others on the Escheat question, *Royal Gazette*, 8 March 1836; *British American*, 13 April 1833

121 PEI, *JHA*, 1836, 114

122 *Royal Gazette*, 30 April 1836

123 Emphasis in the original. *Prince Edward Island Times*, 10 May 1836

124 For a splendid study of the subtle ways by which class understandings are maintained, see Scott, *Weapons of the Weak.*

125 In George Rudé's terms the 'derived' ideas of thinkers such as Locke, Blackstone, and Chitty were being combined with the 'inherent' ideas of rural islanders. Rudé, *Ideology and Popular Protest*, 27–38.

126 For some of the literature concerning the development and significance of this language elsewhere, the producer ideology it sustained, and its ambiguities, see Raymond Williams, *Keywords*, 54; Briggs, 'The Language of "Class"'; Wilentz, *Chants Democratic*, 157–9; Dawley, *Class and Community*, 44, 64–5; Faler, *Mechanics and Manufacturers*, 176–88; Alan Taylor, *Liberty Men*, 7; Summerhill, 'The Farmers' Republic' 55, 127; Huston, *Land and Freedom*, 111–12.

127 Rankin was charged with assault by William Douse in the summer of 1836 and chose to flee the island in the fall, thus bringing the *Prince Edward Times* to a close. Bumsted, 'William Rankin.'

128 De Jong, 'Charlottetown's Good Samaritan,' 24

129 A.B., 'Irregular Stanzas. On a late important event,' see *Prince Edward Island Times*, 24 May 1836.

130 On Prince Edward Island, as in other settings, older facets of an early popular culture – such as the charivari – were adapted to meet plebeian political needs as strategies of protest increasingly focused on the power of the state. McPhee, 'Popular Culture, Symbolism and Rural Radicalism'; Greer, 'From Folklore to Revolution'

131 'Satiricus' to the editor, *Royal Gazette*, 19 April 1836; Hobsbawm and Rudé, *Captain Swing*
132 MacDonell, *The Emigrant Experience*, 118–25
133 'The Fox and the Bear,' *Prince Edward Island Times*, 10 May 1836
134 MacDonell, *The Emigrant Experience*, 114–19
135 *Legislative and Other Proceedings on the Expediency of Appointing a Court of Escheats in Prince Edward Island*, 93
136 MacDonell, *The Emigrant Experience*, 116–17
137 Philanthropist to the editor, *Royal Gazette*, 22 Nov. 1836

8. Harvey and the Escheators, 1836–1837

1 On Harvey's career prior to his appointment as lieutenant-governor of Prince Edward Island, see Buckner, 'Sir John Harvey.'
2 *Royal Gazette*, 18 Oct. 1836
3 According to the 1833 census there were roughly 5,800 males over sixteen in the two counties.
4 *Royal Gazette*, 18 Oct. 1836
5 Harvey to Grey, 30 Oct. 1836, Harvey Letterbooks, RG1, R.S. 344/B/1/5, PANB
6 Harvey to Grey, 23 April 1836, CO 226/53/148–9, NAC; Harvey to Grey, 29 April, 1836, CO 226/53/150–1, NAC
7 Harvey to Ready, 3 Jan. 1837, Harvey Letterbooks, RG1, R.S. 344/B/1/45, PANB
8 Robert Stewart to Harvey, 11 May and 8 June 1836, Stewart Letterbooks, Stewart Family fonds, Acc. 2316/2/448 and 452–3, PARO
9 Robert Stewart to Waller, 11 May 1836, to Colvile, 7 and 21 June 1836, to Harvey, 8 and 21 June and 2 Aug. 1836, Stewart Letterbooks, Stewart Family fonds, Acc. 2316/2/447–8, 451–6, 482–9, PARO; Seymour to Harvey, 5 July 1836, Private Letter Books, Seymour of Ragley Papers, 114A/508/2, WCRO
10 Harvey to Grey, 23 May 1836, CO 226/53/151–3, NAC
11 Harvey to Glenelg, 5 Sept. 1836, CO 226/53/165–6, NAC
12 Harvey to Glenelg, 16 Oct. 1835, CO 226/53/216–17, NAC; Harvey to Hubert Taylor, 4 Nov. 1836, Harvey Letterbooks, RG1, R.S. 344/B/1/9, PANB
13 *Royal Gazette*, 18 Oct. 1836
14 *Royal Gazette*, 25 Oct. 1836
15 Harvey to Glenelg, 27 Sept. 1836, CO 226/53/181–3, NAC

16 Harvey to Glenelg, 29 Oct. 1836, CO 226/53/236–7, NAC; Harvey to Green, 28 Oct. 1836, Harvey Letterbooks, RG1, R.S. 344/B/1/1–3, PANB
17 Harvey to Glenelg, 3 Oct. 1836, CO 226/53/207–8, NAC; Harvey to Bowles, 30 Oct. 1836, Harvey Letterbooks, RG1, R.S. 344/B/1/10–11, PANB
18 Unidentified diary, Smith, Alley Collection, Acc. 2702/900, PARO
19 David Ross Diary, 3, PEIC, Robertson Library, UPEI
20 Peake to Mssrs Cunard, 13 Dec. 1836, Peake Letterbooks, Peake, Brecken fonds, Acc. 2881, PARO; *Royal Gazette*, 26 July and 13 Sept. 1836
21 Extract of a letter, *Royal Gazette*, 25 Oct. 1836
22 *Royal Gazette*, 14 March 1837
23 *Royal Gazette*, 25 April 1837
24 Common Sense to the editor, *Royal Gazette*, 11 Oct. 1836
25 *Royal Gazette*, 20 Sept. 1836
26 Morrow, 'James Bagnall'
27 Christman, *Tin Horns and Calico*, 20; Alan Taylor, *Liberty Men*, 5–6; Alan Taylor, 'Agrarian Independence,' 225
28 *Royal Gazette*, 22 Nov. 1836
29 Harvey to Hubert Taylor, 29 Oct. 1836 and 7 Jan. 1837, Harvey Letterbooks, RG1, R.S. 344/B/1/6, 59, PANB; FitzRoy to the Duke of Richmond, 8 Nov. 1837, Correspondence of Lady Mary FitzRoy, Acc. 3786/116, PARO
30 *Royal Gazette*, 7 Feb. 1837
31 *Royal Gazette*, 22 Nov. 1836
32 Cooper to T.H. Haviland, 24 Jan. 1837, *Royal Gazette*, 7 Feb. 1837
33 Macintosh to T.H. Haviland, 25 Jan. 1837, ibid.
34 See, too, the advice of Cooper, Macintosh, and Le Lecheur to their followers in *Colonial Herald*, 14 April 1838, and Cooper's comments on resistance at the James Douglas auction in Cooper to 'The Electors of Prince Edward Island,' *Colonial Herald*, 12 March 1842.
35 See Alexander Rae's comments on his reasons for adopting a more radical stance in this period in *Royal Gazette*, 16 Feb. 1841.
36 See Peter McCallum's comments in Cooper to T.H. Haviland, 24 Jan. 1837, *Royal Gazette*, 7 Feb. 1837; Harvey to Glenelg, 24 Jan. 1837, CO 226/54/18, NAC; Rev. John McLennan to FitzRoy, 24 Nov. 1837, ibid., 323; Bishop Macdonald to FitzRoy, 23 April 1838, CO 226/55/329–40.
37 Cooper to T.H. Haviland, 24 Jan. 1837, *Royal Gazette*, 7 Feb. 1837
38 *Royal Gazette*, 22 Nov. 1836
39 When the meeting got underway in the early afternoon of the 20th Joseph Coffin reminded those present that the petition and four resolutions he

was presenting were those which had been in circulation 'amongst the people from last night until now'; *Royal Gazette*, 10 Jan. 1837.

40 The three fundamental propositions are drawn from Alan Taylor, 'Agrarian Independence.' The broader patterns are explored as well in Brown, 'Back Country Rebellions,' Countryman, '"Out of the Bounds of the Law,"' and Karsky, 'Agrarian Radicalism.'

41 *Royal Gazette*, 17 Jan. 1837

42 Harvey to Glenelg, 24 Jan. 1837, CO 226/54/15–16, NAC

43 Cooper to T.H. Haviland, 24 Jan. 1837, *Royal Gazette*, 7 Feb. 1837

44 T.H. Haviland to Gentlemen, 12 Jan. 1837, *Royal Gazette* 7 Feb. 1837

45 *Royal Gazette*, 7 Feb. 1837

46 The accused were unaware that Harvey had consulted law officers about the possibility of prosecuting them and had been informed that they had not committed an indictable offence. FitzRoy to Glenelg, 13 Feb. 1838, CO 226/55/96, NAC

47 *Royal Gazette*, 7 Feb. 1837

48 *Royal Gazette*, 21 Feb. 1837

49 Harvey to Glenelg, 26 Jan. 1837, CO 226/54/26, NAC

50 Ibid.

51 FitzRoy to Glenelg, 13 Feb. 1838, CO 226/55/96, NAC

52 See the Bay Fortune resolutions in *Royal Gazette*, 29 May 1832 and 29 March 1836

53 *Royal Gazette*, 7 Feb. 1837, 21 Feb. 1837

54 *Royal Gazette*, 14 Feb. 1837

55 *Royal Gazette*, 21 Feb. 1837

56 *Colonial Herald*, 27 Jan. 1838

57 Harvey to Glenelg, 26 Jan. 1837, CO 226/54/25–6, NAC. Lieutenant-Governor Huntley forgave Joseph Coffin and made him a commissioner of the peace again in 1842: Haviland to Coffin, 4 Oct. 1842, RG7, Provincial Secretary fonds, 3/25, PARO

58 Emphasis in the original. Harvey to Taylor, 7 Jan. 1837, Harvey Letterbooks, RG1, R.S. 344/B/1/60–1, PANB

59 Emphasis in the original. Harvey to Taylor, 7 Feb. 1837, Harvey Letterbooks, RG1, R.S. 344/B/1/76, PANB

60 *Royal Gazette*, 14 Feb. 1837

61 His argument, which is rooted in an intentional and misleading conflation of the objectives of advocates of developmental politics who had adopted the notion of a partial escheat with the objectives of those whose primary aim was the redress of tenant grievances, lives on in interpretations of

island history that portray Dalrymple – and Reformers more generally – as men who sought to advance the real interests of the Island's tenantry. Escheat's leaders are cast as unrealistic men who led the rural population astray.

62 PEI, *JHA*, 1837, 44, 97, 111–13, 121, 145; *Royal Gazette*, 28 March 1837, 4 April 1837, and 18 April 1837

63 PEI, *JHA*, 1837, 19, 44; *Royal Gazette*, 28 March 1837 and 14 Feb. 1837

64 In the 1840s, tenants in New York received from the state legislature similar advice concerning the primacy of contract and the need to appeal to landlords: Huston, *Land and Freedom*, 103

65 *Royal Gazette*, 7 Feb. 1837

66 On the broader propositions informing Cooper's position on land reform, see in particular 'Cooper's speech on the Escheat Question,' *Royal Gazette*, 15 March 1831 and 3 April 1832; *British American*, 13 April 1833.

67 *Royal Gazette*, 14 Feb. 1837

68 Ibid.

69 *Royal Gazette*, 21 March 1837

70 *Royal Gazette*, 20 June 1837. When the tenantry of New York came to employ political tactics in their struggle for land reform in the 1840s and made their presence felt in the state legislature, the sanctity of the individual contract would prove an insurmountable point of contention. See McCurdy, *The Anti-Rent Era*, 103, 110–15; Ellis, *Landlords and Farmers*, 243–4, 278.

71 Emphasis in the original. Harvey to Glenelg, 24 Jan. 1837, CO 226/54/15–9, NAC

72 The draft in his letterbooks, and in the Colonial Office papers, is dated 15 Feb. 1837, but it was not posted until 7 March: Harvey Letterbooks, RG 1, R.S. 344/B/1/99, PANB; CO 226/54/62–4, NAC.

73 On his use of pamphlets, see Harvey to Glenelg, 7 Feb. 1837, CO 226/54/42, NAC.

74 *Royal Gazette*, 21 March 1837

75 *Royal Gazette*, 14 March 1837

76 *Royal Gazette*, 21 Feb. 1837

77 *Royal Gazette*, 21 March and 11 April 1837

78 *Royal Gazette*, 21 March 1837

79 Harvey to the Honourable Chief Justice, 22 March 1837, Harvey Letterbooks, RG 1, R.S. 344/B/1/115, PANB

80 *Royal Gazette*, 14 March 1837

81 *Royal Gazette*, 25 April 1837

82 Petition to Harvey, CO 226/54/95, NAC
83 Harvey to Glenelg, May 1837, CO 226/54/134–8, NAC
84 Harvey to Glenelg, 7 February 1837, CO 226/54/48–9, NAC

9. Agrarian Institutions and the March to Power, 1837–1838

1 The brevity of the appointment and the shift to government house in New Brunswick was, however, in keeping with Harvey's intentions from the very beginning. See Harvey to Taylor, 29 Oct. 1836, Harvey Letterbooks, RG1, R.S. 344/B/1/6, PANB.
2 Buckner, 'Sir Charles Augustus FitzRoy'
3 FitzRoy to Harvey, 12 July 1837, Ganong Collection, 29/2/3, NBM
4 *Royal Gazette*, 4 July 1837
5 Executive Council Minutes, 13 July 1837, RG 5, PARO; Hodgson to T. Owen, 13 July 1837, Owen Family fonds, Acc. 3744/25, PARO; *Royal Gazette*, 25 July 1837
6 *T.S. Sorell v. J. McInnis*, Supreme Court Records, 1834, RG 6, PARO
7 *T.S. Sorell v. J. Robertson*, Supreme Court Records, 1834, RG 6, PARO; Lane to FitzRoy, 30 Sept. 1837, CO 226/54/316–18, NAC
8 Return of Township Lands in Prince Edward Island, CO 226/54/267–9, NAC
9 Executive Council Minutes, 5 Sept. 1837, RG 5, PARO
10 This form of maiming destroyed the status value of the horse while leaving it intact as a working animal. A reward authorized by the Executive Council was posted in the *Royal Gazette*, 5 Sept. 1837.
11 On Prince Edward Island, as in the British Isles and the United States, animal maiming was a tactic in personal disputes as well as a weapon of social protest. The distinction is not always easily made. See *Royal Gazette*, 22 Sept. 1835 and 19 April 1836. Archer, '"A Fiendish Outrage?"; Huston, *Land and Freedom*, 93.
12 FitzRoy to Glenelg, 3 Oct. 1837, CO 226/54/257–63, NAC
13 Address presented to His Excellency the Lieutenant-Governor Sir Charles Augustus FitzRoy, 8 Sept. 1837, CO 226/54/263–4 , NAC
14 His Excellency's Reply, 8 Sept. 1837, CO 226/54/264–5, NAC
15 FitzRoy to Glenelg, 3 Oct. 1837, CO 226/54/257–63, NAC
16 To the Proprietors of Prince Edward Island, 3 Oct. 1837, CO 226/54/266, NAC
17 FitzRoy to Glenelg, 3 Oct. 1837, CO 226/54/261, NAC
18 To the Proprietors of Prince Edward Island, 3 Oct. 1837, CO 226/54/265–6, NAC

19 R. Hodgson to T. Owen, 30 Sept. 1837, Owen Family fonds, Acc. 3744/26, PARO

20 His Excellency's Reply, 8 Sept. 1837, CO 226/54/265, NAC

21 The interactions between those associated with the Prince Edward Island Association and FitzRoy are noted in Seymour to Robert Stewart, 28 March 1837; Seymour to Robert Stewart, 19 April 1837; Seymour to FitzRoy, 12 May 1837, all in Private Letter Books, Seymour of Ragley Papers, 114A/508/2, WCRO; George Seymour, Personal Diaries, entry for 26 March 1837, CR 114A/374/14, WCRO.

22 FitzRoy to Harvey, 19 Nov. 1837, Ganong Collection, 29/2/4, NBM

23 William Cooper to John Le Lacheur, 14 Sept. 1837, Correspondence concerning Cooper/FitzRoy Dispute, Acc. 2524/20, PARO

24 *Royal Gazette*, 10 Oct. 1837. FitzRoy was furious with Haszard for this and threatened to strip him of his government contracts. See FitzRoy to Glenelg, 23 Oct. 1837, CO 226/54/270–3, NAC.

25 The issue appears to have been a general topic of conversation among Islanders. Note the mention of a 5 per cent reduction of rents in Hodgson to Owen, 30 Sept. 1837, Owen Family fonds, Acc. 3744/26, PARO; Bay Fortune Committee to Cooper, 7 Feb. 1838, Correspondence concerning Cooper/FitzRoy Dispute, Acc. 2524/20, PARO. See also McCallum's statements in the house and the various sworn accounts that emerged concerning what the governor was saying after FitzRoy challenged Cooper on the matter. *Royal Gazette*, 6 March 1838; Bay Fortune Committee to Cooper, 7 Feb. 1838, Correspondence concerning Cooper/FitzRoy Dispute, Acc. 2524/20; Sworn statement of Robert [?], 30 Jan. 1838, Material concerning Cooper/FitzRoy Dispute, Acc. 2552/55, PARO

26 Alexander Rae raised the issue of the statements in Cooper's circular letter at the 15 Nov. 1837 Meeting of Delegates; *Colonial Herald*, 25 Nov. 1837, in CO 226/56/141, NAC

27 To the Proprietors of Prince Edward Island, 3 Oct. 1837, CO 226/54/265–6, NAC

28 Responding to charges that Coun Douly Rankin was reading and mistranslating the Governor's letter at public meetings in the Belfast area, John Arbuckle indicated that it was he who had done the translations as it was necessary to read the governor's circular in Irish Gaelic as well as Scots Gaelic. John Arbuckle to T.H. Haviland, 25 Jan. 1838, CO 226/55/298, NAC

29 Cooper to John Le Lacheur, 14 Sept. 1837, Correspondence concerning Cooper/FitzRoy Dispute, Acc. 2524/20, PARO

30 *Colonial Herald*, 25 Nov. 1837, in CO 226/56/141–2, NAC

31 Ibid.
32 Ibid.
33 *Colonial Herald,* 10 Feb. 1838
34 *Colonial Herald,* 13 Jan. 1838 and 10 March 1838. Chartists too used a 'boycott' tactic in the late 1830s and early 1840s. See Dorothy Thompson, *The Chartists,* 77.
35 *Colonial Herald,* 10 Feb. 1838
36 *Colonial Herald,* 13 Jan. 1838
37 *Colonial Herald,* 5 Feb. 1838
38 *Colonial Herald,* 10 March 1838
39 Ibid.
40 *Colonial Herald,* 4 July 1838
41 *Colonial Herald,* 10 March 1838
42 *Colonial Herald,* 17 Feb. 1838
43 Lord Townshend's tenants on Lot 56, for instance, had been notified in the summer of 1837 that if all their arrears were not paid up immediately they could expect to be evicted en masse. The total sum demanded of the sixty-eight families resident in the township amounted to roughly £1,500. Waller to the Tenantry of the Township Number 56, June 1837, CO 226/56/189–92, NAC; Rent Roll of Lot or Township No. 56, CO 226/54/455–6.
44 On the proprietorial role in establishing the legislative framework permitting tenant labour to be used directly to meet landlord costs on state-organized projects, see chapter 6.
45 Douse to Colvile, 7 Jan. 1838, Selkirk Papers, MG 19, E1/73/19257–9, NAC
46 Haviland to FitzRoy, 26 April 1838, CO 226/55/291–4, NAC
47 Douse's complaints that FitzRoy's circular had been central to tenant unrest on the Selkirk estate in 1837–8 and that the governor was not adequately responding to the problem and to his needs led to a major conflict between Douse and the governor and ultimately between Colvile, who managed the estate and who wanted FitzRoy – and his close adviser, T.H. Haviland – removed, and the Colonial Office, which ultimately stood by them. FitzRoy to Glenelg, 29 Nov. 1837, and enclosures, CO 226/54/302–25, NAC; FitzRoy to Glenelg, 2 April 1838, and enclosures, 152–75; FitzRoy to Glenelg, 30 April 1838, and enclosure, CO 226/55/277–305; FitzRoy to Glenelg, 21 May 1838, and enclosures, CO 226/55/331–9; Colvile to Glenelg, 21 Feb. 1838, CO 226/56/131–2; Colvile to Glenelg, 3 March 1838, with enclosures, CO 226/56/135–8; Colvile to Selkirk, 7 April 1838, Selkirk Papers, MG 19, E1/73/19279, NAC.
48 As with most such confrontations, there was much controversy concerning what precisely happened as those on either side of the dispute experi-

enced the events from different positions and were seeking to sustain differing agendas with their descriptions. 'One of the Party' to the editor, *Colonial Herald*, 27 June 1838; George R. Young, *A Statement of the 'Escheat Question' in the Island of Prince Edward: Together with the Causes of the late Agitation and the Remedies Proposed*, 2; 'O.P.Q.' to the editor, *Colonial Herald*, 23 Jan. 1841; 'Plain Common Sense' to the editor, ibid., 6 Feb. 1841; John Myrie Holl to the editor, ibid., 20 Feb. 1841; 'The only clergyman resident within the bounds of the district' to the editor, ibid. 20 March 1841; Charles Stewart and W.P. Grossard to the editor, ibid., 27 March1841; William Douse to the editor, ibid., 3 April and 10 April 1841

49 Donald Macdonald to William Waller, 5 Feb. 1838, CO 226/56/110, NAC
50 Address to the Association of Proprietors in London, CO 226/55/98–101, NAC
51 FitzRoy to Glenelg, 30 Jan. 1838, CO 226/55/79, NAC
52 FitzRoy to Glenelg, 29 Nov. 1837, CO 226/54/304, NAC
53 FitzRoy to Glenelg, 30 Jan. 1838, CO 226/55/76–81, NAC
54 The minutes and drafts are contained in CO 226/55/82–4, NAC
55 Deposition of Angus McPhee, George Farmer, and Robert Bell, 27 Feb. 1838, CO 226/55/176–180, NAC
56 Collins to Douse, 10 March 1838, CO 226/55/172–5, NAC
57 H.D. Morpeth to FitzRoy, 18 Sept. 1837, to FitzRoy, 24 Nov. 1837, CO 226/54/616–17 and 310, NAC; Address to the Association of Proprietors in London, CO 226/55/98–101
58 Robert Stewart to John Lawson, 6 Aug. 1834, Stewart Letterbooks, Stewart Family fonds, Acc. 2316/2/413–15, PARO; John Arbuckle to T.H. Haviland, 25 January 1838, CO 226/55/297
59 Resolution 16, Tenant Meeting Lots 18 and 19, *Colonial Herald*, 10 Feb. 1838; Hodgson to Owen, 30 Sept. 1837, Owen Family fonds, Acc. 3744/26, PARO; PEI, *JHA*, 1840, appendix P
60 FitzRoy to the Duke of Richmond, 20 March 1838, Correspondence of Lady Mary FitzRoy, Acc. 3786/117, PARO
61 Douse to Colvile, 12 Oct. 1837, MG 19, E1/73/19226, NAC
62 Hatvany, '"Wedded to the Marshes"'
63 Bittermann and McCallum, 'The One That Got Away'
64 John Lawson to Robert Stewart, 25 March 1836, Ira Brown Collection, Acc. 2810/128, PARO
65 FitzRoy to Glenelg, 8 Jan. 1838, CO 226/55/27–34, NAC
66 William Douse claimed that he drew the issue to the governor's attention and in so doing ensured that he did not grant the requests: Douse to Colvile, 7 Jan. 1838, MG 19, E1/73/19254, NAC

67 *Colonial Herald*, 20 Jan. 1838; *Royal Gazette*, 23 January 1838
68 *Royal Gazette*, 30 Jan. 1838
69 Ibid.
70 *Royal Gazette*, 6 Feb. 1838
71 Once he found out about it and obtained a copy – sometime *after* the assembly convened at the end of January – FitzRoy was able to make good use of it both to attack Cooper's credibility and to defend himself against proprietorial charges that it had been his own circular letter to landlords which had induced a revival of Escheat activism in the winter of 1837–8. FitzRoy to Glenelg, 2 April 1838, CO 226/55/152–65, NAC. There were many copies in circulation. Included in the network receiving letters were John Le Lacheur, Coun Douly Rankin, Daniel Campbell, William Clark, John Macintosh, and John Leslie. John McIntosh to John Leslie, 23 Sept. 1837, Selkirk Papers, MG 19, E1/73/19259–61, NAC; Cooper to Le Lacheur, 14 Sept. 1837; John Le Lacheur to Douly Rankin, 22 Sept. 1837, Correspondence concerning Cooper/FitzRoy Dispute, Acc. 2524/20, PARO; *Royal Gazette*, 6 March 1838
72 *Royal Gazette*, 6 March 1838
73 FitzRoy to Glenelg, 2 April 1838, CO 226/55/157, NAC; *Colonial Herald*, 10 March 1838
74 *Royal Gazette*, 30 Jan. 1838
75 *Colonial Herald*, 24 Feb. 1838
76 *Colonial Herald*, 14 April 1838
77 Waller to Secretary of State, 19 Aug. 1837, Waller to Secretary of State, 19 Aug. 1837, CO 226/54/433 and 435, NAC; to Waller Glenelg, 14 Sept. 1837, to Glenelg, 14 Sept. 1837, CO 226/54/437 and 451–2; Memorial of Proprietors of Land in Prince Edward Island ...,' 13 Aug. 1837, CO 226/54/439–46; Henry Hill to Glenelg, 20 Sept. 1837, CO 226/54/457–8
78 *Royal Gazette*, 30 Jan. 1838
79 Report of the Joint Committee of the Council and the Assembly, 29 Jan. 1838, CO 226/55/200–232, NAC
80 Douse to Colvile, 12 Oct. 1837, Selkirk papers, MG 19, E1/73/19231–2, NAC
81 Douse to Colvile, 18 Nov. 1837, Selkirk papers, MG 19, E1/73/19235, NAC
82 Robert Hodgson's judgment on the election act, 10 March 1838, CO 226/55/136–7, NAC
83 FitzRoy to Glenelg, 6 May 1838, to Glenelg, 9 April, CO 226/55/319 and 234, NAC
84 *Royal Gazette*, 10 April 1838
85 FitzRoy to Glenelg, 9 April 1838, CO 226/55/234–5. It is not clear whether this included Irish Gaelic.

86 G. Edward Macdonald, 'Bernard Donald Macdonald'; Bishop Macdonald to FitzRoy, 23 April 1838, CO 226/55/329–40, NAC
87 Harvey to Bishop McDonell, 30 April 1837, Harvey Letterbooks, RG 1 RS/344/B/1/163, PANB; Rea, 'Alexander McDonell'
88 Abercrombie to Palmerston, 25 Oct. 1837, CO 226/54/365, NAC
89 Ibid.; Abercrombie to Palmerston, 7 Nov. 1837, CO 226/54/379, NAC
90 Harvey to Bishop McDonell, 30 April 1837, Harvey Letterbooks, RG 1 RS/344/B/1/163, PANB. The Catholic Church assumed a similar role in Lower Canada at this time. Young, 'Positive Law, Positive State,' 58
91 FitzRoy to Glenelg, 9 April 1838, CO 226/55/240–1, NAC
92 See the minutes on FitzRoy to Glenelg, 9 April 1838, CO 226/55/238, NAC
93 *Colonial Herald*, 14 April 1838; J.W. Le Lacheur, John Macintosh, Edward Dunn, and Patrick Walker to Glenelg, 16 April 1838, CO 226/56/145–6, NAC
94 It is useful to know that FitzRoy painted others whom he crossed swords with that year in similar terms. He described George Young as 'a very tricky schuffling fellow' and William Douse as the member of an 'ignorant and uneducated' class who could not be trusted and who lied about his conversations with the governor. FitzRoy to Richmond, 7 Sept. 1838, Ms 3786/119, PARO; FitzRoy to Glenelg, 30 April 1838, CO 226/55/277–91, NAC
95 FitzRoy to Glenelg, 6 May 1838, CO 226/55/318–21, NAC
96 See James Stephen's minute on FitzRoy to Glenelg, 6 May 1838, CO 226/55/321, NAC
97 Cooper to Glenelg, 30 June 1838, CO 226/56/147, NAC
98 Petition of Oliver Thomas LeBone, Chieftain of the MicMac tribe of the Indian Inhabitants of Prince Edward Island, May 1838, CO 226/56/228–9, NAC
99 James Stephen Minute, Cooper to Glenelg, 30 June 1838, CO 226/56/148, NAC
100 Cooper to Glenelg, 30 June 1838, CO 226/56/147, NAC
101 Young to Glenelg, 29 Jan. 1838, CO 226/56/406, NAC
102 Young to Glenelg, 22 Jan. 1838, CO 226/56/395–8, NAC; Young to Glenelg, 29 Jan. 1838, CO 226/56/406–7
103 Glenelg to FitzRoy, 16 March 1838, CO 227/8/135–7, NAC
104 Cooper to Glenelg, 16 Aug. 1838, PEI, *JHA*, 1839, appendix A, 21
105 T.H. Haviland contended that if the proprietors associated with the Prince Edward Island Association had made their offer sooner it would have met with success. While flattering to Harvey, whose circular had

prompted the response, and correct insofar as it notes that delay in the proprietorial response affected its reception, Haviland's argument falls well short of the truth. Haviland to Harvey, 16 Jan. 1838, Hazen Collection, 10/64/2, NBM

106 David Stewart to John Stewart, July, to Colvile, 6 Dec. 1831, Stewart Letterbooks, Stewart Family fonds, Acc. 2316/1/39 and 71–3, PARO; PEI, *JHA*, 1842, appendix, N, 80

107 By the second half of the 1830s this was equal to roughly 1/6 currency. In the previous decade the exchange rate had typically involved a 10 per cent discount, so by specifying sterling the proprietors were proposing a rate of rental that was higher than what had been expected of island tenants at the turn of the decade. John MacGregor, *Historical and Descriptive Sketches of the Maritime Colonies of British America*, 81; *Report on the Affairs of British North America from The Earl of Durham*, appendix B, 170

108 George Grey to Cooper, 25 Aug. 1838, PEI, *JHA*, 1839, appendix A, 21–2

109 FitzRoy to Glenelg, 24 May 1838, CO 226/55/347–53, NAC

110 FitzRoy to Glenelg, 9 April 1838, CO 226/55/236–7, NAC; FitzRoy to Richmond, 7 Sept. 1838, Correspondence of Lady Mary FitzRoy, Acc. 3786/119, PARO

111 George Grey to Cooper, 25 Aug. 1838, PEI, *JHA*, 1839, appendix A, 21–2

112 Michael Cross, 'Conclusion,' in Wait, *The Wait Letters*, 151

113 *Colonial Herald*, 8 Dec. 1838; Joseph Hume to William Cooper, 13 Aug. 1842, *Colonial Herald*, 18 March 1843

114 S. Cunard to Colvile, 13 Aug. 1838, Selkirk Papers, MG 19 E1/73/19070–3, NAC

115 *Report on the Affairs of British North America from The Earl of Durham*, appendix B, 146

116 S. Cunard to Colvile, 15 Sept. 1838, Selkirk Papers, MG 19 E1/73/19084–5, NAC

117 Young and Brooking, along with Samuel Cunard, and Colvile, had just signed a £12,000 indenture in May to purchase the massive Cambridge estate. Indenture, 14 May 1838, George Young Papers, MG 2 725/F2/1248, PANS

118 George Young to Colvile, 14 Aug. 1838, Selkirk Papers, MG 19 E1/73/19065–6, NAC

119 Ibid., E1/73/19066

120 George Young to Colvile, 14 Sept. 1838, Selkirk Papers, MG 19 E1/73/19078–80, NAC. William Young was, according to Joseph Howe, the only Reform voice in the Nova Scotia delegation. Beck, *Joseph Howe*, vol. 1, *Conservative Reformer, 1804–1848*, 196.

121 FitzRoy to Durham, 7 July 1838, Durham Papers, MG 24/A27/18/49–59, NAC

122 *A Few Observations shewing the Errors and Misstatements contained in Mr Young's Pamphlet on the 'Escheat Question' in the Island of Prince Edward by an Independent Settler*, 26–7. The pamphlet was a defence of FitzRoy and his closest allies and was written by someone very close to Government House. Indeed, the similarity between its contents and some of FitzRoy's dispatches is striking. See too, Hatvany, 'Almanacs and the New Middle Class.'

123 *Report on the Affairs of British North America from The Earl of Durham*, appendix B, 169–75

124 George Seymour bitterly noted the hypocrisy of his own agent, T.H. Haviland, calling for better terms despite his having 'governed my property himself.' George Seymour, Private Diaries, Entry 14 April 1839, Seymour of Ragley Papers, CR 114 A/374/15, WCRO

125 *Royal Gazette*, 3 July and 4 Sept. 1838

126 *Report on the Affairs of British North America from The Earl of Durham*, appendix B, 167

127 Le Lacheur to Hanson, 4 Oct. 1838, *Colonial Herald*, 17 Oct. 1838

128 John Le Lacheur report to the General Committee, *Colonial Herald*, 17 Oct. 1838

129 John Le Lacheur to 'The Independent Electors of Prince Edward Island,' 26 Sept. 1838

130 Lucas, ed., *Lord Durham's Report on the Affairs of British North America*, 2: 198

131 *Report on the Affairs of British North America from The Earl of Durham*, appendix B, 19, 21

132 Hodgson to the editor, *Colonial Herald*, 26 Sept. 1838

133 Ibid.; *Royal Gazette*, extra, 27 Sept. 1838

134 Durham to FitzRoy, 22 Sept. 1838, *Colonial Herald*, 3 Oct. 1838; *Royal Gazette*, extra, 27 Sept. 1838

135 Le Lacheur to Durham, 4 Oct. 1838, to Hanson, 4 Oct. 1838, *Colonial Herald*, 17 Oct. 1838

136 *Colonial Herald*, 24 Oct. 1838

137 John Le Lacheur to the Independent and Loyal Constituencies of Prince Edward Island, *Colonial Herald*, 7 Nov. 1838

138 'A settler' to the editor, *Colonial Herald*, 7 Nov. 1838

139 *Royal Gazette*, 30 Oct., 6, 13 and 20 Nov., 18 Dec. 1838

140 John Le Lacheur went to the assembly as an incumbent representing a Queens district after the election, but he had previously been a Kings County member.

141 Taylor, 'Francis Longworth'; Accounts of Vessels Launched and Registered, PEI, *JHA*, PEI, *JLC*

142 Thomas Gorman was not, as Greenhill and Giffard speculated, 'a creature of Yeo's' but an Escheat partisan. Greenhill and Giffard, *Westcountrymen in Prince Edward's Isle*, 141

10. The Limits of Democratic Power, 1838–1842

1 Belchem, 'Republicanism, Popular Constitutionalism, and the Radical Platform,' 11–12

2 The correspondence was republished in PEI, *JHA*, 1839, appendix B.

3 *Royal Gazette*, 5 March 1839

4 John Lawson to Robert Stewart, 25 March 1836, Ira Brown Collection, Acc. 2810/128, PARO; CO 226/67/170–6, Case; PEI, *JHA*, 1839, appendix S; Bittermann and McCallum, 'The One That Got Away'

5 *Colonial Herald*, 23 Feb. 1839, Supplement

6 *Royal Gazette*, 30 April 1839; PEI, *JHA*, 1839, 2nd Session, 64–9

7 See Ready to Huskinson, 26 May 1828, CO 226/45/52, NAC; Harvey to Glenelg, 11 March 1837, ibid., 54/75–6; FitzRoy to Glenelg, 15 Sept. 1837, ibid., 225.

8 FitzRoy to Glenelg, 5 Sept. 1838, CO 226/55/476, NAC

9 *Royal Gazette*, 5 March 1839

10 Report of a Select Committee of the Inhabitants of Lot or Township number Fifty-Six, 16 January 1838, CO 226/56/181; Robertson, 'Thomas Heath Haviland'

11 Robertson, 'Sir Robert Hodgson'

12 Holman, 'John Brecken' FitzRoy to Glenelg, 5 Sept. 1838, CO 226/55/476, NAC

13 M. Brook Taylor, 'Charles Worrell' Robertson, 'Donald Macdonald'

14 M. Brook Taylor, 'George Dalrymple'

15 FitzRoy to Glenelg, 5 Sept. 1838, CO 226/55/476, NAC

16 Bumsted, 'George Wright'; Holman, 'John Brecken'; Holman, 'Joseph Pope'; Robertson, 'John Small Macdonald'; Leard, 'Political Relations'

17 The council's decision to reject the supplementary land tax bill passed by the assembly in 1832 was a significant exception. See chapter 4.

18 PEI, *JHA*, 1839, 2nd Session, 6–7. By contrast, Nova Scotia's Reformers – despite their disputes with Government House and its allies – rallied around the flag and authorized the governor to call out the entire militia and spend £100,000 if necessary. Beck, *Joseph Howe*, vol. 1, *Conservative Reformer*, 189

19 *Royal Gazette*, 12 and 19 Feb. 1839; PEI, *JHA*, 1839, 1st Session, 35, 42–5, 2nd Session, 47

20 *Royal Gazette*, 2 April 1939

21 PEI, *JHA*, 1839, 2nd Session, 20–1, 27–32

22 Like those advocating reforms elsewhere, Escheators had more faith in the utility of a delegation and the provision of accurate accounts of colonial grievances than was merited by imperial performance. See Beck, *Politics of Nova Scotia*, vol. 1, *Nicholson-Fielding, 1710–1896*, 113–14

23 FitzRoy to Normanby, 7 May 1839, CO 226/58/106–22, NAC

24 On the problems besetting the Melbourne government, see Gash, *Aristocracy and People: Britain, 1815–1865*, 169–86

25 On Normanby's discussions with Cooper see the minutes on the cancelled draft of a letter from the Colonial Office to Cooper, CO 226/59/75, NAC and Cooper to Russell, CO 226/59/218; Cooper to Committee of Correspondence, 20 Sept. 1839, PEI, *JHA*, 1840, appendix A, 3; Cooper to Normanby, 2 Sept. 1839, CO 226/59/213. Most accounts of Cooper's mission to Britain in 1839 fail to mention that this was his *second* trip and that he engaged in discussions with Glenelg and others at the Colonial Office in 1838. As well, while correctly noting that Lord Russell did not see him in 1839, they neglect to mention that Russell was not the Colonial Secretary at the time of Cooper's arrival and that Lord Normanby, like Glenelg before him, did in fact meet with Cooper.

26 Cooper to Russell, 9 Sept. 1839, CO 226/59/215–21, NAC

27 Minutes, CO 226/59/222–3, NAC

28 Stephen to Cooper, 20 Sept. 1839, CO 226/59/224–5, NAC

29 An additional request on these grounds for some indication of the Colonial Office's response was denied. See Cooper to Russell, 23 Sept. 1839, CO 226/59/233–4, NAC.

30 See 'The Delegate's Statement' and Cooper's published correspondence, *Royal Gazette*, 3 March 1839.

31 Hutch and Ziegler, *Joseph Hume*

32 *Royal Gazette*, 26 Nov. 1839

33 See John Thomson's comments at the Sentiner's meeting of 3 January 1840. *Colonial Herald*, 18 Jan. 1840. Thomson's advice would have been in keeping with that given by FitzRoy's close ally Robert Hodgson, who advocated a buy-back scheme in his testimony before the Durham Commission. *Report on the Affairs of British North America from The Earl of Durham*, appendix B, 170

34 FitzRoy, 6 May 1839, Heads of Proposed Plan for Removing the Discontent at Present Existing in Prince Edward Island from a Monopoly of Lands by Absentee Proprietors, CO 226/58/142, NAC

35 Ibid., CO 226/58/141–52, NAC
36 *Royal Gazette*, 26 Nov. 1839
37 Russell to FitzRoy, 17 Sept. 1839, CO 227/8/178–80, NAC
38 FitzRoy to Russell, 27 Nov. 1839, CO 226/58/263–6, NAC
39 On the functioning of Nova Scotia's system, see the testimony of J.W. Nutting, Commissioner of the Nova Scotia Court of Escheat, *Minutes of Evidence Taken Under the Direction of a General Commission of Enquiry for Crown Lands and Emigration appointed on the 21st of June 1838 by his Excellency the Right Honorable The Earl of Durham*, 26–8.
40 *Colonial Herald*, 18 Jan. 1840
41 Rae's commentary on Cooper's performance is contained in *Royal Gazette*, 25 Feb. 1840. The broader debate was reprinted in *Royal Gazette*, 4 Feb. and 3 and 10 March 1840.
42 *Royal Gazette*, 3 March 1840
43 *Royal Gazette*, 18 and 25 Feb. 1840
44 *Royal Gazette*, 27 March 1840; *Colonial Herald*, 4 April 1840. Young, like James Peters, had come to the island in expectation of being made solicitor and manager of the new land company that his brother George was establishing with Cunard, Colvile, the Stewarts, and others. These expectations, though, were dashed by Cunard's rival plans and by the dissolution of the original corporate framework in the face of growing conflict between Cunard and George Young. In the event, while James Peters moved into the ranks of those associated with the governor, Charles Young initially lent his support to their opponents. On Young's projected role in the land company plans and the Young/Cunard dispute, see Cunard to A. Colvile, 13 Aug. 1838, George Young to Colvile, 14 Aug. 1838, Selkirk Papers, MG 29 E1/73/19070–3 and 19065–6, NAC. See too, Robertson, 'James Horsfield Peters.'
45 PEI, *JHA*, 111
46 PEI, *JHA*, 1840, 142
47 PEI, *JHA*, 1840, 112–16, 120
48 'An act to authorize the Crown to purchase the Lands, and to regulate the settlement of the Inhabitants of this Island, and to repeal certain Sections of an Act entitled "An Act for levying an Assessment on all Lands in this Island,"' *Royal Gazette*, 12 May 1840
49 PEI, *JHA*, 1840,145–6
50 *Royal Gazette*, 5 May 1840
51 FitzRoy to Russell, 4 and 5 May 1840, CO 226/60/109–13 and 146–8, NAC
52 FitzRoy to Russell, 4 May 1840, CO 226/60/112, NAC
53 Russell to FitzRoy, 22 Sept. 1840, Appendix B, PEI, *JHA*, 1841

54 For reports of some of the local meetings held to discuss ongoing legislation see *Colonial Herald*, 16 and 23 March 1839
55 Vernon Smith to Waller, 24 Sept. 1841, CO 226/60/453–6, NAC
56 Stewart to Russell, 3 Oct. 1840, CO 226/60/457–9, NAC
57 Cunard to Russell, 13 Nov. 1840; Seymour to Russell, 26 Nov. 1840; Worrell to Russell, 17 Dec. 1840, CO 226/60/467–70, 542–6, and 550–1, NAC
58 Meeting of the Proprietors of Land in Prince Edward Island, 6 April 1841, CO 226/62/213–14, NAC
59 Melville to Robert, 30 March 1834, Ann Melville to Robert, 3 Sept. 1834, GD 51/8/7/23; Melville to Robert, 25 July 1835, GD 51/8/7/24; Henry to Robert, 20 Nov. 1837, GD 51/8/7/29; Ann Melville to Robert, 10 Jan. 1838, GD 51/8/7/30, NAS
60 *Colonial Herald*, 29 Aug. 1840
61 Ibid.
62 *Colonial Herald*, 24 Oct. 1840
63 *Colonial Herald*, 19 Jan. 1839
64 *Colonial Herald*, 27 July 1839
65 *Royal Gazette*, 14 Jan. 1840
66 Ibid.
67 PEI, *JHA*, 1840, appendix P
68 *Flora Townshend v. James Douglas*, Supreme Court Records, 1840, RG 6, PARO; Executive Council Minutes, 28 Jan. 1840, RG 5 PARO; PEI, *JHA*, 1840, appendix P; *Royal Gazette*, 4 Aug. 1840; James Douglas to the editor, *Colonial Herald*, 15 Feb. 1840
69 PEI, *JHA*, 1841, 123
70 William Cooper to the electors of Prince Edward Island, *Colonial Herald*, 12 March 1842
71 *Royal Gazette*, last July issue 1840
72 *Royal Gazette*, 4 Aug. 1840
73 Ibid.
74 *Colonial Herald*, 17 Oct. 1840
75 PEI, *JHA*, 1840, 139
76 Douse to Colvile, 7 Jan. 1838, Selkirk Papers, MG 19, E1/73/19262, NAC; Seymour to Russell, 20 Nov. Worrell to Russell, 17 Dec. 1840, CO 226/60/546 and 550–1, NAC
77 See, for instance, Rae's comments in the house on 5 February, *Royal Gazette*, 16 Feb. 1841.
78 *Royal Gazette*, 16 Feb. 1841
79 *Royal Gazette*, 9 March 1841; PEI, *JHA*, 1841, 62
80 *Royal Gazette*, 23 March 1841; PEI, *JHA*, 1841, 158–61

81 *Royal Gazette*, 27 April 1841; Macfarlane and Forbes to Hume, 1 May 1841, PEI, *JHA*, 1842, appendix K. The assembly was forced to drop the appropriation of money for Hume's salary.
82 PEI, *JHA*, 1841, 155–6
83 *Royal Gazette*, supplement, 1 May 1841
84 Resolution of the Legislative Council, 29 April 1841, CO 226/61/145–6. In New York, too, attacks on anti-rent leaders accused them of demagoguery and of deluding their followers into thinking that leasehold land tenure could be eliminated through political action. Huston, *Land and Freedom*, 136–7.
85 FitzRoy to Russell, 3 May 1841, CO 226/61/114, NAC
86 FitzRoy to Russell, 5 May 1841, CO 226/61/175, NAC
87 James Stephen minute, 15 June 1841, CO 226/61/180, NAC
88 FitzRoy to Russell, 5 May 1841, CO 226/61/166–79, NAC
89 *Royal Gazette*, supplement, 1 May 1841
90 James Stephen minute, 15 June 1841, CO 226/61/180, NAC
91 The discrepancy was noted in the late 1820s when the council and assembly locked horns over the handling of appropriations bills. See Huskisson to Ready, 30 Oct. 1827, CO 227/7/145–7, NAC
92 FitzRoy to Russell, 29 March 1841, CO 226/61/63–7, NAC; Russell to FitzRoy, 2 July 1841, CO 227/8/220–2.
93 Stephen minute, 15 June 1841, CO 226/61/180, NAC
94 Russell minute, 19 June 1841, CO 226/61/180, NAC
95 *Colonial Herald*, 24 July 1841
96 Cunard to Vernon Smith, 20 Aug. 1841, CO 226/62/226, NAC
97 Hume to Russell, 18 June 1841, CO 226/62/235, NAC
98 Bowring to Macfarlane, 23 Nov. 1841, PEI, *JHA*, 1842, appendix K; Fladeland, *Abolitionists and Working-Class Problems*, 98
99 Buckner, 'Sir Charles Augustus FitzRoy'; Robertson, 'Sir Henry Vere Huntley'
100 Rae to the Constituency of the Second Electoral District of Prince County, *Colonial Herald*, 1 Jan. 1842
101 *Royal Gazette*, 8 March 1842
102 Huntley to Stanley, Feb. 16, 1842, CO 226/63/55, NAC
103 PEI, *JHA*, 1842, 133–5; appendix, N, 80–5
104 Hume to Cooper, 20 Jan. 1842, PEI, *JHA*, 1842, appendix L
105 *Royal Gazette*, 19 April 1842
106 Their judgments, as well as the election results of 1842, are a reminder that Russell's refusal to see Cooper in 1839 did not kill the Escheat challenge, as some Island histories have suggested.

107 Huntley to Stanley, 26 Dec. 1841, CO 226/62/157–8, NAC

108 Huntley to Stanley, 16 Feb. 1842, CO 226/63/57, NAC

109 Ibid., CO 226/63/56–7

110 FitzRoy to Russell, 27 Feb. 1841, CO 226/60/51–2, NAC

111 William Cooper et al., To the Electors by Whose Votes the Subscribers Were Elected, *Colonial Herald*, 23 April and 7 and 14 May 1842. Clark ultimately chose to run, but he was denounced as a questionable Escheat ally and failed in his bid. See Duncan MacLean's remarks *Colonial Herald*, 2 July 1842.

112 Speech of His Excellency Sir Henry Vere Huntley, 16 April 1842, CO 226/63/117, NAC

113 An Elector of King's County to the Electors of Prince Edward Island, *Royal Gazette*, 8 Feb. 1842

114 William Cooper, To the Electors of Prince Edward Island, *Colonial Herald*, 14 May 1842

115 *Royal Gazette*, 19 July 1842

116 Huntley, Construction of the House of Assembly, 13 Aug. 1842, CO 226/64/30, NAC

117 *Colonial Herald*, 18 June 1842

118 Coles's position on the political spectrum was not altogether clear at this time. In the winter of 1837–8 he had chaired a banquet at Cornelius Little's house for Cooper, Le Lacheur, and Macintosh and toasted them for their 'noble stand against tyranny.' Huntley, though, not without reason, classed him not as an Escheator or even as 'uncertain' but as an opponent of Cooper's party. *Colonial Herald*, 10 March 1838; Huntley, Construction of the House of Assembly, 13 Aug. 1842, CO 226/64/30, NAC

119 *Colonial Herald*, 4 June 1842

120 *Royal Gazette*, 19 July 1842; *Colonial Herald*, 23 July 1842

121 Although Donald Montgomery was re-elected in Princetown, he had distanced himself from the Escheat cause. So too had Alexander MacLean in Queens who had stepped into Charles Young's shoes when the latter assumed a seat on the Legislative Council.

122 Francis Bolger's contention that Escheat leaders lost control of the house in 1842 because 'the tenantry largely abandoned them' is misleading. The only rural riding that fits this description was the 3rd District of Queens. Bolger, ed., *Canada's Smallest Province*, 114

123 Huntley to Stanley, 10 Aug. 1842, CO 226/64/5, NAC

124 William Cooper et al., To the Electors by Whose Votes the Subscribers Were Elected, *Colonial Herald*, 23 April 1842; One of the Tenantry to the

Electors of the First District of Queen's County, ibid., 18 June 1842; An Independent Elector to the Electors of Second District Queen's County, ibid., 2 July 1842

125 William Cooper, To the Electors of Prince Edward Island, *Colonial Herald*, 14 May 1842

126 Gunn, *The Political History of Newfoundland*, 77–88

127 The statements of Michael Lacey before the 1861 Land Commission concerning proprietorial persecution rooted in his Escheat politics (and the intervention of his landlord during his testimony) provide evidence of a broader pattern. Such is the case as well with James Warburton's testimony concerning Yeo's use of his rent rolls. See Robertson, *The Prince Edward Island Land Commission of 1860*, 115, 64.

Conclusion

1 James Stephen minute, 15 June 1841, CO 226/61/180, NAC

2 Jarvis to Robert Hazen, 2 Aug. 1843, MG 24, B 13, Edward James Jarvis Papers, vol. 2, NAC

3 Robertson, *The Tenant League*

4 Huston, *Land and Freedom*, 8

5 Dorothy Thompson, *The Chartists*, 1

6 Emphasis in the original. William Cooper to the editor, *Colonial Herald*, 15 Jan. 1842

7 Dundas to Buckingham, 20 May 1868, CO 226/104/289–90, NAC

8 To the Proprietors of Prince Edward Island, 3 Oct. 1837, CO 226/54/265–6, NAC

9 Douse to Colvile, 7 Jan. 1838, Selkirk Papers, MG 19, E1/73/19262, NAC; Seymour to Russell, 20 Nov. Worrell to Russell, 17 Dec. 1840, CO 226/60/546 and 550–1, NAC

10 *Kelly v. Sulivan* (1877), 1 Supreme Court Reports, 34–5

Selected Bibliography

Archives

National Archives of Canada, Ottawa (NAC)
CO 226. Prince Edward Island, Original Correspondence.
CO 227. Prince Edward Island, Entry Books.
CO 231. Prince Edward Island, Miscellanea.
CO 188. New Brunswick, Original Correspondence.
Selkirk Papers. MG 19, E1.
DesBarres Papers. MG 23, F1–5.
Durham Papers. MG 24, A 27.
Edward James Jarvis Papers. MG 24, B13.
Prince Edward Island Public Archives and Record Office, Charlottetown (PARO)
RG 1. Lieutenant Governor fonds.
RG 2. Legislative Council of Prince Edward Island fonds.
RG 3. Prince Edward Island House of Assembly fonds.
RG 5. P.E.I. Executive Council fonds.
RG 6.1. Supreme Court fonds.
RG 6.6. Court of Chancery.
RG 7. Provincial Secretary fonds.
RG 15. Commissioner of Public Lands fonds.
RG 16. Land Registry fonds.
Prince Edward Island, *Journals of the House of Assembly.*
Prince Edward Island, *Journals of the Legislative Council.*
Stewart Family fonds. Acc. 2316.
Miscellaneous Papers. Acc. 2334.
Billings/Cundall Correspondence. Acc. 2518.

Correspondence concerning Cooper/FitzRoy Dispute. Acc. 2524/20.
Material concerning Cooper/FitzRoy Dispute. Acc. 2552/55.
Pope Family fonds. Acc. 2574.
Miscellaneous Papers. Acc. 2659.
MacDonald Papers. Acc. 2664.
Smith, Alley Collection. Acc. 2702.
Sundry Papers of James and Samuel Marchbank. Acc. 2720.
H.D. Morpeth fonds. Acc. 2794.
McLellan Family fonds. Acc. 2802.
Ira Brown Collection. Acc. 2810.
Palmer Family fonds. Acc. 2849.
Peake, Brecken fonds. Acc. 2881.
Miscellaneous Papers. Acc. 3002.
Catherine St John Collection. Acc. 3023.
Alice Fraser fonds. Acc. 3073.
Mr and Mrs Clinton Stewart Collection. Acc. 3209.
George and Alexander Birnie business fonds. Acc. 3269.
Owen Family fonds. Acc. 3744.
Correspondence of Lady Mary FitzRoy (from Goodwin Ms WSRO) Acc. 3786.
Letters of John Ready to the Duke of Richmond. (from Goodwin Ms WSRO) Acc. 3968.
Peter Magowan letter – 1807. Acc. 4082.
Cambridge family genealogical works / by John Bradley. Acc. 4430.
A Short Description of the Island of St John, in the Gulph of St Lawrence, North America, 25 June 1779. Acc. 4437.
Peter MacGowan Letterbooks. Ms HF 73/191/01.

Robertson Library, University of Prince Edward Island, Charlottetown
Prince Edward Island Collection. David Ross Diary.

Public Archives of Nova Scotia, Halifax (PANS)
George Young Papers. MG 2, 725.

Nova Scotia Crown Lands Record Centre
Grant Books.

Public Archives of New Brunswick, Fredericton (PANB)
RG1.
RS 107, Department of Natural Resources: Crown Lands.

New Brunswick Museum, Saint John (NBM)
Ross-Ross Collection.
Ganong Collection.
Hazen Collection.

National Register of Archives, London (NRA)

British Library, London (BL)
Liverpool Papers.
Peel Papers.
Guildhall Library (London)
Post Office London Directory.
Pigot's Directory.
Robson's London Directory.
London Directory.
Minutes of the Proceedings of the Court of Common Council.
Noble Collection.
Lincolnshire Archives Office, Lincoln, UK (LAO)
Langton Papers.
Warwickshire County Record Office, Warwick, UK (WCRO)
Seymour of Ragley Papers.
National Archives of Scotland (NAS)
Blackwood and Smith Collection. GD 293.
Bonar Mackenzie and Kermack Collection. GD 235.
Melville Castle Muniments. GD 51.
Montgomery Papers. GD 293; GD 409.
Register House Plans. 2096; 23401; 23223.
Ross Estate Muniments. GD 47.
Scottish National Library, Edinburgh
Melville Papers. Ms. 3847.
National Library of Ireland, Dublin (NLI)
O'Hara Papers. Ms. 20287.
Northern Ireland Record Office, Belfast
Belfast Directory.
Matin's Belfast Directory.
Matier's Belfast Directory.

Periodicals

Bee (Pictou).
British American (Charlottetown).
Colonial Herald (Charlottetown).
Gentleman's Magazine (London).
London Gazette.
Nation (Dublin).
Prince Edward Island Register (Charlottetown).
Prince Edward Island Times (Charlottetown).
Royal Gazette (Charlottetown).
Vindicator (Montreal).

Government Publications

Abstract of the Proceedings before the Land Commissioner's Court, held during the summer of 1860 to inquire into the differences relative to the rights of landowners and tenants in Prince Edward Island. Reporters J.D. Gordon and David Laird. Charlottetown: *The Protestant*, 1862.

Acts of the Privy Council of England, Colonial Series, ed. James Munro. London, 1912.

Journals of the Commissioners of Trade and Plantations. Reprint ed. Nendeln/Liechtenstein, 1970.

Minutes of Evidence Taken Under the Direction of a General Commission of Enquiry for Crown Lands and Emigration appointed on the 21st of June 1838 by his Excellency the Right Honorable The Earl of Durham. Quebec: Fisher and Kemble, 1839.

Report of the Public Archives of Canada for the year 1923. Ottawa: King's Printer, 1924.

Report on the Affairs of British North America from the Earl of Durham. London: House of Commons, 1839.

Contemporary Published Material

A Few Observations shewing the Errors and Misstatements contained in Mr Young's Pamphlet on the 'Escheat Question' in the Island of Prince Edward by an Independent Settler. Charlottetown: James B. Cooper, July 1838.

'A Proprietor.' *Facts versus Lord Durham.* London: Madden and Co., 1839.

A Short Account of Prince Edward Island Designed Chiefly for the Information of the Agriculturalist and Other Emigrants of Small Capital. London: Madden and Co., 1839.

Buckingham, James S. *Canada, Nova Scotia, New Brunswick and the Other British Provinces in North America with a Plan of National Colonization.* London: Fischer and Son, 1843.

Chitty, Joseph. *A Treatise on the Law of the Prerogatives of the Crown and the Relative Duties and Rights of the Subject.* London: J. Butterworth, 1820.

[Cooper, William]. *Legislative and Other Proceedings on the Expediency of Appointing a Court of Escheats in Prince Edward Island.* Charlottetown: J.D. Haszard, 1836.

Lewellin, J.L. *Emigration: Prince Edward Island: A Brief but Faithful Account of this Fine Colony; Showing Some of its Advantages as a Place of Settlement; Addressed to those British Farmers, and Others, who are determined to Emigrate, and Try their Fortune in a New Country.* Charlottetown: James D. Haszard, 1832.

Lucas, Sir. C.P., ed. *Lord Durham's Report on the Affairs of British North America.* 2 vols. Oxford: Clarendon Press, 1912.

Marryat, Captain. *Frank Mildmay; or, the Naval Officer*. London: Henry Colburn, 1836.

McGregor, John. *Historical and Descriptive Sketches of the Maritime Colonies of British America*. London: Longman, Rees, Orne, Brown, and Green, 1828.

Stewart, John. *An Account of Prince Edward Island in the Gulf of St Lawrence, North America*. London: Winchester and Son: 1806.

Young, George R. *A Statement of the 'Esheat Question' in the Island of Prince Edward; Together with the Causes of the Late Agitation and the Remedies Proposed*. London: R. & W. Swale, 1838.

Secondary Works

Abernethy, Thomas Perkins. *Western Lands and the American Revolution*. New York: Russell and Russell, 1959.

Acheson, T.W. 'The Great Merchant and Economic Development in Saint John 1820–1850.' *Acadiensis* 8:2 (Spring 1979): 3–27.

– *Saint John: The Making of a Colonial Urban Community*. Toronto: University of Toronto Press, 1985.

Archer, John E. '"A Fiendish Outrage?": A Study of Animal Maiming in East Anglia, 1830–1870.' *Agricultural History Review* 33:2 (1985): 147–57.

Arsenault, Georges. *The Island Acadians, 1720–1980*. Trans. Sally Ross. Charlottetown: Ragweed Press, 1989.

Baglole, Harry. 'The Legacy of William Cooper.' *Cooper Review* 3 (1988): 16–20.

– 'William Cooper.' *DCB*. Toronto: University Press, 1976. 9:155–8.

– 'William Cooper of Sailor's Hope.' *Island Magazine* (Fall/Winter 1979): 3–11.

– ed. *Exploring Island History: A Guide to the Historical Resources of Prince Edward Island*. Belfast, PEI: Ragweed Press, 1977.

Baglole, Harry, and David Weale. *The Island and Confederation: The End of an Era*. Summerside, PEI: Williams and Crue, 1973.

Bagster, C. Birch. *The Progress and Prospects of Prince Edward Island*. Charlottetown: John Ings, 1861.

Bailyn, Bernard. *The Ideological Origins of the American Revolution*. Cambridge: Harvard University Press, 1967.

– *Voyagers to the West: A Passage in the Peopling of America on the Eve of the Revolution*. New York: Alfred A. Knopf, 1986.

Beames, Michael. *Peasants and Power: The Whiteboy Movements and Their Control in Pre-Famine Ireland*. Sussex: Harvester Press, 1983.

Beaven, Reverend Alfred B. *The Aldermen of the City of London*. London: Corporation of the City of London, 1913.

Beck, J. Murray. *Joseph Howe*. Vol. 1. *Conservative Reformer, 1804–1848*. Kingston and Montreal: McGill-Queen's University Press, 1982.
– 'Jotham Blanchard.' *DCB*. Toronto: University of Toronto Press, 1988. 7: 81–5.
– *Politics of Nova Scotia*. Vol. 1. *Nicholson-Fielding, 1710–1896*. Tantallon, NS: Four East Publications, 1985.
Beck, James V. *The Descendants of Vere Beck*. Summerside, PEI: Williams and Crue, 1983.
Beckett, J.C. 'Introduction.' In *A New History of Ireland*. Vol. 4. *Eighteenth-Century Ireland, 1691–1800*, ed. T.W. Moody and W.E. Vaughan. Oxford: Clarendon Press, 1986.
– *The Making of Modern Ireland, 1603–1923*. London: Faber and Faber, 1981.
Belchem, John. 'Henry Hunt and the Evolution of the Mass Platform.' *English Historical Review* 93 (1978): 739–73.
– *Industrialization and the Working Class: The English Experience, 1750–1900*. Aldershot: Scolar Press, 1990.
– *'Orator' Hunt: Henry Hunt and English Working-Class Radicalism*. Oxford: Clarendon Press, 1985.
– 'Republicanism, Popular Constitutionalism, and the Radical Platform in Early Nineteenth-Century England.' *Social History* 6 (1981): 1–32.
Bell, D.G. *Early Loyalist Saint John: The Origin of New Brunswick Politics 1783–1786*. Fredericton: New Ireland Press, 1983.
– 'Sedition among the Loyalists: The Case of St John, 1784–6.' In *Canadian State Trials: Law, Politics, and Security Measures, 1608–1837*, ed. F. Murray Greenwood and Barry Wright, 223–40. Toronto: University of Toronto Press, 1996.
Bell, Marilyn. 'Mr Mann's Island: The Journal of an Absentee Proprietor, 1840.' *The Island* 33 (Spring/Summer 1993): 17–24.
Bellot, Leland J. *William Knox: The Life and Thought of an Eighteenth-Century Imperialist*. Austin: University of Texas Press, 1977.
Bercé, Yves-Marie. 'Rural Unrest.' In *Our Forgotten Past: Seven Centuries of Life on the Land*, ed. Jerome Blum, 135–6. New York: Thames and Hudson, 1982.
Bird, Isabella Lucy. *The EnglishWoman in America*. Toronto; reprint ed. 1966.
Bittermann, Rusty. 'Agrarian Protest and Cultural Transfer: Irish Emigrants and the Escheat Movement on Prince Edward Island.' In *The Irish in Atlantic Canada*, ed. Tom Power, 96–106. Fredericton: New Ireland Press, 1991.
– 'Economic Stratification and Agrarian Settlement: Middle River in the Early Nineteenth Century.' In *The Island: New Perspectives on Cape Breton History, 1712–1990*, ed. Kenneth Donovan, 71–87. Fredericton and Sydney: Acadiensis Press and UCCB Press, 1990.

– 'Farm Households and Wage Labour in the Northeastern Maritimes in the Early 19th Century.' *Labour/Le Travail* 31 (Spring 1993): 13–46.

– 'The Hierarchy of the Soil: Land and Labour in a 19th-Century Cape Breton Community.' *Acadiensis* 18:1 (Autumn 1988): 33–55.

– 'Rural Protest on Prince Edward Island in Transatlantic Context: From the Aftermath of the Seven Years' War to the 1840s.' In *Transatlantic Rebels: Agrarian Radicalism in Comparative Context*, ed. Thomas Summerhill and James C. Scott, 21–53. East Lansing: Michigan State University Press, 2004.

– 'Women and the Escheat Movement: The Politics of Everyday Life.' In *Separate Spheres: The World of Women in the 19th Century Maritimes*, ed. Sue Morton and Janet Guildford, 22–38. Fredericton: Acadiensis Press, 1994.

Bittermann, Rusty, and Margaret McCallum. 'The One That Got Away: Fishery Reserves on Prince Edward Island.' *Dalhousie Law Journal* 28:2 (Fall 2005).

– 'When Private Rights Become Public Wrongs: Property and the State in Prince Edward Island in the 1830s.' In *Despotic Dominion: Property Rights in British Settler Colonies*, ed. John McLaren, A.R. Buck, and Nancy E. Wright, 144–68. Vancouver: UBC Press, 2004.

Bittermann, Rusty, Robert MacKinnon, and Graeme Wynn. 'Of Inequality and Interdependence in the Nova Scotian Countryside.' *CHR* 74:1 (March 1993): 1–43.

Blakeley, Phyllis R. 'Sir Samuel Cunard.' *DCB*. Toronto: University of Toronto Press, 1976. 9:172–84.

Blanchard, J. Henri. *The Acadians of Prince Edward Island, 1720–1964*. Ottawa: Leclerc, 1964.

Bloch, Marc. *Feudal Society*. 2 vols. Chicago: University of Chicago Press, 1961.

Blum, Jerome. *The End of the Old Order in Rural Europe*. Princeton: Princeton University Press, 1978.

Blumin, Stuart M. *The Emergence of the Middle Class: Social Experience in the American City, 1760–1900*. Cambridge: Cambridge University Press, 1989.

Bock, Phillip K. 'Micmac.' In *Handbook of North American Indians*. Vol. 15. *Northeast*. Ed. Bruce Trigger, 109–22. Washington: Smithsonian Institution, 1978).

Bolger, Francis, ed. *Canada's Smallest Province: A History of Prince Edward Island*. Charlottetown: Prince Edward Island 1973 Centennial Committee, 1973.

Bolland, O. Nigel. 'Systems of Domination after Slavery: The Control of Land and Labor in the British West Indies after 1838.' *Comparative Studies in Society and History* 23:4 (October 1981): 591–619.

Bond, Beverly W. *The Quit-Rent System in the American Colonies*. New Haven: Yale University Press, 1919.

Bottomore, Tom, ed. *A Dictionary of Marxist Thought*. Cambridge: Harvard University Press, 1983.

Bourne, Kenneth, ed. *The Letters of the Third Viscount Palmerston to Laurence and Elizabeth Sulivan, 1804–1863*. London: Royal Historical Society, 1979.

Bremner, Benjamin. *Memories of Long Ago: Island Scrap Book*. Charlottetown: Irving, 1932.

Briggs, Asa. 'The Language of "Class" in Early Nineteenth-Century England.' In *The Collected Essays of Asa Briggs*. Vol. 1. *Words, Numbers, Places, People*, 3–33. Brighton: Harvester Press, 1985.

Broeker, Galen. *Rural Disorder and Police Reform in Ireland, 1812–36*. London: Routledge and Kegan Paul, 1970.

Brown, Richard Maxwell. 'Back Country Rebellions and the Homestead Ethic.' In *Tradition, Conflict, and Modernization: Perspectives on the American Revolution*, ed. Richard Maxwell Brown and Don E. Fehrenbacher, 73–98. New York: Academic Press, 1977.

Buckner, Phillip. 'Charles Douglass Smith.' *DCB*. Toronto: University of Toronto Press, 1985. 8: 823–8.

– 'The Colonial Office and British North America, 1801–50.' *DCB*. Toronto: University of Toronto Press, 1985. 8: xxiii–xxxvii.

– 'Sir Aretas William Young.' *DCB*. Toronto: University of Toronto Press, 1987. 6: 820–2.

– 'Sir Charles Augustus FitzRoy.' *DCB*. Toronto: University of Toronto Press, 1985. 8:295–7.

– 'Sir John Harvey.' *DCB*. Toronto: University of Toronto Press, 1985. 8: 374–84.

– *The Transition to Responsible Government: British Policy in British North America, 1815–1850*. Westport, CT: Greenwood Press, 1985.

Bumsted, J.M. 'Angus Macaulay.' *DCB*. Toronto: University of Toronto Press, 1987. 6: 412–5.

– 'Caesar Colclough.' *DCB*. Toronto: University of Toronto Press, 1987. 6: 160–4.

– 'Edmund Fanning.' *DCB*. Toronto: University of Toronto Press, 1983. 5: 308–12.

– 'George Wright.' *DCB*. Toronto: University of Toronto Press, 1988. 7:924–5.

– 'John Hill.' *DCB*. Toronto: University of Toronto Press, 1988. 7: 406–9.

– 'Joseph Robinson.' *DCB*. Toronto: University of Toronto Press, 1983. 5: 720–1.

– 'The Land Question on Prince Edward Island and the Quitrent Controversy of 1802–1806.' *Acadiensis* 29:2 (Spring 2000): 3–26.

– *Land, Settlement, and Politics on Eighteenth-Century Prince Edward Island*. Kingston and Montreal: McGill-Queen's University Press, 1987.

– 'Liberty of the Press in Early Prince Edward Island, 1823–9.' In *Canadian State Trials: Law, Politics, and Security Measures, 1608–1837*, ed. F. Murray

Greenwood and Barry Wright, 522–46. Toronto: University of Toronto Press, 1996.
– 'The Loyal Electors of Prince Edward Island.' *Island Magazine* 8 (1980): 8–14.
– 'The Loyalist Land Question.' *Island Magazine* 25 (Spring/Summer 1989): 21–8.
– 'The Origins of the Land Question on Prince Edward Island, 1767–1805.' *Acadiensis* 11:1 (Autumn 1981): 43–56.
– 'Parliamentary Privilege and Electoral Disputes on Colonial Prince Edward Island.' *Island Magazine* 26 (Fall/Winter 1989): 22–6 and 27 (Spring/Summer 1990): 15–21.
– 'Peter Stewart.' *DCB*. Toronto: University of Toronto Press, 1983. 5:776–9.
– 'Robert Hodgson.' *DCB*. Toronto: University of Toronto Press, 1983. 5: 424–5.
– 'Scottish Emigration to the Maritimes, 1770–1815: A New Look at an Old Theme.' *Acadiensis* 10:2 (Spring 1981): 65–85.
– 'Settlement by Chance: Lord Selkirk and Prince Edward Island.' *CHR* 59 (1978): 170–88.
– 'Sir James Montgomery and Prince Edward Island, 1767–1803.' *Acadiensis* 7:2 (Spring 1978): 76–102.
– 'William Rankin.' *DCB*. Toronto: University of Toronto Press, 1988. 7:734–5.
– 'William Roubel.' *DCB*. Toronto: University of Toronto Press, 1987. 6:662–3.
Calhoun, Craig. *The Question of Class Struggle: Social Foundations of Popular Radicalism during the Industrial Revolution*. Chicago: University of Chicago Press, 1982.
Callbeck, Lorne C. *The Cradle of Confederation: A Brief History of Prince Edward Island from Its Discovery in 1534 to the Present Time*. Fredericton: Brunswick Press, 1964.
Campbell, Duncan. *History of Prince Edward Island*. Charlottetown: Remner Bros., 1875.
Cashin, Edward J. *The King's Ranger: Thomas Brown and the American Revolution on the Southern Frontier*. Athens: University of Georgia Press, 1989.
Chabot, Richard. 'Cyrille-Hector-Octave Coté.' *DCB*. Toronto: University of Toronto Press, 1988. 7: 208–11.
Chase, Malcolm. *'The People's Farm': English Radical Agrarianism*. Oxford: Clarendon Press, 1988.
Christman, Henry. *Tin Horns and Calico: A Decisive Episode in the Emergence of Democracy*. New York: Henry Holt, 1945.
Clark, Andrew Hill. *Three Centuries and the Island: A Historical Geography of Settlement and Agriculture in Prince Edward Island, Canada*. Toronto: University of Toronto Press, 1959.

Clark, S.D. *Movements of Political Protest in Canada, 1640–1840*. Toronto: University of Toronto Press, 1959.

Cooper, John W. 'A Pioneer Family from Prince Edward Island to California in 1849 & 50' [1895]. Available at http://www.islandregister.co/cooperbook.html

Cotton, W.L. *Chapters in Our Island Story*. Charlottetown: Irwin Printing Co., 1927.

Countryman, Edward. '"Out of the Bounds of the Law": Northern Land Rioters in the Eighteenth Century.' In *The American Revolution*. Ed. Alfred F. Young, 39–61. DeKalb: University of Northern Illinois Press, 1976.

– *A People in Revolution: The American Revolution and Political Society in New York, 1760–1790*. Baltimore: Johns Hopkins University Press, 1981.

Cowan, Helen I. *British Emigration to British North America: The First Hundred Years*. Toronto: University of Toronto Press, 1967.

Craig, Gerald. *Upper Canada: The Formative Years, 1784–1841*. Toronto: McClelland and Stewart, 1963.

Creighton, Donald. *The Empire of the St. Lawrence*. Toronto: Macmillan, 1956.

Daigle, Jean, and Robert Leblanc. *Historical Atlas of Canada*. vol. 1: *From the Beginning to 1800*. Ed. R. Cole Harris, plate 30. Toronto: University of Toronto Press, 1987.

Dawley, Alan. *Class and Community: The Industrial Revolution in Lynn*. Cambridge: Harvard University Press, 1976.

De Jong, Nicolas. 'Charlottetown's Good Samaritan of the Deep.' *Island Magazine* 21 (Spring/Summer 1987): 24–6.

– 'John Mackintosh.' *DCB*. Toronto: University of Toronto Press, 1982. 11: 566–8.

Devine, T.M. 'Unrest and Stability in Rural Ireland and Scotland, 1760–1840.' In *Economy and Society in Scotland and Ireland 1500–1939*, ed. Rosalind Mitchison and Peter Roebuck, 126–139. Edinburgh: John Donald, 1988.

Dictionary of National Biography. London: Smith, Elder, and Co., 1908.

Eden, Peter, ed. *Dictionary of Land Surveyors and Local Cartographers of Great Britain and Ireland, 1550–1850*. Supplement. Chatham, UK: W. and J. Mackay, 1979.

Elliott, Bruce. *Irish Migrants in the Canadas: A New Approach*. Kingston and Montreal: McGill-Queen's University Press, 1988.

Ellis, David Maldwyn. *Landlords and Farmers in the Hudson-Mohawk Region, 1790–1850*. Ithaca, NY: Cornell University Press, 1946.

Ellis, Richard E. *The Jeffersonian Crisis: Courts and Politics in the Young Republic*. New York: Oxford University Press, 1971.

Ells, Margaret. 'Clearing the Decks for the Loyalists.' Canadian Historical Association, *Annual Reports* (1933): 43–58.

Faler, Paul. *Mechanics and Manufacturers in the Early Industrial Revolution: Lynn, Massachusetts, 1780–1860*. Albany: State University of New York Press, 1981.

Field, Daniel. *Rebels in the Name of the Tsar*. Boston: Houghton Mifflin, 1976.

Fingard, Judith. *The Dark Side of Life in Victorian Halifax*. Halifax: Pottersfield Press, 1989.

Fischer, Lewis. 'The Shipping Industry of Nineteenth Century Prince Edward Island: A Brief History.' *Island Magazine* 4 (Spring/Summer 1978): 15–21.

Fladeland, Betty. *Abolitionists and Working-Class Problems in the Age of Industrialization*. Baton Rouge: Louisiana State University Press, 1984.

Foner, Eric. 'Abolitionism and the Labor Movement in Antebellum America.' In *Anti-Slavery, Religion, and Reform: Essays in Memory of Roger Anstey*. Ed. Christine Bolt and Seymour Drescher, 254–71. Folkestone, UK: William Dawson and Sons, 1980.

Frank, David. 'Richard Smith.' *DCB*, Toronto: University of Toronto Press, 1976, 9: 731–2.

Galbraith, John S. *The Little Emperor*. Toronto: Macmillan, 1976.

Galarneau, Claude. 'Jacques-Ladislas-Joseph Calonne.' *DCB*. Toronto: University of Toronto Press, 1987. 6: 105–7.

Garner, John. *The Franchise and Politics in British North America, 1755–1867*. Toronto: University of Toronto Press, 1969.

Gash, Norman. *Aristocracy and People, Britain, 1815–1865*. Cambridge: Harvard University Press, 1979.

Gates, Lillian. 'The Decided Policy of William Lyon Mackenzie.' *CHR* 40:3 (September 1959): 185–208.

– *Land Policies of Upper Canada*. Toronto: University of Toronto Press, 1968.

Gates, Paul Wallace. *The Farmer's Age: Agriculture, 1815–1860*. New York: Holt, Rinehart and Winston, 1960.

Gerriets, Marilyn. 'The Impact of the General Mining Association on the Nova Scotia Coal Industry, 1826–1850.' *Acadiensis* 21:1 (Autumn 1991): 54–84.

Ginsberg, Carlo. *The Cheese and the Worms: The Cosmos of a Sixteenth-Century Miller*. Trans. John and Anne Tedeschi. Hammondsworth: Penguin, 1982.

Goodwin, Albert. *The Friends of Liberty: The English Democratic Movement in the Age of the French Revolution*. London: Hutchinson, 1979.

Goodwyn, Lawrence. *The Populist Moment: A Short History of the Agrarian Revolt in America*. Oxford: Oxford University Press, 1978.

Gray, John Morgan. *Lord Selkirk of Red River*. London: Macmillan, 1963.

– 'Thomas Douglas,' *DCB*. Toronto: University of Toronto Press, 1983. 5: 264–9.

Greenhill, Basil. 'James Yeo.' *DCB*. Toronto: University of Toronto Press, 1976. 9: 855–7.

Greenhill, Basil, and Ann Giffard. *Westcountrymen in Prince Edward's Isle: A*

Fragment of the Great Migration. Toronto: University of Toronto Press, 1967.

Greer, Allan. 'The Birth of the Police in Canada.' In *Colonial Leviathan: State Formation in Mid-Nineteenth-Century Canada*, ed. Allan Greer and Ian Radforth, 17–49. Toronto: University of Toronto Press, 1992.

– 'From Folklore to Revolution: Charivaris and the Lower Canadian Rebellion of 1837.' *Social History* 15:1 (January 1990): 25–43.

– *The Patriots and the People: The Rebellion of 1837 in Rural Lower Canada*. Toronto: University of Toronto Press, 1993.

– *Peasant, Landlord, and Merchant: Rural Society in Three Quebec Parishes, 1740–1840*. Toronto: University of Toronto Press, 1985.

Griffiths, Naomi. *The Contexts of Acadian History: 1686–1784*. Montreal and Kingston: McGill-Queen's University Press, 1992.

Gunn, Gertrude E. *The Political History of Newfoundland, 1832–1864*. Toronto: University of Toronto Press, 1966.

Harris, Marshall. *Origin of the Land Tenure System in the United States*. 1953. Westport, CT: Greenwood Press, 1970.

Harris, Richard Colebrook. *The Seigneurial System in Early Canada: A Geographical Study*. Kingston and Montreal: McGill-Queen's University Press, 1984.

Harrison, J.F.C. *The Common People: A History from the Norman Conquest to the Present*. Glasgow: William Collins, 1984.

– *Robert Owen and the Owenites in Britain and America: The Quest for the New Moral World*. London: Routledge and Kegan Paul, 1969.

Harvey, D.C. 'Early Settlement and Social Conditions in Prince Edward Island.' *Dalhousie Review* 11 (1931/2): 448–61.

– '"The Loyal Electors."' *Royal Society of Canada* 24:2 (1930): 101–10.

– ed. *Journeys to the Island of St John*. Toronto: Macmillan, 1955.

Hatvany, Matthew. 'Almanacs and the New Middle Class: New England and Nova Scotian Influences and Middle-Class Hegemony in Early Prince Edward Island.' *Histoire sociale/Social History* 30 (1997): 417–38.

– 'The Proprietary Burden?' *The Island* 44 (Fall/Winter 1998): 3–19.

– '"Wedded to the Marshes": Salt Marshes and Socio-Economic Differentiation in Early Prince Edward Island.' *Acadiensis* 30:2 (Spring 2001): 40–55.

Head, C. Grant. *Eighteenth-Century Newfoundland: A Geographer's Perspective*. Toronto: McClelland and Stewart, 1976.

Hirsch, Susan E. *Roots of the American Working Class: The Industrialization of Crafts in Newark, 1800–1860*. N.p.: University of Pennsylvania Press, 1978.

The History of Deleware County, Iowa. Chicago: Western Historical Co., n.d.

Hobsbawm, E.J. *The Age of Revolution 1789–1848*. New York: New American Library, 1962.

– 'History from Below – Some Reflections.' In *History from Below: Studies in Popular Protest and Popular Ideology in Honour of George Rudé*, ed. Frederick Krantz, Montreal: Concordia University Press, 1985.

– *Primitive Rebels: Studies in Archaic Forms of Social Movement in the 19th and 20th Centuries*. New York: W.W. Norton, 1959, 1965.

Hobsbawm, Eric, and George Rudé. *Captain Swing: A Social History of the Great English Agricultural Uprising of 1830*. New York and London: W.W. Norton, 1975.

Hof, Ulrich Im. 'German Associations and Politics in the Second Half of the Eighteenth Century.' *The Transformation of Political Culture: England and Germany in the Late Eighteenth Century*, ed. Eckhart Hellmuth, 207–18. London: Oxford University Press, 1990.

Holdsworth, W. S. *A History of English Law*. 3rd ed. London: Methuen, 1944.

Hollis, Patricia. *The Pauper Press: A Study in Working-Class Radicalism of the 1830s*. Oxford: Oxford University Press, 1970.

Holman, H.T. 'John Brecken.' *DCB*. Toronto: University of Toronto Press, 1988. 7: 103–4.

– 'John Cambridge.' *DCB*. Toronto: University of Toronto Press, 1987. 6: s107–10.

– 'Joseph Pope.' *DCB*. Toronto: University of Toronto Press, 1990. 12: 855–8.

Hornsby, S.J. *Nineteenth-Century Cape Breton: A Historical Geography*. Kingston and Montreal: McGill-Queen's University Press, 1992.

– 'Scottish Emigration and Settlement in Early Nineteenth Century Cape Breton.' *People, Places, Patterns, Processes: Geographical Perspectives on the Canadian Past*, ed. Graeme Wynn, 110–38. Toronto: Copp Clark Pitman, 1990.

Hunter, James. *The Making of the Crofting Community*. Edinburgh: John Donald, 1976.

Huston, Reeve. *Land and Freedom: Rural Society, Popular Protest, and Party Politics in Antebellum New York*. New York: Oxford University Press, 2000.

– 'Multiple Crossings: Thomas Ainge Devyr and Transatlantic Land Reform.' In *Transatlantic Rebels: Agrarian Radicalism in Comparative Context*, ed. Thomas Summerhill and James C. Scott, 137–66. East Lansing: Michigan State University Press, 2004.

Hutch, Ronald K., and Paul R. Ziegler. *Joseph Hume: The People's M.P.* Philadelphia: American Philosophical Society, 1985.

Jones, David. *Before Rebecca: Popular Protests in Wales, 1793–1835*. Bristol: Allen Lane, 1973.

Jones, Matt Bushnell. *Vermont in the Making, 1750–1777*. Hamden, CT: Archon Books, 1939, 1968.

Joyce, Patrick. *Visions of the People: Industrial England and the Question of Class 1848–1914*. Cambridge: Cambridge University Press, 1991.

Judd, Gerrit P. *Members of Parliament, 1734–1832*. Hamden, CT: Shoe String Press, 1972.

Karr, Clarence. *The Canada Land Company: The Early Years; An Experiment in Colonization, 1823–1843*. Ottawa: Ontario Historical Society, 1974.

Karsky, Barbara. 'Agrarian Radicalism in the Late Revolutionary Period (1780–1795).' In *New Wine in Old Skins: A Comparative View of Socio-Political Structures and Values Affecting the American Revolution*, ed. Erich Angermann, et al., 87–114. Stuttgart: Ernst Klett, 1976.

Kennedy, Michael L. *The Jacobin Clubs in the French Revolution: The First Years*. Princeton: Princeton University Press, 1982.

Kilbourn, William. *The Firebrand: William Lyon Mackenzie and the Rebellion in Upper Canada*. Toronto: Clarke, Irwin, 1956.

Kim, Sung Bok. *Landlord and Tenant in Colonial New York: Manorial Society, 1664–1775*. Williamsburg, VA: Institute of Early American History and Culture, 1978.

Kulikoff, Allan. *From British Peasants to Colonial American Farmers*. Chapel Hill: University of North Carolina Press, 2000.

Laurie, Bruce. *Working People of Philadelphia, 1800–1850*. Philadelphia: Temple University Press, 1980.

Lawrence, Joseph Wilson. *The Judges of New Brunswick and Their Times*. Fredericton: Acadiensis Press, 1985.

Leard, Waldron. 'Political Relations.' *The Island* 52 (Fall/Winter 2002): 15–18.

Lebergott, Stanley. 'The Demand for Land: The United States, 1820–1860.' *Journal of Economic History* 45:2 (1985): 181–212.

Lefebvre, Georges. *The Great Fear of 1789: Rural Panic in Revolutionary France*. Trans. Joan White. Princeton: Princeton University Press, 1973.

Lefler, Hugh T., and William S. Powell. *Colonial North Carolina: A History*. New York: Charles Scribner's Sons, 1973.

Little, J.I. *Nationalism, Capitalism, and Colonization in Nineteenth-Century Quebec: The Upper St Francis District*. Kingston and Montreal: McGill-Queen's University Press, 1989.

Livingstone, J. Ross. *Responsible Government in Prince Edward Island: A Triumph of Self-Government under the Crown*. Iowa City: University of Iowa, 1931.

Lockerby, Earle. 'The Deportation of the Acadians from Île St-Jean, 1758.' *Acadiensis*, 27:2 (Spring 1998): 45–94.

Macdonald, G. Edward. 'Bernard Donald Macdonald.' *DCB*. Toronto: University of Toronto Press, 1985. 8: 528–30.

Macdonald, Norman. *Canada, 1763–1841: Immigration and Settlement: The Administration of the Imperial Land Regulations*. London: Longmans, 1939.

MacDonell, Margaret. *The Emigrant Experience: Songs of Highland Emigrants in North America*. Toronto: University of Toronto Press, 1982.

MacKinnon, D.A. and A.B. Warburton, eds. *Past and Present of Prince Edward Island*. Charlottetown: B.F. Bowen [1906].

MacKinnon, Frank. *The Government of Prince Edward Island*. Toronto: University of Toronto Press, 1951.

MacKinnon, Kenneth A. 'Coun Douly Rankin.' *DCB*. Toronto: University of Toronto Press, 1985. 8: 740–2.

MacKinnon, Neil. *This Unfriendly Soil: The Loyalist Experience in Nova Scotia, 1783–1791*. Kingston and Montreal: McGill-Queen's University Press, 1986.

MacLean, Marianne. *The People of Glengarry: Highlanders in Transition, 1745–1820*. Montreal and Kingston: McGill-Queen's University Press, 1991.

MacLeod, Ada. 'The Glenaladale Pioneers.' *Dalhousie Review* 11 (1931–2): 311–24.

MacMillan, John C. *The Early History of the Catholic Church in Prince Edward Island*. Quebec: Evenement Printing, 1905.

MacNutt, W.S. *The Atlantic Provinces: The Emergence of Colonial Society 1712–1857*. Toronto: McClelland and Stewart, 1965.

– 'Fanning's Regime on Prince Edward Island.' *Acadiensis* 1:1 (Autumn 1971): 37–53.

– *New Brunswick, A History: 1784–1867*. Toronto: Macmillan, 1984.

MacPhail, Sir Andrew. 'The History of Prince Edward Island.' In *Canada and Its Provinces: A History of the Canadian People and Their Institutions by One Hundred Associates*, ed. Adam Shortt and Arthur Doughty, Toronto: T. & A. Constable, 1913. 13: 305–75.

Macqueen, Malcolm A. *Skye Pioneers and 'The Island.'* Winnipeg: Stovel, 1929.

Martell, J.S. 'Early Coal Mining in Nova Scotia.' In *Cape Breton Historical Essays*, ed. Don Macgillivray and Brian Tennyson, 41–53. Sydney: College of Cape Breton Press, 1980.

Martin, Chester. *Dominion Lands Policy*. Toronto: McClelland and Stewart, 1973.

Mather, F.C. *Public Order in the Age of the Chartists*. Manchester: Manchester University Press, 1959.

McCallum, Margaret E. 'Prairie Women and the Struggle for a Dower Law, 1905–1920.' *Prairie Forum* 18:1 (Spring 1993): 19–34.

– 'The Sacred Rights of Property: Title, Entitlement, and the Land Question in Nineteenth-Century Prince Edward Island.' In *Essays in the History of Canadian Law*. Volume 8. *In Honour of R.C.B. Risk*, ed. G. Blaine Baker and Jim Phillips, 358–97. Toronto: University of Toronto Press for the Osgoode Law Society, 1999.

McCann, Larry. '"Living a Double Life": Town and Country in the Industrialization of the Maritimes.' *Geographical Perspectives on the Maritime Provinces*, ed. Douglas Day et al., 93–113. Halifax: St Mary's University Press, 1988.

McCurdy, Charles W. *The Anti-Rent Era in New York Law and Politics, 1839–1865*. Chapel Hill: University of North Carolina Press, 2001.

McGee, Harold F. 'The Micmac People: The Earliest Migrants.' In *Banked Fires: The Ethnics of Nova Scotia*, ed. Douglas F. Campbell, 14–40. Port Credit: Scribblers' Press, 1978.

McPhee, Peter. 'Popular Culture, Symbolism, and Rural Radicalism in Nineteenth-Century France.' *Journal of Peasant Studies* 5 (January 1978): 235–53.

Meeman, James, and Desmond Clarke, eds. *The Royal Dublin Society, 1731–1981*. Dublin: Gill and Macmillan, 1981.

Meinig, D.W. *The Shaping of America: A Geographical Perspective on 500 Years of History*. Vol. 1. *Atlantic America, 1492–1800*. New Haven: Yale University Press, 1986.

Merrill, Michael, and Sean Wilentz, '"The Key of Libberty": William Manning and Plebian Democracy.' In *Beyond the American Revolution: Explorations in the History of American Radicalism*, ed. Alfred F. Young, 246–82. DeKalb: Northern Illinois University Press, 1993.

Miller, Kirby. *Emigrants and Exiles: Ireland and the Irish Exodus to North America*. New York: Oxford University Press, 1985.

Miller, Virginia. 'The Micmac: A Maritime Woodland Group.' In *Native Peoples: The Canadian Experience*, ed. R. Bruce Morrison and C. Roderick Wilson, 324–52. Toronto: McClelland and Stewart, 1986.

Molloy, Pat. *And They Blessed Rebecca: An Account of the Welsh Toll-Gate Riots 1839–1844*. Llandysul: Gomer Press, 1983.

Morgan, R.J. 'Joseph Frederick Wallet DesBarres.' *DCB*. Toronto: University of Toronto Press, 1987. 6: 192–7.

– 'Orphan Outpost: Cape Breton Colony, 1784–1820.' PhD dissertation, University of Ottawa, 1972.

Morrow, Marianne. 'James Bagnall.' *DCB*. Toronto: University of Toronto Press, 1985. 8: 35–7.

New, Chester. *Lord Durham: A Biography of John George Lambton, First Earl of Durham*. London: Oxford University Press, 1929.

Nobles, Gregory H. 'Breaking into the Backcountry: New Approaches to the Early American Frontier, 1750–1800.' *William and Mary Quarterly* 46:4 (October 1989): 641–70.

Noel, Françoise. *The Christie Seigneuries: Estate Management and Settlement in the Upper Richelieu Valley, 1760–1854*. Kingston and Montreal: McGill-Queen's University Press, 1992.

Olney, R.J. *Rural Society and County Government in Nineteenth-Century Lincolnshire*. Lincoln: History of Lincolnshire Committee, 1979.

Ouellet, Fernand. *Lower Canada 1791–1840: Social Change and Nationalism*. Trans. Patricia Claxton. Toronto: McClelland and Stewart, 1980.

Owen, Arthur C. *Arthur Owen, Master Builder, and Elizabeth Lee: Their Children and Grandchildren, a Partial Genealogy of an Island Family*. Privately printed, 1990.

Palmer, R.R. *The Age of the Democratic Revolution: A Political History of Europe and America, 1760–1800*. Princeton: Princeton University Press, 1959.

Palmer, Stanley H. *Police and Protest in England and Ireland, 1780–1850*. Cambridge: Cambridge University Press, 1988.

Parssinen, T.M. 'Association, Convention, and Anti-Parliament in British Radical Politics, 1771–1848.' *English Historical Review* 88 (1973): 504–33.

Pessen, Edward. *Most Uncommon Jacksonians: The Radical Leaders of the Early Labour Movement*. Albany: SUNY Press, 1967.

Pigot, F.C. 'John MacDonald of Glenaladale.' *DCB*. Toronto: University of Toronto Press, 1983. 5: 514–17.

– 'John Stewart.' *DCB*. Toronto: University of Toronto Press, 1987. 6: 735–8.

– *John Stewart of Mount Stewart*. Charlottetown: P.E.I. Heritage Foundation, 1974.

– 'Thomas Desbrisay.' *DCB*. Toronto: University of Toronto Press, 1983. 5: 249–50.

Polanyi, Karl. *The Great Transformation: The Political and Economic Origins of Our Time*. Boston: Beacon Press, 1968.

Pollard, J.B. *Historical Sketch of the Eastern Regions of New France, from the Various Dates of Their Discoveries to the Surrender of Louisbourg, 1758. Also Prince Edward Island: Military and Civil*. Charlottetown: John Coombs, 1898.

Rea, J.E. 'Alexander McDonell.' *DCB* Toronto: University of Toronto Press, 1988. 7: 544–51.

Read, Colin, and Ronald J. Stagg, eds. *The Rebellion of 1837 in Upper Canada*. Don Mills, ON: The Champlain Society, 1985.

Reader, W.J. *Professional Men: The Rise of the Professional Classes in Nineteenth-Century England*. New York: Basic Books, 1966.

Richards, Eric. *A History of the Highland Clearances*. Vol. 1. *Agrarian Transformation and the Evictions 1746–1886*. London: Croom Helm, 1982.

– 'How Tame Were the Highlanders during the Clearances?' *Scottish Studies* 17 (Spring 1973): 35–50.

Riddell, R.G. 'A Study in the Land Policy of the Colonial Office, 1763–1855.' *CHR* 18 (1937): 385–405.

Robb, Andrew. 'Rioting in 19th Century P.E.I.' *Canadian Frontier* (1978): 30–4.

Robertson, Ian Ross. 'Daniel Brenan.' *DCB*. Toronto: University of Toronto Press, 1972. 10:90.

– 'Donald Macdonald.' *DCB*. Toronto: University of Toronto Press, 1985. 8: 530–3.

– 'Highlanders, Irishmen, and the Land Question in Nineteenth-Century Prince Edward Island.' In *Comparative Aspects of Scottish and Irish Economic and Social History 1600–1900*, ed. L.M. Cullen and T.C. Smout, 227–40. Edinburgh: John Donald, 1977.

– 'James Douglas Haszard.' *DCB*. Toronto: University of Toronto Press, 1972. 10: 339.

– 'James Horsfield Peters.' *DCB*. Toronto: University of Toronto Press, 1990. 12: 838–42.

– 'John Small Macdonald.' *DCB*. Toronto: University of Toronto Press, 1988. 7: 541–2.

– 'Recent Island History.' *Acadiensis* 4:2 (Spring 1975): 111–18.

– 'Reform, Literacy, and the Lease: The Prince Edward Island Free Education Act of 1852.' *Acadiensis* 20:1 (Autumn 1990): 52–71.

– 'Sir Henry Vere Huntley.' *DCB*. Toronto: University of Toronto Press, 1976. 9: 400–2.

– 'Sir Robert Hodgson.' *DCB*. Toronto: University of Toronto Press, 1972. 10: 251–2.

– *The Tenant League of Prince Edward Island, 1864–1867: Leasehold Tenure in the New World*. Toronto: University of Toronto Press, 1996.

– 'Thomas Heath Haviland.' *DCB*. Toronto: University of Toronto Press, 1976. 9: 375–7.

– ed. *The Prince Edward Island Land Commission of 1860*. Fredericton: Acadiensis Press, 1988.

Romney, Paul. 'From the Types Riot to the Rebellion.' *OH* 79:2 (June 1987): 113–44.

Rose, R.B. 'The "Red Scare" of the 1790s: The French Revolution and the "Agrarian Law."' *Past and Present* 103 (May 1984): 113–30.

Royle, Stephen A., and Caitriona Ni' Laoire. 'DesBrisay's Settlers.' *The Island* 51 (Spring/Summer 2002): 19–23.

Rudé, George. *The Crowd in History: A Study of Popular Disturbances in France and England, 1730–1848*. London: Lawrence and Wishart, 1981.

– *Ideology and Popular Protest*. London: Lawrence and Wishart, 1980.

Ryan, Mary. *Cradle of the Middle Class: The Family in Oneida County, New York, 1790–1865*. Cambridge: Cambridge University Press, 1981.

Sakolski, Aaron M. *Land Tenure and Land Taxation in America*. NewYork: Robert Schalkenbach Foundation, 1957.

Samson, Danny. 'Industrial Colonization: The Colonial Context of the General Mining Association, Nova Scotia, 1825–1842.' *Acadiensis* 29:1 (Autumn 1999): 3–28.

Saunders, Ivan J. 'The New Brunswick and Nova Scotia Land Company and the Settlement of Stanley, New Brunswick.' MA thesis, University of New Brunswick, 1969.

Scott, James C. *Weapons of the Weak: Everyday Forms of Peasant Resistance*. New Haven: Yale University Press, 1985.

Sewell, William H., Jr. *Work and Revolution in France: The Language of Labor from the Old Regime to 1848*. Cambridge: Cambridge University Press, 1980.

Sharpe, Errol. *A Peoples' History of Prince Edward Island*. Toronto: Steel Rail Publishing, 1976.

Slaughter, Thomas P. *The Whiskey Rebellion: Frontier Epilogue to the American Revolution* Oxford: Oxford University Press, 1986.

Smitheram, Verner, David Milne, and Satadal Dasgupta, eds. *The Garden Transformed: Prince Edward Island, 1945–1980*. Charlottetown: Ragweed Press, 1982.

Sobey, Douglas. 'Prince Edward Island in 1840: The Travel Journal of Sir George Seymour.' *The Island* 54 (Fall/Winter 2003): 26–33 and 55 (Spring/Summer 2004): 2–7.

Stewart, Deborah. 'Robert Bruce Stewart and the Land Question.' *Island Magazine* 21 (Spring/Summer 1987): 3–11.

Summerhill, Thomas. 'The Farmers' Republic: Agrarian Protest and the Capitalist Transformation of Upstate New York, 1840–1900.' PhD dissertation, University of California, San Diego, 1993.

Sutherland, David. 'The Merchants of Halifax 1815–1850: A Class in Pursuit of Metropolitan Status.' PhD dissertation, University of Toronto, 1975.

Sutherland, George. *A Manual of the Geography and Natural and Civil History of Prince Edward Island for the Use of Schools, Families, and Emigrants*. Charlottetown: John Ross, 1861.

Szatmary, David P. *Shay's Rebellion: The Making of an Agrarian Insurrection*. Amherst: University of Massachusetts Press, 1980.

Taylor, Alan. 'Agrarian Independence: Northern Land Rioters After the Revolution.' In *Beyond the American Revolution: Explorations in the History of American Radicalism*, ed. Alfred F. Young, 221–45. DeKalb: University of Northern Illinois Press, 1993.

– *Liberty Men and Great Proprietors: The Revolutionary Settlement on the Maine Frontier, 1760–1820*. Chapel Hill: University of North Carolina Press, 1990.

Taylor, E.G.R. *Mathematical Practitioners of Hanoverian England, 1714–1840*. Cambridge: Cambridge University Press, 1966.

Taylor, M. Brook. 'Charles Binns.' *DCB*. Toronto: University of Toronto Press, 1988. 7: 76–7.

– 'Charles Worrell.' *DCB*. Toronto: University of Toronto Press, 1985. 8: 953–5.

– 'Francis Longworth.' *DCB*. Toronto: University of Toronto Press, 1988. 7: 511.

– 'George Dalrymple.' *DCB*. Toronto: University of Toronto Press, 1985. 8: 197–8.

Tebeau, Charlton W. *A History of Florida*. Coral Gables: University of Miami Press, 1971.

Thompson, Dorothy. *The Chartists: Popular Politics in the Industrial Revolution*. New York: Pantheon, 1984.

Thompson, E.P. *The Making of the English Working Class*. Middlesex: Penguin, 1982.

Tilly, Charles. 'Britain Creates the Social Movement.' In *Social Conflict and the Political Order in Modern Britain*, ed. James E. Cronin and Jonathan Schneer, 21–51. London: Croom Helm, 1982.

– *From Mobilization to Revolution*. Reading, MA: Addison-Wesley, 1978.

Thorne, R.G. *The History of Parliament*. Vol. 5. *The House of Commons, 1790–1820*. London: Secker and Warburg, 1986.

Topoloski, Jerzy. 'Revolutionary Consciousness in America and Europe from the Mid-Eighteenth to the Early Nineteenth Century as a Methodological and Historical Problem.' In *The American and European Revolutions, 1776–1848*, ed. Jaroslaw Pelenski, 75–93. Iowa City: University of Iowa Press, 1980.

Townshend, Adele. 'Drama at Abell's Cape.' *Island Magazine* 6 (Spring/Summer 1979): 33–7.

Trevelyan, George Macaulay. *England in the Age of Wycliffe*. London: Longmans, 1935.

Tuck, Robert. 'St. Eleanors: The Veneered Village.' *Island Magazine*, 18 (Fall/Winter 1985): 3–8.

Upton, L.F.S. 'Thomas Irwin.' *DCB*. Toronto: University of Toronto Press, 1988. 7: 436–8.

Vass, Elinor. 'John Ready.' *DCB*. Toronto: University of Toronto Press, 1988. 7: 740–2.

– 'The Ready Touch: John Ready and Prince Edward Island, 1824–1831.' *Island Magazine* 28 (Fall/Winter 1990): 30–7.

Wait, Benjamin, *The Wait Letters*. Don Mills, ON: Press Porcépic, 1976.

Warburton, A.B. *A History of Prince Edward Island*. Saint John: n.p., 1923.

Ward, J.T. *Chartism*. London: Batsford: 1973.

Warman, Arturo. *'We Come to Object': The Peasants of Morelos and the National State*. Trans. Stephen K. Ault. Baltimore: Johns Hopkins University Press, 1980.

Watson, Harry L. *Liberty and Power: The Politics of Jacksonian America*. New York: Hill and Wang, 1990.

Weaver, John C. *The Great Land Rush and the Making of the Modern World, 1650–1900*. Kingston and Montreal: McGill-Queen's University Press, 2003.

Webber, David. 'Robert Shuttleworth: The Opulent Gentleman from Morell.' *Island Magazine* 31 (Spring/Summer 1992): 3–10.

– *A Thousand Young Men: The Colonial Volunteer Militia of Prince Edward Island, 1775–1874*. Charlottetown: Prince Edward Island Museum and Heritage Foundation, 1990.

White, Patrick C., ed. *Lord Selkirk's Diary, 1803–4: A Journal of His Travels in British North America and the Northeastern United States*. Toronto: Champlain Society, 1958.

Whitelaw, William Menzies. *The Maritimes and Canada before Confederation*. Toronto: Oxford University Press, 1966.

Wilentz, Sean. *Chants Democratic: New York City and the Rise of the American Working Class, 1788–1850*. New York: Oxford University Press, 1984.

Williams, David. *The Rebecca Riots: A Study in Agrarian Discontent*. Cardiff: University of Wales Press, 1955.

Williams, Raymond. *Keywords: A Vocabulary of Culture and Society*. New York: Oxford University Press, 1976.

Wilson, David A. *Paine and Cobbett: The Transatlantic Connection*. Kingston and Montreal: McGill-Queen's University Press, 1988.

Wilson, Catharine Anne. *A New Lease on Life: Landlords, Tenants, and Immigrants in Ireland and Canada*. Montreal: McGill-Queen's University Press, 1994.

Wood, J.D. 'Transatlantic Land Reform: America and the Crofters Revolt.' *Scottish Historical Review* 63:1 (1984): 79–104.

Wynn, Graeme. *Timber Colony*. Toronto: University of Toronto Press, 1981.

Young, Alfred F., ed. *Beyond the American Revolution: Explorations in the History of American Radicalism*. DeKalb: Northern Illinois University Press, 1993.

Young, Brian. 'Positive Law, Positive State: Class Realignment and the Transformation of Lower Canada, 1815–1866.' In *Colonial Leviathan: State Formation in Mid-Nineteenth-Century Canada*, ed. Allan Greer and Ian Radforth, 50–63. Toronto: University of Toronto Press, 1992.

Index

www.ingramcontent.com/pod-product-compliance
Lightning Source LLC
LaVergne TN
LVHW090803070826
844660LV00022B/1062
9780802072290